ADVANCE PRAISE FOR *KARL BARTH & THE PIETISTS*

"With his customary thoroughness and flair for the important and often unknown historical detail and its theological ramification, Professor Busch's work *Karl Barth & the Pietists* expands our understanding of this crucial period in the development of Barth's theology in the 1920s: the two versions of the Romans commentary and their significance for Barth's interaction with Continental Pietism. Busch's scholarship sharpens our awareness that there is much to the Barth legacy that has yet to be fully understood and unpacked, especially in its English-language reception. Daniel Bloesch and IVP are to be commended for presenting this capable and very readable translation, and for making this significant research and analysis available to the growing and curious Barth audience in English."

DARRELL L. GUDER, HENRY WINTERS LUCE PROFESSOR OF MISSIONAL AND ECUMENICAL THEOLOGY, PRINCETON THEOLOGICAL SEMINARY

"*Karl Barth & the Pietists* is the history of a 'troublesome friendship' in which author Eberhard Busch lets each party to the friendship articulate just what is troublesome about it. What emerges is a focused masterpiece in historical theology with foundational significance for the integrity of Christian experience (a troubling word to Barth, a touchstone for Pietists) and the Christian life (more public and social to Barth, more individual and personal to Pietists). Serving as a laboratory for ecumenical conversationalists, this work shows how easily and quickly issues can get subverted or co-opted by stereotypes, snap judgments and the use of common words without common meanings. As Busch shows, Barth the interpreter is never isolated from Barth the interlocutor. That makes for interesting history."

JOHN WEBORG, PROFESSOR EMERITUS OF THEOLOGY, NORTH PARK THEOLOGICAL SEMINARY

Karl Barth & the Pietists

The Young Karl Barth's Critique of Pietism and Its Response

Foreword by Donald W. Dayton

Eberhard Busch

Translated by Daniel W. Bloesch

InterVarsity Press
Downers Grove, Illinois

InterVarsity Press
P.O. Box 1400, Downers Grove, IL 60515-1426
World Wide Web: www.ivpress.com
E-mail: mail@ivpress.com

English translation ©2004 by InterVarsity Christian Fellowship/USA®. Original German edition published as Karl Barth und die Pietisten *by Eberhard Busch, ©1978 Chr. Kaiser Verlag, Munich.*

InterVarsity Press® is the book-publishing division of InterVarsity Christian Fellowship/USA®, a student movement active on campus at hundreds of universities, colleges and schools of nursing in the United States of America, and a member movement of the International Fellowship of Evangelical Students. For information about local and regional activities, write Public Relations Dept., InterVarsity Christian Fellowship/USA, 6400 Schroeder Rd., P.O. Box 7895, Madison, WI 53707-7895, or visit the IVCF website at <www.intervarsity.org>.

All Scripture quotations, unless otherwise indicated, are taken from the Holy Bible, New International Version®. NIV®. *Copyright ©1973, 1978, 1984 by International Bible Society. Used by permission of Zondervan Publishing House. All rights reserved.*

"Hope for the Conversion of the Converted" is translated from the original "Hoffnung auf Umkehr der Bekehrten: Karl Barth und der Pietismus" by Eberhard Busch. Used by permission.

Design: Kathleen Lay Burrows

Images: Roberta Polfus

ISBN 0-8308-2741-2

Printed in the United States of America ∞

Library of Congress Cataloging-in-Publication Data

Busch, Eberhard, 1937-
  [Karl Barth und die Pietisten. English]
  Karl Barth and the pietists: the young Karl Barth's critique of pietism and its response / Eberhard Busch; foreword by Donald W. Dayton; translated by Daniel W. Bloesch.
      p. cm.
Includes bibliographical references.
  ISBN 0-8308-2741-2 (pbk.: alk. paper)
  1. Barth, Karl, 1886-1968. 2. Pietism. I. Title.
  BX4827.B3B86213 2004
  230'.044'092—dc22

                                                              2003023201

P	18	17	16	15	14	13	12	11	10	9	8	7	6	5	4	3	2	1
Y	18	17	16	15	14	13	12	11	10	09	08	07	06	05	04			

Contents

Outline

Foreword

I am delighted that InterVarsity Press has undertaken to publish an English translation of *Karl Barth und die Pietisten*—and that it has been translated by Dan Bloesch, a veteran of my seminar on the doctrine of reconciliation in Karl Barth. I first became aware of the importance of this book almost a quarter of a century ago in Tübingen, during my first sabbatical leave in the spring of 1980, less than two years after its publication in 1978. Over the years since that time in Germany, I have become increasingly convinced that it has not been given the attention that it deserves, especially in the English-speaking world.

I had chosen Tübingen for my sabbatical because of the presence of Jürgen Moltmann, Eberhard Jüngel and Hans Küng, but my real interest was in thinking through the much disputed relationship between Karl Barth and "evangelicalism." I had been reared in the Holiness variety of American "evangelicalism," but it had not taken for me. It was the reading of Søren Kierkegaard and Karl Barth in graduate school that mediated faith to me, and I needed time to sort all this out. In Tübingen a group of "left-wing evangelicals" in the SMD (Studenten Mission Deutschland—the German counterpart of InterVarsity Christian Fellowship) welcomed me into their community (which published *Unterwegs*, the German counterpart to *Sojourners* magazine) and shared their more advanced experience of pilgrimage in dialogue with the theology of Karl Barth. In the process they introduced me to this book by Barth's last assistant, who was to emerge as the biographer and a major interpreter of Barth's thought.

This experience reoriented my thinking at a number of points. Most important, I discovered a major difference between the German and the American "evangelical" experience. In the United States we generally assume what I call the conservative-liberal paradigm for the interpretation of "evangelicalism," equating it with Protestant orthodoxy. In Germany they speak much more of the reaction to that stream that we call Pietism. I was somewhat prepared to track this issue by a seven-year sojourn in the Evangelical Covenant Church and North Park Theological Seminary, one of the few American seminaries to self-consciously assert that they stand in this tradition (many others have pietistic roots but don't claim them). But this semester in Germany sharply focused these questions in a new way.

I was used to the typical American distinction between "conservative" and "liberal" theology. They spoke of the contrast between "academic" theology *(Universitätstheologie)* and "church" theology *(Gemeindetheologie)*. They took their clues not so much from the fundamentalist-modernist controversy as from the earlier Pietist currents of the seventeenth and eighteenth century as they were reshaped in the nineteenth century into the various *Gemeinschaften* ("fellowship" groups in the Lutheran national churches) by the ministry of Robert Pearsall Smith (husband and coworker of Hannah Whitall Smith, author of the classic *The Christian's Secret of a Happy Life)*—as Dan Bloesch indicates in his helpful notes to this book. I soon discovered I was in quite a different theological culture, one that actually assumed Kierkegaard was a Christian and took seriously Schleiermacher's claim to be a "Herrenhutter [the center of the Pietism of Count Zinzendorf] of a higher order." Such an orientation was unthinkable in American "evangelicalism," especially in the age of the ascendancy of Francis Schaeffer.

Reflecting on such themes led me to distinguish meanings of the word *evangelical* that are kept separate in German but collapsed in popular English usage. I began to distinguish the Reformation use of the word *(evangelisch)* from the eighteenth century use in the awakening tradition of the "evangelical revival" *(pietistisch,* or rooted in the *Theologie der Erweckungsbewegung* or *Gemeinschaftsbewegung)* and even from the modern neo-evangelical use derived from the twentieth century fundamentalist-modernist controversy *(evangelikal)*. Each of these meanings of the word has a separate and different dialogue with Barth.[1]

Without making these distinctions, one cannot understand the theological discussion in this book. Busch is concerned primarily with Barth's discussion with those who stand in the more pietistic and even Holiness line of the of the "fellowship movement." In this discussion the issues are not so much those of the confessional traditions of the Reformation (who tend to be most concerned about Barth's rethinking of such themes as election and predestination) or of the twentieth century (concerned more about "orthodoxy" and the doctrine of Scripture) as they are the efficacy of grace in "conversion" and whether this produces an empirically observable difference between Christians and non-Christians. These questions are at the center of Busch's book, in which he not only traces Barth's sharp critique of Pietism in general but works through in great detail the reviews of Barth's work in the literature of the *Gemeinschaften*.

---

[1]Donald W. Dayton, "Karl Barth and Evangelicalism: The Varieties of a Sibling Rivalry," *TSF Bulletin* 8 (May-June 1985): 18-23, the major published product of my sabbatical term.

It is important to realize that Busch expected his book to be followed by another treating the late, mature Barth on these questions. As far as I know, this volume was never written as originally envisioned. For this reason, this volume includes another essay by Busch which attempts to survey the whole of Barth. This is important because a substantial case can be made that in the fourth volume of the *Church Dogmatics* Barth has mellowed somewhat in his criticism of Pietism. He comments that IV/2 is intended to treat the issues of Pietism in a still critical but systematic way. There one will find positive references to Bengel's *Gnomon*, the great Pietist commentary, more sympathetic treatment of such Pietist figures as Count Zinzendorf of the Moravians (for his "Christocentrism" and linking of Christ and "creation," as well as other themes), and some level of retraction of the attacks of the "early Barth" on the sentimentality, subjectivism and even eroticism of Pietist hymnody. Most astonishing of all is the extent to which Barth grounds his thought in the slogan "Jesus ist Sieger" (Jesus is Victor) of the radical Pietists in southwest Germany, especially the Blumhardts, father and son, of Möttlingen and Bad Boll.[2]

I am convinced that further attention to the late Barth will bring to awareness a number of points in which Barth may be said to be making an unexpectedly positive appropriation of the Pietist tradition, given his earlier criticisms. Perhaps the earlier fights with Pietism are a form of "sibling rivalry" in which Barth is working out his own struggle with his family's roots in Pietism. It seems to me, at least, that Barth is moving beyond Pietism by going through it rather than around it or against it, as we have often assumed. Such themes obviously need careful exploration, but Busch's book refocuses the "evangelical" discussion with Barth along such lines.

One of the most interesting of these questions would be whether some of the broad outlines of Barth's doctrine of Scripture might not have more affinity with Pietism than Orthodoxy in the post-Reformation era. Many Pietists warned against the doctrine of the "inerrancy" of Scripture that was so dear to the "orthodox" and to contemporary "evangelicalism." They felt that the orthodox did their theologizing in too close a dialogue with philosophy. The Pietists advocated a sort of "Bible piety" that pulled the Scripture out from under the control of the creeds and put it to "devotional" use, founding Bible societies and other agencies to bring the Bible into the life of all Christians. If we were to view Barth in this line, we might make more sense of his radical (and antiphilosophical) biblicism combined with a noninerrantist, but genuinely authoritative, doctrine

---

[2]This stream of influence is being studied (in his Drew University dissertation) by Christian T. Collins Winn, one of the translators of the essay appended to this volume.

of Scripture. Likewise, it is possible to argue that many key figures that shape Barth's hermeneutic are modern-day Pietists attempting to work out the logic of the move toward biblical theology that developed at Pietist Halle University.

Even the usual evangelical attack on Barth's doctrine of Scripture (that for him the Bible *becomes* the Word of God) is clarified by attention to the question of Pietism. Many of the dominant streams of American "evangelicalism" are deeply influenced by orthodoxy, especially through the Princeton theology of the nineteenth century. B. B. Warfield, for example, presupposes the tradition of Protestant orthodoxy in his exegesis of 2 Timothy 3:16. For him and the "orthodox" the Greek word *theopneustos* ("God-breathed") is to be understood as past tense, and it is characteristic of this tradition to draw a sharp line at the end of the canonical period, so that God acts (and speaks) differently now. This results in a careful distinction between the "inspiration" that produced the biblical text and the "illumination" that occurs as the Holy Spirit speaks through the text to us today. The Pietists (as in Bengel's *Gnomon* and other writings in that line, including John Wesley's *Explanatory Notes on the New Testament*) tended to muddy this distinction by speaking of an ongoing act of "inspiration," arguing that Jesus is the same, yesterday today and forever and thus minimizing the distinction between the canonical era and our own (whether in miracles of healing, contemporary speaking or an ongoing "inspiring" of the biblical text by the Holy Spirit).

If there is any truth to this analysis, Barth might be seen not as the great enemy of "evangelicalism" (in the sense of "orthodoxy") but perhaps as a great friend of "evangelicalism" (in the sense of "Pietism"), in spite of the power of his critique of the subjective tendency of Pietism. And if, as I am becoming increasingly convinced, the American interpretation of evangelicalism is based on some horrendous category mistakes caused by the almost total neglect of the influence of Pietism, then this book makes not only a significant contribution to Barth studies but also helps us gain more clarity on the nature of evangelicalism itself. It is for these reasons that I am happy to commend this book to an English readership.

Donald W. Dayton
Haggard School of Theology
Azusa Pacific University
Thanksgiving 2003

Translator's Introduction

Karl Barth and the Pietists is a translation of a work published by Christian Kaiser Verlag under the title *Karl Barth und die Pietistin*. It was written in 1978 by Dr. Eberhard Busch, a leading authority on the life and theology of the Reformed theologian Karl Barth, who has been called an authentic "church father" of the Post-Reformation era and one of the foremost theologians of the twentieth century. Dr. Busch is presently a professor of theology at the University of Göttingen in Germany who has served as a pastor in his native Switzerland and as the curator of the Barth archives in Basel. This work traces Barth's dialogue with an important segment of the church in Europe, the movement of Pietism in Germany and Switzerland. The first part of this book deals with Barth's critique of Pietism, and the second part with the Pietistic responses to this critique in the period up to 1930. The third part focuses on the learning process that took place on the part of both Barth and the Pietists as a result of this ongoing dialogue.

Dr. Busch's work is here preceded by the table of contents, a more detailed outline of the work (which includes the subheadings of the original German edition), a foreword written by Dr. Donald Dayton, professor of theology at Azusa Pacific University, California, and Dr. Busch's introduction. We have also included several valuable features at the end of the book, including an essay written by Dr. Busch at a later date, "Hope for the Conversion of the Converted," which supplements his original book and brings it to a fitting conclusion.

In the book itself Busch goes into detail on the first three stages of Barth's journey in his relationship with Pietism. The first stage covers Barth's early period, when he was a liberal theologian. The second stage covers the period marked by his first *Epistle to the Romans,* written in 1919. This is followed closely in the third stage by the period that began with the publication of a very different second *Epistle to the Romans* in 1922 and continued up to 1930.

In the epilogue Busch takes up the discussion of the final three stages not considered in the book. The fourth stage of Barth's journey led him to take a more critical view of Pietism, expressed in his lecture on the history of Protestant theology in 1932-1933. The fifth stage of the relationship is characterized by a profound shift in his thinking, in which he shows a new appreciation for the central concern of the Pietists, summarized by the key terms *conversion, new birth, spir-*

itual awakening, sanctification and *discipleship.* Barth develops these themes in his *Church Dogmatics* IV/2, written in 1955. Although his response to Pietism is more positive, he still defines the terms differently and says he is not one of them. In the 1960s, the sixth and final stage of the relationship, Barth moves even closer to Pietism as he seeks to develop a "theology of the Holy Spirit." Although he was critical of the "No Other Gospel" confessing movement that arose in Germany in opposition to Bultmann's theology, Barth hoped for a "new kind of Pietism" that would testify to the Lord Jesus Christ in the transforming power of the Holy Spirit, able to confront the idols of a secularizing church and society drifting even further into the waters of unbelief and skepticism.

An understanding of these final three stages is essential to gaining a more comprehensive, well-rounded picture of Barth's relationship with Pietism. Busch concludes the essay by addressing to modern-day Pietism several questions, raised by Barth's thought-questions, that seek to establish common ground between Pietism and Barthian theology: their understanding of the objective and subjective reality of salvation, the issue of grace and sin, the significance of the individual's decision of faith and the continuing conversion of believers. Finally, he asks probing questions on their view of the contemporary church and its ministry to the world.

The epilogue is followed by two appendices. The first is a brief history of German Pietism in the nineteenth and twentieth centuries. What is Pietism? What is the origin of the movement that became such an important dialogue partner for Karl Barth throughout his academic career? This history seeks to offer a backdrop for a better understanding of the dialogue by providing a thumbnail sketch of the key events and figures of the spiritual awakenings in German-speaking Europe that led to the emergence of modern-day Pietism. The story begins with the post-Napoleonic spiritual awakening that swept through Germany from the 1820s through the 1840s and planted the seeds for a second spiritual awakening that occurred in the 1880s and continued through the early part of the twentieth century. This revival is the actual origin of the community movement *(die Gemeinschaftsbewegung)* that united the various Pietistic regional associations, foreign missionary agencies and social ministries into the Gnadau Association of Pietistic Communities *(Gnadauer Gemeinschaftsverband)* and led also to the formation of the German Evangelical Alliance. It was these community people who felt they were being addressed in Barth's critique of Pietism and who became his primary interlocutors. The second appendix is a brief explanation of two key terms, *Landeskirche* and *Gemeinschaftsbewegung,* and why I have translated them respectively as "established Protestant church" and "community movement."

The book concludes with a bibliography of Barth's works cited in this study and their English translations (where these are available), a list of abbreviations for the periodicals cited in Busch's footnotes, and indexes of names and Scriptures.

I would like to thank Dr. Gary Deddo, associate editor at InterVarsity Press, for his enthusiastic support of this translation project, as well as his wise counsel and patience in shepherding this work to completion over the course of several years. In addition, I would like to thank Ruth Rhenius and Christian T. Collins Winn for their input on the translation of the epilogue. I owe a debt of gratitude to Dr. Darrell Guder for reviewing the manuscript and offering helpful suggestions. Any errors in the translation are my own.

Finally, I would like to dedicate this translation to my cousin Dr. Donald Bloesch, professor of theology emeritus at Dubuque Theological Seminary, my theological mentor and friend.

Daniel W. Bloesch

Introduction

The publication of Karl Barth's *Epistle to the Romans* can be seen as the most significant event in church history in the decade following World War I, according to a Pietistic account of church history published by K. Deitenbeck in 1962.[1] The fact that an eminently theological book is judged to be so significant by the Pietistic side testifies to the impact of the earlier Barth's theology and shows to what degree this Christian group clearly paid attention to it. According to Deitenbeck, the turnaround in theology triggered by that book can be attributed to this decisive fact: "The structure of liberal theology erected over the course of more than 100 years collapsed like a house of cards under the weight of the arguments made by Barth. What still seemed progressive yesterday was shelved today."[2] If we disregard the exaggeration of the last sentence, what is still striking about this statement from the lips of a Pietist is that he apparently overlooked or forgot the fact that Barth's attack also somehow opposed the "structure" of Pietism erected over the course of more than two hundred years.

This ignorance is even more remarkable because the Pietists of that era clearly understand his attack in this way. The critical movement of thought that marked the second interpretation of the epistle to the Romans published in 1922 in fact provoked a diverse, lively echo from supporters of the Pietistic community movement. They did not at all feel that Barth's theses were just peripheral criticism of Pietism. "The community movement is in the dock."[3] It is "an inquisition of the utmost severity"[4]; "Barth has made a decisive declaration of war against Pietism."[5] "Barth is putting a probe into position to strike Pietism at its roots."[6] The Pietistic camp indicated with such statements that it heard Barth's critique and found it to be so fundamental that they felt provoked to launch a counterattack. If this camp's memory of that confrontation between the author of the *Epistle to the Romans* and the community movement seems to be clouded

---

[1] K. Deitenbeck, *Das Feld muss er behalten: Der Weg des Evangeliums durch zwei Jahrtausende,* 1962, pp. 163-64.
[2] Ibid., p. 163.
[3] H. Oltmann, essay of the same name, in *Im Kampf um die Kirche,* 1930, p. 75.
[4] E. Schick, *Die Botschaft des Pietismus,* 2nd ed., p. 19.
[5] G. F. Nagel, *Karl Barth und der heilsgewisse Glaube,* 1929, p. 10.
[6] W. Hützen, *Biblisches Glaubensleben,* 1928, p. 4.

(and Deitenbeck's account creates this impression) we may wonder whether the confrontation was perhaps not as fruitful and promising as the general situation then appeared. We may conclude from this that Pietism—however this situation is evaluated—did not by any means collapse like a house of cards because of Barth's attack. Instead, it withstood the attack and has now put it on the shelf. The course of the following study should demonstrate whether this was the proper course of action. This study is interested in calling to mind the fact of the confrontation between Karl Barth's theology and the Pietists in the 1920s.

This confrontation is a fact. The first and second interpretation of the epistle to the Romans implied among other things a definite argument with Pietism. Above all, the group that understood itself as Pietism viewed the second edition of the book as a critical question addressed to them, jeopardizing their movement. Therefore, from that point in time they dealt extensively with Barth's theology and grappled with it quite vigorously, at times offering their own sharp criticism. It can be noted here that Barth's attack was not just provocative for the Pietists because of its contradiction of them. What made this attack so confusing for them, and what made it necessary for them to examine themselves and come up with a response to Barth, was the fact that the attack was actually aimed at the address of liberal theology as well. Thus this attack was not launched from a liberal position. The Pietists were used to facing opposition from this position, and they believed they were furnished with suitable weapons to wage the battle against liberalism.

What made this attack so confusing for them was that they encountered opposition not in the name of modern man, reason or intellectual honesty but— let us put it in problematic but succinct terms—from the perspective of the Bible, from God, thus from a position where they thought they themselves stood, a position they thought they had to defend against the liberals and could claim as their own, actual domain.[7] The recognition that only those moved by the Spirit are the children of God was especially important to them. If they claimed to understand themselves as children of God who were moved by the Spirit in dealing with Barth, they confronted the question, whose children were they actually? Was the spirit moving them actually the Spirit of *God*? This kind of ques-

---

[7]It is amazing that even after and in spite of Barth's question, G. Bergmann still sees the situation unfailingly in such dualism: *either* the false, unbiblical position of liberalism *or* the position of the Bible, of the people of God, of possessing the Word of God in its fullness, which is identical to the position of Pietism. "There is only one common front line in all denominations," and in all these situations there is the driving force of Pietism—against the unbiblical and corrupting neo-rationalism of our day. Here God's people must join forces to attack and must not wave the white flag of peace. War is necessary here, relentless war and the hard times it brings" (*Gottes Leute im Angriff,* 1964, p. 30).

tioning was extremely unsettling for them. Here was a person who seemed to stab them in the back from a direction in which they thought they were covered. They considered Barth's critique of Pietism unreasonable and a challenge with which they could not easily cope. Indeed, they had trouble even understanding it. It was an obvious temptation for them to render this questioner harmless by reshaping his question until it sounded exactly like all the criticism they had been accustomed to hearing for a long time, criticism they had already handled from the beginning.

However, the fact remains that they could not simply slip past the theology of the *Epistle to the Romans*. Instead, it put pressure on them to listen carefully and reflect on it and then to take various positions on it and reflect on their own position. When we describe this confrontation, we will discuss these two issues. One issue is the meaning and thrust of the critique leveled at the Pietistic dialogue partner by the author of the *Epistle to the Romans,* linked to the question, on the one hand, to what extent the critique actually arose from the place it claimed as its basis, and on the other, to what extent it really confronted those who were its object. The second issue is the manner in which the Pietists on their part sought to cope with the question addressed to them, linked to the question of whether they accurately understood Barth and whether the counter-position they advocated and defended against Barth was able to satisfactorily respond to that question. The following work is essentially devoted to treating both of these points.

We would first like to start by precisely defining the boundaries of our subject. On the one hand the *author* of the *Epistle to the Romans* will have his say in this study. We will primarily describe Barth's critique of Pietism found in the second edition of this book because the Pietistic argument with Karl Barth primarily and in part even exclusively dealt with it for years. In addition, the early history of the critique of Pietism found in this book will be included in our study although it was largely not in view to the authors of the Pietistic responses as far as the first *Epistle to the Romans* is concerned, and not at all as far as the even earlier history is concerned. But today that early history must be considered especially since the sources that enable us to know it have become increasingly accessible. It is essential that we pay attention to them in order to understand and evaluate the critique of Pietism found in the second *Epistle to the Romans*. Barth's publications subsequent to his second *Epistle to the Romans* written in the further course of the 1920s when he was a professor in Göttingen and then in Münster will be cited only in passing, mainly to examine the question whether his position on Pietism changed, perhaps under the influence of the reactions from this side. There are two reasons that the cutoff point of our study is set approximately at the beginning of the 1930s: (1) the subsequent Pietistic reactions still focused on the second *Epistle to the Romans* and thus were not able to bring in any new points of view, and (2) a new phase in the relationship between Barth and Pietism began when Barth started his work on his *Church Dogmatics* and when the church struggle of the Confessing Church took center stage.[8]

Therefore Barth's only extensive and direct discussion of historical Pietism in his lecture of 1932/33 will not be included in our account.[9] It is worth a separate study. We will only be able to hint at the fact that we understand this lecture as the conclusion of the earlier phase because it summarizes and unfolds in detail all the important elements of Barth's position on Pietism from the first *Epistle to the Romans* through the second *Epistle to the Romans* to the end of the 1920s.

On the other side *Pietism* will have its say. The difficulties of a historical or substantive definition of this phenomenon, especially the problem of bringing together an abundance of diverse views and concerns under this heading, are very familiar to us. So is the problem of describing the interrelationships and distinctions between the Pietism of the eighteenth century, the spiritual awakening of the ninteenth century and the community movement of the twentieth century. These difficulties can be summed up in Kurt Aland's dictum: "There never was *one* Pietism."[10] So we will be pragmatic in our study and understand Pietism as that phenomenon whose supporters felt they were addressed and targeted by Barth's critique of Pietism and thus felt goaded into replying to Barth's address. As a rule they are members of the more recent community movement within the established Protestant church. Barth did not simply make an impermissible mistake when he summarized the three aforementioned historical phenomena with the concept of "Pietism." This analysis is confirmed by the fact that in their responses to him, these community people identified themselves with baroque Pietism and the revivalist movement, sharing their essential concerns without overlooking the differences between these three phenomena. They viewed Barth's critique of both of these historical movements as a critique of themselves.

Therefore, in what follows we think we can use the concepts "Pietists" and "community people" synonymously. Once again we must qualify our study by saying that when the voice of the Pietists is heard in the second part of our

---

[8]Here I gladly point out that Mr. Ulrich Weidner in Göttingen is presently writing a treatise on the relationship of the middle-aged and later Barth to Pietism.

[9]The lecture was printed in 1946 as the first part of the book *Protestant Theology in the Nineteenth Century,* pp. 16-152.

[10]K. Aland, *Kirchengeschichtliche Entwürfe,* 1960, p. 545.

treatise, it will certainly not be the voice of the Pietists that speaks there but actually only the voice of those who felt that they were being called and pressured to take issue with Karl Barth as members of the community movement within the established Protestant church during the 1920s. Therefore, we must keep an open mind to the possibility that these spokespersons only represented *one* particular view of "Pietism," alongside of which still other unarticulated options were possible in this context. For example, the historical Pietism of the eighteenth century or "the prevalent mood in the rank and file" of the community movement may have been somewhat different from the impression these spokesmen made. Furthermore, there is a simple reason for restricting ourselves almost exclusively to allowing the *German* supporters of the community movement to speak when we describe the Pietistic responses to Barth. The Pietistic discussion with Barth took place most intensively and most extensively in the German-speaking area of Europe.[11] Here the Pietists took an in-depth look at the theology of the *Epistle to the Romans,* especially in the period from 1926 to 1929.

---

[11]I could not discover a corresponding preoccupation of the community people in Switzerland. Joh. Schneider in his lecture "Sanctification" seems to have implicitly distanced himself from Barth at the Baden Conference in 1924; at any rate, he presented the same arguments for "sanctification" that were important to German Pietists who shared his views especially in relationship to Barth. Presumably G. Weisman had Barth in mind at the Baden Conference in 1929, but he did not mention the name when he said, "Because sanctification understood in strictly Pietistic terms was 'reformational,' an objection to it could not be raised in principle, unless Calvinistic ideas were stressed, which limit the possibility of the assurance of salvation breaking through on the basis of stressing the sovereign, hidden rule of God. By stressing this alone, one enters into conflict with the clear, divine commission" ("Die Bekehrung im Lichte der Heil: Schrift und der christlichen Erfahrung," in *Badener Konferenz,* 1929, p. 13). For J. Gubler, K. Barth simply does not exist in this story (*Kirche und Pietismus: Ein Gang durch die neuere ev. Kirchengeschichte der Schweiz,* 1959).

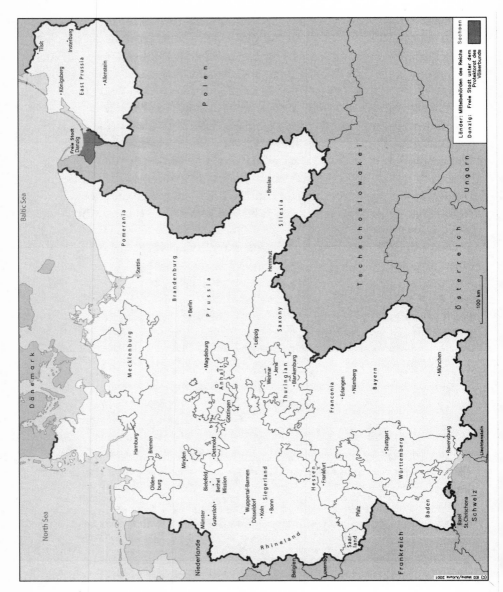

Germany, circa 1937

Part A

Barth's Position on Pietism Up to 1921

I. The Background of Karl Barth's Critique of Pietism

Pietistic Influences in Barth's Upbringing

It meant a lot for a Pietist when H. Oltmann conceded that the author of the *Epistle to the Romans* discussed Pietism in a critical manner but without being guilty of ignorance, a lack of understanding or ill will.[1] This view was by no means undisputed in his camp. For example, W. Knappe, a Pietist who diligently tried to understand Barth's theology and was relatively open-minded toward it, found Barth's "passionate position against Pietism" questionable because "it is blind and thus is not based on real, and above all, practical knowledge of the movement. . . . He only has a caricature of Pietism in view."[2] As late as 1936, after Barth had given his lecture on the eighteenth century, F. Mund simply denied that Barth was able to understand Pietism and relate to its "secret" (which was identical to "the Holy Spirit!").[3] The *background* of Barth's critique of Pietism has crucial significance not the least because it considerably relativizes if not refutes this objection to his *critique of Pietism*. For this early history shows that Pietism was not foreign to his background but was very familiar to him so that he got to know it in the best light in the environment in which he was first at home. And even more it shows that for years, stretching up to Barth's first theological writings, Pietism was one of the experiences that had a positive influence on him and that he consciously affirmed. He knew it not only from the outside with the eyes of the enemy but also from the inside with the eyes of a friend.

Let us be clear about some facts! Many of his ancestors and relatives took a positive attitude toward this movement; in fact, they counted themselves as a part of it.[4] Let me mention only a few names. His great-great-grandfather, the

---

[1]*Die Gemeinschaftsbewegung auf der Anklagebank in Im Kampf um die Kirche,* 1930, p. 71. Oltmann mentions no name here but clearly means Barth.

[2]*Karl Barth und der Pietismus,* 1927, p. 13.

[3]*Pietismus-eine Schicksalsfrage an die Kirche heute,* 1936, pp. 17ff.

[4]Compare Barth's remark in a letter from October 30, 1963, in which he calls Pietism the "great tradition in its own way," "knowing that I am seriously obligated to it in spite of all my reservations because some of my ancestors were Pietists, but then also on the basis of my studies" (*Briefe* 1961–1968, 1975, p. 205).

Basel pastor Joh. Rud. Burckhardt (1738–1820), was the founder of the Society of Christianity and a friend of the Herrnhurt community,[5] indeed "a key figure among all the pious believers in the country."[6] For a while he was the son-in-law of Hieronymus Annoni, and as a vicar he was quick and eager to learn from him. Annoni was called the "father of Basel's Pietism,"[7] and associated with Tersteegen, Zinzendorf and the Pietists of Halle. He was a representative of a "mystic, ascetic individualism" that remained within the orbit of the church.[8] The son given to this great-great-grandfather, Johannes, became a close friend of Ludwig Hofacker, A. Knapp and also of G. D. and Emil Krummacher. His great-grandson Karl Barth confessed later that he was "an edifying and joyous Pietist in the best sense of the word." Of all his ancestors Johannes was the one who made "the strongest spiritual impression" on him.[9] His daughter Johanna was strongly influenced by her father. Even in his old age Karl Barth preferred "the gentle Pietism" of this woman who was his highly respected grandmother to the rigid, conservative orthodoxy of her husband.[10]

It was especially this Pietistic line in his ancestry which influenced the young Karl Barth's upbringing in an unobtrusive but impressive way. His mother, the daughter of Johanna, nee Burckhardt, used the children's songs of Abel Burkhardt as a textbook from which her son received his first theological instruction. Once he understood it, it was, in his words, eminently suited "to carry

---

[5] P. Wernle, *Der schweizerische Protestantismus im 18. Jahrhundert*, vol. 2, 1924, p. 396.

[6] A fragment of K. Barth's autobiography, 1967 (typewritten in the Karl Barth archives, Basel).

[7] Wernle, *Der schweizerische Protestantismus im 18. Jahrhundert*, vol. 1, 1923, p. 339.

[8] Ibid., p. 327. A Bible was in Karl Barth's possession—the well-known Pietists' Bible from H. Horche—which Annoni once gave to his great-great-grandfather with this handwritten dedication: "As long as Mr. and Mrs. EGO lives/the Savior will always be opposed," etc.

[9] Barth's characterization of his great-grandfather (in the fragment of his autobiography, 1967) goes into detail: He was "a decided Pietist. Even if he was clearly theologically conservative, which was taken for granted at that time, he was not a Pietist who believed in doctrine, but in the Scriptures, existing in a living relationship to the living Lord Jesus Christ—therefore he was not a dark, pessimistic Pietist, but a joyous one. Indeed he rejoiced right up to his final days, even in the throes of death, which was a difficult struggle for him. He was not a narrow-minded Pietist, but open-minded especially toward nature and natural science. Moreover, he continued his work in academic theology to the end. He was not a hard, legalistic Pietist who was oppressive to his surroundings, but an edifying and pleasing Pietist in the best sense of the word. It seems to me that he was an exemplary type of this special variety of the true children of God." These informative sentences document the final phase of Barth's relationship to Pietism, where Pietism in itself and as such was no longer problematic to him. Instead, assuming that there are also Pietists in Christendom, this question alone seemed interesting to him: What does a Pietist do with his inheritance? Does he give way to the gospel on the basis of his tradition and thus move forward on this basis or not? In Barth's view both are clearly possible, and what can be said about Pietism is decided only *here*.

[10] Epilogue, in *Schleiermacher-Auswahl*, Siebenstern-Taschenbuch 113/114, 1968, p. 292.

us through whole oceans of historicism and anti-historicism, mysticism, rationalism, orthodoxy, liberalism and existentialism—certainly not untried and unchallenged, but relatively unharmed—and sooner or later to bring us back to the point." What was characteristic of these songs with their remarkable Pietistic slant was the warm and comfortable way they spoke of the "Savior" and his deeds and sufferings as something "present," happening now.[11] What is also worth mentioning about Karl Barth's upbringing is the so-called Lerber school in Bern, which he attended during his entire time in school. It was a "school established to promote the cause of Pietism" in conscious and emphatic opposition to the "reforming," liberal state schools.[12]

The thought of his father, Fritz Barth, was clearly influenced by the concern of the Pietistic circles in Switzerland and Germany, despite his not uncritical independence which occasionally brought him the disapproval of these Pietistic circles. He was above all grateful to the Swabian T. Beck, who had also been a guiding light for his father and had led him "out of the barren heath of a self-sufficient critique into the green meadows of the Word of God."[13] His "conversion," understood as a "new birth," as "the beginning of a new life in man," as the transformation of his personal life from its deepest roots, as an entrance into lasting "personal contact with Jesus," was "the most wonderful and glorious of all God's works" for him.[14] He viewed Romans 7:14ff. as a description of our spiritual condition *before* conversion, and he expected a "state of conversion" in which we "experience God as our God" in a decisive way and "have been equipped for fruitful service by the power of God's Spirit."[15] Thus he considered orthodoxy an "ossification of church life that Pietism has successfully protested."[16]

In his Bern lecture on recent church history in the summer of 1905, which his son attended shortly after he had advanced to the study of theology, Fritz Barth on the whole presented a quite favorable view of Pietism. "We must truly know the subject we study, not only from hearsay." For "even today it is a major force that must be respected." Above all, "its moral earnestness" and "its insistence on the central truth of the gospel is highly commendable." Therefore "the pastor must beware of having a falling out with his Pietists who make up the best part of his congregation."[17] To be sure, F. Barth saw certain sectarian, anti-

---

[11]KD 4/2, p.125.
[12]A. Tavel, *70 Jahre Freies Gymnasium,* 1934, p. 70.
[13]F. Barth, *Christus unsere Hoffnung: Sammlung von religiosen Reden und Vorträgen,* 1913, p. 4.
[14]Ibid., pp. 194-95.
[15]Ibid., pp. 183, 195, 198.
[16]Ibid., p. 401.
[17]Ibid.

intellectual, legalistic and enthusiastic tendencies in Pietism as negatives. But he emphasized its positive features more strongly. He saw its strengths in four areas: (1) the priority of life over doctrine; (2) its view of spiritual rebirth; (3) the close connection of justification to sanctification; and (4) the idea of the coming kingdom of God, both limiting and expanding the church as an institution. Ritschl's critique was rejected by F. Barth, who declared Pietism both Lutheran and biblical.[18]

Even when the young Karl Barth became increasingly more open to the liberal theology of his era during his years of study, detaching himself from his father's instruction, he actually did not enter a totally different environment in the lecture hall of Wilhelm Herrmann, who became his most important teacher when he changed his thought. To be sure, with the radical conclusions Herrmann drew from his rejection of the orthodox concept of faith, he proved to be a liberal theologian in his own way, and his fundamental rejection of that concept of faith was based on liberal premises.

However, when in his view "all Christian faith is an expression of confidence in an event that has been personally experienced,"[19] it is evident that his ideas had strong overtones of his Pietistic heritage. It was not just words that he adopted from it. He was also closely following this tradition when he chose the subject matter for his writings. Chapters on "rebirth" and "conversion" are located at the dominant center of his *Ethics,* and in this context we read the following sentences: Faith is a "personal conviction gained as a result of seriously taking stock of oneself"[20] or "wherever real Christian faith emerges, man becomes conscious of the fact that he has been wonderfully renewed"[21] or "if Jesus is to be our Redeemer, his person in its redemptive power must be a fact not only others tell us about, but we ourselves experience."[22] Thus it is understandable that twenty years after Karl Barth completed his university education, he could describe the atmosphere in Herrmann's lecture hall with the words of Mackintosh: "Conversions must have taken place frequently as a result of his instruction." Years later Barth himself praised Herrmann's "Pietism in the best sense of the word."[23] We may say that Herrmann's theology offered the young Barth the opportunity to affirm liberal thought without sacrificing Pietistic concerns.

---

[18]Ibid.

[19]W. Hermann, *Der Verkehr des Christen mit Gott,* 7th ed., 1921, p. 180.

[20]W. Hermann, *Ethik,* 5th ed., 1921, p. 113.

[21]Ibid., p. 98.

[22]Ibid., p. 120.

[23]K. Barth, *Die Theologie und die Kirche, Ges. Vorträge* 2, 1928, p. 271.

Pietistic Ideas in Barth's First Theological Framework

The first theological work Barth did in his Geneva and then in his Safenwil pastorate proves that this subheading is not wrong. We can conclude from it that this possibility became a dominant theme in his thought for some time. The foil for his thought was orthodoxy, an understanding of faith seen as "an acceptance of external facts, considering them to be true," using Herrmann's terminology.[24] His critique of this understanding of faith went far beyond classical Protestant orthodoxy, but he believed it was only targeted at a few views held by Reformational theology, in particular its understanding of the Bible as a source of revelation.[25] He also yielded the field of "knowledge" in its entirety to "critical Rationalism": There is only *one* body of knowledge, and that is "the knowledge of critical Rationalism."[26] For Barth the decisive reason for this anti-orthodox thesis was the modern concept of autonomy behind which theology could not, he thought, return. "And thus the classical Protestant version of the concept of historical authority is impossible in every sense. . . . This renders the idea of authoritative statutes in a hierarchical institution invalid, as well as the idea of an authoritative canon, authoritative ideas, propositions and narratives, even if an angel from heaven had brought them."[27]

Here Barth was intentionally continuing the tradition of Romanticism.[28] True faith is not knowledge but "a developmental process in the life of the individual,"[29] "individual liveliness,"[30] "the actualization of heightened states of consciousness given in an a priori function,"[31] in short, "an inner experience" that as such is immediate, yet at the same time irrefutable and unprovable. It cannot be analyzed; it cannot actually be expressed in words but can only be experienced, or to put it in religious terms, "faith is an experience of God,"[32] it is "intuitive," "a reception of the impression that the eternal substance makes on our self-consciousness."[33] Therefore God is determinative for faith "not as any external norm, but as an individual inner certainty and authority."[34] In Barth's

---

[24]"Ob Jesus gelebt hat?" *Gemeinde-Blatt Geneva,* April 23, 1910.
[25]"Der christliche Glaube und die Geschichte," in *Schweizer Theologische Zeitschrift,* 1912, pp. 14ff. The lecture was already given in 1910.
[26]Ibid., p. 17.
[27]Ibid.
[28]"Moderne Theologie und Reichsgottesarbeit," in *ZTK,* 1909, p. 320.
[29]"Der christliche Glaube und die Geschichte," p. 63.
[30]Ibid., p. 59.
[31]Ibid., p. 72.
[32]Ibid., p. 5.
[33]Ibid., p. 51.
[34]"Answer to D. Achelis and D. Drews," in *ZTK,* 1909, p. 485.

view this understanding of faith is not subjective[35] since faith as experience and receptivity is not essentially closed in on itself. However, this understanding of faith is distinctly individualistic to the degree that not any one external factor in itself but only inner "emotion" is normative for faith in such receptivity.[36] Thus it is always only one's *own* experience that counts.[37] In this view religion has to be strictly located in the realm of the individual. "Religion knows only individual values, history knows only universally valid facts."[38] Of course religion is not merely one special "province" of life; rather it is life itself, individual life, a living development and realization of the individual.

Barth encountered two difficulties in developing this understanding of faith. (1) How is faith imparted to human beings? On the one hand, the communication of "knowledge" in terms of Barth's radical description is ruled out, but on the other hand, as Barth stressed,[39] the assumption that faith is a natural condition in human beings is also ruled out! Barth's answer was simple and logical. "It is through people who have become alive that the living person is imparted to people."[40] A christology and—inextricably tied to it—ecclesiology had their place for him within the framework of this answer. (2) How can a faith understood as unguarded receptivity protect itself from false, unwholesome influences, from arbitrariness and fanaticism? His answer in terms of Herrmann's theology is that the prerequisite for religion is the "morality" of man. But it is also an individual morality, since it is not obedience to norms that confront persons externally, but reflection on and decisional orientation to a truth and authority that manifests itself in the individual.[41]

In the period between 1907 and 1912, the young Barth acted in an emphatically *liberal* way in this understanding of faith and understood himself to be liberal. Not only his rejection of the doctrines of the early church[42]—the Bible as the source of revelation,[43] the decalogue as the norm for behavior,[44] etc.—demon-

---

[35]Rather, he even considers it to be an "inner corrective" to the danger of degenerating into "subjectivism" (ibid.).

[36]Ibid., p. 484: "The normative, the objective, the eternal is found only in the 'emotion' of this inner experience—everything entering into thoughts and words is itself a part of the relativistic current of history."

[37]Ibid., p. 485: "No one else stands up for him/he stands all alone on himself."

[38]"Moderne Theologie und Reichsgottesarbeit," p. 319.

[39]"Der christliche Glaube und die Geschichte," p. 51.

[40]Ibid., p. 66.

[41]"Moderne Theologie und Reichsgottesarbeit," p. 317.

[42]Compare his derision of the Chalcedonian language in sermon nr. 51, October 30, 1910.

[43]"Der christliche Glaube und die Geschichte," pp. 10ff., 65.

[44]"Moderne Theologie und Reichsgottesarbeit," p. 319: "Both the one table of Moses and the other has slipped out of our hands."

strates this liberal stance, but also his intellectual home in the world of Kant and Schleiermacher, as well as of Goethe and Schiller, and especially his use of Kant's concept of autonomy and the Romantic concept of individuality as his starting point. Moreover, Barth thought he could establish a synthesis of Kant and Schleiermacher by linking "morality" and "religion" as Herrmann already intended to.

However, at the same time Barth thought he agreed with the *Pietists* in this understanding of faith—this is important here. For he was able to explicitly pick up a number of Pietism's central concerns from his starting point in liberal theology. A lecture from 1910 made these concerns clear: the assurance of salvation,[45] "Christ in us" who is certainly not in us by nature but who comes into our life by first personally influencing us,[46] the interpretation of sanctification as "the content of justification,"[47] the understanding of divine righteousness as "an inner condition of life"[48] and consequently the interpretation of the Christian congregation in terms of "individuals who have become believers or whose faith has come alive."[49] Similar linkages can also be observed in Barth's early sermons. "Whatever is to have value in our time must be a fact."[50] Faith must also be a fact, and it is a fact by being inner life. In the words of Angelus Silesius, "It is not outside, the fool seeks it there/It is in you, you bring it forth eternally."[51] Therefore Christians believe "what they themselves have experienced,"[52] what "they can affirm as a fact in their own life."[53] Those who themselves are alive experience that God lives, and wherever we experience this, "God awakens in us."[54] For "the most inward and greatest truth is what takes place in our hearts." Of course, "they have not drawn from themselves what has emerged in them, but it is an effect of . . . Christ."[55] So it is of utmost importance to become "personally acquainted with Jesus of Nazareth" in order to become "a new creation," because you then have the mind of Christ, because you yourself have become a small part of Christ."[56] Again, "to accept that Christ was the Son of God, performed mir-

---

[45]"Der christliche Glaube und die Geschichte," p. 57.

[46]Ibid., p. 51.

[47]Ibid., pp. 59-60.

[48]Ibid., p. 63.

[49]Ibid., p. 66.

[50]Sermon nr. 4, August 18, 1907 (this sermon, like all the others quoted here, are handwritten and located in the Barth archives in Basel).

[51]Sermon nr. 21, November 21, 1909.

[52]Sermon nr. 66, May 28, 1911.

[53]Sermon nr. 63, April 14, 1911.

[54]Sermon nr. 47, August 7, 1910.

[55]Compare n. 64.

[56]Sermon nr. 27, January 1, 1910.

acles, died for our sins, was resurrected" does not help us at all; rather "Christ wants to live in you."[57]

Barth's *explicit,* positive position on Pietism in this period can no longer be a surprise after all this. In contradistinction to orthodoxy, "the most terrible disaster of theological thought imaginable"[58] that cannot be condemned strongly enough, true Protestant theology continued to "live" in the circles of the mystics and Pietists, "although clad in strange garments."[59] Is that strange? Yes. "Albrecht Ritschl can tell us that. But the internal principle of this school of thought was simply the Reformational and Protestant one. Although it looked untheological, the correct position on the question of historical theology was renewed in it and kept alive within Protestantism."[60] Barth pledged his allegiance to this historical heritage, especially in Geneva, where he was at loggerheads with the subconsciousness of the Genevans who had a surfeit of "Pietist-complexes."[61] In his sermons he called attention to the "mystics of the Middle Ages" and even quoted from their work, signaling his agreement.[62] And he presented the Pietists to the Genevans as exemplary in their demand that "true piety must be *life* and true life must be *piety.*"[63]

Among the figures of the older Pietism, Annoni from Basel[64] and Zinzendorf[65] (who was not understood in Reformational terms) enjoyed Barth's respect. In contrast to his later condemnation of Angelus Silesius's aphorisms on the birth,

---

[57]Sermon nr. 43, July 3, 1910. See his statement on this in "Der christliche Glaube und die Geschichte": Not "Christ in himself," not his external life, not his words, not his deeds, but "the inner life of Jesus," the divine work in man given through him, in which this happens, "He turns into I"—this is the source and content of faith; this (alleged) view of Calvin has been renewed, Barth thinks, by Pietism and by Schleiermacher (pp. 58-59, 63).

[58]"Der christliche Glaube und die Geschichte," p. 56.

[59]Ibid., p. 64.

[60]Ibid.

[61]"Pour la dignité de Geneve," in *Basler Nachrichten,* 1911, nr. 119. "Momier" is the French expression for Pietists.

[62]Compare sermon nr. 40, June 1910: "Brave German men got on the trail of truth anew in the 14th century, then once again in the 16th century. . . . At that time the mystics of the Middle Ages called us to contemplate the one thing needful." Compare in sermon nr. 19, November 1909, his praise for the same "profound German thinkers, who . . . assert that all our perfection and all our bliss is due to the fact that man passes through and overcomes all creaturliness and all contingency and all being goes into the depths that are bottomless." On both poems, *Gemeinde-Blatt Geneva,* nr. 34, 1910.

[63]On both poems, *Gemeinde-Blatt Geneva,* nr. 34, 1910.

[64]Ibid. Barth had Annoni's poem printed there: "If only the washerwomen/would think good thoughts while working . . ."

[65]"Der christliche Glaube und die Geschichte," p. 64. His recognition of Zinzendorf is all the more conspicuous because Fritz Barth strongly criticized him; in his lecture from 1905 ("feeling and imagination are dangerously predominant") he did not treat him under the title "Pietism" but under the title "separatism."

crucifixion and resurrection of Christ "in you" as "outrageous pieties,"[66] he stressed that they had their "completely rightful place."[67]

Above all, he was impressed by Tersteegen, for his path was "not from confession to experience, but from experience to confession," which keeps faith free of illusions because it is at the same time "not the way of seeking happiness, but the way of self-denial." It is also not the way of self-effort but the way of allowing God to work. And where does this path lead? "To the dizzy heights of inwardness and truthfulness," "into the paradise of the soul's holy seclusion with God," where God "as the breath from the eternal stillness/gently penetrates the depth of the soul." Even though Tersteegen unfortunately tended to turn self-denial into a denial of the world, Barth considered him to be "one of the greatest men we have, a prophet of *concentration* in life and thought, of *inwardness* of the soul and its redemption, of the *superiority* of God who made us and not we who made him."[68] However, in Barth's view Novalis avoided Tersteegen's one mistake. At that time he also dealt with Novalis and believed that he belonged at the side of Tersteegen as a "proclaimer of redemptive self-denial."[69] Early on in Safenwil, Barth had a similar relationship to the figures of Pietism where he could occasionally give a whole sermon on W. Booth and his Salvation Army,[70] where he mentioned the books of a Tersteegen or a Jung-Stilling and recommended them to his congregation as "books whose views I endorse."[71] He also actually had his congregation sing Pietistic songs over and over again.[72]

His First Attempts to Critique Pietism

Of course, although Barth was open to this side, he was not himself a Pietist at that time. He was a liberal theologian who as such nevertheless thought he could integrate his Pietistic inheritance into his liberal framework. Because his understanding of faith as inner life and experience was at the heart of his theological framework—in contrast to all claims of propositional truth—he could think that he had come back to a genuine Pietistic tradition. But he was also

---

[66]KD II/1, p. 316.

[67]"Der christliche Glaube und die Geschichte," p. 57. Compare also sermon nr. 43, July 3, 1910.

[68]Gerhard Tersteegen, in *Gemeinde-Blatt Geneva*, nr. 40, 1910. The article presents a summary of a lecture by Karl Barth given in Geneva.

[69]Novalis, in *Gemeinde-Blatt Geneva*, nr. 43, 1911.

[70]Sermon nr. 129, August 25, 1912; Booth is strongly seen here, though, through the lens of his religious-social involvement.

[71]*Sermons*, 1913, 1976, p. 62.

[72]A few examples (so far as they can still be discovered): "Die Sach ist dein" by S. Preiswerk, "Eine Herde und ein Hirt" by Fr. A. Krummacher (*Sermons*, 1914, 1974, p. 544), "Kommt, Brüder, lasst us gehen" comes from Tersteegen (in *Gemeinde-Blatt Geneva*, p. 564), "O Durchbrecher . . . " by G. Arnold (in *Gemeinde-Blatt Geneva*, p. 223), etc.

able to take this understanding of faith as a yardstick to examine whether and to what extent Pietism met this criterion. And in fact he had to notice that in many figures of Pietism this understanding of faith was not developed with the purity and rigor he had in mind, especially with regard to the negative consequences of rejecting a faith based merely on claims of propositional truth. Instead, elements of an orthodox, supernatural or fundamentalist understanding of faith often continued to be interspersed in it, more or less strongly. Because he intended to develop a consistent, liberal understanding of faith, a critique of Pietism had to readily come to mind wherever he felt this Pietism was "burdened" by just such elements. The roots of the thesis of the "consistent" or "original" Pietist later written down by Barth are presumably found here. It claims that many figures of Pietism actually gave inconsistent support to their own concern. However, when it is supported in a consistent way this concern is identical with the pure form of what modern Christianity pursued as "the humanization" of faith.[73]

In fact in his view Barth came across an example of such an inconsistent Pietism tied to the recognition of "dogmas" when he had to review a book by the evangelist Elias Schrenk in 1909. That is why he flatly rejected the content of the book and could not recognize it as an "edifying book" because it asks the reader to accept this dogma.[74] However, it is interesting to see that he had unmistakable respect for the Pietist himself in spite of his rejection of this book. Evidently his teaching on the necessity of imparting faith not by doctrine but by living personalities, which was a consequence of Pietistic views, offered him a practical opportunity to interpret even "inconsistent" Pietists in the most favorable light. It offered him the opportunity in Schrenk's work to distinguish between his doctrine and its author. On the one hand Barth denied that his doctrine had the "persuasiveness of rational and biblical evidence." On the other hand he was at the same time able to admire "the inner spiritual aliveness of the significant man who stands behind it."[75] In 1911 Barth evaluated John Mott, the "apostle to the students," in the same way. Mott stood in the evangelistic tradition of Dwight L.

---

[73]Compare the lecture on the eighteenth century from 1932/33. In *Die prot. Theologie in im 19. Jahrbundert,* 1946, p. 93. Here this distinction, however, finds a new evaluation: whereas the Barth of 1910 sees a shortcoming in the inconsistency of Pietism, the Barth of 1932-1933 now sees, conversely, an advantage in this.

[74]Review of E. Schrenk, "Seelsorgeliche Briefe für allerlei Leute," *Christliche Welt,* vol. 23, nr. 50, column 1204. Ironically, Barth accuses himself here of being one of those who "suffer" from the "dogmatic softening of the bones" incriminated by Schrenk, to then seriously add that nothing is won in matters of faith with an authoritative recourse to one or another "biblical teaching or individual verse."

[75]Ibid.

Moody, and after meeting him in Geneva, he largely rejected Mott's ideas.[76] But at the same time he was deeply moved by Mott's "superior personality" as one who was "in a living relationship with the man from Nazareth, which we can certainly *describe* well . . . but very seldom *experience*."[77] It was obviously the application of a consistently held Pietistic idea which enabled him to find "believing individuals" among its supporters despite his reservations about certain Pietistic doctrines. Pietism is actually "consistent" in these men. Even though to some extent he condemns those "rational and biblical evidences" as inconsistent, at the same time Pietism is excused for its inconsistency. In these reflections by Barth I discern an initial form of his later conviction that something else was "alive" in Pietism beyond what it actually said.[78]

If Barth's critique of Pietistic doctrine moved along the lines of his liberal theology, there was an element in his theology whose application led him to begin a critique of Pietism that at the same time called his "liberal" framework into question. We mean the element that can be labeled "self-denial," a concept that Barth initially found in Tersteegen, Angelus Silesius and Novalis. He thought he could also somehow link it to Herrmann's understanding of faith, but he emphasized it more strongly that Herrmann did. It seems to us that the conclusions he drew from this idea soon led him to have reservations about the Pietists that were not in the least peripheral. At the same time they were also misgivings about his "liberal" starting point.

As we have said, Tersteegen's path of self-denial was impressive to him, but he found it problematic that Tersteegen confused *self*-denial with a denial of the *world*. In fact, Barth thought "even as good a Calvinist as Gerhard Tersteegen was in this respect fully Catholic. For him the world was only a deafening noise from which one must escape!"[79]

Barth sensed that Tersteegen put less emphasis on the "denial" and more on the "self that was to be denied. For Barth the opposite was the case; self-denial, by objecting only to the "ego," to egotism, ruled out all attempts to take flight from the world. If this idea is taken seriously, redemption had to mean "redemp-

---

[76]"John Mott und die christliche Studentenbewegung," *Centralblatt des Zofingervereins*, 1911, pp. 487ff. Quote from P. Gruner, *Menschenwege und Gotteswege im Studentenleben,* 1942, pp. 437ff. Compare p. 439: Mott "addressed his auditorium in globo . . . as children," preached at it "from the pulpit of a truth that is fixed from the outset" with "pseudo-scientific tricks," with ideas we have largely "thrown overboard as unusable," etc.

[77]Ibid., pp. 443-45.

[78]Compare, for example, *Die prot. Theologie im 19. Jahrhundert,* 1946, p. 103: "One can not possibly read his documents without having to say to oneself that the faith he really lived out was always beyond the bounds marked out by all these categories."

[79]Sermon nr. 85, November 5, 1911.

tion from self, from one's own person." Thus we suddenly hear that redemption was now considered to be impossible as long as it was marked by a desire to say, "*I* would like to be saved," just as other people are used to saying, "*I* would like to have a strong personality."[80] If this idea is taken seriously, then it stands to reason that Barth would stress the fact that redemption is not merely for a few but for *all*, not just the private fulfillment of an individual longing for salvation, rather redemption is about the salvation of the *world*.[81] For this reason it was not a coincidence that we hear even the early Barth make explicitly critical remarks about Pietism. He objected to their "unpleasant habit of smelling and sniffing at their fellow human beings to find out if they are converted,"[82] to their unnatural rules about what we call "Christian" and "non-Christian," which they used to harass people, and thus to their pious separation from the world,[83] and their individual blessedness which was indifferent to earthly distress.[84]

The same idea of self-denial unleashed another series of ideas in Barth's reflections that can also certainly be found in many Pietists. However, if they were thought out logically, they could also be used to critique Pietism. We could reduce them to the common denominator of "spiritual poverty." If Barth appreciated Novalis as a "proclaimer of redemptive self-denial," as he boldly put it, it is important to see that in this context Barth does not mean by self-denial any kind of pious exercise of virtue but a basic characterization of the way in which

---

[80]Sermon nr. 53, November 20, 1901. Compare sermon nr. 58, January 29, 1911: "We think the higher life actually means overcoming all egoism; however not only overcoming sensuous but also intellectual and pious egoism."

[81]Compare sermon nr. 27, January 1, 1910: "There is in Christianity no secret teaching at all which would only be meant for Pietists, but only one truth, and it is for everyone." Sermon nr. 134, September 29, 1912: "Paul says, 'you are all children of God' and does not say: 'you should be children of God!' and this means also: 'not because we are converted are we children of God,' but this is also true of innumerable crowds of sinners, the indifferent and those who deny God." And therefore: "Thank God, it does not matter if I am converted, but it does matter if Christ is working on me." Sermon nr. 136, October 13, 1912: "Jesus said: Come to me, all you . . . it does not say: Come to me, all who have the inner light."

[82]Sermon nr. 134, September 29, 1912.

[83]Sermon nr. 58, January 29, 1911; Barth develops the idea in dialogue with the work of Ch. M. Sheldon, *In the Footsteps of Jesus.*

[84]Compare *Sermons,* 1913, 1976, p. 191: "We have perhaps even experienced a conversion . . . And [nevertheless have] certain inclinations, for example, to sow discord, or the principle: money is more important than anything else!" *Sermons,* 1914, 1974, p. 70: "Look, you are here, and perhaps you say to me: I am saved, I know and love God, I have joy, peace, tranquility and am fully sufficient in him. But now listen: there are besides you so many who are prevented from coming to the place where you are now, certainly through their personal guilt, but in any case, through the conditions in which they live as well: Insufficient or meager income, poor housing, bad habits . . ." The same idea is also found on pages 351-52, but here it is linked to a conclusion that is critical of religion: "We think we have God, but his Spirit and his power are far from us. Our life looks deceptively like a good, godly life, but it is not."

we relate to God. We encounter "Christ in the darkness, in death, in the extinction of the earth spirit"[85] (clearly not in the affirmation, fulfillment, elevation or perfection of human conditions). The idea of self-denial understood in these terms had to have critical consequences for his view of Pietism. When starting from this point of view Barth came to the conclusion: Faith or, as he puts it here, "the soul begins where interest ceases."[86] Here he was arguing along the lines of the "disinterested" faith of certain mystically oriented Pietists. But then he went beyond the scope of this group or any theology that identifies faith with a certain kind of human consciousness and experience. He went further, turning the self-denial of the Christian into a relinquishment of any *consciousness* of being a Christian. Suddenly we can find surprising sentences in the early Barth such as this: "Blessed are those who know they are not pious! . . . They *are* the people of God because they know that they are not."[87]

It should be clear that both of these series of ideas included critical barbs hurled at both Pietism and liberalism. Indeed, it is obvious that they had an explosive force that was able to attack the liberal framework of a "religious individualism" as such, a concept that was favorable to Pietism and that was supported by the early Barth. The first series of ideas stressed "religious *individualism,*" the second "*religious* individualism." We may even venture to assume that the beginnings of Barth's later critique of Pietism are found in these two series of ideas. The first one led to his critique in the first *Epistle to the Romans,* the second one to his critique in the second *Epistle to the Romans.* Again it can be said that the latent explosive force of these series of ideas in Barth's early theology hardly had an effect and for the time being did not

---

[85]Compare n. 69.

[86]Sermon nr. 53, November 20, 1910.

[87]These sentences could be found in the second *Epistle to the Romans,* but they come from sermon nr. 58, from January 29, 1911, in which it says in more detail: "Think of an evangelistic meeting . . . on the one side there are the faithful and those who are convinced. They endeavor to draw the others over, those who are not convinced, the 'unbelievers.' Imagine that Jesus would come into such a meeting and would speak the one word: Blessed are those who are spiritually poor. Indeed, we at least have reason to ask: On what side does he stand, on the side of the 'believers' who know that they are pious, or on the side of the 'unbelievers' who know that they are not pious?" No, there is no doubt: "In reality the situation is such that by far the most sincere, pious people of our time probably would have belonged to the Pharisees." For "we would say like the Pharisees of old: Blessed are those who are spiritually rich." But Jesus says: "Blessed are those who know that they are not pious." This sounds "like a tune from another world. It startles us all the more because we thought we were already in the other, better world with our piety and diligence. We are no longer frivolous and superficial . . . but we do what is right and have the proper awareness of it and now all of a sudden all the standards are reversed" when Jesus stands up for the impious: "You *are* the people of God because you know that you are not."

touch his liberal framework. Perhaps it can be clearly understood only in retrospect and recognized as seeds of a new theological framework and a con-
comitant critique of Pietism that would point the way ahead. Since in our opinion they both grew from the root of the idea of self-denial, Barth could for the
time being continue to believe in good faith that he was basically in harmony
with Tersteegen's path not "of seeking happiness, but of self-denial" on the
one hand and with Hermann's teaching about faith as an "inner submission to
God" on the other hand.

The Significance and Problematic Nature of Barth's Early Position on Pietism

We have assembled a few facts from Barth's development and his own theological beginnings in the period between 1907 and 1912. In summary what can we
conclude from these facts that are clearly a quite determinative part of the early
history of his critique of Pietism?

1. Barth indeed *knew* Pietism, and not just from the outside. Not only were
the factors that influenced his intellectual development at least not anti-Pietistic;
to a large degree they were in a rather close relationship to this Christian movement. He himself thought that he was by no means in opposition to "the mystics
and Pietists" in his early theology. Instead he fundamentally *affirmed* their concern. That is why from the start we can rule out the idea that in his later critique
of Pietism he made his judgments simply from ignorance or a lack of understanding for the Pietists' cause.

2. If Barth's largely positive relationship to Pietism later grew critical, as we
will demonstrate, this critique—and this is highly significant—cannot simply be
that Barth wanted to see a greater emphasis placed on the "superiority of God
who made us and not we who made him" instead of an egocentric attitude, or
allowing God to work instead of working ourselves, or self-denial instead of
seeking our own happiness. Therefore a construct that seeks to take his later
critique of Pietism into account and then tries to combine a Barth interpreted *in
these terms* with the Pietistic concern is invalid from the outset. If Barth had intended to stress those viewpoints in his later critique of Pietism, he could have
done so without his criticizing Pietism. In fact, he was able to say this in his early
period when he was favorable to Pietism, following the thought of Tersteegen,
for example.[88]

3. However, Barth's praise for Pietsim depended on a certain interpretation
of this phenomenon. He basically saw it as a quite *modern* movement—not co-

---

[88]See n. 68 above.

incidentally the soil in which Schleiermacher was rooted![89] He saw it as a modern movement which took seriously the discovery, emerging in the Renaissance and climaxing in Romanticism, of, on the one hand, the difference between the historical and scientific realm and the vital individual realm, and on the other hand, the location of religion not in the former but firmly in the latter realm.[90] This interpretation is all the more remarkable because it differs, for example, from H. Stephan's understanding of Pietism as an antimodern movement in his book on the modern era (1909).[91] Interestingly, Karl Barth collaborated with Stephan on this book. Of course, we must be clear that Barth's praise for Pietism is tied to two assumptions, setting aside the question of whether Barth's interpretation is completely accurate or whether one really should see reactionary elements in Pietism. Barth assumed that (1) the modern concept of autonomy and individuality is considered to be a fact of history in Western thought, making it impossible to go back to the premodern era.[92] That is why this fact definitely has a *theological* quality. Thus Barth articulated a thesis on which the final word cannot be spoken so simply because of its problematic nature. At any rate, it is enormously far-reaching in its theological consequences because it virtually attributes the character of revelation to "intellectual stages of development." (2) Barth's praise for Pietism is tied to his simple characterization of orthodoxy as "heteronomy" and to his radical rejection not only of orthodoxy but wide swaths of "premodern" church history. The fact that such an understanding of orthodoxy is totally superficial, achieved without opening one orthodox book, and at the same time that one ruins any chance of gaining an understanding of the Reformation with such an understanding of orthodoxy (or at best can "save" it by associating it with the Renaissance) is so patently obvious that the final word cannot be spoken about these problematic assumptions.

4. In those days Barth thought that he could reduce the concerns of Pietism to the common denominator of "*religious individualism*." This characterization of Pietism is so significant because the same phrase will reappear in Barth's later critique of Pietism. Of course then it will be fraught with negative connotations, especially in the first *Epistle to the Romans* and then in the lecture of 1932/33 where he covered himself by making a stronger case. We will identify our reservations about this characterization in more detail later, but at this point we must agree that this phrase is certainly accurate as far as it goes, but it is not sufficient.

---

[89]"Der christliche Glaube und die Geschichte," p. 64.
[90]Ibid., pp. 49ff.
[91]Compare Stephan's praise for Barth's "valuable notes" on this book in his preface.
[92]"Der christliche Glaube und die Geschichte," p. 17.

What makes it insufficient is not that the Pietistic idea of community would be overlooked by stressing this "religious individualism." Barth himself showed how a particular understanding of community is inextricably linked to such individualism. What makes this common denominator insufficient is that it encompasses too many different ways of thinking at one time (for example, at least for the young Barth, the thinking of the Reformation, mysticism, Pietism and Romanticism) to be able to grasp what was unique in Pietism. But we could also say that this phrase is too general to notice more than just *one* aspect of Pietism.

5. Barth declared his support for the Pietists in a way that enabled him to simultaneously declare his support for the principles of *liberalism*. In fact, his support for these principles became the key to access his understanding of the Pietistic concern. Under the heading "religious individualism" he thought he could affirm the Pietistic tradition together with the liberal tradition and thus link both together. This view also had far-reaching consequences for Barth's later critique of Pietism because it is a (biographical) prerequisite for understanding his later thesis about the affinity of Pietism and the Enlightenment. Barth certainly was able to marshal several factual reasons for this thesis that was meant to be critical of Pietism. In addition, it takes on a captivating quality because we now know that it was articulated by Barth in the awareness that he himself had tested the possibility of achieving a synthesis of these two traditions. Again we must not overlook the fact that this thesis at least in its early form has its limitations, because it affirms and grasps Pietism only when it harmonizes with liberal principles and can be categorized with them. In Barth's early period he was not a Pietist but a supporter of a liberal position who as such believed that the concern of the Pietists (in Hegel's well-known terms) was "synthesized" in liberalism. From this perspective we must look for the possibility that in his later critique of Pietism, Barth distanced himself from Pietism only inasmuch as it was "related" to the other phenomenon, if in fact this thesis of the affinity between these two phenomena was a component of his critique.

6. It is striking that the early Barth primarily appealed to the so-called *radical,* spiritualistic Pietists such as Angelus Silesius or Tersteegen. By contrast he appealed less or not at all to the so-called church Pietists such as Spener, Francke and Bengel or to figures of contemporary Pietism in the community movement. This fact can be taken as a sign that clearly only this "radical Pietism" was suitable for seeing "Pietism" in conjunction with liberalism and for appealing to Pietism in favor of a sharply anti-orthodox understanding of faith in terms of "religious individualism." Thus ecclesiastical Pietism had to appear "inconsistent" to him and could only be included in that he presumed that "its logical consequence" would lead to the radical, individualistic anti-orthodox understanding

of faith held by an Angelus Silesius. There is no doubt that it actually tended to move in that direction. This tendency comes out very forcefully in many statements. However the real question is whether this interpretation does justice historically to the church Pietism of the eighteenth century or to the more recent community movement. Are not important aspects of church Pietism that was in fact shaped by orthodoxy left out of consideration? Were there not perhaps other, more solid reasons why it did not turn into such a "radical Pietism" other than a lack of consistency? And finally, did not Barth's interpretation fail to appreciate a series of meaningful "pious desires" for the reform of the church, such as the promotion of Bible reading or lay ministries which were also part of the essence of ecclesiastical Pietism? These aspects of Pietism play a significant role in giving it proper recognition. If Barth mainly addressed "the consistency" of Pietism in his later critique as well, this would shed light on why church Pietism could rightfully feel that it was not "fully" targeted by it. Rather it felt that his critique called attention to possible consequences that could pose a threat to it.

7. We have seen that Barth was not simply uncritical toward this phenomenon even at the beginning of his theological career when he was quite favorable to Pietism. But if our assumption is correct that Barth's first critical remarks about Pietism can be understood as conclusions drawn from the idea of "self-denial," an idea first found in Pietism's own supporters, and that the first signs of Barth's late critique of Pietism are found in them, a question comes to mind from this dual perspective: Could Barth ever become an anti-Pietist even in his later critique of Pietism? In fact did not a Pietistic root secretly survive in his later theological thought to a certain extent in spite of all the criticism of this phenomenon implied by it?

II. Barth's Critique of Pietism in the First Epistle to the Romans

1. His Preparation to Critique Pietism in the First Epistle to the Romans

Notes on Barth's Change Between 1912 and 1916

A change in Barth's theological thought took place in the years between 1912 and 1916. It came out in his first interpretation of the Pauline Epistle to the Romans that he began in 1916. In the course of this interpretation not only the understanding of faith we just sketched out but especially Pietism was subjected to a fundamental critique. The question of what factors brought about this change is discussed a lot today. However, it has not yet been clarified, and it is questionable if it can ever be answered from a historical, immanent perspective. So it can only be dealt with here in passing.

It is certain that Barth himself was aware of a fundamental change in his thought during this period. Based on his self-understanding,[1] the following factors were at work in this situation, listed in chronological order: (1) His preoccupation with the labor issue and socialism, in association with his encounter with religious socialism. In this context his thought was especially stimulated by the differences of opinion between H. Kutter and L. Ragaz, the main representatives of this movement in Switzerland. (2) The shock he felt at the outbreak of World War I and especially his disappointment at the failure of his liberal theological teachers as well as the socialists at the outbreak of the war, in conjunction with the issue of a new starting point. (3) His encounter with the message of both Blumhardts and consequently his new focus on the issue of preaching and on the Bible, culminating in his study of the Epistle to the Romans. Barth's sincerity in listing the factors that triggered a change in his thought cannot be doubted. Nevertheless, we must think of this change as being more

---

[1] K. Barth, "Autobiogr. Skizze," in K. Barth/R. Bultmann, *Briefwechsel 1922–1966,* 1971, pp. 306-7.

complicated and not necessarily tied to this chronological pattern. We must also not conceive of it as a secondary conversion,[2] and not at all as the occurrence of a radical break with his earlier thought that would have simply negated what he had previously affirmed.

However, a bewildering fact is that Barth's earliest thought shows insights that did not at all fit the position of a "religious socialism" he held then and that would presumably not be found in his thought at that time based on the afore-mentioned chronological pattern. We will cite a few examples to illustrate this point. The view of social democracy as a movement heading "toward the kingdom of God" is actually found in his first sermon in the summer of 1907, far earlier than his contact with the labor problem in Safenwil.[3] His critique of religious individualism with its "I want to be saved" mentality is already clearly expressed in his Geneva sermon from November 1910, at a time when he considered religious individualism alone to be theologically legitimate.[4] Therefore, he recognized even then that the individual is nothing at all "without the whole," except as a "link in the chain of the whole, in the Kingdom of the living God."[5] Even his awareness of the "crisis," the view that "a dark mood, an oppressive atmosphere of inner decay weighs on our era" and that in fact it must grow completely dark over us . . . so that the Day of God can dawn anew," is already found in his thought in this early period and thus long before the shockwave of World War I.[6] Indeed, even the insight that the kingdom of God is not a heightening of existing reality but can now only be affirmed by "making crucial *negations*" was already present in his thought at the beginning.[7] These examples are certainly only one piece of a larger, still confusing puzzle. But they can show that significant insights Barth talked about after or during his change were already present or latent in his thought before the change.

If this was so, if the young Barth believed he could harmonize his position of "religious individualism" with such statements—and he somehow must have believed this—we must at least raise the question of whether conversely his in-

---

[2]Compare the description of this change by the old K. Barth in *Letzte Zeugnisse*, 1969, p. 19: "In the course of this work as a pastor I gradually grew attentive to the Bible."

[3]We must consider the fact that Barth was already familiar with the social issue from his father and his confirmation teacher, R. Aeschbacher (compare E. Busch, *Karl Barths Lebenslauf,* 1975, 42.81). He was also familiar with it from Marburg, where the Neo-Kantianism advocated there was considered to be the "political philosophy of Socialism" (in *Ges. Aufsätze*, 1923, pp. 463ff.). Barth's reading of Kant and Schleiermacher as well as his reading of Socialist authors in his Marburg period is documented.

[4]Sermon nr. 53, November 11, 1910 (manuscript in the K. Barth archives, Basel).

[5]Sermon nr. 56, January 1, 1911.

[6]Ibid.

[7]"We do not want him to rule over us!" In *Kirchenblatt für die ref. Schweiz,* May 27, 1911, p. 83.

sights *after* his change could be linked to certain elements in his understanding of his earlier position.[8] The question of what factors triggered his change will thus have to be tied to the question of how far-reaching his change actually was, what elements of his previous thought were changed and which ones remained constant. It seems to me as if there are several reasons for assuming that we can expect such continuity and thus definite limits to the change Barth made in his thinking in spite of all the changes that did occur, especially in view of both interpretations of the *Epistle to the Romans*. This is so even if we can only point them out in passing within the framework of our study.[9] Perhaps these indications are sufficient to call our attention to the task that must still be solved.

Nevertheless, we cannot overlook the fact that a theologically changed Barth, or one who was in the process of change, began to speak in the first *Epistle to the Romans*. Here he contested what had previously been dear to his heart: "religious individualism." We must point out his Safenwil lecture from October 9, 1917, in order to clarify the nature and extent of the change that occured. He held this lecture immediately before he wrote the section of the first *Epistle to the Romans* in which he explicitly took issue with Pietism and which can be seen as Barth's attempt to give an account of his present intellectual position. The subject, "Religion and Life," is unmistakably reminiscent of the problem the young, "liberal" Barth faced. But his development of this subject shows just as unmistakably the change that occurred in his thinking. The change can be summed up in the phrase "Religion *is* Life." This synthesis has turned into an antithesis (religion and life mutually exclude each other) to such an extent that Barth now votes against "religion" and for "life": "The *curse* is that what is called *religion* is completely out of touch with reality. *Redemption* is *life* itself."[10] Barth understands by "life": (1) it is "the universal, the all-encompassing reality," (2) it is corporeality, "sheer inwardness that has become external," and (3) it is "dynamism." In contrast to this he understands by "religion": (1) it is merely a "private matter," the salvation of the "individual soul," personal experience; (2) it is mere "inwardness," "an emotional condition"; (3) it is a mere "attitude."[11] Be-

---

[8]Compare J. Fangmeier, *Erziehung in Zeugenschaft-K. Barth und die Pädagogik,* 1964, p. 30: "It is not as if all the old strains had suddenly fallen silent . . ." I think that even this is perhaps phrased too cautiously.

[9]An indication of this (certainly not evidence in itself) can be seen in the fact that Barth studied and consulted anew the works of Kant which he appreciated so much in his early period when he undertook the two interpretations of the *Epistle to the Romans*. Compare K. Barth/E. Thurneysen, *Briefwechsel 1, 1913-1921,* 1973 (in their further correspondence 1), pp. 145, 148-49, 241. Also compare *Autobiogr. Skizze* (see n. 1), p. 308.

[10]First published in *EvTh* 1951-1952, p. 449.

[11]Ibid., pp. 444ff.

cause "religion" is something "comfortable," people like to stay in it "as in a thick tank turret," practicing "religion, religion, religion and not wanting to notice that it is all about life, life, life."[12] In Barth's view, what makes a smashing of the tank turret necessary is the simple fact that religion is out of touch with reality and passes life by.[13] "Life" is *"different."* Religion sees to that.

First of all, we understand that from this perspective Barth's separation from Pietism could seem obvious. Pietism could especially suggest itself as an obvious paradigm for what was understood by "religion" and thus was rejected. Conversely, we understand how Pietism had to be understood in this case and how it had to be criticized for what was considered to be questionable about it. Undoubtedly it can be reduced to the common denominator of "religious individualism." At any rate, the battle line in Barth's thought is clear—it is clearly targeted at the position once advocated by himself.

But the position he took on this battle is a bit vague. What kind of phenomenon is "life"? Barth simply answers: "Life in the world and life in the Bible."[14] Was it thus a phenomenon that could be found both in the "world" as well as in the Bible? How does Barth come to assume that life in the world and life in the Bible are congruent and that both phenomena oppose "religion" and are superior to it? And how does he come to reduce what is unique in the Bible to this common denominator? Moreover, how does he come to assert that individualism as such is both the main characteristic and the problematic aspect of "religion"? And how does he come to consider the social structure of the phenomenon of "life" as such to be something fundamentally different from the individualism of "religion," something superior to it and able to overcome it? Barth's own position is somewhat unclear and unsettled. If in fact he criticized Pietism from this position, we must now ask if he was only partially able to capture its essence or if he was able to do more than that, thus enabling him to really put it behind him?

To appreciate Barth's position we must recognize that he was evidently looking for an opportunity to make theological statements in which the divine was no longer understood as a part of the human individual and his self-awareness. Thus he had gained insight into the problematic nature of this concept. This was really something new in his understanding. But we cannot recognize this without at the same time seeing that the level on which he thought it was possible to make such statements was not necessarily so different from the level on which his thinking had previously operated. For example, what

---

[12]Ibid., p. 450.
[13]Ibid., p. 443.
[14]Ibid., p. 450.

was problematic for him about "religion" in this phase was not "experience" in itself but only the individualistic aspect of it! Perhaps we could even be permitted to view his new position as such not merely as a break with the theology of Hermann but also as the attempt to synthesize what was learned from it with the newly discovered insights of "religious socialism." Precisely this concept of "life" made such an outstanding bridge, combining the understanding of faith Herrmann called "experience," the idea of an unanalyzed, self-evident, spontaneous, not "contrived" but "living" reality with the religious, social understanding of Christianity as a supra-individual, holistic, dynamic reality. If this interpretation would prove to be correct, both the direction and the limits of the "progress" Barth made in moving beyond his earlier position would become apparent.

The Influence of Christoph Blumhardt and T. Beck

How did Barth arrive at the new position we have just described? It should have become clear that one particular line of thought in Barth's first attempt at making a critique of Pietism which we pointed out above had gained a major influence in his thought in the period before he began his first *Epistle to the Romans*. This was his separation from "religious *individualism*." Undoubtedly Barth's involvement with socialism also played a significant role in this development.[15] When he said in his Safenwil lecture of December 17, 1911, on "Jesus Christ and the Social Movement" that what Jesus brought was not the requirement to "believe or accept this or that" but "to live a certain way,"[16] he was still clearly following liberal thinking as defined by Hermann. But he set out on a new path when he defined in greater detail what he meant by "living a certain way." He saw it closely linked with the intentions but not the actual situation of the "social movement." In other words, he rejected a "useless Christianity that only wants to get into heaven." By stressing that the end of God's ways is "corporeality," the gospel for Barth could be summed up in these words, "You are to be set free from all things that begin with 'I' and 'mine,' absolutely free, in order to be free to offer social assistance."[17] It is obvious that the position of "religious individualism" had become impossible for him. But it would be superficial, in my opinion, to simply replace it with the concept of "the social movement" or "social assistance." If Barth was initially

---

[15]F. W. Marquardt is especially preoccupied with illuminating this relationship; compare *Theologie und Sozialismus: Das Beispiel K. Barths,* 1972, pp. 70ff., 114ff. Also compare U. Dannemann, *Theologie und Politik im Denken K. Barths,* 1977, pp. 25ff.

[16]"Jesus Christus und die soziale Bewegung," *Der freie Aargauer,* December 23-30, 1911.

[17]Ibid.

of the opinion that he could reduce his alternative to this phrase, various factors, including the failure of the socialists when the world war broke out, but also the difference between the "religious socialists" Kutter and Ragaz, led him to understand that he still needed to clarify what could be considered as an alternative to "religious individualism."

His clarification of this question not only preceded his interpretation of the epistle to the Romans but his interpretation of the epistle to the Romans served to clarify it as well. In my view two figures in particular pointed the way for him in clarifying this question. Both of them had their roots in Pietism and surprisingly found a number of admirers there, although both of them took a critical turn in their relationship with Pietism. They were Christoph Blumhardt and T. Beck. Barth discovered Blumhardt about one year before he began his interpretation of the epistle to the Romans, when he visited Bad Boll in April 1915.[18] He felt that Blumhardt's message was "immediately true."[19] Blumhardt's ideas, reinforced by his careful study of Christoph's father, Johann Christian Blumhardt,[20] and by reading the books of Fr. Zundel,[21] gave Barth much food for thought in the following years. His influence was so great that Barth wanted to "gratefully" confess in the forward to his first book, published in 1917, "that we received . . . crucial stimulus to our thought from *Blumhardt,* both the elder and the junior."[22] A few days before he began his interpretations of the epistle to the Romans, he summarized in a review of Blumhardt's *House Devotions* (1916) what this stimulus was. It met with rejection among the reli-

---

[18]Compare Busch, *Karl Barths Lebenslauf,* 1975, pp. 96-97. Christoph Blumhardt was greatly admired by several of Barth's relatives (for example, Karl and Elizabeth Sartorius), which may have motivated the theology student Karl Barth to visit Blumhardt "several times," the first time on December 27, 1907, but "without gaining any profound insight" (compare Busch, *Karl Barths Lebenslauf,* 1975, p. 55). If Barth "discovered" Blumhardt in 1915, part of his discovery was that he now saw Blumhardt positioned beyond Pietism and beyond what Pietistic admiration made of him. Thus we could ask whether the following remark in the first *Epistle to the Romans* was not also targeted at his Pietistic relatives' admiration for Blumhardt. The church "is given Blumhardt [by God] . . . and it takes notice of everything, knows how to make something of everything for its purposes, it knows how to discover what is religious, human, interesting, 'piety' in every demonstration of God's existence and to leave behind what is divine, the message itself, that which could become dangerous, God's call to repentance" (p. 314).

[19]*Briefwechsel* 1, p. 107

[20]In June 1915 Barth read Zundel's book on Blumhardt "in great consternation" (ibid., p. 51), "primarily with the feeling of shame" (p. 53).

[21]In January 1916 Barth mentions that he was edified by reading his books, in conjunction with the suspicion that "modern theology could possibly become obsolete" (ibid., p. 121). Compare his mentioning of Zundel in the first *Epistle to the Romans,* pp. 1, 12, 14, 117.

[22]*Briefwechsel* 1, pp. 232-33. In the forward of this book *Suchet Gott, so werdet ihr leben* (1917), edited with Thurneysen, this sentence, though, is missing. Barth's reading of the Bad Boller "Briefblatter" of 1887 can be documented for July 1917 (*Briefwechsel* 1, p. 216).

gious socialists,[23] whereas Blumhardt stated that he was "highly satisfied" with it.[24] Furthermore, soon after the publication of the first *Epistle to the Romans* (1919), he wrote an obituary of Blumhardt, and its essential points were in harmony with that review.

Two things became important for Barth through the influence of Blumhardt. (1) *Hope* for the "completion" of all things by God became a key viewpoint for him. "The great future of God is behind everything."[25] However, in the view of Barth and Blumhardt this future means that the universal salvation of humanity takes the place of a self-centered interest in the salvation of the individual,[26] the linkage of "eternity" to the "earth" takes the place of a mere belief in the afterlife,[27] a redemption of the physical nature takes the place of a mere spiritual redemption,[28] and faith in the renewal of all things takes the place of faith in the need for only some things to be renewed.[29] In this line of thought God is understood not as something beside life but as "the living God"[30] himself or as the "life-bringing God"[31] and as the One who can provide something completely *new*. This new thing is *life*.[32] But only a supra-individual, universal, holistic "life" is considered to be "real life." If Barth believed that he had overcome the problematic aspect of Pietism with this view that was partially influenced by the tradition of religious socialism, he especially believed he had gotten beyond the problematic aspect of religious socialism with the ideas that had become important to him through Blumhardt's influence. (2) How does this new order come about? Barth and Blumhardt answered that it comes "from God himself."[33] First of all, the battle raging between Kutter and Ragaz about the way the kingdom of God comes, which Barth reduced to the phrase "wait or hurry," was relativized by this answer. Both of them have their place, and both of them are right.[34]

---

[23]*Briefwechsel* 1, pp. 146-47. Ragaz refused to print it.

[24]Ibid., pp. 158-59.

[25]"Auf das Reich Gottes warten," *Der freie Schweizer Arbeiter,* 1916, nr. 47 (in what follows briefly quoted as 1916, based on the reprinting of the review in *Suchet Gott, so werdet ihr leben,* 2nd ed., 1928, pp. 175ff). Thus 1916, p. 190. Compare "Vergangenheit und Zukunft," *Neuer Freier Aargauer,* 1919, nr. 204/5 (in what follows briefly quoted as 1919, based on the reprinting of the obituary, in J. Moltmann, *Anfänge der dialektischen Theologie* 1, 1962, p. 37ff). Thus 1919, p. 45.

[26]1916, pp. 186-87; 1919, p. 45.

[27]1916, p. 186; compare p. 184, 1919, p. 45.

[28]1919, pp. 45-46.

[29]1919, p. 46; compare 1916, p. 191.

[30]1919, p. 44.

[31]1916, p. 179.

[32]1919, p. 44.

[33]1916, p. 190.

[34]1916, pp. 188-89; 1919, p. 48.

However, both of them have their limitations because action "coming from man" is not itself the solution. Because this new order "coming from God" is life, it does not come abruptly but is being prepared and starts to develop in "our waiting and hurrying." Now Barth emphasized that in its essence this gradual development (as Barth liked to put it) does not take place "mechanically, but organically."[35] This new order is not forced upon the world from the outside or stuck on the old order as a foreign object but "desires to be born from the old order,"[36] and shows itself as "a seed" in humankind "that is to take root and grow."[37] Thus by its very nature it comes "quietly and gently."[38] It comes in such a way that we are not "seeking anything of our own" and do not want to grow ourselves. Rather we "allow God to grow in us."[39]

It will become apparent that these two viewpoints actually became major ideas in Barth's interpretation of the Epistle to the Romans. We see the creative aspect of it precisely in the way Barth combines both viewpoints. We also assume that Barth, like Blumhardt, believed he was making a contribution to laying a new theological foundation by combining them. Through Blumhardt's influence it also dawned on him that "our dialectic has reached a dead end" and "if we want to be healthy and strong, we must start over again and expect solutions to the conflicts and problems that move us so deeply on a different foundation," beyond what is important "to us all, also to those of us who are socialist theologians."[40]

It seems to me that Barth's understanding of both these viewpoints was enriched and his idea about the possibility of combining them was strengthened by his discovery of the other theologian I mentioned: T. Beck.[41] After reading

---

[35]1916, p. 190.

[36]1919, p. 46.

[37]1916, p. 180.

[38]1916, p. 186.

[39]1916, p. 188.

[40]1916, pp. 176-77.

[41]Of course, the name was familiar to him from his father, Fritz Barth, whose "life's work" he later called "the result of the profound influence" of Beck's theology (*Die prot. Theologie im 19. Jahrhundert,* 1946, p. 568). It is no coincidence that when Barth turned his attention to Beck in the first *Epistle to the Romans,* he was also focusing theologically on his own father (compare the foreword to this book and furthermore the quotes there from F. Barth's work on pp. 99, 124, 151, 179, which all conspicuously breathe the spirit of Beck). Compare the psychologically interesting remark of the old Barth about the origin of the first *Epistle to the Romans:* "Only then did I begin to remember my father who died in 1912 with the proper respect and gratitude. . . . And I do not want to conceal the fact that for a moment the thought crossed my mind that I wanted to and would now take retaliatory action of sorts against those who had so outshone my father!" (epilogue, in *Schleiermacher-Auswahl.* Siebenstern-Taschenbuch 113/114, 1968, p. 294).

B. Riggenbach's biography of Beck in May 1916,[42] he came across his writings in July during his work on the interpretation of the epistle to the Romans. He said, "I have discovered a treasure chest, J. T. Beck! He is simply head and shoulders above the rest of the crowd as an expositor of the Bible. . . . He is also (in part) easily accessible and exemplary for us in his systematic ways. I got on his trail by studying the epistle to the Romans."[43] It was a new experience for Barth to find "something there that was quite different and more fruitful than ordinary positive Christianity."[44] It was in sharp contrast to what he knew about Beck from word of mouth until then. He believed he could essentially see Beck in close conjunction with Blumhardt.[45] What he found in Beck was in fact closely related to what he found in Blumhardt, and he gave his attention (only) to what was closely related in their thought. It focused on the goal of the kingdom of God, understood not as the fulfillment of the desire for an individual salvation of the soul but as a comprehensive, holistic, spiritual and physical "living organism" that leads humanity out of its isolation, as a complete world organization[46] that is established by divine "forces," by vital cosmic energies. In Beck's thought this central expectation was linked to the idea that "the simple, quiet and earnest way is the one that leads to the goal, it is not achieved by hustle and bustle."[47] This goal is being prepared not by mechanical activity but by organic growth alone, by the forces of the future world penetrating the present one, not by our own building but by the blossoming of divine seeds.[48] In this line of thought Christ is understood as the first seed of the new world,[49] and justification is seen as growth in the process of being made righteous.[50]

These ideas not only noticeably shaped the thought and even the language of the first *Epistle to the Romans* and helped Barth express his own inten-

[42]*Briefwechsel* 1, p. 138.
[43]Ibid., p. 148.
[44]Ibid., pp. 160-61, where Barth refers to Beck's article in *RGG* 1, pp. 996-97, which emphasizes Beck's sharp "critique of the empirical church and not least its Pietistic manifestations."
[45]*Briefwechsel* 1, p. 160: here Barth resists Thurneysen's distinction between them.
[46]*RGG* 1, p. 997. Compare also G. Weth, *Die Heilsgeschichte: Ihr universeller und ihr individueller Sinn in der offenbarungsgeschichtlichen Theologie des 19. Jahrhunderts,* 1931, pp. 72ff., 137ff. Moreover, it is remarkable to see how in Weth's view the Barth of the 1920s fails to take this tradition into account, yet it escapes Weth's notice that Barth once stood firmly in this tradition. Compare also Beck's interpretation of Romans 5:12ff. in *Erklärung des Briefes Pauli an die Römer* 1, 1884, pp. 396ff. It especially impressed Barth; see *Briefwechsel* 1, p. 229.
[47]T. Beck, *Treu und frei,* 1915, pp. 212-13.
[48]Compare *RGG* 1, p. 997, and Weth, *Die Heilsgeschichte,* pp. 191ff.
[49]Weth, *Die Heilsgeschichte,* pp. 126ff.
[50]T. Beck, *Erklärung des Briefes Pauli an die Römer* 1, pp. 85ff.

tions,[51] but he made Beck's influence explicitly visible by using a number of quotations from Beck (a practice that is typical of the book itself). For example, in Beck's words he said "that an inherent force of disorganization is prevalent in the whole earthly system of life which undermines and dissolves the vital energies of organisms."[52] And with Beck he said that the Spirit of God is nothing other than "the principle that determines the whole new organization of the future in its cosmic expansion"[53] and that "the new humanity of the sons of God forms the heart of the renewal of the world that is now beginning."[54] He also said with Beck that the new age of God is starting to develop "in the organic growth of living seeds," of "fertile seeds from the age of consummation."[55] We conclude from all this that Barth was stimulated by Beck's thought to stress both of these viewpoints and combine them and that in this regard he found a similar pattern of thought in Blumhardt. It should be easy to see that Barth's earlier liberal concept of a "religious individualism" had to change under the influence of these ideas. It is at least clear in outline what was now to take its place. And it should also be obvious not only that this change implied a critical abandonment of Pietism but also in what sense this occurred.

Encounters with Pietists

Barth actually made this abandonment of Pietism explicit in his book when he interpreted Romans 7:14ff. in a whole chapter under the title "The Law and Pietism" (pp. 204-17). Today the date when this chapter was written can be precisely determined today. After Barth had begun his first *Epistle to the Romans* in the summer of 1916, his interpretation of Romans 5 came to a standstill in March 1917. Only after a break of six months did he continue to write this book.[56] In the period between the end of October and December 1917 he wrote the chapter in which he took issue with Pietism in his interpretation and at the same time dealt with it thematically.[57]

---

[51]A few examples of how Barth could fully speak Beck's language in the first *Epistle to the Romans* without quoting him: Christ is "the seed of the new world," "The divine grows organically" (p. 62). Justification is "being rooted and growing" in the soil of God's righteousness (p. 66). The Spirit is "the growing energy of the coming world of God" (p. 221), transforming "our total existence subject to death . . . into an organism of life," "transforming the bonds which still hold you captive into freedoms and conquests, advancing organically" (p. 219), etc.

[52]*Römerbrief* 1, p. 127.

[53]Ibid., p. 231.

[54]Ibid., pp. 240-41; compare further pp. 130, 212, 282, 291, 414.

[55]Ibid., p. 2.

[56]Compare E. Busch, *Karl Barths Lebenslauf,* 1975, p. 113.

[57]Compare *Briefwechsel* 1, pp. 238, 254.

To appreciate the position he held there, it is useful to make clear in what way he was specifically prepared for this discussion. *A literary preoccupation* with Pietism preceded his discussion with it. His reading of A. Ritschl's *History of Pietism* at the beginning of 1916 had been quite a while earlier, and it was evidently more important for Barth to get to know the author than the object of his study in order to prepare a "great strike against the theologians" (especially of that school).[58] In November of the same year he used an evangelistic meeting by J. Vetter in Safenwil as an opportunity to do extensive reading "in the old Pietists."[59] In this respect his library had been enriched from the inheritance of his grandmother Sartorius, who had died at the end of 1915.[60] While interpreting the Epistle to the Romans himself he continually used the interpretations of the old Schwabian Pietists Bengel and C. H. Rieger, whom he still called "my true friends" at the beginning of 1919.[61] However, he also used the interpretation of A. Tholuck.[62]

Barth dealt with Pietism in more detail especially during that six-month break. In particular, his reading of Hofacker's sermons can be verified during this period, and they made a strong impression on him although he clearly sensed the difference between them and sermons of Blumhardt.[63] In addition he read a number of biographies of Pietistic figures: the ones about David Spleiss,[64] Ludwig Hofacker,[65] August Tholuck[66] and the one about the biblicist Gottfried Menken.[67] It is also possible that he got to see the biographies of Sixt

---

[58]Ibid., p. 121.

[59]Ibid., p. 162.

[60]Based on an oral report of Barth to the author.

[61]*Briefwechsel* 1, p. 320.

[62]Ibid., p. 148.

[63]Ibid., pp. 205, 216.

[64]C. Stokar and David Spleiss, *weil. Antistes of the Schaffhausen church,* 1858; compare *Briefwechsel* 1, pp. 199-200.

[65]A. Knapp, *Leben von Ludwig Hofacker mit einer Auswahl aus seinen Briefen,* 6th ed., 1895; compare *Briefwechsel* 1, p. 200.

[66]L. Witte, *Das Leben D. Friedrich August Gotttreu Tholucks,* 1884/6; compare *Briefwechsel* 1, p. 215. Consider what kind of Christianity and what impression of Pietism Barth encountered in this book and in the two previously mentioned ones! Everything centered on the "earnestly wrestling soul fighting the most intense battles of rebirth," the sinner in search of the Savior "looking at himself in the mirror of self-understanding" (Knappe, ed., 1860, 1864), preoccupied with a change "that is all about his own salvation" (p. 52). His desire is "to become acquainted with myself, to examine, view, purify and compare all my works and words in order to finally enjoy the reflection of your imperishable life that has penetrated deeply into my heart" (Witte, 1, pp. 114-15). Spleiss also delights in feeling "the balsam of heaven flow . . . into my constricted heart" (Stokar, *Leben von Ludwig Hofacker,* p. 108).

[67]C. H. Gildemeister, *Leben und Wirken des Dr. Gottfried Menken,* 1861; compare *Briefwechsel* 1, p. 215. Reading this book evidently made no little impression on Barth, and we may assume that it confirmed what he found in Beck when he read there about the "whole," the kingdom of God and Christ as the King.

Karl von Kapff and of Christian Gottlieb Barth.[68] I think it is very likely that he also read the peculiar work of D. F. Strauss's friend Christian Märklin, *A Portrayal and Critique of Modern Pietism.*[69] Its praise for Pietism somewhat confused the revivalist theologians of that era. Märklin praised them because Pietism was striving for "internalization," that is, for taking the object of faith into the pious subject in a thoroughly liberal sense, although it was unfortunate that Pietism was inconsistent in not completing the attempt.[70] In any case, Märklin's work was strikingly similar to Barth's interpretation of Pietism, although Barth's praise and criticism had different emphases.[71] After dealing with Tholuck, Barth wrote on July 17, 1917, "My image of Pietism . . . is gradually being rounded off and soon I will be able to read something else again."[72]

In summary, the following points can be made about Barth's literary treatment of Pietism, especially in the summer of 1917. (1) He thoroughly *prepared* for the critique of Pietism he began to make in the fall by asking the representatives of this movement about its concerns. (2) He especially read *biographies* of Pietists and considered this genre to be an appropriate way to access an understanding of their concern. By so conspicuously preferring this form of access to Pietism, he clearly assumed that its intentions had to come to expression in a special way through biographies. (3) In the summer of 1917, Barth dealt exclusively with *revivalist theology* from the beginning of the nineteenth century, as far as it can be proven. His reasons for limiting his reading to this period can only be surmised.[73] At any rate, it can be assumed from his reading material that in his discussion with Pietism in the first *Epistle to the Romans* this "revivalist movement" was first and foremost in his mind.

Several personal *encounters* with representatives of this group preceded this discussion. Three encounters are especially worth mentioning. The first

---

[68]At least Thurneysen points out that he read the biographies of both of these men. In *Briefwechsel* 1, pp. 218-19, 221.

[69]Thurneysen mentions it (ibid, pp. 218-19). I remember from Barth's oral report that he also knew it well.

[70]Chr. Märklin, for example, pp. 27-28, 272.

[71]Märklin's view of Pietism obviously fit in well with the view of the young, "liberal" Barth and is remarkably similar to the view of the first *Epistle to the Romans* but especially to his view in "The History of Protestant Theology" (lecture, 1932-1933, printed 1946).

[72]*Briefwechsel* 1, p. 215.

[73]Did the revivalist movement as one of the various epochs of Pietism especially interest him as a foil to the message of the older Blumhardt? Or did it interest him as a sideshow to Romanticism, which had long been dear to his heart and which is then treated in the *Epistle to the Romans* in the section preceding the chapter on Pietism? Or did he see it as part of the environment of Schleiermacher's theology or as the strongest, most impressive representation of what he understood by "Pietism"?

one, with E. von May, an officer of the Salvation Army, in the fall of 1915 took the most positive course. To be sure, Barth thought he was a "true spiritual individualist," but "there was a joyous streak in his whole personality that made a strong impression on me."[74] He said even more: "I actually felt ashamed in the presence of this man who lived a perfectly natural, simple life in the love of God, in which everything is so organic and nothing at all is feigned. Everything this man said was without the slightest trace of methodical thinking, but radiant and alive from within, true because he experienced it first hand. I had never actually heard such a thing before except once from Herrmann and then from Blumhardt."[75]

On the other hand, the second encounter, the one with Jakob Vetter, a member of the staff at the Pilgrim Mission St. Chrischona, during an evangelistic campaign in November 1916 in Safenwil, turned out to be a quite negative experience: "The cause he proclaimed there is really not the gospel, but a very bad type of mechanical religion. If that is Pietism, then we should no longer believe there are even minimal points of contact between us and the Pietists. They really mean something *totally* different than we. This is psychological religion in its worst form, the vain description of a series of psychological events in the soul of the Christian . . . no, this is really not it."[76] Barth probably also saw the Safenwil community people (brothers of Albrecht) along these lines, and occasionally he came into conflict with them.[77] When a sympathizer of theirs complained to

---

[74]*Briefwechsel* 1, p. 95.

[75]Ibid., pp. 106-7.

[76]Ibid., p. 164.

[77]Ibid., p. 315. Several of Barth's parishioners wandered off, some to the Salvation Army, some to those brothers of Albrecht (p. 325): "The people at the Pietistic chapel are mobilizing against me." At the same time they are collaborating with the (political) "liberals"! The Safenwil community (the brothers of Albrecht, in common parlance called the "chapel" or the "gathering") can be traced back to the work of the Methodist Jakob Albrecht in Pennsylvania, whose missionaries had been establishing "evangelical communities" in Switzerland since 1866. Their members as a rule remained in the established Reformed church but usually attended the gatherings of the local evangelical community instead of the church services of the Swiss Reformed Church. However, according to their church polity only those individuals could join the community who "declare that they confess Jesus Christ as their Lord and Savior and have the earnest desire to be redeemed from sin and to live in the community of the Spirit" (according to S. Schaffner, *Die evangelische Gemeinschaft,* 1953, p. 9). A report on the founding of the Safenwil Pietistic community at the end of the nineteenth century states: "The Lord likewise gave us entry in Safenwil. . . . The preaching of the gospel proved to be powerful everywhere and resulted in the revival, illumination, and conversion of many souls. He who has the keys of David opened the doors, therefore, in quick succession one soul after another could be received into membership" (F. Schweingruber, *Ebenezer: Eine Gedenkschrift zur Feier des 50 jährigen Bestehens der Ev. Gemeinschaft in der Schweiz und im Elsass,* 1916, pp. 69-70).

Vetter about him, Vetter angrily remarked in his "mission tent greeting" that the sympathizer was right.[78]

The third encounter that once again took a more positive course was with the Schaffhausen pastor H. Gelzer, whom Barth met for the first time in April 1917 and with whom he remained in rather close contact for some time.[79] "I really can't take his Pietism so seriously because he has something so genuinely positive, joyful and peaceful about him, something that I have been struggling to attain with great difficulty, like Ernst von May."[80] Barth made some critical remarks to him about Pietism, but only because "he 'gave' me something, as they say in his jargon." Barth thought: "Perhaps I fall for such intense people too quickly. There is something very direct about him that makes a strong impression on me in spite of all my reservations."[81]

The facts we have cited show that Barth not only dealt with this phenomenon by reading its literature. He personally reached out to it in the form of various "intense" figures. He had more or less strong reservations about all of them, but they all related to the same point: he objected to the "individualism" in Pietism. But in his criticism Barth was obviously not blind to the differences between the Pietists and not willing to "throw them all into one grave." Rather it is striking that several of them even "gave" him something in a surprisingly positive sense. This was true to such a great extent that we have to wonder how Barth on the whole could express such a thorough rejection of Pietism in the first *Epistle to the Romans* after having experienced such valuable encounters with representatives of this line of thought a short time earlier. In fact, he had encounters that even "shamed" him. In addition, how could he make this critique after admitting that men such as Hofacker and Spleiss had impressed him when he read their works?[82] It is hard to imagine that he had already forgotten the positive things that had been "given" to him in these encounters or that he had suddenly interpreted them differently. Thus there is only one other explanation. In spite of all the criticism of Pietism presented in the *Epistle to the Romans* Barth did not want to question the possibility that the Christian faith could truly be lived out on this basis. To a certain degree

---

[78]*Briefwechsel* 1, p. 259. This incident reported by Thurneysen took place at about the same time Barth wrote the chapter on Pietism in the *Epistle to the Romans*.

[79]Gelzer visited with the B. K. Group of Safenwil in April 1917 to listen to a lecture by Barth. And Barth attended the Baden Conference sponsored by Pietistic circles in May to listen to Gelzer's lecture there about "Reflections on Repentance" on the anniversary of the Reformation. Compare *Briefwechsel* 1, pp. 192-93, 201.

[80]Ibid ., p. 193.

[81]Ibid., p. 203.

[82]Ibid., pp. 199-220, 216.

his critique applied only to the problematic nature of this basis. But he clearly started with the tacit assumption that something can be present in a Pietist that cannot be criticized in spite of all other criticism of it. If we see this correctly, this would mean that Barth's sharp criticism of Pietism in the first *Epistle to the Romans* was not meant to be the last word on it.

Of course, it is an open question whether the "immediate truth" he found in certain but not all Pietists was still "Pietism" for Barth or something else. Was it something that is in harmony with Pietism or something that basically goes beyond its limits? In the *Epistle to the Romans* Barth seems to have meant the latter since what he found in certain Pietists, such "life . . . in which everything is so organic and nothing at all is feigned," was an important factor in his own understanding of faith and played a role in his separation from Pietism. Again it can be said, if I'm not very much mistaken, that when he now recognizes an "immediately true" life of faith in the Pietists beyond the problematic statements they had made, he goes back to an earlier thesis in which he could critique their teaching but nevertheless let the "living personalities" "behind" it appeal to him. If this is correct, this would mean that precisely at this not unimportant point a certain amount of *continuity* has been discovered between Barth's early, liberal concept and his first *Epistle to the Romans* and that even in Barth's present understanding of faith (and even in his application of it in distancing himself from Pietism!) a *Pietistic* motive can still be recognized.

2. THE IMPLEMENTATION OF HIS CRITIQUE OF PIETISM IN THE FIRST *EPISTLE TO THE ROMANS*

The Individualism of Pietism

We can say and have already implied it. In Barth's first exegesis of Romans it is his negative concern to directly criticize an understanding of faith in terms of "religious individualism," an understanding once claimed to be absolutely necessary. His separation from Pietism, to which he devoted a special chapter, is especially illuminated by how this understanding of faith had now become the dominant *foil* in Barth's thought. What does he understand by Pietism? He now says "Pietism" is essentially the attempt to find "an individual solution to the meaning of life"![83] It is "personal life as an end in itself."[84] The issue of an *individual* breakthrough, *individual* conversion, *individual* sanctification, *in-*

---

[83] *Der Römerbrief,* 1st ed., 1919 (hereafter Ro 1), p. 250.
[84] Ibid., p. 206

dividual salvation, *individual* happiness takes the place of a life lived in response to the answer given to the *world*.[85] It is the *"religious method whose presupposition is the distant, commanding God and thus whose content is the subject 'God and the soul.'"*[86] Its question is *"What should I do to be saved?"*[87] Its goal is *"that the soul* may find its 'true home and inner peace.'"*[88] In short, it is "religious individualism," and that is precisely the charge brought against it now. How is this charge to be understood, and how does Barth come to judge this idea as problematic?

At the time Barth was writing the manuscript of the first *Epistle to the Romans,* a new insight began to assert itself in his thought, the insight that God or, as he used to say at that time, "the world of God is something new compared to the world of human beings with all of its opportunities and structures."[89] Therefore none of these opportunities and structures must be identified with that new divine world. Rather the fact "that God is *God"* must stand against all attempts to make such an identification.[90] "Will we never allow ourselves to hear the warning that God's righteousness is his own and is not a Jewish, Catholic, Lutheran, Calvinistic, Pietistic, democratic, socialist righteousness?"[91] In this most general sense the concern of the first and second *Epistle to the Romans* is the same. Not only in the second Romans commentary but already here in the first one, Barth seeks to understand how human beings are called away from a preoccupation with themselves—be it a Jewish, Catholic, Lutheran, Calvinistic, or Pietist self—to see God in a new way and to recognize and acknowledge him in his uniqueness and distinctiveness. But in both the first and second commentaries Barth goes his own way to assert this same concern. Thus we must first ask in what way he tries to implement this concern in his first *Epistle to Romans.*

The human world's difference from God, indeed, the fact that it is adverse to the world of God is proven for the Barth of the first *Epistle of the Romans* above all by the existence of *individualism.* "Precisely the importance and glory human beings ascribe to the sphere of their own soul, to their personal, individual life, is a falling away from the living God."[92] The dark nature of this world originated in the splintering of a living whole into a chaos of separate

---

[85]Ibid., p. 205.
[86]Ibid.
[87]Ibid., p. 208.
[88]Ibid., p. 216.
[89]Compare *Das Wort Gottes und die Theologie, Ges. Vorträge* 1, 1924, pp. 29ff.
[90]Ro 1, pp. 47, 97.
[91]Ibid., p. 298.
[92]Ibid., p. 216.

endeavors and individuals who gained their own importance so that now every human being exists as an individual, "cut off from the living, divine organism of humanity and the world. The whole human race, the whole world, lives in this isolation, disintegration, fragmentation, and disorganization."[93] This is why the difference between these various endeavors and individuals is ultimately unimportant: they all *as such* participate in the dark nature of this world.[94] If they *all* participate in it *as such,* they are still connected to one another in their splintering, but in a new way: "in the totality of nature" that in a way forms the demonic counterpart to that living, divine world organism.[95] In this "natural world" they are all simultaneously linked together, "jointly responsible" for the world's falling away from God. "The individual who desires to evade this joint responsibility falls victim to it even more."[96] This train of thought sounds like Schelling and is surely in part drawn from him via H. Kutter and T. Beck, as the language itself shows.[97]

Barth draws the following conclusions from these thoughts. (1) If the nature of this dark world consists of individualism, then any movement whose express concern is to find an individualistic solution to the problems of mankind only proves it belongs to this world, and nothing but that. (2) If any individualistic solution to the problems is nothing but a confirmation that it belongs to this world, then one cannot have a part in God's new world in the form of individualism; it is fundamentally impossible. For what is new about the world of God is that the dark nature of the present world and its individualism, its "disorganization," is overcome in it, that the original "organic unity between God and man and between man and the world that had been lost is now restored in it."[98] That is why we can have a part in the new world of God only by overcoming its (individualistic) nature, not by affirming its nature as a world that is adverse to God. Thus Barth dares to make these most radical statements: "God and personal life have nothing to do with one another. God's will cannot be done in individuals."[99] "The truth is nothing for the individ-

---

[93]Ibid. p. 202.

[94]Ibid., p. 35: "The difference between mountain and valley becomes insignificant when the sun at its zenith fills both with its light."

[95]Ibid., p. 216.

[96]Ibid., p. 25. Compare p. 184: "O we poor idealists and Pietists, theologians, ethicists and educators, indeed we were and are all 'brothers,' bound together in solidarity by the problem of the law . . . when we forget—and we forget it every day—that we 'are in Christ.'"

[97]As Barth himself later admitted in his autobiographical sketch of 1927. In K. Barth/R. Bultmann, *Briefwechsel 1922–1966,* 1971, p. 307.

[98]Ro 1, p. 58.

[99]Ibid., p. 196.

ual."[100] "As a soul, as an isolated individual, as an unorganized part of a chaotic whole I am qualitatively not suited to enter into a positive relationship with divine objectivity."[101] "Personal life as an end in itself is *against* God."[102] "Whatever I may undertake and experience on this basis has poison in it, it is done without God."[103] "There is no such thing as salvation of the individual and salvation of the soul."[104] In short, "nothing comes from nothing," for "the soul that wants to be something for itself and refuses to grasp that in Christ it is redeemed precisely from this existence for the self, is and remains in the body of death."[105]

All of this is also said against Pietism, in particular and explicitly in the context of these quotations. For according to Barth its essence is *individual* conversion, *individual* sanctification, *individual* salvation, thus it is individualism, and it is especially so in the sense that it is individualistic consciously and intentionally. As individualism it shares in the nature of this dark world by definition because as such this is a falling away from God, it is being distant from God and being unredeemed. On the basis of its individualistic questions it can essentially have nothing to do with God and his redemption, but only represents nothing but a part of the unredeemed world that is far from God. On this basis the individual remains "unredeemed in spite of all his redemptive skills. It cannot be any other way."[106] There is no communion with God that stops at inwardness. "This would be the old individualistic horror of Pietism, whose dead ends and mistakes we have escaped in Christ."[107]

In Barth's view Pietistic individualism is expressed especially by its tendency to foster *separation* instead of solidarity, be it an external or internal separation, be it a general separation from the world, be it a specific separation from the "worldly" church.[108] And in this context we find the famous sentence, "I would rather be in hell with the world church than in heaven with Pietism, be it of a lower or higher order, of an older or more modern observance. In this case Christ is with us in hell."[109] The concept "world church" is decisive for an un-

---

[100]Ibid., p. 202.
[101]Ibid., p. 205.
[102]Ibid., p. 206.
[103]Ibid., p. 217.
[104]Ibid., p. 207. Compare also p. 215: "There is a question for which there is *no* answer and this is the question about my personal righteousness and salvation . . . in which the whole wretchedness of the Pietistic dialectic slumbers undeveloped."
[105]Ibid., p. 216.
[106]Ibid.
[107]Ibid., p. 247.
[108]Ibid., p. 269.
[109]Ibid., pp. 269-70.

derstanding of this statement. The stress does not lie on "church," since Barth also criticizes it, aiming at a breakup of the church's institutional structure that is not there "for the sake of humanity."[110] Barth also does not say "the church of sinners," which would have an advantage over the pious in God's view, since a doctrine of the justification of the sinner is not even in view in the first *Epistle to the Romans*.[111] When Barth says the "world church," he clearly sees a parable of the "new world of God," making the point that a greater opportunity to practice solidarity with the "children of the world" is given in the established Protestant church than in Pietistic separation. Moreover, Barth's reference to the location of this world church in "hell" can probably be understood as a polemical, ironic rejoinder to the Pietist charge that a church embracing every Tom, Dick and Harry is "of Satan."[112] Barth's dictum could be paraphrased like this: If you Pietists care to think such a church is in hell, it is in vain that you think you will be in "heaven" compared with it. For you are also still living on the basis of this *world*, because the nature of this world is shaped by "individualism." "This separation of yours has taken place only within the framework of this sinful world and its orders."[113]

This thesis is developed logically, but its consequences are surprising. The problematic nature of Pietism is traditionally seen in its flight from the world, its lack of attention to this world with its focus on "redemption" from this world and for the world beyond. Yet Barth accuses Pietism of conforming to the world, just the opposite of what one would expect. Barth mainly has the compelling logic of his argumentation as proof of this surprising thesis. It renders a verdict on the thought Pietism itself has of course viewed differently. The historical evidence Barth cites for his thesis can be viewed less as a demonstration than as an illustration of this thesis: "The alleged triumphal appearance of Jesus Christ at the end of time turns into a simple, natural phenomenon, as in that cautionary dream of the young Tholuck."[114] "Strongly developed religiosity . . . has always been an especially powerful support for the dark powers. The idealists of 1825

---

[110]Ibid., pp. 87-88.

[111]In his understanding of "justification" he emphasized in the first *Epistle to the Romans* that the person is not left "as he is" but is "fully reshaped"; compare ibid., p. 151.

[112]As it seems to me, a preparation for that sentence quoted above is found in Barth's remark to Thurneysen on May 26, 1917 (in *Briefwechsel* 1, p. 203): "After reading Spleiss I wrote a letter to Gelzer about the church as the Satan of the Pietists, with the observation that I see this Satan at least waving at the end in the N.T."

[113]Ro 1, p. 212.

[114]Ibid., p. 216. On July 17, 1917, Barth called Thurneysen's attention to this dream in a letter in which he "quasi denies . . . the return of Christ" and remarked about this: "It becomes rather clear what they basically had to think of themselves!" In *Briefwechsel* 1, p. 215.

are members of William IV's consistory in 1850."[115] Or stated in more general terms: "How is the Pietist supposed to say something or know how to do something against mammon, war, sickness, fate or death when his deepest nature consists in the same falling away from God as the nature of those forces? He encounters the same arrogance everywhere in the world."[116] As I have said, these are only indicators, but certainly they are astonishing indicators that support Barth's thesis, although not actual evidence. Perhaps it is not coincidental that they are mainly aimed at the phenomenon of the revival of the early nineteenth century. (In comparison with the older Pietism it was more conservative because it was related to the restoration of the pre-Napoleonic status quo.) However, a discussion of this thesis could only begin by examining its actual presuppositions instead of these illustrations.

The "Mechanical" Aspect of Pietism

Barth's position has not yet been fully discussed. He occasionally says, "What Pietism, with all of its fallacies seeks in vain to attain will only become possible and true in the new *world*."[117] In spite of all of his criticism, Barth at least concedes to Pietism that it is aiming for something that is right. Yes, it even has a legitimate reason for its separation in that it demonstrates and knows that a new world must emerge. However, in Barth's view its error at this point can be seen in its desire to bring about, to "make" this new world, precisely by separating itself from this world of sin and cultivating its individualistic "redemptive techniques." This is correct: we must be redeemed from this sinful world; but this cannot happen in such a way that *"I" do* it, because we remain captive to the pattern of this sinful world while attempting to achieve redemption in *this* form. Clearly, for Barth *religious* individualism is tied to the conviction that redemption can be produced "mechanically," that is, by one's own doing. Thus for Barth a critique of individualism becomes a critique of *religious* individualism because it objects to such human technique. Sin means that human beings

---

[115]Ro 1, p. 215. A preliminary form of these sentences is found in Barth's correspondence with Thurneysen (1, p. 200): "I see from all my biographies of Pietists what a *tragic* moment it was 100 years ago when they began to be desired and heard and could leave the wilderness to become antistes. . . . Death can lurk in the logic of *every* step precisely because it goes to the essence of Christianity that God must let the door that had just snapped into the lock slam shut again with a loud bang" (May 16, 1917). This passage differs from the similar one in the *Epistle to the Romans* in that Barth *here* clearly anticipates a phase in the revivalist movement, namely, when it had not yet found any recognition but was still in the wilderness, in which there was "a door that had just snapped into the lock" in it in a good sense of the word.

[116]Ro 1, p. 214.

[117]Ibid., p. 237.

want to manage their own cause instead of living for God's cause[118] (whether it is a good cause or bad cause is at first totally unimportant). Therefore "arrogant human endeavor"[119] takes over precisely where we should instead be "growing in Christ."[120]

The "assumption" of this "religious method" is in fact "the alien, commanding God."[121] And this is actually the essence of *religion* itself: In the view of the first *Epistle to the Romans* unity with God, the new world of God is God's *demand*[122] and its way to God is decisively the way of the law. And God is always *only* an alien, distant God for it, and that goal is always *only* a demand for it, never a reality. It can never become a reality because it wants to achieve it "mechanically," by its own doing. Yet no matter how much we desire to get beyond the sinful world, we cannot get away from it because we always accept sin as a given and do not do away with it under such "law,"[123] or in other words, because we avail ourselves of the techniques of this old world time and again when we try to overcome the old world in this way. We get beyond it only "when God *on his own initiative* has really created and brought forth what the religious world (it is, after all, the world too) seeks in vain and only says it seeks."[124] And *because* God has actually given the beginning of the new world as a seed and because God is no longer "the God who is so distant from us, but the God in whom we live and move and have our being," we get beyond the old world only by being rooted "and growing organically" in this given, this seed, in connection with Christ's life. Thus we dare to begin with hope and not with fear and trembling, as the Pietists do.[125] On the contrary, "the human effort, the desire to be something only ruins it . . . all your struggling and climbing, 'nearer my God to thee' will perhaps lead you to the highest summits of the earth, but not into the kingdom of heaven."[126]

Two things especially characterize Pietism in Barth's view, in that it has chosen the legalistic way of religion by "human effort." First, it persists in a dichotomy, a "dialectic" and a "dualism."[127] The basic structure of "Pietist dialectics" is based on its *desire* to achieve this new world, but it does not *achieve* it. On the

---

[118]Ibid., p. 210.
[119]Ibid., p. 215.
[120]Ibid., p. 205.
[121]Compare n. 4.
[122]Ibid., pp. 67, 184.
[123]Ibid., p. 168.
[124]Ibid., p. 67.
[125]Ibid., pp. 97-98, 120.
[126]Ibid., p. 304.
[127]Ibid., pp. 211, 208.

one hand it *knows* about our need to be redeemed from chaotic nature as a whole; on the other hand it cannot be redeemed from it because it actually remains captive to the "world of flesh" as an individual "soul" who wants to share in the "spiritual world" but as such cannot do it.[128] This dualism gives birth to new, further dualisms in which it is reflected: the tension between a "higher self focused on God" and "my unredeemed total existence" or the fluctuation between the bad and "the comforting experiences I have with myself"[129] or going back and forth between writhing "in the struggle of repentance" and reveling in the "wonderful feeling of sinlessness."[130] This is what the religious individualism of Pietism achieves: It entangles itself in such a dialectic. But what it does not achieve in this way is redemption. Instead it stands apart from redemption with its dialectic. And therefore its questions are truly "hellish problems."[131] They lead into the "inferno of Pietism . . . , where the demons do their work."[132] "The method of Pietism is . . . possible only under the wrath of God."[133]

The second thing that characterizes Pietism when it chooses the legalistic way of human technique is that its piety is a contrived and *artificial* one. Thus a mark of Pietistic faith is the frenetic activity which in Barth's opinion proves that it lacks what it strives for: "I am so zealously religious and so strictly moral because I do not possess truth and goodness in a living way. As a fighter for God, . . . I join his side precisely because the divine in my existence can not become true life, but must be and remain unmoved inwardness, dully brooding only to itself. . . . If I were a living person, a fully redeemed person, I would no longer have to be so heated in my piety."[134] Of course, Pietism sees the necessity of redemption, but it does not achieve it; it cannot because the way it seeks to do it continues to be in the "world" and avails itself of its techniques. So at best it seeks to cure the ailment by treating the symptoms but not the root cause. "In Pietism there is smoke, but no fire."[135] It has the proper knowledge but the wrong "method." And what is wrong about it is that it does not lead to the goal it should lead to based on that knowledge, but remains captive to that from which it knows it should be liberating. And for Barth it follows that "being redeemed" in Pietism not only has something artificial about it, but is only a contrived, an imagined redemption that does not correspond to reality. Because it

---

[128]Ibid.
[129]Ibid., p. 211.
[130]Ibid., p. 210.
[131]Ibid., p. 205.
[132]Ibid., p. 216.
[133]Ibid., p. 213.
[134]Ibid.
[135]Ibid., pp. 214-15.

is not rooted and growing in the new beginning that has been given by God, Pietism finds itself *outside* of redemption in all of its expressions and is still in the world. "All that Pietism calls 'experience' is uncertain and easily refutable."[136] Its "assurance of salvation" is only an "imaginary one."[137] Whatever experiences there may be within it, whatever I "have been through in terms of spiritual awakening, illumination, conversion, sanctification, etc.," is "vain pretense and imagination"[138] and "takes place in hell."[139]

Those are hard sentences marked by a wounding stridency. Are they not too strident, suspect because of the "heat" of his repudiation? We can state right away that Barth will later never speak of Pietism in such a harsh and negative way, even in the second *Epistle to the Romans*. It is clear that his argument with the individualism of Pietism developed into a critique of its *religious* individualism under the second aspect outlined above. In this critique Barth at least takes into consideration what seemed at first to be lacking in his position on this phenomenon: the element that has been labeled "Pietism's flight from the world." Of course this element is given an interpretation in Barth's critical examination that sees the element only as new evidence for Pietism's continued captivity to the "world." Through its attempt to move beyond the solidarity of all who are caught in that unredeemed "totality of nature," there arises in Pietism a new, more powerful "religious" individualism over against that individualism for which all those in the "totality of nature" are jointly responsible. But what is problematic about this in the first *Epistle to the Romans* is basically only its individualism, and Barth's argument with this is actually only a variation and reinforcement of his one critical thesis: On this basis of individualism, within the framework of my existence as an individual, redemption is impossible; one remains "unredeemed in spite of all redemptive skills." In spite of a promising beginning, the first *Epistle to the Romans* basically does not include any direct critique of religion. And if Barth does object to "religious individualism," then only because he will show that it is just a special case of "individualism" and thus will condemn it. Therefore "experience" and "possession" of the divine in particular are not a problem in themselves. They only become one if it is an individualistic, contrived experience whereas Barth does not question it as an organic, living experience. To be sure, Barth once labeled the immediacy of the "I in you and you in me" as an

---

[136]Ibid., p. 168.
[137]Ibid., p. 249.
[138]Ibid., p. 206.
[139]Ibid., p. 215.

excessive Pietistic claim and as "the original act of sin." However, as the context shows, he does not object to this claim per se, but only if it cannot live
up to reality within the assumptions of Pietism.[140] There is salvation not *in* my
existence as an individual but only *out of* my existence as an individual. There
is no individualistic redemption but only redemption from individualism. This
is the heart of Barth's thesis with regard to Pietism.

Its Proximity to Liberalism

It is as plain as day that at the same time this thesis represents a critical separation from the framework of a "religious individualism" Barth himself supported
several years earlier even if we must not view his comment at the beginning of
the chapter on Pietism as an indication of this fact there. He wrote, "We are by
nature Pietists and are speaking on our own behalf."[141] This fact is illuminated
and confirmed by the fact that Barth continues to see liberalism and Pietism as
being linked together even in the critical stance of the first *Epistle to the Romans*.
It is no coincidence that a chapter on "the Law and Romanticism" precedes the
section on "the Law and Pietism." Both his analysis and critique of Romanticism
corresponds to his evaluation of Pietism. Likewise, both are reduced to the common denominator of "religious individualism." However, under the title "Romanticism" Barth discusses not only the so-called limited historical phenomenon, but clearly the liberal theology of the nineteenth century as a whole, that
is, "the idol of the century, 'personality.'"[142] It is apparent that Barth is taking
issue here with his own theologically liberal past when we encounter statements
in this chapter that sound biographical: "There we stood with our personal life,
with our . . . individuality. We did not know anything of importance except our
personal life. We were overly important to ourselves: as individuals. Of course
we still had no inkling of the character of the rule we live under, but lovingly,
as if it had to do with God, we lowered our gaze into the abyss of our ego" until
"God's working from afar" opened our eyes as we dealt with Kant (we must undoubtedly understand this phrase as a reference to Kant, although Kant's name
is not mentioned directly).[143]

Of course Pietism and "Romanticism" are two different things for Barth. For
him the Romantist is the naive individualist who has now awaked from his
dream and has been "roused from his naive confidence."[144] Roused by an en-

---

[140]Ibid., p. 213.
[141]Ibid., p. 205.
[142]Ibid., p. 202; compare his mention of Schleiermacher, p. 200.
[143]Ibid., p. 196.
[144]Ibid., pp. 195-96.

counter with the Kantian Law (Barth came back to it again but understood it in a new way) that commands him to take action, "the value of which is found only in the universal validity of its norm, it forbids what he is obviously devoted to: his natural isolation, the naive importance of his own personal existence, the cheerful arbitrariness of his conscious thoughts and his unconscious feelings."[145] This "law's" encounter with the "individual trapped in his subjectivity"[146] must end in disaster because the human being "as a self who is only I," as "an equable individual who fends for himself," is not at all a subject "who can obey the imperatives of morality" (of the "You should!" correctly recognized by Kant as divine).[147] This encounter destroys "such naiveté," leads to a separation between nature and spirit and to a "struggle against nature in the name of spirit,"[148] but it does not lead to a conquest of individualism.

Rather it is the heart of Romanticism, just as it is of Pietism in its own way. "The fall [is] already complete with Romantic individualism." The generally prevalent sin, which consisted in our isolation, breaks forth [here] as the actual essence of our personal life as well."[149] Here God is "just good enough to be 'experienced' by us, to help us continue to build our individualistic tower of Babel."[150] And the problems that are prevalent in the individualism of Romanticism are the same in Pietism. They both intend to overcome apostasy from God, but the way they do it, their "religious, moral" individualism, cannot overcome but only confirms the apostasy. By combining Romanticism and Pietism (in both cases he is obviously thinking of the nineteenth century) Barth asserts that both of them basically share the same intention and suffer from the same problem, as we can read in the first *Epistle to the Romans*. This assertion is the earliest form of the dual thesis presented in detail in Barth's history of "Protestant theology." (1) Pietism in its basic form is "individualism." (2) Pietism and the Enlightenment are "different forms of one essence that vary more externally than internally" (here Barth mainly has the eighteenth century in mind).[151]

---

[145]Ibid., p. 198. Already in 1910 in Geneva Barth was occasionally able to intimate such a "social" interpretation of the categorical imperative: "Thinking socially and wanting to think in these terms means . . . learning to so direct his thoughts and decisions into the most subtle stirrings of our inward being that *our* motives can at all times claim the dignity of being definitive for *all others*" (*Gemeinde-Blatt Geneva,* September 24, 1910).

[146]Ro 1, p. 198.

[147]Ibid., p. 201; on Kant, compare p. 197.

[148]Ibid., p. 199.

[149]Ibid., p. 196.

[150]Ibid., p. 197.

[151]*Die prot. Theologie im 19. Jahrhundert,* 1946, pp. 93, 65.

The "Organism" of the Kingdom of God and Its Organic Coming

What then is the positive premise of Barth's critique of "religious individualism"? What does it mean when he juxtaposes the statement "salvation is only in Christ" with the Pietistic idea of the "individual's salvation"?[152] What does he mean when he says, "Faith begins with what in the best case Pietism ends on shaky ground"?[153] We have already touched on Barth's positive counter-position in the previous section and thus would like to summarize it in a few sentences. We could sum up his positive view in these terms: Redemption is not one of the possibilities of *this* "world" but only in the "*new* world of God." And Barth basically understands this new world as the "coming world of God."[154] It is *future,* and we are always still going toward it. But the fact that this new world has already begun in seminal form, is already a given, plays a large role in Barth's thought. And by emphasizing this point, a concept of God suggests itself to him that differs markedly from the one stressed in the second *Epistle to the Romans.* God is not the "wholly other," the One who dwells in the world to come, the incomprehensible One, the One who is not a given, the unknown One. These are not the terms he uses here. On the contrary, the "unknown, commanding God" is considered here as the "premise" of the religious method of Pietism.[155] No, God is not "wholly other," but the world of God is only a different kind of world from ours. And its difference is shown by the fact that since "it has already begun it no longer makes any sense to *look for* or to *create* a distant, strange, unknown divine being, rather it is a matter of *taking* and growing out of the abundant life that is here."[156]

"The truth we as idealists know and proclaim is always [only] demand and promise, never the discovery and creation of a life from and with God."[157] What is real is missing under the "law," in morality, in religion. But "the question of reality Idealism raises and leaves unsolved has found its essential answer at *one* place in the world for the *whole* world."[158] "In Christ all surrogates are conquered and brushed aside . . . including the viewpoints of religion, church, . . . morality and all idealist philosophies, to the extent that the divine merely confronts man as demand . . . for in Christ the fulfillment has appeared,"[159] fulfillment primarily as "the growing energy of the coming world of God."[160] But in

---

[152]Ro 1, p. 207.
[153]Ibid., p. 115.
[154]Ibid., p. 221.
[155]Ibid., p. 205.
[156]Ibid., p. 218.
[157]Ibid., p. 52.
[158]Ibid., pp. 57-58.
[159]Ibid., p. 181.
[160]Ibid., p. 221.

this form, a "world of divine life" has appeared on earth in Christ. In him the divine being is present. Notice the coexistence of three concepts clearly understood to be synonyms: "nature, gift, growth,"[161] "the breakthrough of a divine seed through anti-God husks,"[162] as "the seed of a new world."[163] Now there is both. First, there is *existence in Christ*. This means that you are "organically planted in the living growth of the divine righteousness,"[164] allowing the new or rather the oldest nature of life, its nature in God to work naturally and without confusion. This existence in Christ means being under an order that is internal and not external to you, natural and not remote. It simply means "being natural."[165] At the same time there is *Christ's existence in us*, meaning that we have the "redemptive" power in ourselves that will "transform the ties still binding us into freedoms and conquests, a process that will advance organically . . . until your total existence is transformed into an organism of life."[166]

We can easily picture Barth's special insight in his first *Epistle to the Romans* and especially his positive concern in relation to Pietism by looking at the concept of the "organic" that has been so characteristic of the author of this book. This concept implies two statement complexes whose outlines become clear by examining what Barth regards as their opposite: on one hand it is the concept of the "mechanical," on the other hand, the concept of "disorganization." On the one hand he describes a living organism with its "quiet growth," which cannot "produce" as it emerges from itself and from the inside. And that is precisely what we can say about the way the divine being comes now: "it grows organically and no longer needs any mechanical construction."[167] All of our own private, independent, self-made ventures to redeem the world would be "mechanical." But our human efforts, "our richly developed life," hinder "the quiet growth of divine life in the world."[168] "We would not have to be so religiously busy if we would stand before God in steady growth."[169] "Do we still want to become mechanical where we simply ought to grow in Christ?"[170] The divine being is only present where it works in "quiet growth" whereby its human equivalent is "quiet waiting."

On the other hand, the concept of "organic" life describes a living system with

---

[161]Ibid., p. 218
[162]Ibid., p. 264.
[163]Ibid., p. 62.
[164]Ibid., p. 80.
[165]Ibid., pp. 220-21.
[166]Ibid., p. 219.
[167]Ibid., p. 62.
[168]Ibid., p. 299.
[169]Ibid., p. 213.
[170]Ibid., p. 205.

regard to the inner, essential *connection* between all its "parts." This connection is so essential that they are no longer merely parts, "no longer monads in the midst of chaos."[171] Rather all these parts form a whole as they are linked together. This is what can be said about life in the coming "new world of God" as the *goal* of all God's ways: It is an existence where all the parts are vitally linked together[172] in a "living, divine organism of humanity and the world"[173] in God's "organization." If a human being is "cut off" from it, as it is often said, he or she exists "as an unorganized member of a chaotic whole,"[174] in isolation, in "disorganization."[175] If there is redemption only "in Christ," this means for the author of the first *Epistle to the Romans* that there is redemption "only from my unorganized life, from isolation, and self-importance, from the fatal context of life or rather death in which the self is only I"[176]; there is redemption only in the organic context of a new world,"[177] in a "changed world context into which our life is grafted."[178] In this new world we are liberated from the "isolation of personal life" because the organs and powers of the new world of which you are a part are in solidarity with you and support you."[179] Therefore be willing to "place yourself in the *context* of life; for only when you are and become organic are you *alive*."[180]

Both of these aspects of an "organic" understanding of the "new world of God" clarify the meaning and grounds of Barth's critique of Pietism found in the first *Epistle to the Romans*. For it is in line with both of these aspects when Barth sees Pietism as "individualism" in thrall to a "disorganization" in conflict with the new world of God and as "*religious* individualism" in thrall to a "mechanical" misunderstanding of the organically growing divine realm.

3. AN ANALYSIS OF BARTH'S CRITIQUE OF PIETISM IN THE FIRST *EPISTLE TO THE ROMANS*

His Relationship to W. Herrmann

The ideas that had an impact on Barth's thought in this era become apparent in his critique of religious individualism in the first *Epistle to the Romans*. He makes

---

[171]Ibid., p. 221.
[172]Ibid., p. 198.
[173]Ibid., p. 202.
[174]Ibid., p. 205.
[175]Ibid., p. 202.
[176]Ibid., p. 206.
[177]Ibid., p. 211.
[178]Ibid., p. 149.
[179]Ibid., p. 221.
[180]Ibid., p. 357.

this critique from the perspective of an understanding of God and faith that is shaped by the concepts of "life" and "organic whole." Especially the exemplary ideas of Christoph Blumhardt but also of T. Beck exerted an unmistakable influence on him in his view of the divine world as a holistic, living organism and in his view of the way in which it comes, in the form of lively, peaceful growth. And with this dual view Barth certainly finds himself in a different place theologically than in his early years.

We cannot avoid the question of whether there is still a positive memory of the theology of W. Herrmann in the theology of the first *Epistle to the Romans* and especially in its focus on the concept of "life," since Herrmann's theology focused on the idea of "experience." At first glance it does not look like it. First of all, his opposition to it is so abundantly clear that it seems to exclude the possibility of a positive link. This is what could be heard in Herrmann's theology: Religion is rooted in an experience that belongs to the individual.[181] "Religion has its place in this individual experience."[182] If Barth opposes anything in his first *Epistle to the Romans,* it is this statement. On the whole he undoubtedly represents a movement that seeks to distance itself from Herrmann.

But that is not all there is to say. Herrmann's basic position was associated with two battle lines. On the one hand he opened a front against a Christianity for which faith is *doctrine* or a recognition of its importance, "something handed down by tradition" instead of "something growing in the present,"[183] a system of thought instead of "something really alive."[184] However, not the affirmation of others' ideas but only the experience of being touched by a living faith can "put me into a situation where new spiritual life is possible."[185] The other front on which he fought was the mystical view of Christianity[186] in which "God's influence on the soul is sought and found merely in an inner experience of the individual, in other words, in emotional excitement."[187] Herrmann actually condemned this view as well because the mystic subjectively separates himself from

---

[181] *Ges. Aufsätze,* 1923, p. 129.

[182] Ibid., p. 143.

[183] *Der Verkehr des Christen mit Gott,* 7th ed., 1921, p. 32.

[184] Ibid., p. 31.

[185] Ibid., p. 33.

[186] I am not sure whether Herrmann also has Pietism in mind here. As far as I can see, he otherwise talked little about Pietism. Once he accuses it of knowing and applying a "technique" in gaining access to faith (*Ges. Aufsätze,* p. 83). Another time he praises its turning away from an intellectualistic Christianity which, however, it is not able to overcome because it "did not take hold of the evil at its roots" (*Christlich-protestantische Dogmatik,* in P. Hinneberg, *Die Kultur der Gegenwart,* Teil 1, Abt. 4, Halfte 2, 1906, p. 619).

[187] *Der Verkehr des Christen mit Gott,* p. 17.

all external influences and withdraws only to God and himself. In this way he passes by the "living God of revelation" and does not get beyond the stage in which "human consciousness still clings to the world[188]—all the while asserting that God is not the world. Thus all such experiences come under suspicion of being mere illusion."[189]

It is astonishing to see that a similar hostile stance can be recognized in the author of the first *Epistle to the Romans*. On the one hand he kept the anti-orthodox attitude of his early years: it is not a question of doctrine but life, "something living," therefore not "theory" or "dogma," not the communication of intellectual clarity, not an escape into the secure heights of pure ideas."[190] On the other hand, Barth's critique of Pietism resembles both points of Herrmann's critique of mysticism. It rejects an inwardness achieved by separation from the world and it sees the problematic nature of such inwardness in the fact that human consciousness still clings to the world (and thus comes under "suspicion of being mere illusion" as an experience of *God*).

Herrmann could put his positive ideas about those two front lines in these terms: God "is not recognized as a dead thing, for there is nothing about him that is not life. Thus he is only recognized where he reveals his life."[191] Where this happens, the good is actually *life* given by God, in contrast to Kant, where humanity encounters the good as an ideal, as something that merely ought to be.[192] Proceeding from this Herrmann quotation, which could fit in the first *Epistle to the Romans* without editing, we could at least consider the possibility of associating the idea of the "living God" in Herrmann and Kutter with Barth's thought. If Herrmann could express his concern in this way, then we can probably say this is basically the concern of the first *Epistle to the Romans* as well. To go one step further: it is striking that, in his argument with "Romanticism" and idealism, and indirectly in his criticism of the Pietist attempt to satisfy a "distant and demanding God" through one's own action, Barth adopts Herrmann's unusual attempt to surpass Kant by "asserting an organically growing divine existence and posses-

---

[188]Ibid., p. 25.
[189]Ibid., p. 30.
[190]Ro 1, p. 264.
[191]W. Herrmann, *Ges. Aufsätze*, pp. 199ff.
[192]Compare W. Herrmann, *Ethik*, 5th ed., 1921, p. 94: Kant did not "get beyond the horizon of orthodox religious instruction"; that is why he knew the "life" of religion as "something merely wanted," not as "an experience given to man as a gift, freeing him inwardly." Compare *Ges. Aufsätze*, p. 146. Under the "law" and, among other things, in Kant's understanding of religion as a duty and demand "he [man] lacks the inner unity of the truly lively one."

sion in man in contrast to the emptiness of the Idealists' demand."[193]

Of course, when Herrmann let this idea lead to the crucial thesis that the knowledge of God is "the unguarded expression of individual experience,"[194] it is immediately clear where the author of the first *Epistle to the Romans* goes his own way in contrast to Herrmann. As a matter of principle Barth wants to overcome the prevailing, basic individualism that is so dominant in Herrmann's theology (especially the aspect of holism and solidarity in Barth's concept of "organic growth" makes this clear). In his first *Epistle to the Romans* Barth goes beyond Herrmann in that he thinks he has found a position he describes with the phrase "in Christ," interpreted antisubjectively in terms of "organic growth." From this position he can now turn Herrmann's critique of mysticism against Herrmann himself in a radicalized form. Yet in his first *Epistle to the Romans* Barth does not go beyond Herrmann in that Herrmann's thought forms have remained useful to him in describing this "new position." Especially an aspect of the complex "living-experiencing" that is so important to Herrmann is preserved in Barth's concept of "organic growth": what Herrmann called "unguarded" is kept untouched and included in Barth's idea of God's working in the world by way of vital, quiet, growth that is contrary to everything "mechanical."[195] Thus Barth learned from Herrmann. It could also be said that he stays with him at an essential point while trying to get beyond his "individualism."[196] And this significant point makes itself felt in Barth's argument with Pietism, especially in the

---

[193]Barth summarized this thesis of his first *Epistle to the Romans* in this way in the second edition of his *Epistle to the Romans,* 1922, p. 223. Compare Ro 1, pp. 52-53: "The truth which we as idealists know . . . is always demand . . . , never the discovery and creation of a life from and with God." "Idealism set up excellent programs, but to carry them out, a new spirit, which is not present, must be postulated as an additional program point . . . which [however] tragically can *not* be postulated. . . . Idealism probably postulates this as well . . . to testify to the fact that precisely this ultimate, crucial event does *not* take place." Compare p. 168.

[194]In *Christliche Welt,* 1917, nr. 44, p. 842.

[195]As late as 1925 Barth commented on Herrmann's statement quoted last with the following typical words: "'Defenseless' is very good. But 'the expression of individual experience' is decisively not good" (*Die Theologie und die Kirche, Ges. Vorträge* 2, 1928, p. 269). This commentary by Barth faithfully reproduces the dual, dialectical attitude of the author of the first *Epistle to the Romans* with regard to Herrmann. He also calls attention to the fact that it is to be expected that Herrmann will exert a positive influence on Barth beyond the period of the first *Epistle to the Romans.*

[196]It is not so wrong, if put too one-sidedly, when Mayne said about Barth's theology in the stage of 1919 in *ZTK* 1922 ("Kritische Berichte," p. 460): "Seen as a whole, it seems to me that Barth has nothing more profound to offer than W. Herrmann, and also nothing clearer." I wonder if Barth in the first *Epistle to the Romans* did not have something in mind like a synthesis of the "sharply different forms of our existence (*Ges. Aufsätze,* p. 151), the universally valid form and the individual form by defining both phenomena from the perspective of the concept of "living faith." I would think that from the vantage point of this attempt it becomes understandable what continued to link him with Herrmann *and* to what extent he moved beyond Herrmann.

thesis that it remains captive to the world in spite of its separation from the world and that the divine being does not disclose himself in this ("mechanical") way, but only as the Living One.

His Relationship to Religious Socialism

Barth clearly found new teachers, namely, in *religious socialism,* by seeking to move beyond Herrmann's "individualism" and especially because in this school of thought "individualism" appeared to him to be the characteristic and decisive problem of Pietism. In this regard his critique of Pietism in his first *Epistle* bears striking resemblance to the critique of Kutter and Ragaz. According to Ragaz, Pietism only has "this one great concern: how his soul can be saved from the corruption of sin,"[197] and always only "the soul of the individual."[198] But this is "nothing but pious selfishness! You want to save your soul, but you let the devil have the world."[199] A new insight is set against it: not "the rule of self," but "the rule of God!"[200] However, for Ragaz this means immediate action without beating around the bush. "Conversion must not only be a conversion of the individual soul, but of the *world*. It must not even take place in the individual soul without being intentionally linked to the world."[201]

Kutter sees it in similar terms. He has a Pietist describe his concern in the following terms. "I related everything, the whole gospel, God, Christ, grace, eternal life to myself—God for *me,* Christ for *me,* grace and eternal life for *me!"* "I never heard them speak about God and Jesus except in connection with the salvation of my own soul; I knew nothing of a Kingdom of God." "I lived my life in this naive egotism, or better pious, spiritual egotism."[202] In contrast to such Pietism, Kutter affirms a "universal Christianity that seeks to perfect the world, something the Christianity of the individual soul does not know," "hope for the whole world" instead of for one's own salvation.[203] Here, "like Christ, I am open

---

[197]"Gespräch zwischen Quidam und einem Pietisten" (1919), in *Weltreich, Religion und Gottesherrschaft* 2, 1922, p. 82 /E. Thurneysen, *Briefwechsel* 1, 1913–1921, 1973, p. 358). In this work by Ragaz "we," that is, Barth/Thurneysen, are "killed as Pietists." He presumably understood Ragaz's argument as being targeted at Barth. He especially took issue with the Pietistic objection to the religious Socialists who mistook the kingdom of God for new political conditions and who wanted to establish it by political means. It seems doubtful to me, though, that the thrust of Ragaz's work went against Barth.

[198]"Gespräch zwischen Quidam und einem Pietisten," p. 86.

[199]Ibid., p. 89.

[200]Ibid., p. 90.

[201]Ibid., p. 86.

[202]*Not und Gewissheit: Ein Briefwechsel,* 1927, pp. 24ff. Although the book was published only in 1927, we may assume that Kutter here expresses an opinion he had held for a long time to which he remained true throughout the years.

[203]Ibid., p. 61.

to the whole world," whereas in Pietism "I am closed to it for the sake of *my* soul. In the former case a human being for all is in view, in the latter case one person for himself."[204] And Kutter can say as sharply as Barth: Individualism grasps not only too little, but as such nothing at all of God—"mere individual piety" is actually the "greatest godlessness."[205]

Of course, the well-known difference between Ragaz and Kutter also becomes apparent in their critique of Pietism. The issue for both of them is conversion that moves away from a salvation understood in individualistic terms. But in what direction does it move? Ragaz stresses that it moves in the direction of the God of the *world;* Kutter on the other hand sees it moving in the direction of the *God* of the world, "to God himself, to *God . . .* to God as he is."[206] And whereas from his location Ragaz above all misses Pietism's advocacy for "overturning the system of violence and oppression, and stopping war,"[207] Kutter not only misses that, but even more an understanding of faith in terms of "letting God do it . . . He will do it."[208] On the other hand, an amazing agreement between Kutter and Ragaz can be observed. It is typical of both of them—and this would hardly be a coincidence—to portray their conflict with Pietism in the form of a dialogue. It is hardly a coincidence because both are convinced that in criticizing Pietism they are not so much advocating a position opposing it as drawing the proper conclusions from Pietism itself. Kutter puts it in explicit terms: His concern is "not simply to brush it off. It is not a matter of either-or, but of both-and."[209] Ragaz puts it the same way. He stands very close to Pietism. "I could express my intentions in such a way that they are a fulfillment of Pietism."[210]

If we compare Barth's critique of Pietism to that of Ragaz and Kutter, we can affirm the following points. (1) Barth is in agreement with Ragaz and Kutter in their view that the total complex of "Pietism" can be reduced to a common denominator—Christianity focused on the individual soul. On principle they all reject a Christianity understood in these terms. (2) If Ragaz's critique of Pietism's religious individualism has the nuance of objecting to its sanctioning of the status quo and Kutter's thought is nuanced more in the direction of objecting to its denial of the "living God" and "letting God do what he wants," Barth's critique

---

[204]Ibid., p. 30.

[205]Ibid., p. 53.

[206]Ibid., p. 55.

[207]"Gesprach zwischen Quidam und einem Pietisten," p. 93.

[208]*Not und Gewissheit,* p. 53.

[209]Ibid., p. 50; compare p. 62. It is unclear to me, though, how Kutter could combine this irenic statement with his polemical one that the (Pietistic) preoccupation with their own piety is the greatest "godlessness."

[210]"Gespräch zwischen Quidam und einem Pietisten," p. 84; compare p. 101.

of the Pietistic position distinguishes itself by clearly seeking to combine both of these aspects. This assumption is confirmed by the fact that in this period Barth makes an effort to pick up Kutter's insight without dropping Ragaz's special concern.[211] Above all, it is confirmed by the fact that the linkage of these two aspects corresponds to his attempt to synthesize these two basic ideas in the concept of "the organic" learned from Blumhardt and Beck. (3) It is important for Barth to say with Ragaz against Pietism (and to some extent against Kutter's talk about "God himself") that a "new *world*" is at stake, "comprehensive change, a new situation in the world." Yet Ragaz's critique of Pietism lacks the other side of the coin that marks Barth's critique of Pietism: his separation from the "mechanical," the "contrived," the "machine" nature of Pietism, stressing that the way to the new world of God is rather the way of organic, secret growth. Ragaz sees no problems here, whereas Barth actually turns what he has said against Pietism, mutatis mutandis against Ragaz's "religious socialism" as well.[212] This "other" viewpoint he advocates here is inspired by Kutter and mainly by Blumhardt. But since this viewpoint also includes Herrmann's inheritance, we may assume that in the first *Epistle to the Romans* Barth not only wants to correct this inheritance by what he learned in "religious socialism" but also the latter by what he learned from Herrmann. (4) On the whole, Barth's critique of Pietism appears to be sharper and more irreconcilable than the critique of Ragaz and Kutter. They both do not talk as vehemently as Barth about the "inferno of Pietism" and its "hellish problems," and when they accuse Pietism of succumbing to the charge of an "illusion," it does not carry the same weight for them as it does for Barth. We see this fact as an indication that he clearly does not just want to support Pietism more *consistently;* instead he wants to support something different in contrast to it. And he clearly intends to do more than just expand religious *individualism* into a religious *socialism*. It seems clear to me that he *wants* to do this. But it is a legitimate question to ask whether he *can* do it,

---

[211]Compare E. Busch, *Karl Barths Lebenslauf,* 1975, p. 98. It seems to me that Barth not only wanted to combine Kutter and Ragaz but also wanted to *correct* Kutter by Ragaz and Ragaz by Kutter and that he even then was striving to go beyond the position of Ragaz *and* Kutter.

[212]Barth's interpretation of Romans 13 that is so well-regarded today can in my opinion primarily be read as a discussion with Ragaz, who rightfully found himself as the one personally addressed in Barth's talk there about the "man in the prophet's cloak" and about the "pretentious pose of an agent of the world's judge" (pp. 384-85). And the emphasis of Barth's "political" view portrayed here seems to me to be decisively placed on his thesis: "What is at stake is the great work of building a new world that must take place . . . inwardly and objectively . . .by all people [in Christ!] peacefully and together becoming accustomed to the divine atmosphere and that must not be disturbed by individual, anarchic eruptions, . . . not by individual bungling" (p. 380).

rebus sic stantibus, whether his viewpoint goes beyond Pietism as fundamentally as he thinks or whether Kutter and Ragaz have not seen the situation more clearly when they understand their new viewpoint as an expansion and "fulfillment of Pietism," a viewpoint shared by Barth at key points.

The Problem of Barth's Understanding of Pietism

Let me now deal directly with Barth's critique of Pietism in the first *Epistle to the Romans* and ask how well founded it is! First, it should not be denied that Barth has accurately articulated a truly characteristic aspect of Pietism with his reference to *"individualism"* (individual conversion, individual sanctification, individual salvation). Whoever inquires of the revivalist theologians, as Barth has done, cannot overlook (as they have said themselves!) what a large role the "heart" (Tholuck), the "individual soul" (Hofacker), in short, the individual played for them. No one will be able to say that Barth has simply missed the central thrust of Pietism. And it should also not be denied that by propounding the idea of the greatness of *God's kingdom* he has pointed out a biblical perspective in which even all pious, self-centered thinking seems to be exposed to necessary as well as constructive criticism (even if he expresses the idea in rather peculiar terms). If what we have said under the first point is correct, then it would not be unfair to accuse Pietism of neglecting this perspective in its thinking, as Barth has done.

And there also seems to be no question that with his critique of *contrived* faith Barth has asked Pietism a question which it had to recognize as one that should certainly be of concern to it, the truly profound question: Does not its heated piety (similar to the famous instructions given to public speakers "if your argument is weak, speak loud!") reveal that it is deeply uncertain of its cause? Could it cope with this situation other than by deceiving itself? And this question could easily be linked to the thesis drawn from the history of Western thought that Pietism not coincidentally originated in the Cartesian age. And there seems to be no question that in contrast to the Pietist approach Barth has pointed out a genuine criterion of faith that is certain of its cause by speaking of "secret growth" (again expressed in a peculiar way). Such faith is well founded when it does not seek to "achieve" evidence to support it, but when it comes from a solid foundation that has been given to it as a gift.

In summary, in the general sense we have outlined it seems to us that in Barth's critique Pietism was both clearly addressed as such and called to make a biblically based, fruitful self-correction. This will not be questioned in our further discussion. Nevertheless we have reason to question whether Pietism could feel that it had been fully understood or fully dealt with by

Barth's critique. This question could only be affirmed under two conditions: only if the essence of Pietism is sufficiently covered by the concept of "religious individualism" and only if at the same time Barth's position in its focus on the concepts of organic life and organized wholeness is acceptable as an appropriate articulation of the biblical-Reformational message. However, both are open questions.

Now to the first point! Whom did Barth actually have in view when he used the label of "Pietism"? In the chapter on Pietism in the first *Epistle to the Romans* Johann Arnd[213] is quoted twice from the pre-Pietistic devotional literature. Spener[214] is quoted twice from the Pietism of the eighteenth century, C. H. Rieger[215] once, and without mentioning any name, a line from a song by G. Arnold.[216] Finally, Barth alludes to the English revivalist song "Where Does the Soul Find Its Home?"[217] and to a dream of the young Tholuck[218] and to the Pietists who had become members of Frederick William IV's consistory in 1850.[219] The quotations and allusions show that Barth actually wanted to speak of the historical Pietism represented by Spener and the movement that was intellectually committed to it. If we examine the quotations more closely we can first observe that Barth considered it possible to interpret the Rieger quotation in a positive light. Furthermore, he put Arnd and Spener on an equal footing with Luther in his criticism of the idea that there is a continual struggle between the Spirit and the flesh. Either Luther appears as an early Pietist or this view is covered by Reformational theology.[220] Since only certain allusions to "Pietism" are present in the other references we have mentioned, we cannot help thinking that Barth has made a somewhat vague use of the

---

[213]Ro 1, pp. 207, 211.

[214]Ibid.

[215]Ibid., p. 212.

[216]Ibid., that "my spirit at times prepares for something better."

[217]Ibid., p. 216.

[218]Ibid.

[219]Ibid., p. 215. It is hard to say whom Barth exactly meant by the Pietists who had become members of Friedrich Wilhelm's consistory. In 1850 this ruler in fact appointed a member to the highest administrative body in the established Prussian church (Oberkirchenrat), but it was not noticeably occupied by revivalist theologians. Probably Barth simply meant by his remark the biographical change that could in fact be observed in several revivalist theologians who became conservative figures while at the same time they ascended to high church office: for example, E. W. Hengstenberg, whose path went from the revival to a "throne and altar theology"; F. W. Krummacher, who became the court preacher in Berlin in 1853; H. Krummacher, who became a consistory member in Stettin during this period; K. S. von Kapff, who likewise became a member of the consistory in Stuttgart in 1850, etc.

[220]Ro 1, pp. 206-7, 211.

label "Pietism." This impression is reinforced when the reader finds out right at the beginning of the chapter that "we are all by nature Pietists."[221] This statement probably also reveals that Barth the critic identified with the object of his criticism to such a degree that he subjected himself to the criticism he had made. However, if we take it seriously, the statement can also be understood in terms of a typical "religious" attitude Barth speaks of in this context. This attitude reaches far beyond the form of its historical phenomenon or the sociological grouping called "Pietism," as the inclusion even of Luther shows. This attitude very clearly came to light in the historical phenomenon. These quotations and allusions prove that this was also Barth's view. But we can conclude from this statement that in examining this phenomenon Barth also used the concept of Pietism primarily as an ideal type, as Troeltsch did.[222] This would mean that his critique of Pietism affects *historical* Pietism only to the extent that it agrees with the *attitude* called Pietism by Barth. Barth believed that both were actually two different things. This can be gathered from the fact that he repeatedly referred to Pietists, Spener,[223] Tersteegen[224] and Tholuck[225] in an affirmative way throughout his whole book. Nevertheless Barth clearly thought he saw this attitude emerge particularly in historical Pietism. Thus he believed he could reduce its dominant thrust to the common denominator of "religious individualism." However, the question is whether this is legitimate.

In the first *Epistle to the Romans* we come across a fact that has to raise doubts about the validity of reducing Pietism to this common denominator. To be specific, Barth clearly excluded a group of Pietists from his critique: the Swabian Pietists, including J. A. Bengel, C. H. Rieger, F. C. Steinhofer, and from the nineteenth century T. Beck (if we may mention him once in this context). This is no coincidence. Not only did he quote them frequently and find himself in

---

[221]Ibid., p. 205.

[222]It is interesting how Barth in his lecture from the winter semester of 1932/33 on the history of Protestant theology in the eighteenth century prefaces his argument with the "individualism" of Pietism by providing this hermeneutical explanation: individualism in its pure form was only espoused by the "original Pietist"; however, the older Pietism of which Barth wants to speak "only partially manifested its characteristics" (*Die prot. Theologie im 19. Jahrhundert,* 1946, p. 93).

[223]Ro 1, pp. 177, 179-80. He refers to Spener for the statement that we *are* righteous and *stand* in the victory of life.

[224]Ibid., pp. 89, 361, 396. All these passages are quotations from the song "Kommt, Kinder, lasst uns gehen . . ."

[225]Ibid., pp. 242, 244. Tholuck confirms Barth's view that we now live in a temporary phase of history before the end times and that the goal is not destruction but perfection. Compare further p. 421.

substantial agreement with them;[226] beyond this it is impossible to ignore the fact that the theology of the first *Epistle to the Romans* has also been shaped by the tradition of Swabian Pietism with its unique insights. Since this tradition was centered around the idea of the "kingdom of God," a critical barb against "individualism" had been part of it for a long time, at times even against Pietistic forms of individualism. Therefore Barth harnessed this tradition in his critique of Pietism not without historical justification.[227] Again it was precisely a *Pietistic* tradition Barth appealed to here. He thoroughly placed himself in this camp to differentiate himself from "Pietism." If this is correct, then two things follow from it. (1) As Barth himself could know, if there are dimensions of Pietistic thought that cannot be covered by the concept of "individualism," then there are legitimate doubts about the suitability of this concept to adequately define the essence of Pietism. And (2) this is more consequential here: By fighting Pietism *only* as "individualism," he did not get away from it in the way he thought. As he himself later remarked,[228] he continued to be rooted in it in one respect while

---

[226]Ibid., pp. 8, 113, 269, 403, 420 (Bengel); 112, 212, 243, 278, 336, 378, 400, 403, 414-15, 435, 436 (Rieger); 2, 127, 130, 212, 231-32, 282, 291, 414 (Beck). We can examine here the problem Barth mentioned in the foreword of the second edition of the *Epistle to the Romans* (1922, xviii): "The explanation of the Epistle to the Romans by C. H. Rieger (1726–1791) in his 'Reflections on the New Testament 1828' mentioned in the first edition literally correspond to the explanation of Fr. Chr. Steinhofer (1706–1761) edited in 1851 from the third chapter to the end of the book. At any rate, the plagiarism can not be blamed on the worthy Rieger himself." Steinhofer too was certainly a "worthy" man, a highly original theologian who was influenced by Zinzendorf in his christocentrism; yet he remained largely unknown, a lonely figure in his time. However, it is quite unlikely that the explanation of the epistle to the Romans used by Barth comes from him. An explanation of the epistle to the Romans is missing in the bibliography by J. Chr. Storr (in F. C. Steinhofer, *Explanation of the First Letter of John*, 1762, XVIIIff). At least it is certain that several of his "talks" on selected passages of Romans were written down and parts of them were published in a small book after his death. It is also certain that the book was reprinted in 1857 (with a foreword by Beck), considerably expanded from "unknown sources." Then in 1871 a further edition was published, this time reduced to the sections that were "undoubtedly of Steinhofer origin." This latter edition contained only sermons on a few verses from the epistle to the Romans (all this according to the foreword in Steinhofer's *Christian Talks on the Believers' State of Grace, Based on the Testimonies of Paul's Letter to the Romans*, 1871). Thus everything speaks for the fact that the explanation of the epistle to the Romans used by Barth came from C. H. Rieger—especially since the history of the transmission of his "reflections" is clearly unproblematic (compare the foreword to the edition of 1847, p. 19).

[227]Compare, for example, Ro 1, p. 269. Barth appeals to Bengel in connection with the idea that Pietism leads to separation instead of to solidarity: "That *ego* must be thoroughly eliminated (Bengel)."

[228]The first *Epistle to the Romans*, Barth says in 1927, was strongly influenced more than I myself noticed by the ideas of Bengel, Otinger and Beck and (via Kutter also by Schelling). "Afterwards these ideas did not prove to be a firm enough foundation for what had to be said" ("Autobiographical Sketch from 1927," in K. Barth/R. Bultmann, *Briefwechsel 1922–1966*, 1971, p. 307).

at the same time he sought to distance himself from it in another respect. And this is not all. His labeling of Pietism as "religious individualism" has another problematic aspect. It not only fell short of aptly describing the *whole* of Pietism. At the same time it was so superficial that it not only described Pietism, but in the same breath, the Reformers as well, as K. Müller gleefully exclaimed in his joyous approval of the first *Epistle to the Romans*.[229]

We can see more clearly how much Barth's critique of Pietism was in fact targeted against the Reformers when we consider that his critique of individualism was still linked to the idea of the "mechanical" production of the new life. Barth *thought* he was in harmony with the Reformers on this point, for it was obviously important to him that the new life was not to be understood as a "human effort" but as a gift. We have already indicated that an issue was raised at this point that Pietism took seriously. On the other hand, when Barth stressed the idea of "organic growth" he was influenced by those Swabian authorities in whose Pietism (especially defined by J. Böhme) precisely this idea played an important role: the idea of "the organic," the concept of "life," "powers," "seed" all applied to understanding the unique nature of God's world as well his view of the fall as a fragmentation of humanity. And could not a prime example of this idea be found in Tersteegen? ("as the gentle flowers gladly come to bloom . . . so let me, quietly and gladly . . . let thee work"). Therefore did not Barth want to distance himself from Pietism by using something that was defined by Pietism? Did he not align himself here with one Pietistic school of thought only to object to another, but only *one* other Pietistic school of thought?

In addition, he criticized Pietism for failing to understand that salvation cannot be found in an individualistic way and that human beings are thus always caught up in the conflict between "Spirit" and "flesh."[230] This thesis became an arrow that was crucially aimed at the Lutheran "simultaneously justified and a sinner" *(simul justus et peccator)* and actually not at Pietism as much as Barth tried to interpret Pietism along these lines. Precisely at this point Pietism wanted to go beyond the Reformation, whether it understood itself either as the true interpreter of the Reformation or as the initiator of a "second Reformation." For a long time the *simul justus et peccator* had been offensive to Pietism, and its interest in the growth of the *justus* beyond the *peccator* had long been its heartfelt concern. Thus in his review of the first *Epistle to the Romans* Pietist E. Gerber from Bern had little difficulty brushing off Barth's objection

---

[229]K. Müller, "K. B., *Der Römerbrief*," in *RKZZ* nr. 18, March 1, 1921.

[230]Ro 1, p. 211: Barth documents this view in *one* breath with a quote from Luther and J. Arnd. Compare also p. 207!

on this point. Only "so-called Pietists" cannot get beyond the turmoil so accurately described by Paul. It is not a characteristic of Pietism to get stuck in Romans 7:14-24. When we keep the founders of Pietism in mind—A. H. Francke, Bogatzky, Baron von Kottwitz and in Switzerland F. Godel, Father Zeller and many others—we find that in their life and in their writings they described the state of grace found in Romans 7:25 and 8:1-2 from their own experience.[231] Pietism could not really feel it was affected by Barth's objections along this line of attack.[232] This means that in spite of all his undeniable efforts to move away from Pietism, Barth was clearly too closely attached to it to be able to attack the innermost bastion of Pietism held by his reviewers. In the following section we will elaborate on the decisive point where he was still closely attached to Pietism in spite of everything.

The Problem of Barth's Theological Self-Understanding

Assuming his critique of "religious individualism" is at least partially true of Pietism, one question still remains. Did the position from which Barth made his critique possess enough persuasiveness to seriously shake a Pietist's convictions and effectively teach him something new? We have already said that by stressing the greatness of the "kingdom of God" and its interpretation as a living, trans-subjective quantity that cannot be orchestrated by man, the theology of the first *Epistle to the Romans* brought a weighty biblical argument into play against individualism. And this should be acknowledged even if at the same time Barth's argument contained a somewhat critical examination of Reformational theology, uncovering its tendency to be preoccupied with a narrow question: "How do *I* get a merciful God?"

Of course, another question must be added. Although Barth articulated this argument in such an exclusive way and was undeniably justified in doing so, did not his approach necessarily conceal *other* equally justifiable, central biblical insights? We must especially raise the question of whether the key themes Paul develops in the Epistle to the Romans such as grace, faith and "justification of

---

[231]E. Gerber, "Ein neues Buch über den Römerbrief," in *Brosamen,* nr. 17, April 27, 1919. Compare also Barth's remark from April 13, 1919 (*Briefwechsel* 1, p. 325): "Again I find applause in the darkest areas of the (Pietistic) 'Evangelical Society.'"

[232]Barth should actually not have acted so surprised as he did at that time that the review "of Pastor Ernst Gerber, the fearsome pope and heresy hunter of this organization," on the whole turned out to be so "astonishingly affirmative" (letter from May 21, 1919, to Thurneysen, in *Briefwechsel* 1, p. 328). In his old age Barth conceded: "I regret and am sorry from the bottom of my heart for all the bad things I wrote about romanticism in the first edition of the *Epistle to the Romans,* just as I did not do justice to Pietism in my holy zeal at that time" (Epilogue, in *Schleiermacher-Auswahl*), 1968, p. 291, Siebenstern-Taschenbuch 113/114.

the godless" which shone anew in the Reformation (in spite of the narrowness of its questions) come into view in their spiritual fullness and clarity when the category of the "individual" is treated as the "first falsehood" (*proton pseudos*)? Is this category really the most reprehensible, the "sin" itself?[233] Is not the baby being thrown out with the bathwater simply to accentuate a proper and important insight? Is not Barth's judgment on "individualism" as the actual fall much too external, formalistic, imprecise and superficial? By rejecting Pietism and making a legitimate critique of the Reformers' narrow question, did he not inevitably leave behind the factually decisive discovery of the Reformation (the question about a "gracious God")?

In fact we believe that a deficit exists in the first *Epistle to the Romans* with regard to the Reformational doctrines of grace and justification. Therefore this book's critique of Pietism has merit, but no conclusive merit. We believe this critique got stuck in a peculiar half-measure in keeping with the half-measure just shown in the preceding section. Barth distanced himself from one Pietistic tradition and form of thought only to be trapped in another. The half-measure consists of the fact that in the first *Epistle to the Romans* "religious individualism" was actually not criticized to the extent that it was "religious." It was only criticized to the extent that it was individualistic. To put it in different terms, Pietism (as well as Romanticism) is problematic not with regard to *what* it would like to achieve and thinks it actually can achieve, but basically with regard to *how* it wants to achieve it—by means of individualism and a "mechanical" process. However, Barth believed Pietism could never achieve it this way. As we pointed out earlier, Barth objected to the Pietists' claim that they were in God and he was in them, but only because this claim cannot be realized by way of "isolation." But if it this claim is still made, then it is "excessive" and "untrue."[234] The immediacy of the "I in you and you in me" and all that Pietism seeks and intends is thus not unachievable in itself. "In the new world everything that Pietism wants to get hold of for nothing in all its rash actions will become possible and true."[235] It is not unachievable in itself, but only in a different way, not in an individualistic and "mechanical" way. It is achievable only by way of the "organic growth" of the divine. And this takes place to such a great degree that a Pietistic reviewer could state with satisfaction that Barth leads "to a joyous possession of God."[236]

---

[233]Ro 1, p. 196.
[234]Ibid., p. 213.
[235]Ibid., p. 237.
[236]Review of Barth's book of sermons and *Suchet Gott, so werdet ihr leben* (1917) by K. E., *Glocke*, 1918, nr. 18.

In fact it was Barth's concern that the divine enters into human life in such a way that something new emerges in it, not in order to "*seek* a distant, strange, unknown divine being" but "to *take* and to *grow* from the fullness of life that is there."[237] According to Barth, the divine powers work in such a way that "as they advance organically, they transform the bondage of the flesh into freedom and give you the ability to overcome temptations. The remnants of your personal existence lived in alienation from God vanish."[238] They create a "life process" in which you "participate," a new order "which is internal and not external to you, natural and not strange."[239] Grace is really an "experience," is "power," indeed it is "the possession of the power that does good." Therefore Barth could say that "the inherent power of grace is the free, good will of man flowing from God and oriented toward God, . . . our will itself. . . . Man under grace is what he will make of himself. . . . He has God's desire and power to do good. He has the gift of activating his good will. . . . Here are the moral imperatives of genuine analysis."[240]

What is actually gained by all these statements in relation to Pietism? Indeed, must we not say instead: his understanding of grace as "possessing the power that does good," his understanding of justification in this sense of making the sinner righteous and of "sanctification" as an organically advancing life process that leaves behind the vanishing remnants of an existence alienated from God—this is at least so analogous to the Pietists' intentions that Barth could not really believe that he had in principle gone beyond Pietism. Again, how do these statements relate to the understanding of the Reformers? It must be said that humankind's relationship to God is seen here in an immediacy which lacks the brokenness implied by the justification of the godless, by the "simultaneously justified and a sinner" *(simul justus et peccator)* and by "faith alone" *(sola fide)*. The objections that Philip Bachmann raised against Barth's concept in his review of the book truly made sense. "In this interpretation Barth talks very little about the fact that God loves us and forgives our sin. God acts not with us or for us, but in us. The basic concept of God's immanence in us takes the place of the basic concept of God's fellowship with us." "The central, primary truth in the concept of justification, forgiveness of sins, is not considered. What occupies Barth's attention is something similar to the concept of righteousness in A. Osiander, spoken in the

---

[237]Ro 1, p. 218.
[238]Ibid., p. 219.
[239]Ibid., p. 221.
[240]Ibid., p. 169.

same terms."[241] New theological insights had to find room in Barth's thought, especially to allow for the Reformers' understanding of Scripture. He dared not close his mind to these objections. As he expressly mentioned in the foreword to his second interpretation of the *Epistle to the Romans,* he did not close his mind to them.[242] Within the framework of this doctrine of grace and justification presented in the first *Epistle to the Romans* and also influenced by Osiander, he shared with the Pietists a particular basic theological conviction that would have made it impossible for him to challenge Pietism in principle, even though his massive argument against the "inferno of Pietism" may have given that impression.

---

[241]"Ph. Bachmann, Der Römerbrief verdeutscht und vergegenwärtigt: Ein Wort zu K. Barths *Römerbrief,*" *Neue kirchliche Zeitschrift,* 1921, pp. 547, 523. In my opinion J. Fangmeier accurately remarks on the first *Epistle to the Romans:* "Here he makes too thorough a break with the old conditions, but makes too small a break with the old self."

[242]*Der Römerbrief,* 2nd ed., 1922, viii, on the review of Bachmann: "Here objections are raised in a very gentle way, objections I must recognize as correct and essential."

III. Barth's Critique of Pietism in the
Second Epistle to the Romans

1. THE CHANGE IN HIS CRITIQUE OF PIETISM IN THE SECOND
EPISTLE TO THE ROMANS COMPARED WITH THE FIRST ONE

Notes on Barth's Change Between 1919 and 1920

More than two years after he finished writing the first *Epistle to the Romans,*
Barth began to review his interpretation for a new edition of the book. H. U.
von Balthasar commented on the result of the revised edition: "No one could
have had any idea what the second edition would look like on the basis of the
first book."[1] Aware of the difference between the two books, Barth himself said
in the preface to the second *Epistle to the Romans,* which was written in the period between October 1920 and September 1921 and published in 1922: "No
stone from the first book, so to say, was left standing in the second one." However, he added that "what the two editions have in common can and must not
be overlooked."[2] When G. Heinzelmann made the remark that Barth should actually have expressed his regret in the new book that he misinformed his readers about God and the world in the first edition of the *Epistle to the Romans,*[3]
that remark was probably just meant as a joke, although the following points
were overlooked. (1) In any case, there was clearly common ground between
the two books. (2) All theologizing is only human knowledge about God and
thus is not timeless but time-bound knowledge that is capable of change and in
need of change. This is not just true in general but was also seen by Barth with
regard to his own theology.[4] (3) What Barth wanted to say about the prevailing
theology of his time from which he himself came and by which he was shaped
was so unusual and new that it was understandable when he was not able to
say it how he wanted to in his first attempt. (4) In his second *Epistle to the Ro-*

---

[1]*Karl Barth, Darstellung und Deutung seiner Theologie,* 2nd ed., 1962, p. 71.
[2]*Der Römerbrief,* 2 Aufl. (hereafter Ro 2), pp. vii-viii.
[3]In *Neue kirchliche Zeitschrift* 35, p. 539.
[4]Ro 2, p. ix.

mans Barth explicitly expressed his regret about several theses in his first interpretation. He specifically mentioned them at a number of places in the second edition, and we will list them below.

Research into the reasons for the change in Barth's thought is still in its infancy both with regard to the change between the first and second *Epistle to the Romans* and with regard to the change from being a disciple of liberal theology to the author of the first *Epistle to the Romans*. In the preface to the second interpretation Barth himself points out four factors "that contributed to his further movement and the shifting battle lines": (1) his further Pauline studies; (2) his discovery of Overbeck; (3) the stimulation of his thinking by an understanding of Plato and Kant developed anew by Heinrich Barth as well as by his reading of Kierkegaard and Dostoyevsky accompanied by Thurneysen's interpretations; and (4) the response to the theology of the first *Epistle to the Romans*. The widespread approval of it puzzled him.[5] The following texts elucidate and verify Barth's statements for the brief time span of only two years in which this change in his thinking between the first and the second *Epistle to the Romans* took place. Besides his informative correspondence with E. Thurneysen there were three lectures: "Christian Life" (June 1919 in Aarburg; unprinted), "The Christian in Society" (September 1919 in Tambach) and "Biblical Questions, Insights and Prospects" (April 1920 in Aarau).[6] In addition to these lectures there were two essays: "The Past and the Future" (Fr. Naumann and Chr. Blumhardt) from September 1919[7] and "Unresolved Problems in Modern Theology" (following F. Overbeck) from January and February 1920.[8] He probably returned to his Pauline studies of 1919 on Ephesians and 1 Corinthians in his later lectures (research still has to illuminate to what degree this happened). Moreover, his lectures in the first half of 1920 on 2 Corinthians bore fruit in a sermon series. Seven of them were included in a book of sermons titled *Come, Holy Spirit!*[9]

Allow me to make a few comments on these texts which document Barth's preparation for his second interpretation of the Epistle to the Romans and the change in his thinking between the first and second editions of his book! We can expect his thinking to be developed and changed not only by his reading and studies during these two years, but also by his *encounters* primarily with a number of lively minds in postwar Germany with whom he made contact only after the end of the war. Especially his Tambach lecture opened the door over-

---

[5]Ibid., p. viii.
[6]*Ges. Vorträge* 1, 1924, pp. 33-34, or 70ff.
[7]Reprinted in J. Moltmann, *Anfänge der dialektischen Theologie* 1, 1962, pp. 37ff.
[8]*Ges. Vorträge* 2, 1928, pp. 1ff.
[9]1924, pp. 190-265.

night to making these contacts.[10] Indeed, we must expect that not only did his theological studies lead to certain encounters but also that these encounters guided him in selecting his reading material and the kind of studies he pursued and stimulated his thinking as well. The significance of the Tambach lecture for Barth was essentially this: "All at once I found a group of people and the prospect of further groups for whom my theological experiments addressed their uneasiness as answers address questions—answers which quietly turned into questions again in the dialogue that ensued with these German contemporaries. Welcoming more than one of these minds hungering[11] for reality made me feel perplexed and forced me to raise the issue of the biblical meaning of the 'kingdom of God' a second time." Thus the significance of these encounters for the emergence of a new, radical line of questioning cannot be minimized. We can even draw the conclusion that the first document of Barth's change is not the Tambach lecture that was the beginning of those encounters, and even less the lecture "Christian Life" from June 1919 which evidently was the model for the Tambach lecture.[12] Although his view had become more critical, although the *totaliter aliter,* the life to come in the kingdom of God is more strongly emphasized than in the first *Epistle to the Romans,*[13] this Tambach lecture is in fact still largely a systematic summary of the insights of the first *Epistle to the Romans.* Barth speaks there as here of being conscious of the "immediacy of God" given "in Christ,"[14] of an "activity of God in man,"[15] of a "breakthrough of the divine into humanity."[16] Barth also operates here as there with an anti-individualistic, organic concept of life when we hear, for example, this statement: "The awakening of the soul is the movement we participate in, . . . the movement in life toward life. . . . An independent life *besides* life is not life, but death . . . our personal life is dead even if it were the most noble, the finest and most pious life imaginable. . . . All juxtaposition of parts is dead. . . . God himself would be dead if he only pushed from outside, if he were a 'thing in itself' and not the One in all . . . it is the revolution of life against the forces of death clutching it;

---

[10]On the wealth of encounters at that time, compare E. Busch, *Karl Barths Lebenslauf,* 1975, pp. 124ff.

[11]"Karl Barth, Autobiographical Sketch from 1927," in K. Barth/R. Bultmann, *Briefwechsel 1922–1966,* 1971, p. 308.

[12]According to F. W. Marquardt in a typewritten "Report on the Socialist Speeches from the Unpublished Works of Karl Barth."

[13]Compare K. Barth/E. Thurneysen, *Briefwechsel* 1, 1913–1921, 1973, p. 325. Also compare *Ges. Vorträge* 1, 65-66 (Tambach lecture): "the *wholly* other of the Kingdom, which is the Kingdom of *God*"!

[14]*Ges. Vorträge* 1, p. 42.

[15]Ibid., p. 43.

[16]Ibid., p. 44.

we are in the process of defeating them. . . . There is something in us that fundamentally contests these forces." Now everyone can "himself become a *living person* and enter into the *victory* of life." "We *are* moved by God. . . . Divine history is taking place in us and to us." "The great syntheses of the Epistle to the Colossians, they can not be completely foreign to us. They are evident in us. . . . They are lived out. We ourselves live them out."[17] This is still clearly the language of the first *Epistle to the Romans*. Thus Barth's remark that the "answers" of this lecture, only later turned into new questions for him, must be taken seriously. It is significant that he himself did not call this lecture, but only the Aarau lecture from April 1920, "the first document of this change" in his thinking between the first and second *Epistle to the Romans*.[18]

As far as Barth's own *study* in the period between both of these books is concerned, it can be ascertained from the sources that he initially read Tertullian in June 1919 (besides the previously mentioned Pauline studies) and gained the following impression: "The questions and the battles, the dangers and the prospects are always remarkably the same wherever it gets serious."[19] He added: "He is highly necessary to gain an understanding of genuine Pietism. Apart from a few peculiar things . . . I am rediscovering all these good minds: Oetinger's realism, Menken's resistance to the Zeitgeist, Kierkegaard's protest against the reality of the world, Blumhardt's spiritual ideas and his thoughts[20] on the return of Christ." The positive sense in which Barth speaks here of "genuine Pietism" is striking! It is especially the anti-secular streak in Pietism that impresses him here. Of course, he mentions only those "Pietists" by name who can be addressed as critical crossover theologians.

Barth's study of *Plato* is attested from the same period,[21] undoubtedly defined by Heinrich Barth's understanding of Plato.[22] In studying Plato, especially the "Socrates of Phaidon" seemed to grow in importance for K. Barth.[23] We must gain a clear understanding of Phaidon's thesis to see how it actually influenced Barth's thinking. The divine as "the reality that always stays the same" is opposed to "everything that changes" and to all phenomena that are problematic because they are so changeable.[24] On the one hand, that divine reality is their

---

[17]Ibid., p. 50.

[18]See n. 11.

[19]*Briefwechsel* 1, letter from June 26, 1919, p. 334.

[20]Ibid., letter from June 28, 1919, p. 336; his reading of Oetinger in May 1919 (pp. 327ff.).

[21]Ibid., p. 334.

[22]Ibid., pp. 404, 446. In 1921 H. Barth published his book *The Soul in the Philosophy of Plato* and gave his inaugural lecture on "The Problem of Origins in Platonic Philosophy" (attended and appreciated by Karl Barth).

[23]Compare *Ges. Vorträge* 2, p. 8.

[24]Plato, *Phaidon,* quoted in the translation by Schleiermacher, 1958, p. 30.

origin, establishing life in this world as the wholly Other. This is why all "learning . . . is memory."[25] However, that divine reality is also at the same time their radical boundary. This is why humankind can recognize the divine reality in no other way than "very close . . . to death."[26] This is why all pure knowledge is merely "wisdom when we are dead," possible only beyond this present life.[27] One can sense how he was instructed by Plato when the crucial thesis of the Aarau lecture from April 1920 is heard: "The one single source of an immediate, real revelation of God is found in *death*,"[28] or when we read in a sermon on 2 Corinthians 2 that was preached at about the same time: "The Word of God . . . . is the memory of eternity in man. It reminds us . . . of familiar things we have forgotten and have to relearn . . . completely anew."[29]

The Impetus Given by Overbeck

The fact that Barth's thinking changed between the two interpretations of the *Epistle to the Romans* can be most clearly understood and documented in his preoccupation with Franz Overbeck, whose posthumous work *Christianity and Culture* was published in 1919 and who was then hailed by Barth as his "Melchizedek."[30] His reading of Overbeck paralleled his studies on 2 Corinthians and resulted in an essay, "Unresolved Problems," which was finished at the end of February 1920.[31] It seems to me that Barth's subsequent reading of Kierkegaard,[32] of Ibsen, Nietzsche and Dostoyevsky was very much on his mind and stimulated his thinking but on the whole only confirmed the discovery he made by reading Overbeck.[33] What did he discover in his reading? "He urgently impressed on us the commandment: You shall not misuse the name of the Lord your God." He impressed it on Barth by using nothing but negations and radically questioning modern Christianity and especially its theology,[34] "calling us away

---

[25]Ibid., p. 27.
[26]Ibid., p. 18.
[27]Ibid., p. 19.
[28]*Ges. Vorträge* 1, p. 86.
[29]Komm, "Schopfer Gott!" p. 204.
[30]*Briefwechsel* 1, p. 364.
[31]Ibid., p. 372.
[32]Ibid., pp. 395, 400.
[33]I believe that Barth's remark during his work on the second *Epistle to the Romans* in a letter to Thurneysen from December 6, 1920, must be taken seriously: There are many things he does not yet see, but he is happy "that we are already so far along—primarily because of Overbeck." Compare Thurneysen's observation in his letter to Barth from May 5, 1920: "that we have reached a first important step through our insight into Overbeck's Stop! and No!, which takes us beyond religious socialism and probably beyond Kutter as well."
[34]*Ges. Vorträge* 2, p. 3.

from all the fleshpots of Egypt out into the desert, driving us to a place where we can neither acquire nor possess, neither feast, nor be lavish, but can only hunger and thirst, seek, ask and knock."[35] This is why the concept of *death* became characteristic of the knowledge of God. It not only marks the "boundary of human knowledge" but at the same time "its transcendental origin."[36] It defines all earthly things, though it is defined as "unfathomable, incomparable prehistory that is beyond time."[37] But used in this way, the concept mainly characterizes the *boundary* of human knowledge and signifies that the divine "things" are "*last things,*" beyond all this-worldly things, and that all this-worldly things are nothing but "world" and "of this world," even Christianity insofar as it is "historical" or can become "historical."[38] From this vantage point the whole history of the church was viewed as a single "history of decline,"[39] and the sharpest criticism was especially leveled at "a Christianity that has become worldly-wise, at the whole of modern theology that seeks to force Christianity on the world under the sanctified cover of modern culture by making its basically ascetic character invisible and even denying it."[40]

One is taken aback by these bold statements: impress the third commandment on us, good, but why then must the whole history of the church be a "history of decline"? Is this a *fact* because of a certain failure? Or is this a *necessity* simply because it is temporal in itself? Or is this not a thesis about church history at all but a critique of a modern, Christian *view* of church history? In this essay by Overbeck as well as in Barth's second *Epistle to the Romans* it is somewhat vague how his critical negations are to be viewed. Does Barth speak so emphatically about the wisdom of death, etc., because he is actually facing a Christianity that he must judge to be in danger of betraying Christianity and losing its subject? Is that why he wants to contest it with those critical theses and appeal anew to the church to get serious with God (and thus with the third commandment)? Or is the root of Barth's critical posture initially not his insight into an actual failure of modern Christianity but the equally modern thesis of "historical relativism" that is taken up and turned theologically into the idea that on the one hand everything historical is understood a priori as "world" and as "of this world," but on the other hand the fulfillment of the third commandment is seen exclusively in

---

[35]Ibid., p. 4. Barth adds, evidently still sympathizing with Angelus Silesius, though appreciating him from another side: "not a little comparable to the unsettling sayings of the 'Cherubic Wanderer'"!

[36]Ibid., pp. 6-7.

[37]Ibid., p. 6.

[38]Ibid., p. 5.

[39]Ibid., p. 12.

[40]Ibid., p. 19-20.

recognizing the otherworldliness of God in relation to the whole historical plane? Or is this critique a radical actualization of early Christian apocalyptic for which all that exists seems destined for destruction in expectation of the end?

It seems to me that what Barth meant here is vague. These three factors were probably closely connected in his thinking. But this would mean that following Overbeck, he wanted to once again impress the third commandment on Christianity. This is, in fact, a good idea! But he did it in *such a way* that his argument was also tied to a certain *interpretation* of modern Christianity and at the same time to his conviction that *"historical relativism"* had a certain theological justification. The question that must be asked is whether impressing the third commandment on Christianity can in principle only take place in this form. Or did the commandment have to at least temporarily be inculcated in this way in the specific theological situation of that time? This much is certain: If the final word has not been spoken on Barth's interpretation of modern Christianity and also not on the way he took up the subject of "historical relativism" and overcame it, the final word has also not been spoken on the way he impressed the third commandment on Christianity at that time.

However, it is not vague but clear that a certain *change* occurred in Barth's thinking under the influence of Overbeck. We can explain this change by making the following points. (1) How does Barth's relationship to W. Herrmann appear now? We are not wrong in assuming that the concept of "death" that is now so emphasized can be seen in direct opposition to Herrmann's concept of "life" that was so important for Barth up to and including the period of the first *Epistle to the Romans*. The latter concept now takes the place of the former and clearly has the function of directly contesting what is meant by the concept of "life"; it denies that the divine in a human life is an immediate given. There are sharp limits to the visible immediacy of God's relationship to humanity, since for Barth "the sole source of God's immediate, real revelation . . . is now found in *death*."[41] Of course, from this vantage point he can no longer say with Herrmann that religion consists of an individual *experience* (or can only be said when "religion" is sharply distinguished from "God's revelation"). Therefore Herrmann's concern can only be rejected polemically: "Immediate life is invisible, unknown and impossible in the world of human beings."[42] We could still ask whether even now there is still a subtle connection between Barth and his teacher. For we must interpret Herrmann's statement in this way: what he meant by such life is *beyond* our "experience." It is an *event*. Thus we could ask if what Herrmann

---

[41]See n. 28.
[42]*Der Römerbrief* 2, p. 147.

meant by "life" is simply denied by the concept of "death," or did he rather intend to stress its complete unavailability?

(2) How does what he learned from Overbeck relate to what he learned from Blumhardt? Barth expressly discusses this question in an essay. Both stood "back to back," the one looking back critically, the other looking forward hopefully. Blumhardt's "expectation of the return of Christ, the issue of the real powers of God's Kingdom and his attempt to overcome religious subjectivism" had a negative flip side that was represented by Overbeck.[43] Nevertheless Barth's encounter with Overbeck led him to the idea that Blumhardt's ideas really had this flip side. Indeed, it seems to us that Barth encountered something new in Overbeck compared to Blumhardt's message. Now he is convinced that Blumhardt's message not only can *also* be said in such negative form but *must* now be said in this form. One may not speak of Blumhardt's yes without "going through the narrow gate of Overbeck's negation."[44] If one compares how even in September 1919 Barth appreciated Blumhardt as the man who wanted to "seek and expect the living God neither in the individual nor in a distant heaven, but in the life of human beings on the earth,"[45] now a shift of emphasis in Barth's interpretation of Blumhardt is clearly noticeable since Barth in his essay on Overbeck mainly emphasizes Overbeck's "attack on Christendom"[46] and can only talk of such "life" as the dialectical flip side of "death."

(3) How does Overbeck-Barth relate to Pietism, which is of special interest to us in this context? Here we come across the surprising fact that Barth found in the "skeptic" Overbeck someone who had a remarkable liking for this phenomenon. Barth quotes (shortened and somewhat imprecisely) Overbeck's dictum: "For Ritschl the Pietistic form of Christianity is the most detestable. For me it is the only one under whose influence a personal relationship to Christianity would be possible for me."[47] Of course, it is only Pietism in a certain interpretation or only a particular aspect of it which finds recognition here: not the Pietism that participates in the modernistic process of "rediscovering God in oneself" but the Pietism that is aloof from modern culture and against the secularization of the

---

[43]*Ges. Vorträge* 2, pp. 2, 18.

[44]Ibid., p. 45. Nevertheless it is striking that Barth wrote critically about Blumhardt's joining the SP on October 10, 1920: "It can obviously not be said that this was a superior move from his side" (*Briefwechsel* 1, p. 426). And it was probably not far-fetched., even if said too coarsely, when in December 1920 Fritz Lieb spread this statement as Barth's new opinion that he arrived at as a result of his discovery of Overbeck: "We have to be somewhat cautious about Blumhardt's influence" (*Briefwechsel* 1, p. 449).

[45]"Past and Future" (*Ges. Vorträge* 2; see n. 7), p. 44.

[46]*Ges. Vorträge* 2, p. 18.

[47]F. Overbeck, *Christentum und Kultur,* 1919, p. 179, quoted by Barth in *Ges. Vorträge* 2, p. 7.

faith, the Pietism that has an "ascetic" character.[48] Thus Barth discovered in Over-beck an opportunity to see Pietism differently than in the first *Epistle to the Romans*. He was now drawing more distinctions but was not uncritical. He was still critical of some aspects of Pietism, yet he was not just critical of other aspects but also quite positive. However, what could now seem positive to him about Pietism was something different than the Swabian tradition of Pietism on which he was dependent in the first *Epistle to the Romans*. But what made Pietism so question-able for him again in a different respect implied an understanding that had to make him more independent of this tradition.

In order to get a clear picture of the change that occurred in Barth's thought since the publication of the first *Epistle to the Romans,* not just historically but *on the issues,* we had best go back to Barth's Aarau lecture "Biblical Issues" from April 1920 that summarizes his insights presented simultaneously in his sermons on 2 Corinthians. It is his last systematic report before writing the second *Epistle to the Romans*. Here the concept of "death" is in fact centrally integrated into Barth's own thinking. "The one single source of immediate, real revelation of God is found in *death. Christ* has disclosed it. . . . The significance, the power of God dawns on the men of the Bible at the boundaries of humanity. . . . The human correlate to the divine life is called neither virtue nor enthusiasm, nor love, but the *fear* of the Lord, in fact, the fear of death."[49] To be sure, there is also yes and life in God, but they are available for us only in their opposite form. "Whoever does not understand this 'Yes' as the 'Yes' in the 'No', does not understand it at all. Life emerges from *death!*"[50] There is yes and life only "beyond the grave." Therefore, it is an "absolute miracle."[51] It is the unexplainable and unachievable novelty,"[52] "the possibility that in the strictest sense of the word is not a possibil-ity."[53] From this vantage point Barth sharply criticizes "religion" which turns its cause into "a phenomenon comprehensible in psychological and historical terms" instead of letting its truth be the truth of its "otherworldliness." In religion human-kind has "taken possession of the divine, put it into operation and thus turned God into an idol."[54] Barth's critique is now decisively targeted at such idolization, at the reinterpretation of the knowledge of the otherworldly God into a human possession, into "religion," but it is no longer targeted at individualism as such.

---

[48]Overbeck, *Christentum und Kultur,* p. 286, quoted by Barth, *Ges. Vorträge* 2, p. 7; pp. 273ff., quoted by Barth, *Ges. Vorträge* 2, pp.17, 21.
[49]*Ges. Vorträge* 1, p. 86.
[50]Ibid., p. 89.
[51]Ibid., p. 95.
[52]Ibid., p. 96.
[53]Ibid., p. 89.
[54]Ibid., p. 81.

On the contrary! "The individual with his highly personal life comes to assume his duty . . . in God and thus gains his legitimacy."[55] He puts it even more strongly: "Not the cosmos, . . . nor so-called humanity as a crowd or building, as a current or a movement, not even as the organized or unorganized masses of the nations, . . . but the *individual . . . the individual who fears God* is the first mover."[56] Coming from the first *Epistle to the Romans,* we are not really prepared for the tone that he sets here. In the fall of 1920, when a new edition of his *Epistle to the Romans* became necessary, Barth could no longer fully stand by the book he published at the beginning of 1919, so he had to get to work on a far-reaching revision of the first version of his interpretation. At least this fact is illuminated by pointing out the change that occurred in Barth's thinking between the first and second *Epistle to the Romans.*

As far as the subject of Pietism in particular is concerned, this change pointed him in a different direction. The following points must be considered. (1) He will no longer be able to make his critique of Pietism by referring to the central concept of "individualism." (2) If he does criticize it, he will at most see its problem in terms of the idea that the religious person can "possess" God and his truth. (3) He will have the opportunity to recognize not only the negative aspects of Pietism but also its positive aspects. (4) In preparing for his second interpretation of the Epistle to the Romans, Barth no longer directly dealt with Pietism in great detail. Therefore, it can be assumed that in contrast to his first book he will no longer take a thematic interest in this phenomenon and will at most deal with it in passing.

What Both Interpretations of the Epistle to the Romans Have in Common

Let us now look at the second *Epistle to the Romans* to clarify further the change in Barth's thought. First of all, in comparing both books we cannot overlook the fact that his thought not only changed; rather there is also considerable *common ground* in both interpretations. Indeed, we believe that their differences only become clear against the backdrop of the concerns both books have in common. In fact the same basic concern runs through and undergirds both of them. On the one hand, they both emphasize that God must be recognized anew as *God,* God in his uniqueness over against everything else so that "the fear of the Lord is . . . objectively . . . at the beginning of our wisdom,"[57] so that theologians "do" it not without God but with God. This thesis gained its critical profile when

---

[55]Ibid., p. 97.
[56]Ibid., p. 98.
[57]*Der Römerbrief* 1, 1919 ed. (= Ro 1), p. 299.

Barth claimed that God is not recognized as God in the dominant church and theology or that the one who is called God there is not God. The first *Epistle to the Romans* states, "Everything was always ready without God. God was also supposed to be good enough to carry out and crown with success whatever human beings began on their own initiative. . . . Sooner or later it had to come to light when *our* causes collapsed that *God's* cause is exclusively his *own* cause. That is where we stand today."[58] And in the second *Epistle to the Romans:* "God himself is not recognized as God and what is called God is in fact man himself. We serve the Non-God."[59] "What is new is God as *God.*"[60]

On the other hand, both books emphasize that *human beings* are seen as being in such profound "solidarity" over against God that no one can or may take leave of this solidarity, especially the pious or saintly person. This solidarity means that the divine redemption is something new compared with all human possibilities and this new possibility is not a human possibility. This thesis is in line with the criticism that the religiosity present in Christendom rests on an illusion, to the extent that it consists of a disintegration of this solidarity. Thus the first *Epistle to the Romans* states: "The exception as a way out is a terrible self-delusion. He (God) gives no one the right to place himself outside the ranks of the others and on the side of God. God makes humanity responsible in this solidarity."[61] In the second *Epistle to the Romans* he states: "*God's* standpoint is maintained over against *all* of our standpoints. *He* is right and *all* of us are wrong."[62] Whoever knows this is "united in what establishes human solidarity—we all live without the glory of God. Considered from our human vantage point, this solidarity cannot properly have a limit."[63]

This basic dual concern, rather the two sides of basically the sole concern, is the same in both *Epistles to the Romans*. To talk in Barth's terms, "God is God," "man is man." But there is one more thing: the *relationship* of this God to this man, which is in fact the common concern in *both* books, this relationship which has to do with God's revelation to humankind, with redemption and humanity's being God's children, is conceived and interpreted eschatologically in both instances. It is impossible in both editions apart from it being made possible eschatologically; it is possible only in the dawning of a new world beyond the present world with its possibilities. "God is the One who comes, the One

---

[58]Ibid.
[59]Ro 2, p. 20.
[60]Ibid., p. 324.
[61]Ro 1, pp. 24-25.
[62]Ro 2, p. 318.
[63]Ibid., p. 319.

who breaks out of the disguises of a degenerate world and the modern age";
the spirit of adoption is "nothing other than the *coming* world of God in the
form of a seed."[64] In the language of the first *Epistle to the Romans* God's revelation is called the "creation of a new cosmos; the divine seed breaking through
anti-God shells."[65] And in the (certainly different) language of the second *Epistle
to the Romans* we read: "There is no redemption on *this* earth and under *this*
sky . . . redemption comes only with the coming day when heaven and earth
are made new."[66] We can only talk about revelation, the life of human beings in
blessedness only in the "future resurrection": "it takes place as such on the *new*
earth and under a *new* sky."[67] We can indeed say there are weighty, even crucial
points at which the first and second *Epistle to the Romans* agree.

The Difference Between the Two Interpretations of the *Epistle to the Romans*

The difference between the two books is found in the different way he argues for
and explains their common concern that I have just outlined. This difference is
considerable. The change lies in the fact that Barth seeks to gain new insights and
make clarifications at the aforementioned problematic points in the theology of the
first *Epistle to the Romans*. The change first appears in a new understanding of the
phrase *"God is God."* The fact that God is God meant in the first *Epistle to the Romans* that he is different from the world in its disintegration and "disorganization."
It is not that he is a strange, distant God. Rather in the first edition of the book what
is unique about God was portrayed in terms of an organically growing divine being
in human beings in contrast to the emptiness of the idealistic demand and to individualism (a concept borrowed from Beck).[68] In the second *Epistle to the Romans*
the fact that God is God means that God is not only different but the wholly other,
who is not only not "reachable in a mechanical fashion but not obtainable as something that is growing "organically" in human beings because he is not reachable or
obtainable at all. In making this change Barth corrects and criticizes the position of
his first book and breaks away from his "association with Beck."[69]

In short, the concept of the ineffable takes the place of the "organic" concept.
This concept, used and understood in reference to Kierkegaard,[70] should appar-

---

[64]Ro 1, p. 238.
[65]Ibid., p. 264.
[66]Ro 2, p. 147.
[67]Ibid., p. 205.
[68]Ibid., p. 223.
[69]What can be said about his attempt at that time? "Answer: impossible!" (ibid.).
[70]Ibid., p. 14.

ently designate the exact opposite of Schleiermacher's understanding of faith (which the young Barth had adopted) as a "perception,"[71] which as a subjective process of "being affected" does posit something objective, but only in the sense that the objective is "assumed from the outset" in this process.[72] This description of the divine world as "ineffable" is directed against such an assumption of the object of faith in the process of believing. Barth strikes at the heart of his own earlier concept of "religious individualism" by rejecting any inclusion of the object of faith in the act of faith, something Barth had not yet achieved in his first *Epistle to the Romans*. God is "something different, unique, exceptional and new over against all human approaches to God."[73] The God who is not at all different from these human approaches is in truth a part of human beings and is "No-God," even if we assign "him the highest position in our world." Indeed, "by putting God on the world's throne we mean ourselves. By believing in him, we are justifying and enjoying and honoring ourselves."[74] The real God is beyond any human approach or possibility. He is not merely beyond the human in the sense that every "here and now" includes a "beyond" as its flip side (thus rendering God as something "given" for man). Rather God is "the beyond of both our 'here and now' and our 'beyond,'"[75] absolutely not attainable or possessable, ineffable, the "concealed God" *(deus absconditus).*[76] *"If God is an object of the world, an object among objects, he would obviously not be God at all. However, the true God is the origin of the crisis* of all objectivity because he is without any objectivity . . . the non-being of the world (including the God of human logic.)"[77]

But in view of the vehement negation of any inclusion of the divine in humanity, we must not overlook (as so often it happens) what is not negated by doing so. There is a nearness and revelation of God. For example, the thesis advocated by B. Dörries in opposition to the *Epistle to the Romans* that God is not only a "distant" but also a "close God"[78] rests on a serious misunderstanding of the *Epistle to the Romans* and as such is actually not a serious opposing thesis.

---

[71]Compare Schleiermacher's famous statement in his second "talk": "The perception of the universe, I ask you to befriend this concept, it is the hinge of my whole talk, it is the most universal and highest formula of religion." Compare this with Barth's early essay, "Christian Faith and History" (in *Schweizer Theologische Zeitschrift*, 1912), the equation of "perception" and "fides" or better, "fides salvifica" (pp. 52-53).

[72]"Der christliche Glaube und die Geschichte," p. 57.

[73]Ro 2, p. 67.

[74]Ibid., pp. 19-20.

[75]Ibid., p. 118.

[76]Ibid., p.18: "God! we do not know what we are saying by using this word. Whoever believes, knows that we do not know it."

[77]Ibid., pp. 56-57.

[78]B. Dörries, *Der ferne und der nahe Gott,* 1927, passim.

Barth does not mean by the transcendence of God an "objective" being along-side (above, outside) the world. "As the unknown God," he is "not a metaphys-ical being alongside other beings. He is not a second, other, strange being alongside that which would exist without him, rather he is the eternal, the pure source of all that is, as the non-being of all things their true being."[79] As such God is the source, not a "thing in itself," but as such he is *at the same time* the *boundary* of the world as well as in *relation* to it.[80] "A presupposition which does not apply to every living thing and which is not universally valid, is no absolute, final pre-supposition."[81] Barth's concern is not God's otherworldliness in itself but the relationship of *this* God to man, a relationship that is not broken off even by sin.[82] In the "truest transcendence of God, there is the truest imma-nence."[83] So his truth is not merely unavailable but as such the "arrow from the other shore that we will never enter, but that has hit *us*."[84]

But now we come to the decisive point (and I think we encounter Barth's actual discovery here). God's ineffability, holiness, strangeness, unavailability does not cease when God turns his attention to man, as if this were a stage, phase or a partial truth that has been abolished. Rather, God *in* his revelation is removed from human reach. The "positive relationship between God and man" is true only as an absolute paradox.[85] Precisely when he is *recognized*, he becomes "observable as the One who is ineffable."[86] "God is recognized precisely as the unknown God."[87] In contrast to the first edition of this book it must be said here that the "concealed God" *(deus absconditus)* is only *as such* "the revealed God" *(deus revelatus)*.[88] On the one hand, this rules out the mis-understanding that one of those untrue transcendences is being described when Barth speaks of God's otherworldliness. He is clearly not speaking of a transcendence that extends life in this world into the world to come. On the other hand, a misunderstanding of revelation is ruled out that once again as-serts the possibility of including God in a human approach by way of revela-tion. Especially in this regard Barth freed himself from the way of understand-ing God developed in his first *Epistle to the Romans*. Barth now interprets the

---

[79]Ro 2, p. 52; compare pp. 315-16.
[80]Ibid., pp. 410-11.
[81]Ibid., p. 90.
[82]Ibid., p. 232.
[83]Ibid., p. 91.
[84]Ibid., p. 220; compare p. 258.
[85]Ibid., p. 69.
[86]Ibid., p. 67.
[87]Ibid., p. 65.
[88]Ibid., p. 408.

phrase "God is God" with the thesis that God is free not only in relation to humankind but free also in his revelation to humankind. And in such an interpretation of this phrase he is clearly saying something new compared with the first *Epistle to the Romans*.

Furthermore, the change between the two books is apparent in the second aspect of the basic concern found in both books: *the solidarity of all human beings before God.* If this was maintained in the first *Epistle to the Romans* by resolutely distancing himself from any form of *individualism,* it is remarkable that in the second interpretation the fight against this front has been explicitly discontinued and he has once again moved away from Beck's concept. "Why should the concept of the organism and the organic functioning of its parts have the significance of reminding human beings of God, even if this idea vividly describes what *we* call life?"[89] The "religious individualism" he once advocated is no longer attacked because of the "individualism" but because of the concept of *religion* involved in it. The threat to human solidarity is now seen in this concept. The "Man is Man" is now interpreted accordingly. In the second *Epistle to the Romans* how are human beings bound together? By all being sinners. God must not only say no to "something" in them but to each of them as *individuals,* not only to the worst human possibilities but to *all* of them, even the best. Barth stresses both aspects so strongly that he occasionally runs the risk of equating human nature with human sin.[90] But he clearly stresses it to make the point that there is no redemption whatsoever in the form of the disintegration of the solidarity of sinners. And he does not stress it in such a way that he denies there is a redemption of the sinner and thus the "new man" who has escaped sin.[91]

At any rate, this redeemed new man is "absolutely beyond, the radically other compared to all that I am."[92] To be sure, he is not a second being alongside me,[93] but "I am this subject," as a self that is "impossible," "imperceivable," "outside

---

[89]Ibid., p. 426. It continues there: "In opposition to the first edition of this book it must be said . . . man is confronted with the question of God not via the detour of 'the whole,' but in his own dire need and hope. Where do we get the concept of the Christian corporation which as such claims to represent God's justice over against the individual?"

[90]Compare, for example, p. 145. H. U. von Balthasar (p. 77) also points this out.

[91]Ro 2, p. 177.

[92]Ibid., p. 125. Compare p. 272: The new, living human being is "in imperceivable reality. Therefore primarily the daring attempts from Oetinger to Beck to advance toward a perceivable, real spirit/body unity by speculating in terms of natural philosophy, must be rejected as misleading: they falsify . . . the content of the statement that is at issue here. It may and must be ventured only by appealing to the *divinity* of God understood fundamentally as imperceivable, only as the proclamation of the *absolute* miracle. It is the *in itself* reliable statement, which is discredited as unreliable by all . . . efforts to first *make* it reliable."

[93]Ibid., pp. 142, 272.

my control."[94] Barth's understanding of the "new life" in the first *Epistle to the Romans* as natural growth originating from an existing fullness is ruled out. Now it is said that the new life is not something available and thus "given." Man cannot take control of it. Because it is not perceptible to his sight, he remains simultaneously in solidarity with sinners. According to the second *Epistle to the Romans* religion tries to pass off what is not visually perceptible and impossible as a human possibility, making it visually perceptible. This becomes a way "to elevate myself above other people."[95] Barth's critique of religion is targeted at this problem. (1) Religion is an enterprise of unheard of pride in which man does what he should not do under any circumstances when it asserts a position where the religious person sees himself as an exception to sinful human possibilities, claiming a perceivable nearness to God.[96] (2) When religion cannot accomplish what it wants, it is nothing but an expression of a purely *human* possibility.[97] "Feuerbach is right in an insightful way."[98]

Does Barth reject all religion and all religious experiences? As a rule his second *Epistle to the Romans* was understood this way, but this criticism did not accurately reflect his view. Rather Barth declared: "I want no antireligious polemics!"[99] "Religion can and should not be shaken off."[100] There is no grace "without the experience of grace!"[101] Religion "represents the divine, it is its imprint, its negative—outside of the divine itself."[102]

'If only we *may be* religious people . . . ! Awakening religion . . . is a task that is truly worth the sweat of the noble-minded if any task within humanity is."[103] Barth intends a critique of "religion" but not its abolition because it also has a positive meaning for him. When it *wants to* exempt itself from the other human pos-

---

[94]Ibid., p. 125. This is why Barth objects to a reversal of the new reality into a perceivable, pious possession, enjoyment, experience, etc., in the second *Epistle to the Romans*. Compare p. 31 on this issue: "There is no human righteousness which can carry man away from the wrath of God! There is no objective greatness, no physical elevation that would justify him before God! There is no state of mind or attitude, no disposition or mood, no realization and comprehension that as such would be pleasing to God! Man is man and is in the world of humanity. . . . Whatever gains existence and form and expansion *in* man and *by* man is always, everywhere and as such . . . insubordination. The kingdom of man is never the kingdom of God. . . . There are no happy possessors."
[95]Ibid., pp. 32ff.
[96]Ibid., p. 226.
[97]Ibid., pp. 218, 212.
[98]Ibid., p. 218.
[99]Ibid., p. 223.
[100]Ibid., p. 224.
[101]Ibid., p. 212.
[102]Ibid., p. 236.
[103]Ibid., p. 237; compare pp. 105, 163.

sibilities and yet at the same time cannot do so, it is a possibility fraught with "special danger" and "special promise." It is the "apex of humanity in the ominous dual meaning of this word."[104] On the one hand it is the revelation of human sinfulness: "Religious man is a sinner in the most vivid sense of the word."[105] In religion "sin becomes the concrete condition of our existence."[106] On the other hand, it becomes a pointer to the divine possibility that limits all human possibilities[107] and reveals the positive meaning of being human: being in the image of God, being in a relationship with God.[108] Concerning God Barth declared that he is not only free in relation to man but also *remains* free in his love and affection for man. Concerning man, he declared that he is a sinner not only apart from God, but at the same time he also *remains* a sinner before God, as one who has received a pardon. Thus the Barth of the second *Epistle to the Romans* has clearly gone beyond his concept of justification derived from Osiander in the first edition of the book.[109]

The change from the first to the second *Epistle to the Romans* is also apparent in the third aspect of the concern shared by both books. They both affirm an eschatological understanding of the *positive relationship* between God and man. As we have said, in the second *Epistle to the Romans* it is not only a matter of juxtaposing the "God is God" and "man is man," but at the same time "the relationship of *this* God to *this* man and the relationship of *this* man to *this* God."[110] Already in the first *Epistle to the Romans* this relationship was understood as an eschatological reality, though in such a way that the eschatological kingdom of God was understood there as "the rule of the reorganizing principle of God's world," enabling us now to grow into a life *encompassing* the whole breadth of our existence by virtue of a "seed of life that has been planted in us."[111] If this

---

[104]Ibid., p. 213. In a similar fashion it says dialectically on p. 163: "all recognition, representation and defense of religion [has] its relative right," for "the man's relationship with God *necessarily* has its subjective side." But on the other side "all criticism of religion has its relative right as well," for religion is the old world "as a *human* possibility, as an historical phenomenon and reality . . . based on its psychic, intellectual, moral and sociological form that completely conceals the content it claims."

[105]Ibid., p. 152.

[106]Ibid., p. 228.

[107]Ibid., p. 221.

[108]Ibid., pp. 263-64.

[109]His letter from December 3, 1920 (*Briefwechsel* 1, p. 448), shows how much Barth was conscious of this. In this letter he speaks of "going back *beyond* Hofmann and Beck" and further remarks, "My turning away from Osiander to Luther asserts itself like a disaster against the first edition, and I often wonder how I could be so blind then in not seeing it." Compare Ro 2, p. 404: the praise of "God's forensic justification," which Barth rejected in the first *Epistle to the Romans* (as Beck did).

[110]Ibid., p. xiv.

[111]Ro 1, pp. 229ff.

relationship is also understood eschatologically in the second *Epistle to the Romans* as well, the eschatological dimension is now viewed differently. This dimension is envisioned as such a radical disruption of all human possibilities that the idea of the dawning of God's world in man in the form of a "seed of life planted in us" found in the first *Epistle to the Romans* is ruled out.

Eschatology in both the first and second *Epistle to the Romans* is not the final part of the dogmatics but the fundamental dimension in which this positive relationship between God and man is made possible. What is new in the second *Epistle to the Romans* is that eschatology is interpreted by the cross/resurrection, meaning the cross and resurrection of Christ, designating not historical facts but the decisive category of God's eschatological action on behalf of man. "Death" as the quintessence of the "end of all things" in the second *Epistle to the Romans* takes the place of "life" in such a way that the absolute end of human possibilities is paradoxically the beginning of the divine world. But this hope is found exclusively in the "cross" (understood in these terms).[112] Therefore the divine touches man not where "life" emerges in him (as in the first *Epistle to the Romans*) but where man is limited by death. "This hope is not seen in terms of man touching God in *the experience* of death" but actually at the end of all human possibilities, including this one![113] However, man is "touched" in terms of encountering life in the "cross" at the end of his possibilities, encountering the reality of God and the new man![114] It is not as if "death" in terms of mysticism were "a transition" making it possible to intensify or deepen the experience of this world by an experience of the hereafter! For one thing the reality of life in

---

[112]Ibid., p. 289: "Ave *crux* unica spes mea!"

[113]Ro 2, p. 148.

[114]Ibid., p. 126: "The beginning of the new man can become perceivable to us only at the end of the old man, only at the cross of Christ, the meaning and reality of his resurrection." In this sense Barth uses the famous image of the "tangent." In similar fashion the world of God touches the world of man: "It touches it like the tangent touches a circle, without touching it, and precisely by not touching it, it touches it as its boundary, as a *new* world" (p. 6). In this context the equally famous image of the "hollow space" can be understood, in which Barth understands *faith*. "The faith of man is . . . his will to assume a hollow space" (p. 17). The "hollow space" must not be understood in terms of mysticism: that man empties himself to directly take hold of God in this way. Faith as "hollow space" (the image probably also marks a conscious correction of Osiander's concept of faith in the first *Epistle to the Romans*) always *remains* empty, "hollow" at the perceivable level" (p. 12). "Faith" understood in this way is strictly opposed to an understanding of faith as a *possession*. Where faith is not understood as such "hollow space" but as a "possession"—and be it a perceivably filled "hollow space"—it becomes a purely inner worldly phenomenon; indeed, it is not faith at all, but "unbelief" (p. 32). But if it is a hollow space, it is "the turning, the conversion" from the old to the (imperceivable) new man as the final human, no, first divine possibility (pp. 18-19). Faith in this sense corresponds to the touching of God and man in death/resurrection.

death is an absolute paradox and miracle one cannot expect, something that cannot be intentionally reached by way of or by means of "death" because "death" also means the end of all such ways and means.[115] For another thing, such "life" is by no means a reality *alongside* the reality of "death." Rather "life," the reality of God and the new man relates to human possibilities just as "life is contrasted to death, death to life, being to nonbeing and nonbeing to being."[116] Therefore "a transition, a development, an ascent or a building up from here to there is ruled out in principle."[117] There is "no gradual transition . . . but an abrupt disruption here, an unmediated beginning of the wholly other there."[118] "Life is not life if it is not life from *death*. God is not God if his beginning is not the *end* of man."[119] Yet "the final stop! is also the first forward!" and life *is* in death; indeed it is the ineffable *unity* of "Creator and creature," " reestablished by the cross and resurrection of Christ."[120] It is thus grace, redemption, the new man and the new world.

Therefore, for the Barth of the second *Epistle to the Romans* as well there is a positive "contact" and relationship, even a unity of God and humankind, but only as a purely eschatological possibility, meaning that within the framework of their possibilities human beings can at best only *wait* for it. In relation to their possibilities it is only possible as a paradox, as "an impossibility," only in its "death." "Redemption is the ineffable, inaccessible, impossible event we encounter as "*hope*."[121] If Barth had already seen in the first *Epistle to the Romans* that the eschatological possibility (God's Word) is not achievable by human beings but must come from God, then he has now seen in the second *Epistle to the Romans,* going beyond the first, that this possibility, precisely because it comes from God, is not only something absolutely new compared with the whole level of what can be humanly achieved but also always

---

[115]Ibid., p. 299.
[116]Ibid., p. 117.
[117]Ibid.
[118]Ibid., p. 222.
[119]Ibid., p. 166. Compare the strictly eschatological identification of the new world and the new man. See p. 62: Faith is "bowing before what we can *never become, never have, never do,* before what *never becomes world, never man,* unless in the abolition, in the redemption, in the resurrection of all that we now and here call man and world." Barth does not at all deny, as this passage shows, the reality of God's incarnation or the reality of the new creation of humanity. The special aspect of the *Epistle to the Romans* is, however, the way, namely the eschatological way (as shown above), in which he interprets this reality.
[120]Ibid., p. 293; compare p. 189: "The power of the resurrection . . . is . . . the step across the threshold."
[121]Ibid., p. 298.

remains the absolutely new thing and cannot cease to be such a new thing sometime in space and time (gradually).[122]

2. HIS EXPLICIT CRITIQUE OF PIETISM IN THE SECOND *EPISTLE TO THE ROMANS*

By charting the change that occurred from the first to the second *Epistle to the Romans* we have already sketched the basic lines of the theology found in the second *Epistle to the Romans*. As we will demonstrate, if the Pietistic argument with the early Barth mainly concentrated on this theology, there is a valid reason for it: Barth's explicit argument with Pietism strongly recedes in the second *Epistle to the Romans* compared with the first. The concept "Pietism" seldom appears and has disappeared from his exegesis of Romans 7, not only from the chapter heading but also as a critical lead concept for the presentation of the subject. Instead it gives way to a critical reflection on the concept of "religion." That explains why the Pietistic argument with Barth mainly dealt with the theology of his *Epistle to the Romans* in general, but only a little or not at all with the passages where he explicitly took a position on Pietism. If the Pietists took issue with his *Epistle to the Romans* in spite of its relatively few direct references to its concern, they did so because they felt that the book was a challenge apart from its explicit critique of Pietism. They were not wrong to feel that way. For passages that assume a tacit, *implicit argument* with Pietism are found here again and again, and the *Epistle to the Romans* as a whole wanted to be a critical "marginal note" on *all* church trends and a general critique of the domain of the church and religion. Of course, to such an extent it was also an *indirect critique of Pietism*. But it should be clear that the Pietists ran the risk of misunderstanding in what sense Pietism as such was meant if they referred only to this implicit and indirect critique of Pietism in their discussion with him. That is why it is essential to first make clear the *explicit* critique of Pietism in the *Epistle to the Romans* before judging to what degree Pietism was affected by the thesis of this book in other ways as well.

There are three ways to discover the explicit critique of Pietism found in the

---

[122]I would not think that for this reason Barth simply does not know any future eschatology but only an "axiological" one. His battle against an understanding of the eschaton as the lengthening of the present into the future (imaginable for us), which would only be a continuation of human possibilities (ibid., p. 289), is of course clear (compare p. 170). Nevertheless, Barth would like to understand "our future as a parable of our eternity" (p. 175) and thus the eschaton as something we *wait* for and *hope* for (p. 310), something that *will* be (p. 272), though only as a future resurrection, beyond the end of all things and all time, which then "will never ever become time" (p. 294).

second *Epistle to the Romans*. One can identify the quotations of individual Pietistic authors, his explicit position on the phenomenon of "Pietism" and his
treatment of typical Pietistic concepts and concerns.

The Quotations of Pietistic Authors

First of all, it is a remarkable fact that Barth actually used works by Pietistic ex-
egetes in his own exegesis. He mainly quotes two Swabian Pietists, J. A. Bengel,
and F. C. Steinhofer. Without exception he quotes both of them approvingly.
Barth concludes from the combination of the Pauline "they fall short of the glory
of God" and Bengel's aphorism "glory is being able to see God" that "we lack
this ability to see God."[123] Barth translates Bengel's "spes erit res" this way: *"This
hoping is possessing."*[124] In doing so, he affirms Pietism's interest in "possessing"
faith, but at the same time he corrects it by using the words of a Pietist himself.
Barth concludes his whole work[125] with a quotation from Bengel that speaks of
how difficult it is for the seeker of truth to recognize truth, but also of its trium-
phant march "through adversity." He quotes Steinhofer's statement that the same
verses have a different meaning for the one who trusts in grace and the one
who trusts in works, in that it is sweet for the one, hard for the other.[126] And he
cites the statement that one loses grace by boasting of what one has received.[127]
As far as other Pietistic authors are concerned, Philip F. Hiller is quoted approvingly: "Blood is the basic color on the canvas of the Redeemer."[128] He also
quotes from G. Tersteegen: "Let every one turn his face/with a complete turn/
resolutely toward Jerusalem."[129] He quotes the latter to characterize the orientation of agape and to give the reason why it is different from eros. Barth appeals
to S. Preiswerk, "We must compassionately carry the burdens of all our contemporaries," for his understanding of mission as "tearing down all the differences"[130] that divide humankind. Oetinger's concept of the "sensus communis"
is used positively,[131] and he alludes to the sayings of Angelus Silesius, being crit-

---

[123]Ro 2, p. 75.

[124]Ibid., p. 141. The quotation comes from Bengel's *Gnomon* (on Rom 5:5). Further quotations
of Bengel are in Ro 2, pp. 15, 495.

[125]Ibid., p. 521. According to K. Barth/E. Thurneysen, *Briefwechsel* 1, 1913–1921, 1973 (= *Briefwechsel* 1), p. 442, Barth at first wanted to put this statement by Bengel on the front page of
his second *Epistle to the Romans* as his motto: "Bengel actually says everything [here]. Turning to friend and foe, I could only 'roll out' what could be mentioned."

[126]Ro 2, p. 334.

[127]Ibid., p. 396; further Steinhofer quotations, pp. 134, 495.

[128]Ibid., p. 80.

[129]Ibid., pp. 438-39.

[130]Ibid., p. 74.

[131]Ibid., p. 511.

ical of them only to the extent that they are intended or read "as psychological recipes" but leaving open the question of whether they could also be interpreted differently.[132] As far as I can see, Barth comments on only *one* passage of an actually pre-Pietistic author, J. Arnd, clearly rejecting it as a "dangerous statement." It refers to the struggle against sin as such as an "indication of your believing heart."[133]

The affirmative way Barth draws upon Pietistic authors in the second *Epistle to the Romans* is striking. Of course, he prefers certain theologians. And we can surely not overlook the fact that in selecting those quotations, he gives them a certain slant and fits them into the flow of his thought by giving them a particular interpretation. We cannot claim that his thought is being decisively influenced by these authors, but we can claim that he believes he has definite points of contact with them as he pursues his ideas. That is why he believes he can and should refer to them. Moreover, it is clear in what regard he does *not* quote Pietistic literature and cannot quote it approvingly. This can be seen in those passages where he is critical of an understanding of faith that stresses pious "experience" and "possession." But it is again remarkable that even with his different understanding of faith, Barth apparently is convinced that he does necessarily have the Pietists against him in this matter.[134]

But the picture is seen in a somewhat different light when we compare the quotations of Pietistic authors in both interpretations of the *Epistles to the Romans*. Notice the following facts. (1) A large number of the quotations in the second *Epistle to the Romans* are already quoted in the first edition. (The Steinhofer citations are all ascribed correctly to C. H. Rieger, as we have already noted.) Therefore the number of quotations has hardly been increased in the second interpretation.[135] We may conclude from this (and the few new quotations from Pietistic authors only confirm this) (a) that between both of his interpretations of the *Epistle to the Romans* he did not pursue any new study of Pietism on his own and (b) that he no longer has any vital interest in pursuing a

---

[132]Ibid., p. 84.

[133]Ibid., p. 244.

[134]Compare Barth's interesting remark in KD 4/1, p. 701, on a quotation from a song of Zinzendorf: "Have nothing at all, but believe . . .": "Was it actually so new, surprising and terrible when I called faith a 'hollow space' in my explanation of the Epistle to the Romans in 1921?"

[135]The quotations by Hiller and Preiswerk we have already mentioned; the brief references to Angelus Silesius and Oetinger (the only Pietist of whom a study by Barth between the two *Epistles to the Romans* can be documented!) are new. The two Bengel quotations on pages 75 and 521 are also new. Both come from Bengel's *Gnomon:* the latter from his "conclusio operis," the former from the interpretation of Acts 7:2, rendering half of one of the most famous sayings of Bengel: "God's holiness is his hidden glory, his glory is his manifest holiness."

discussion with Pietism in his second interpretation. The latter impression is strengthened by the following remark. (2) An abundance of quotations by Pietist authors in the first *Epistle to the Romans* are dropped in the second edition. All of Tholuck's and all of Spener's quotations are omitted: not only the ones he discussed in a positive light, but also those he discussed in a negative light. He also dropped half of the Rieger/Steinhofer quotations and two of the three from Tersteegen. Of course it is significant that all of the quotations from T. Beck that were so important for the first *Epistle to the Romans* were cut, but also two of Bengel's: one that objects to "individualism" and another that describes the quiet (organic) growth of the kingdom of God.[136] Evidently both of them no longer fit into the theological outline of the second book. Barth no longer seems to be so interested in Pietism when he is making his arguments. (3) It is remarkable that a series of Pietistic quotations he lifted from the text of his first book acquire a new meaning in the context of the second *Epistle to the Romans*. Bengel's phrase "spes erit res," which we mentioned earlier, was translated "Hoping is possessing" in the first book. Its purpose was to support his opinion that "the future is already humanly present" and that this hope "carries its fulfillment within itself," whereas the same phrase in conjunction with the second book signifies that all "possessing" and the new "being" of the Christian are never to be understood as "a direct reality" but "always dialectically, indirectly, based on faith alone."[137] The statement of J. Arnds that hatred of sin proves the faith that overcomes it is under suspicion in Barth's second interpretation for a different reason than in the first. It is no longer because of the separation of a higher from a lower self, but because of the view that a negative work, my "hatred," "my protest" against sin could turn me into a new man.[138] These two examples illustrate how the first *Epistle to the Romans* served as a stone quarry for the second, but in such a way that "no stone was left lying on another." And so they show in what sense not only Barth's theology but also both his view and his critique of Pietism changed.

His Position on Pietism as a Whole

To start with, three things stand out. Pietism is no longer criticized in the second *Epistle to the Romans* (in contrast to the first) because of its individualism. This is no longer surprising in light of the change between the two books that we

---

[136]The deleted quotations from Bengel were found on pages 269 and 420 in the first *Epistle to the Romans*. And the deleted quotations from Rieger/Steinhofer were found there on pages 243, 400, 415, 435.

[137]See Ro 1, p. 113; Ro 2, p. 141.

[138]See Ro 1, p. 211; Ro 2, p. 244.

have discussed. Barth does mention "the Pietism of individual conversion" once,[139] but only in terms of characterizing a specific form of Christianity, not at all in terms of condemning it. Rather Barth discovered the category of the individual mainly by reading Kierkegaard and in "contradiction to the first edition of the book." "Where do we get the concept of the Christian corporation which as such claims to advocate the law of God against the individual?" The human being stands before God as an individual and "not by way of a detour through the whole."[140] Barth saw that Kierkegaard was the representative of a "super-pietism" in this regard.[141] By learning here from Kierkegaard, he largely discontinued his polemics against "individualism." Of course, not completely! For Barth does believe that Kierkegaard "occasionally has to be straightened out by Kant," and this also would apply to "the Pietism of individual conversion," the necessary changes having been made. His point here is that the paradox of faith is not understood as a *private* paradox and the eschatological goal not as "happiness [or also unhappiness!] *in one's own corner.*"[142] In spite of this reservation Barth ceased fire in this direction, so much so that he came to believe in his old age that he had done too much of a good thing on the other side and had become dependent on Pietistic tradition in a new way.[143]

However, what is also dropped in the second *Epistle to the Romans* is the special affinity of his theological thought to Swabian Pietism and its peculiar power theology by which Barth was so profoundly influenced in the first *Epistle to the Romans;* this new turn has also been mentioned in our earlier discussion. In the wake of Barth's separation from semi-Pelagianism stressing "the wisdom of death," his separation from the idea of an immediate filling of humanity with divine "life" was logical, for it was an idea fed from that source. It is striking that Barth's argument with the special tradition of Swabian Pietism in the second *Epistle to the Romans* mainly occurs in conjunction with his critique of his the-

---

[139]Ro 2, pp. 322-23.
[140]Ibid., p. 427.
[141]Ibid., p. 259.
[142]Ibid., p. 453.
[143]"Dank und Reverenz," *EvTh,* 1963, p. 34: A serious "reservation that forty years ago did not at first dawn on us. . . . Kierkegaard was more deeply indebted to the 19th century than we wanted to admit then. Stressing the historical aspect, we may perhaps wonder if his teaching was not the highest, most consistent and most well-thought out completion of *Pietism* which . . . together with rationalism laid the foundation for the kind of Christianity and church that is oriented toward the pious individual into whose cause he so passionately threw himself just as we resolved to throw ourselves anew into its cause forty years ago while calling on his name. But we were not able to attack its foundation, this anthropocentric, Christian thought as such from the perspective of Kierkegaard, because he himself did not attack it, but rather strengthened it enormously."

ology in the *Epistle to the Romans*. Therefore, as a separation from the experiments made from Oetinger to Beck[144] it was at the same time a separation from the experiments also made in the first edition. Of course, we must not overlook the fact that this critique did not prevent Barth from especially using the writings of the Swabian Pietists, as we have shown.

The most remarkable aspect of the second *Epistle to the Romans* in connection with our subject is that Barth did not criticize Pietism where we assume he would after all that has been said (and where the community people actually felt Barth had primarily criticized them): their understanding of faith as a visible, direct, pious "possession" and "enjoyment." When Barth objects to this, he does not as a rule mention Pietism. An exception to this rule is his comment on the religion of Zinzendorf, the Romantics and the Indians, where he objects to the idea of intimacy with the divine being *without* the fear of the Lord,[145] an intimacy that fails to appreciate the distance between God and humankind.[146] But here the critique is limited to Zinzendorf, who in Barth's view has a close affinity to Romanticism. It is no coincidence that Barth does not directly mention Pietism in this context. For in the second *Epistle to the Romans* Barth evidently thinks he is able to agree with the Pietists on this point to a considerable degree. Indeed we are faced with the fact that Barth expresses a quite friendly view of them now in contrast to earlier. It probably has to do with his discovery of Overbeck, in whose writings he found a favorable opinion of the Pietists, praising them for their "ascetic" aloofness from modern culture. On the other hand, it has to do with his discovery of Kierkegaard's scandalous preaching: from the perspective of Kierkegaard's "super-pietism" he could also learn to see Pietism in a new light so that he now actually has a new *and* in part even a *positive* view of this phenomenon. He is clearly convinced that here a knowledge of grace as a nongiven, its no to humankind as it is and its question mark behind any attempt to elevate humanity, had been kept alive. And so he says that true Christianity "at least feels more closely related to the peculiar endeavors of the ascetics and Pietists" than to the "healthy Protestant piety of the people."[147] In contrast to the Romantic, idealistic theologians, they knew that "Christianity

---

[144]Ro 2, p. 272; see also p. 223.

[145]Ibid., p. 127.

[146]I don't know anything about whether Barth even knew Zinzendorf from his own texts. It seems certain to me that Barth did not know him as well as Tersteegen, for example. Even in his *History of Protestant Theology* Barth talks very vaguely about Zinzendorf. I presume that Barth dealt with Zinzendorf in more detail only in the 1950s, where he then quickly found a very positive relationship to him; compare KD 4/1, p. 763. On page 701 (see n. 12 above) he sees Zinzendorf in the vicinity of the theology of the *Epistle to the Romans*.

[147]Ro 2, p. 448.

does not strive for the heights." On the contrary, it recommends that "human beings are to be led down to the depths."[148] The clearly irregular activity of the ascetics and Pietists is not problematic in itself unless the "paradox" becomes a "private paradox."[149] If the possibility of God is hidden in crying out to God from the depths of human need, and only in this, the criticism will stop; "Tersteegen and his followers are *also* right if they really stand *here*."[150] Do they stand here? According to Barth, yes and no. Yes because they have a profound insight—that Christianity does not strive for the heights. No (this must be explained in greater detail) because they do not stop at this insight. In any case, Barth shows with his yes in what terms he now understands Pietism, and also to what extent he has now taken a positive attitude toward it. If he understood Pietism as being "conformed to the world" in the first *Epistle to the Romans* as a part of the secularization of Christianity, he now clearly sees it in a new light. He now understands how Pietism's attempt to flee the culture and the world is typical of it, and he knows how to appreciate this feature of it.

But a definite *critique of Pietism* is also found in the second *Epistle to the Romans*. It presupposes Barth's new understanding of Pietism and starts with what he approved of. He accuses Pietism of not having stayed with their particular insight and of not taking it seriously in a consistent manner. "The seriousness of the ascetics must be more serious to be fully serious."[151] As we have said, Barth sees Pietism's affinity with the "ascetics," and what he now appreciates in it could be called its *ascetic streak,* revealing its knowledge of God's no, of human sin, the necessity of the fear of God and repentance before him and the disruption of all attempts to identify the human with the divine. This is where Barth's criticism begins. It is *not* focused on the fact that Pietism also knows about God's yes, his love, the new man, even a unity of God and human beings. Rather it is focused on the fact that it fails to appreciate this "ascetic," negative knowledge and misuses it as a "way" to attain divine love and the new man, thus in the end taking *possession* of the divine through human endeavor. In Barth's view this use of such knowledge is an abuse of it, and this "way" is a

---

[148]Ibid., pp. 447-48.

[149]Ibid., p. 453.

[150]Ibid., p. 281. The passage on page 234 points in a similar direction, where Barth understands Calvin, Overbeck, Kierkegaard, Dostoyevsky and Blumhardt as radicals who step "to the extreme edge" of all human possibilities, "who, repenting in sackcloth and ashes, struggle for our salvation amid fear and trembling. To be sure, the Pietists are less radical in this but could not hinder the fact that they too bear within themselves and could one day give birth to the determination inexorably pointing to the extreme edge!"

[151]Ibid., p. 501. By asceticism Barth must mean monasticism. The fact that he sees this in conjunction with Pietism probably has to do with the example of Overbeck.

"dead end" because I not only do not take possession of God's grace by "works" but also not by the negation of "works," because such negation would still be a "work."[152] Not only that direct path from humanity to God but even the negation of such paths is not a way to reach God. Even humility, even every form of self-denial, even the knowledge of having no claim to God's grace does not give me any claim to it. So even when I renounce my own "possessing," I do not have God; rather I am still focusing on myself. But according to Barth it is precisely this view that is the "loophole of Pietistic dialectics." They assume, "I can at least reassure myself that I am restless."[153] This is the "Pietistic dialectic," knowing that self-righteous Pharisaism is not valid in God's eyes but then turning this (correct!) negative knowledge into an assured *method* of attaining grace. "The *new* Pharisaism, more dreadful than any previous Pharisaism, could appear as the triumph of a Pharisaism that not only manages to be 'self-righteous,' but humble as well! Human righteousness is capable of anything, even of neutralizing and destroying the self if it must be (. . . mysticism, Pietism). Beware of this misunderstanding more than of anything else. At the last moment it 'excluded' so many who stood directly in front of the gates of God's righteousness. Whoever wants to be right before man and God will still boast of sinking into the deepest oblivion of non-being (possibly even of his uncertainty and brokenness!). As a human being (only as a human being!) he will stand there, insisting that he is in the right. . . . No 'work,' *not even a negative work,* can be a possibility any longer.[154]

Notice two things in this text that are crucial in the critique of Pietism found in the second *Epistle to the Romans.* On the one hand, notice the phrase "directly in front of the gates of God's righteousness" and on the other hand the phrase "more dreadful than any previous Pharisaism."[155] What Barth is objecting to is that the stance under the no of God is not the place at which the person, *remaining* completely without any claim, receives God's word of grace. Instead, it is a *way,* an intentionally, consciously chosen method to take posses-

---

[152]Ibid., p. 299: "We must be aware that we cannot take possession of this power [the Spirit of God] even with sharpest negation. Even the 'negative' way of mysticism is a dead end, just as all 'ways' are dead ends." Compare p. 196.

[153]Ibid., p. 244; compare p. 273.

[154]Ibid., p. 84.

[155]In my opinion Barth's talk at this point about a "new Pharisaism" is the early form of his later often repeated warning against a "Pharisaism of the tax-collector" (compare KD 1/2, p. 282; KD 4/1, p. 688). Moreover, compare as a commentary on the charge of Pharisaism Barth's insightful reflection from February 3, 1919, that "Pharisaism with its holy, critical earnestness is surely only a deviation of prophetic religion, in its own way a phenomenon of advent as well" (*Briefwechsel* 1, p. 315).

sion of God's grace anew, and it is a mere transitional stage the believer can put *behind* him to attain the possession of grace at the same visible level where he was previously not in possession of it. On the basis of possessing grace the "converted" Pietist departs from the solidarity of sinners (from being dependent on *sola gratia*), so that he reads Romans 7 "as his story *before* his conversion,"[156] in contrast to Paul and the Reformers but in harmony with more recent theology that reads it through Pietistic glasses. Therefore, in the end Pietism arrives at an understanding of faith as a visible, pious possession, an understanding criticized by Barth. But this is not actually the key point in his critique of Pietism. Instead he focuses on the *way* in which it arrives at a misunderstanding of an initially correct insight even though a counterweight exists in its thought. To be sure, the Pietists know of "repentance" "and the fear of the Lord," but they do not follow through on it because they exclude certain people from the need to bow to this understanding.

The frequently cited statement that appears in a similar form in the first *Epistle to the Romans* must be understood in these terms. (It is found on page 269 of the *Epistle to the Romans*, first edition.) "I would rather go to hell with the universal church than go to heaven with the Pietists of a lower or higher order, of an older or modern observance! In this case Christ is with us in hell." (The second statement is found on page 231 *Epistle to the Romans*, second edition.) "Precisely the critic of the church would rather be with the church . . . in hell at any moment of time than with the Pietists of a lower or higher observance in a heaven that does not exist. Let those who are able to grasp it do so: Christ is present where we unconsolably know that we are banished away from Christ, but is never present where we know we are safe from this distressing knowledge."

Although this has been largely overlooked,[157] this passage has a different meaning in each of the books. In in the first *Epistle to the Romans* it is simply a statement against all individualistic "separation" and for "solidarity" with the universal church. In the second *Epistle to the Romans* it is about a word addressed to those who legitimately engage in "anti-ecclesiastical polemics" aimed at "religious churchmen" in order to "remind the church of eternity." In spite of its justifiable criticism it is a warning not to forget that the critic himself is a part of this

---

[156]Ro 2, p. 253. And what drives a Pietist, assuming this "holy change," is for Barth tantamount to discrediting grace: "There is no more foolish rule of all too eager new converts shouting all too loudly for ethics than to cast suspicion on grace by making the pardon and action of man two separate functions and going over to so-called 'attempts at life beyond grace'" (p. 416).

[157]Compare O. Knobloch, "Karl Barth und 'unsere Gemeinschafsleute,'" in *Antwort. Festschrift für K. Barth*, 1956, p. 401.

church "at every moment of time," and thus it is a warning not to turn this correct insight into a new viewpoint or even a school of thought. Otherwise the critic may end up standing before God, insisting he is in the right but departing from his solidarity with sinners.[158] This passage in Barth's critique of Pietism in the second *Epistle to the Romans* is targeted at the danger of a "new Pharisaism" emerging from this correct insight into Pharisaism itself. We could summarize Barth's critique of Pietism in the latter book in these terms: he is one with it in separating from Pelagianism but sees it as being prone to semi-Pelagianism. In Barth's view Pietism knows man is dependent on God's grace but does not know that man *remains* dependent on it, or does not know that grace *remains* free; instead it finally reestablishes a pious "possession" of grace in the sight of God.

Barth's Treatment of Pietistic Concerns and Concepts

Since the actual "concern" of the Pietists and the specifically Pietistic conceptuality can only be ascertained with a degree of imprecision, we move here along the boundary between an explicit and an implicit critique of Pietism and must therefore be more cautious in our conclusions. The Pietists, and we will concentrate on this in particular, have been especially interested in a *change* at all times, a changing of one's ways, a conversion, a time on the Damascus Road, a rebirth, etc. Such a change is necessary in a human life, because it is the time when the old self becomes a new self.[159] What can be heard about this in the second *Epistle to the Romans?* In any case, Barth also talks about such a change, not merely in terms of a partial "improvement" but a *radical break.* "Faith is the incomparable, the irrevocable step across the boundary from the old to the new man that cannot be reversed. Faith is the turning point, the final human possiblity, no—the first divine possibility. It is the turning around, the conversion in which the equilibrium of grace and sin is disrupted and abolished . . . the original date marking man's existence in God occurs, the incomparable step occurs. The conversion that can not be reversed, that rules out any looking back, takes place."[160] This is the Damascus hour,[161] the event in which "I am born from above" (Jn 3:3).[162] And this is an

---

[158]One could well ask whether in the context in which this sentence is located in the second *Epistle to the Romans* Barth would even have arrived at this phrasing if it had not already appeared in the text of the first *Epistle to the Romans.*

[159]Compare M. Schmidt, "Pietismus," in *RGG* 5, pp. 370ff.

[160]Ro 2, pp. 181-82.

[161]Ibid., p. 129. Compare pp. 281-82, where Barth says that by no means may "a Damascus conversion" take the place of the Spirit of God. What one can observe as such a Damascus conversion "can only be strong, true and lively as an *answer.*"

[162]Ibid., p. 126.

event that affects human beings *personally,* that affects "you existentially."[163] Furthermore, it is a change that takes place in a way that is not merely imperceptible. "Grace cannot calm down, not stand still, not even in the face of the firm barrier separating what cannot be seen from what can be seen. It cannot leave this visible life of sin, only to be content with another, invisible life of righteousness in the hereafter. Of all things, not that."[164] And furthermore, it is a change in which not only God acts but in which humankind is also involved. "The power of the resurrection *turned* them *around,* turned *them* around. This turnaround was their own personal step, not a mechanical event that happened to them. They took this step themselves in the power of the resurrection."[165] Therefore a person can choose it or reject it. "He can awake or fall asleep, he can understand or fail to recognize God."[166] And finally Barth believes that "this change can be described," of course only in a series of contradictory snapshots (a bird in flight).[167] Therefore it can certainly not be asserted that Barth knows nothing of a change or conversion in contrast to the Pietists.

However, he talks about it in a different way; for him the "new man" is on a completely different level from the old one. He is precisely new because he is on a different level and not merely a changed figure on the same, previous level. Is conversion "a further, higher stage on his inner journey? No, it is the radical breaking off of his journey, the beginning of *God's* journey with him."[168] Is conversion a mere moment on the temporal level? No, it is "a timeless moment encompassing the new characterization of all that has gone before and all that will come after."[169] Is the new man some kind of (changed) version of the same person? No, not even when he seeks to "save the life of the body that cannot be saved" by "mortification, self-denial or spiritualization!"[170] Rather it is "the man who is called into existence by God's creative word, the man who in dying to the old self is renewed day by day."[171] This new man, and even the act of repentance that leads to him, is strictly given only *in faith*. In Barth's thought this

---

[163]Ibid., p. 258. We also find there: "The turning, conversion that took place in Christ Jesus is *yours."*

[164]Ibid., p. 203.

[165]Ibid., p. 201.

[166]Ibid., p. 96.

[167]Ibid., pp. 178-79: namely, in such a way that (1) the old man is observed as such, (2) that I am burdened with this in my identity and (3) as such was condemned by the cross, (4) that the distance between the old and the new is created and (5) my identity is set with the new man.

[168]Ibid., p. 101.

[169]Ibid.; compare p. 253.

[170]Ibid., p. 273.

[171]Ibid., p. 101.

means it is not given in a way that can be seen. It is not as if he bears no relationship to the old one. Rather the invisible gift of grace eludes our human
clutching, but it is the intervention, "the attack," the "crisis," the "disruption" to
which "our life on earth is subject."[172] And it is not as if this new man had nothing to do with me! Rather, "*I am* this subject if faith exists to set the identity between him and me."[173] However, at the same time this is true: "*I am not* this subject, if it is the radically other compared to all that I am."[174] So now this human
choice in turning from the old to the new man is not a choice between two possibilities, but "what is possible . . . visible and comprehensible is always the rejection of God. If man says 'Yes' to God, the impossible occurs, the miracle, the
paradox."[175] So Barth understands the conversion of Paul not as the substitution
of the visible old self by a visibly new self but as the *limitation* of the visibly
old self by the *invisibly* new self. "He was neutralized as Saul. . . . He went blind.
And then he began to love God, then he recognized him. Now he is what he is
. . . however this means he is what he is not; he knows what he does not know,
he does what he can not do (I live, but not I . . .)."[176]

　　Although Barth understands the change from the old to the new self differently from the Pietists, he still expects a "*possession*" of grace, forgiveness, the
Spirit, etc. The Pietists attach great importance to this as the result of that
change, but Barth also views these facts differently. He affirms "the reality that
human beings are pardoned" and can be told that "they *have* forgiveness, that
they *are* pardoned."[177] Of course, such "possession" and "being" is not visible,
not under human control but given in *faith* alone or in *hope*.[178] It is also possible
for Barth to say that "*We have* the Spirit," only it is a paradoxical, wonderful,
"impossible" possibility.[179] In Barth's thought there is even an experience of

---

[172]Ibid., p. 203.
[173]Ibid., p. 125.
[174]Ibid.
[175]Ibid., p. 96.
[176]Ibid., p. 129.
[177]Ibid., p. 201.
[178]Ibid. In this sense, p. 182: "If you believe, you have!" p. 141: "*This* hoping is *having*"; p. 129: "By becoming one waits in relationship to God, he became one who possesses."
[179]Ibid., pp. 256-57. Note the unheard-of dialectic in which Barth accentuates this sentence: "We have the Spirit. . . . We do *not* mean the Spirit in so far as we associate it with '*we*' and with '*have.*' And yet we must, because we are not allowed to see it differently and cannot see it differently. If we do not say it, we nonetheless think it, and if we do not think it, we none-theless feel it: We have the Spirit. What is inadmissible happens in any case. At any rate, we must know of its inadmissibility, that 'we' can only mean 'not we' and 'have' only 'not have.' Perhaps *then* what is inadmissible can be confronted by the truth: a qualified 'we' and a qual-ified 'have' that virtually encompasses every 'we' and all 'having' of human beings without ceasing to face them as critique and question."

God, but this can only be "cultivated by a vigorous critique of all mere experience."[180] In the same way the truth of "*Christ in us*" cannot be denied, but this is by no means identical to any "human act." It strictly and purely describes "our divine condition" (as the Word of God addressed to us!).[181]

Barth takes a position on additional Pietistic concerns and concepts by using a similar dialectic. Revivals? Yes, there are revivals, but if it only means what "a direct observation" as such seeks to ascertain, then we must consider a corrective to that. God "can be found there to the extent that *God* lets himself be found in such lofty heights and religious developments. . . . But he can be found *not only there,* giving offense to all direct observation."[182] "*Assurance of salvation?* Yes, it cannot be denied in itself, but "assurance of salvation" *without* the most exclusive double predestination. Assurance of salvation in terms of more recent Protestantism is worse than paganism,[183] if it gives human beings something that prevents them "from being saved by grace alone."[184] "*Experiences*"? Once again, yes! There is no grace "without the experience of grace!"[185] But no to them "if they desire and claim to be important in and of themselves, great and in any sense divine without bowing to the judgment of *God,* without waiting for *divine* justification."[186] No, "if one wants to forgive one's own sin under the authority of one's own personal experience."[187] "*Election?*" Yes, this happens to human beings. But "whoever is chosen by God will never say that he chose God."[188] Experiences of "*rapture and enlightenment, moments of inspiration and intuition?*" "Blessed are those who are found worthy of such things. But woe to us when we wait for such things. Woe to us when we do not notice that they too are frills and fragments."[189] The Christian's "*relationship* with Christ": there is such a relationship, but in the field of psychic-historical reality there is no other than the one that carries its cross.[190]

We may conclude from the examples shown here that there is room in the theology of the second *Epistle to the Romans* to take up Pietistic concerns and concepts. Barth obviously has nothing against them in themselves but is only against a particular interpretation of them, or he takes up their ideas by giving

---

[180]Ibid., p. 352.
[181]Ibid., p. 268.
[182]Ibid., p. 381.
[183]Ibid., p. 396.
[184]Ibid., p. 83.
[185]Ibid., p. 212.
[186]Ibid., p. 82.
[187]Ibid., p. 101.
[188]Ibid., pp. 34-35.
[189]Ibid., p. 282.
[190]Ibid., p. 176.

them a particular interpretation. He is concerned about a "change" in the life of human beings as are the Pietists, only he understands this turning point more *radically* than they do in the sense that the change associated with it is not a qualitative one on the same level, but a qualitative one that moves to a new level. Thus we could almost dare to make the statement that the theology of the second *Epistle to the Romans* is inwardly very close to that "super-pietism" Barth sees in Kierkegaard. Now Barth understands the new reality occasioned by this change as a reality made accessible purely by *faith* which as such confronts and contin-ues to confront the level of the old reality as an "impossibility," as a "paradox," probably following Kierkegaard as well but interpreting it in a different sense than the Pietists. Thus Barth's position toward Pietistic concerns and concepts is dialectical.[191] He rejects them to the extent that the Pietistic statements on the new reality neutralize the "paradox," transforming it into "possibilities" and into con-crete changes that are tangible and at one's disposal on the level of the old self! However, he does not reject them in themselves, or not in the sense that they are true as descriptions of an invisible, uncontrollable reality. The difference be-tween Barth and the Pietists is not actually that he does not talk about the Pietistic concerns indicated here but that he speaks about them differently, as intangible realities. And by interpreting them in this way, he not only says the same thing in a different way in relation to the Pietists, but he also says something different from them. He corrects their ideas and puts them in new and different terms so that in using them the enduring freedom of God and his grace are preserved, before which man, even the pardoned sinner, continues to stand.

Thus based on his understanding of that change from the old to the new man Barth comes to different conclusions than the Pietists, based on their under-standing of that change. For them the difference between the old and new man becomes the occasion for drawing a distinction between two groups of human beings, between the converted and the unconverted, believers and unbelievers. Although Barth also sharply distinguishes between the old and new man, they can in principle not be divided into two tangible groups of human beings that are opposed to each other. A detectable distinction between certain human be-ings, the "new" man and those who are "old," cannot be made.[192] The infeasi-

---

[191]Compare p. 513, where Barth says he is able to place himself alongside any person and "to say to him the reassuring news: You are right!— under the unsettling condition that you are also wrong."

[192]Ibid., p. 383: "We have pounded into ourselves that these 'elect ones' are not these and those, not here and there, are not called so and so. They are what they are by grace. They cannot be proven." P. 202: "we know that crossing from death to life . . . cannot be said of any par-ticular human being, to be named this or that, that the names of whose bearers this could be said are only written in the book of life."

bility of such a distinction is not an expression of an embarrassment that because of the ambiguity of all earthly phenomena a distinction between "the elect" and "non-elect" cannot be determined. It is an expression of a theological fact which Barth sees in this way: The (invisible) election is the promise, the (visible) rejection is the looming danger for everyone.[193] It follows then that "Christians" are still always called to repentance[194] and the "unbelievers" are always called to hope.[195] And it follows that Christians can at best only be in the state of becoming Christians and that the existence of the old self is not "his story before his conversion" but "the reality of his existence before and after Damascus," just as the existence of the new man is not his biographical existence after conversion but "the preservation of this man in his totality" in Christ.[196] By developing such theological insights rooted in the logic of Barth's different version of the Pietistic concern—the change from the old to the new man—he seems to distance himself so far from central Pietistic interests, such as its interest in a visible difference between the converted and the unconverted or between a before and after of conversion, that one must wonder if his position that has sympathies with Kierkegaard's *super*-pietism can really be called super-*pietism*.

Barth's Changed View of Pietism Compared with the First Epistle to the Romans

All in all, if we compare the view and critique of Pietism in the second *Epistle to the Romans* with the first one, we can say in summary:

1. Pietism is now certainly no longer the primary opponent of Barth's theology. As Barth wrote to Thurneysen at the end of his exegesis of Romans 7, he was aware of this: "As was to be expected, our whole controversy with Pietism

---

[193]Ibid., p. 331: "The secret of eternal double predestination is the secret of *the* human race, *not this or that* human being. It does not distinguish between these and those human beings, but it is their most profound common possession. They are all in one line facing it. Jacob is in every moment of time Esau as well facing it, and Esau is also Jacob in the eternal moment of revelation. Jacob is the invisible Esau, Esau is the visible Jacob." Especially compare this to p. 267 as well.

[194]Ibid., p. 501: "*Everything* is impure before God and therefore *nothing* in particular, and all observations of *special* impurity before God spring from the secret or open illusion that makes it seem as if not *everything* were impure before God, from the secret or open refusal to repent."

[195]Ibid., p. 331: "No one *may* rest assured of eternal election in time, and no one *must* be conscious of eternal perdition in time." Compare p. 356. Precisely for this reason the pious individual must unceasingly be confronted "with the pagans, tax-collectors who are justified before God . . ." (p. 352).

[196]Ibid., p. 305: "There are, seriously understood, no 'Christians.' There is only the eternal *opportunity* to *become* Christians which is equally accessible and inaccessible for all." Further: p. 253.

which was so important to us 3-4 years ago has disappeared although that phase had gotten especially good grades from the reviewers. Now the barrel of the gun is pointed at a different opponent," at Schleiermacher.[197] Barth says that in Schleiermacher's theology, an attempt was made to turn the grace of God into a religion "more consciously than ever before." He turned the grace of God into "one human possibility or necessity among others," and this attempt is "the betrayal of Christ."[198] It is taken for granted that this attempt was made before, but it was never before undertaken so "consciously," so decisively, so clearly and so problematically as in Schleiermacher. If the Pietists were to still understand themselves as the opponents of the theology of the *Epistle to the Romans,* they would actually be placing themselves closer to Schleiermacher than Barth thought they were.

2. Pietism is now no longer *merely* an opponent. It is now seen more positively, and Barth himself seems to be closer to it. His critique of it is clear: it no longer focuses primarily on its "individualism" but on the "Pharisaism of the tax collector" who believes he may no longer possess and be sure of God's grace by "works" but can do so by foregoing them, by repentance, humility and self-denial; and it focuses at the same time on the semi-Pelagianism which knows about the grace of God but not about the grace of God that *remains free.* Thus Barth's critique on the one hand is less external and formalistic, but on the other hand more refined than in the first *Epistle to the Romans.* It is more refined to the extent that he sees Pietism not only critically but also positively. In fact, he turns critical only after first discovering a positive point of contact on an important issue. What Barth appreciates about it is its ascetic streak which *contradicts* the view that sees faith as a visible possession of the divine. What he objects to is that although it upholds this ascetic line, it does not in principle contradict this view of faith. So in the end it can and does end up with this understanding of faith.

3. On the whole, in the second *Epistle to the Romans* Barth also seems to see Pietism historically in a more refined way.[199] The parallel between Pietism and Romanticism in the first *Epistle to the Romans* is now dropped, not only because a historical discussion of Romanticism and Pietism is no longer pursued but because Barth now sees a definite, considerable difference between these two phenomena. To be sure, he now sees an affinity between Pietism and mysticism

---

[197]*Briefwechsel* 1, 491-92 (May 23, 1921).

[198]Ro 2, p. 207.

[199]One must always keep in mind that the second *Epistle to the Romans* does not offer and does not want to offer any historical discussions, let alone historical presentations. Rather all remarks on historical phenomena are made only in passing.

on the basis of the view common to both that affirms the value of self-denial
and the inherent power of humility as a "negative work" by virtue of which they
believe the divine can be grasped.[200] As we have said, Barth judges such negative work dialectically. If he rejects it because of the technique used to grasp
God, he affirms it because of its recognizable feeling for the "line of death" between God and humankind. With regard to the latter, Romanticism is different
from both of these historical phenomena because it does not seem to know how
human thought and action is broken by the line of death. Its concern is "Romantic immediacy," and Barth judges this as a "blurring of the distance between
God and us," as "forgetting that God can not be seen," as "a deification of man
and a humanization of God,"[201] as "the identification of man with God which
inevitably must result in his isolation from God."[202] Nevertheless Barth does not
totally reject the concern of Romanticism. What it intends is true, but only invisibly true. It is right to posit "immediate living" but is wrong in understanding
such life as a visible given.[203]

In Barth's view theological *liberalism* and *rationalism* agree with Romanticism on a crucial point, negatively in a lack of brokenness in its theological
thinking; positively[204] in assuming an immediate, direct path from the "heights"
of humanity to God. However, Barth sees and judges liberalism and rationalism
dialectically (more strongly than Romanticism and formally similar to Pietism).
For on the one side, it is "liberal self-deception to think that such direct paths
lead to the impossible possibility of God from nature and history, from art, morality, science and even religion."[205] On the other hand, liberalism knew that
there is no claim "by virtue of which something human *in* this world would also
not be *of* this world." Thus Barth can say, "Zwingli and liberalism have proven
to be right even though they are under the wrath of God!"[206] On the one hand,
rationalism is wrong to think that it can make a direct inquiry into God by assuming a "religious apriori." On the other hand, when Barth sets the freedom

---

[200]Ro 2, p. 84. Compare p. 299. The goal that they try to reach—*via negationis*—is in Barth's
view clearly introduced differently here as well as there. In Pietism it is the "experience," in
mysticism it is "a secret and true super-religion running parallel to religion" (p. 223), or better,
a super-world heightening this world.

[201]Ibid., p. 145.

[202]Ibid., p. 32; compare also 140, 206, 418, 321-22.

[203]Ibid., p. 147.

[204]Ibid., p. 447-48: "Christianity does not contemplate the heights" is a remark aimed at idealism,
liberalism, romanticism. "On the contrary, it recommends that human beings allow themselves to be led down into the valleys." The "ascetics and Pietists" have noticed something
of this.

[205]Ibid., pp. 321-22.

[206]Ibid., p. 49.

of God against this thesis, he thinks that he is "in reality honoring the spirit of genuine rationalism which indeed knew about the freedom of God in contradiction to this thesis."[207]

Thus it can be said that in the second *Epistle to the Romans* Barth sees the historical difference between Pietism and rationalism/liberalism in a *more refined way*. But it must be added that he sees each of these phenomena dialectically; thus he sees them *in themselves* in a more refined way. He sees that the ascetic streak found in Pietism by which it distinguishes itself from liberalism and rationalism does not prevent it from picking up their idea of a visible, "immediate life." On the other hand, the unbroken thinking of liberalism and rationalism does not prevent it from thwarting its idea of a visible "immediate life." Thus from the perspective of the second *Epistle to the Romans* it cannot be ruled out that Barth could later come back to the thesis of the inner affinity between Pietism and rationalism. If he actually did advocate such a thesis, the example of the second *Epistle to the Romans* should remind us of the fact that this thesis does not have to signify a leveling of these different phenomena but can imply a knowledge of the unique structure and problems of each one.

3. AN ANALYSIS OF BARTH'S CRITIQUE OF PIETISM IN THE SECOND *EPISTLE TO THE ROMANS*

His Indirect Critique of Pietism

Now that we have attempted to sketch the theology of the second *Epistle to the Romans* and its critique of Pietism, a twofold question must be asked: What is the theological legitimacy of Barth's position, and is his critique of Pietism justified?

First of all, let us consider the latter question. Do Barth's view and critique of Pietism do justice to it? As late as 1956 the community man O. Knobloch took for granted that the author of the second *Epistle to the Romans* had several different caricatures of Pietism in view so that he could hardly see the actual picture. He was guilty then of confusing the caricature with the actual picture of Pietism.[208] Is it really so clear that he did not do justice to Pietism at that time? To answer this question we must carefully distinguish between two things, between Barth's *explicit* critique of Pietism (to which we can add his *implicit* cri-

---

[207]Ibid., p. 370. Compare pp. 259-60, where a formally similar dialectical position on rationalism is found.

[208]O. Knobloch, "Karl Barth und 'unsere Gemeinschaftsleute,'" *in Antwort: Festschrift für K. Barth,* 1956, pp. 400-401. Knobloch takes this charge so much for granted that he does not even seek to give more detailed reasons for it.

tique of Pietism at those places where a tacit argument with this phenomenon can be assumed) and his central theological insights in the *Epistle to the Romans* when these insights actually represent an *indirect critique* of all Christian "movements," including Pietism (above all, when he stresses that "God is God and man is man"). We must address this indirect critique all the more because the Pietists felt they were the target of it and took issue with it. It seems to me that this indirect critique of Pietism will be misunderstood if we do not make clear that it is of a different nature from his explicit critique of Pietism. Put in simple terms, his indirect critique wants to argue that Pietism needs a *corrective;* his explicit critique would like to *correct* its theology.

At least in its basic concern, the theology of the second *Epistle to the Romans* understands itself as a formulation of a "corrective" not just of Pietism but of all possible church "schools of thought" and movements in church history.[209] Therefore Barth can boldly say: "We know how to appreciate the possible significance and fruitfulness of all approaches. We are able to position ourselves in a friendly manner alongside the Catholics, the cultural Protestants, the League of Nations theologians (and whoever else) and give them this reassuring message: You are right! on the unsettling condition that you are also wrong!"[210] The corrective applied to all phenomena of church history here is, in short, reminding ourselves that apart from the divine justification "all we do is in vain," "even in the best life," reminding ourselves that "wherever we fold our hands and feel close to God, whenever we speak and write of divine things, wherever there is preaching and building of temples, ministry for ultimate motives, a higher mission and a higher message, we must remember that all of these endeavors are marred by sin if the miracle of forgiveness does not take place."[211] This reminder is not targeted at the Pietistic or liberal form of "folding one's hands" and does not represent a statement against Pietism as such. This reminder is necessary for all because the differences disappear in view of the fact that without the miracle of forgiveness everyone is "unclean" anyway. "*Everything* is unclean before God and precisely for this reason noth-

---

[209]In an early reflection on his theology presented in the *Epistle to the Romans* (in June 1922) Barth declared that this is not to be conceived of "as a competitive enterprise against the positive, liberal theology of Ritschl or the history of religions school of thought. . . . Rather it can be conceived of as a kind of passing remark . . . which is compatible with all these in its own way and yet is also incompatible with them. . . . This is really my opinion—everyone may stay with his school and with his masters, only perhaps put up with my theology as a corrective, for issues of considerable importance are perhaps contained in those passing remarks" (*Ges. Vorträge* 1, pp. 99-100).

[210]Ro 2, pp. 513.

[211]Ibid., p. 112.

ing in particular."[212] In this sense the basic thesis of the theology of the second *Epistle to the Romans* wants to be a corrective to Pietism as well. It is indirect criticism because it applies the "you are right and you are wrong" to Pietism as well.

To what extent is it wrong? Barth's opinion is undoubtedly not that "you are *partially* right and partially wrong." Rather what he wants to say to the various phenomena of church history and indirectly to Pietism as well is that "you are *completely* wrong." But are not all historical phenomena to be seen in a more discriminating light? Are there not legitimate as well as illegitimate aspects to every phenomenon, not only shadows but also light? And could it not even be that in certain phenomena (in Pietism as well) the illegitimate aspect is only peripheral and can be explained only as "an excess" which does not impair the "actual heart" of the matter? Must not Barth actually have "caricatures" in view which prevent him from seeing the "actual picture" when he emphasizes how these phenomena are totally in the wrong? The process of reflection that leads him to insist on his "absolutistic accusations" and to consider them legitimate is this: If the charge of disobedience is true only of a peripheral aspect, of certain "excesses" of a phenomenon, its essence is simultaneously in jeopardy (it can have such aspects and excesses!).[213] This thought is somewhat unsatisfying and seems to invite a fatal logical consistency that leads to generalizations, of course only to the extent that this conclusion is understood as the standard that is used to do historical justice to a phenomenon. The fact that he himself can carefully consider the distinctions between what is legitimate and what is illegitimate when he evaluates a historical phenomenon (for example, "Tersteegen and his followers are also right!") contradicts the idea that Barth could have meant it only in this way. When he asserts a "you are (totally) wrong" against a historical phenomenon, his concern is not to render a *historical* verdict, because he does not intend to do historical justice to it but would like to confront it with *divine* justification. So this statement by no means rules out discriminating, balanced

---

[212]Ibid., p. 501.

[213]Ibid., p. 379: "If Baal peeps out unambiguously at one place, . . . it is clear that *he* is the master of the house. . . . If it is a question of *God* (and in the church it is at any rate a question of God), then this means that everything is at stake in every detail, then even the strongest "exaggeration" of a detail is not strong enough to remind us of the problem of the whole and no whining protest that in addition to this or that Baal-like feature the church would also like to have all kinds of things from Yahweh, can withstand the force of the circumstantial evidence cited here. But this protest may then be a protective shield against the necessity of repenting. Therefore what is necessary here is not patience, but prophetic impatience, not quiet humor, but unrestrained offensive action, not historical justice, but a love for the truth that hits the pommel and does not even skirt the charge of being unjust to this or that person."

consideration of historical phenomena, but it does exclude the use of such a discriminating view, as a "protective shield against the necessity of repenting,"[214] referring to "some legitimate or good aspect" of this phenomenon.

To what extent are they right at the same time? By applying a corrective to the various schools of thought, Barth does not intend to place a further viewpoint, a further school of thought alongside the others, to compete with them or replace them. Applied to Pietism this means that its representatives should not be asked to think something different but to become aware of certain limits to their thinking. They are not expected to stop being Pietists but to expose themselves to the divine "crisis" as Pietists. Making this assumption he can say, "You are right!" But this is not only true of Pietism! In this sense all of them, "mysticism and Pharisaism, piety and high church, Catholicism and Protestantism, epistles to the Romans and other books together with their basically not so radical phenomena of contrasts and protests, can unfold their true nature."[215] This thought too is somewhat unsatisfactory and smacks of sanctioning the existing order. It seems to finally open the door to everything and anything by wiping out all differences, *if* it is understood as a *historical* justification of all these phenomena. This is not his concern here. Arguing on the historical level, Barth was able to appreciate but also to reject certain features of a historical phenomenon such as Pietism. Rather he is concerned to evaluate such a phenomenon in view of the *divine* justification which is targeted at the one to whom the "you are wrong" is said. By applying a corrective to the various phenomena, by not asking them to assume a different viewpoint but to expose themselves to the divine "crisis," Barth seeks to motivate each of them "to go on their own journey to the end,"[216] on their own journey, not on another journey. But they are to go in such a way that they do not remain in self-affirmation on their own journey but go on their journey to the *end* [217] in a self-critical fashion. In short, the corrective that Barth's theology would like to be and that also includes an "indirect criticism" of Pietism does not want to replace Pietism as such

---

[214]Ibid., p. 379.

[215]Ibid., p. 113.

[216]Ibid., p. 502. Barth says a person is "misled" when one induces him to step onto a different path and when, for example, "his decisiveness and earnestness become irrelevant instead of being given their actual object, when he becomes negligent, indifferent and unclear where he was previously strict and decisive, instead of becoming radical." A noteworthy rebuke for those who once came from Pietism and now believe they have overcome it by becoming so "negligent"!

[217]Ibid., p. 377: "One does not get away from Judaism other than as a Jew, and one does not get away from Pharisaism other than as a Pharisee." Once again the meaning of this sentence only becomes clear here: "[Your] earnestness would have to be more earnest to be completely earnest."

partially or totally by another phenomenon but to place it as a whole under the judgment of God.

When Barth claims he can express something that is not a further "viewpoint" but a corrective to all viewpoints, his position is not without its own problems.[218] First of all, *concerning his position as a critic,* his intention not to force another, not even his own theological teaching, on his dialogue partner may sound sympathetic and unobtrusive, but we still must ask: What kind of sovereign location is this where you can say to all: "You are right" and to all "you are wrong" and assume a viewpoint that harmonizes with all of them and yet is beyond all of them? If at times a "prophetic word" can be a corrective in this sense, you must be clear that you are taking a basically unassailable position that is removed from all discussion. It may be that such a prophetic word actually occurs now and then, but the question arises whether a theology can *seek* to be a corrective understood in these terms or whether it is not in this case a theology that articulates a further viewpoint and thus is not removed from further discussion. Does it not run the risk of identifying its own viewpoint with the Word of God where it forgets this?[219] Certainly Barth knew about this danger in the *Epistle to the Romans*[220] and stressed the relativity of the theology found in the *Epistle to the Romans* as well. Yet it must be asked if he knew enough about this danger at that point.

When Barth claims he is expressing no further viewpoint but is applying a corrective to all other viewpoints, he also runs into a problem concerning the *object of his criticism.* As commendable as it is that the critique expressed here is immanent criticism allowing each of them to go on their own journey to the end, we must still ask: Does this criticism do justice to its partner in dialogue? It is certainly proper and important to remind us that all "folding of hands," all "speaking and writing about divine things" is in need of forgiveness, that it is

---

[218]Barth himself seems to have felt this when already in June 1922 he phrases this claim very cautiously: "Everyone would . . . perhaps (!) put up with my theology as a corrective because those passing remarks perhaps (!) contain something of considerable importance" (*Ges. Vorträge* 1, pp. 99-100). Barth completely distances himself from this claim when he declares five years later "that it was not and could not be the intention of his book on the Epistle to the Romans to act as a 'corrective' but that he never had anything else in mind . . . except doing theology" (*Christliche Dogmatik im Entwurf,* 1927, p. ix).

[219]I would think that we should expect there to be a "prophetic" word reminding us in a special way of our foundations, a word that is subject to this danger without succumbing to it and that *must* speak in this way ("Thus says the Lord").

[220]In my view this was not yet the case when he warns against making "this message of Stop! . . . into a new, highly clever theological viewpoint" (Ro 2, p. 363) or making it into a "new idol" (p. 425), for then one's own position is passed off again as one that is beyond all other viewpoints. However, this is the case when Barth saw the Pauline Epistle to the Romans and all "books about the Epistle to the Romans as subject to this life's rule of law and transgression," as attempts "to think the eternal in time."

always tempted to reach for God, to control him, to forget that "God is God and man is man" and to forgive itself under the authority of its own experiences. Barth is right: "When would the church not have been tempted?"[221] Only what does this say against Pietism as Pietism, since this temptation is obvious to all who fold their hands and speak and write of divine things? As we have said, Barth knew this. But we must be clear about what this means. If this is seen as a corrective, the differences between the various schools of thought and views are leveled. Are they not practically being left the way they are? Therefore are they not being affirmed? Even if Barth defends himself against this charge, we must wonder if it is enough to say that all "folding of hands" and "speaking and writing of divine things" is in need of forgiveness. Assuming this common denominator must we not also distinguish between an appropriate and a nonappropriate "folding of hands" and "speaking and writing of divine things" that does or does not take seriously its need of forgiveness? In this way the verdict on the need to forgive all this activity would not be blindly accepted but would leave room for discussion. It would examine and weigh the different kinds of "speaking and writing" from the viewpoint of asking whether its theology is appropriate!

We do not simply deny the possibility of applying such a corrective to the most diverse "viewpoints" but believe that it cannot be discussed because one can only "put up with"[222] a corrective. Otherwise one can no longer take it seriously as a corrective.

His Explicit Critique of Pietism

However, Barth himself distinguished between the point he wanted to make and his *Epistle to the Romans* itself. Thus he also advocated a certain theology, in fact a "viewpoint" in this book whose appreciation for Pietism would not only serve as a corrective for him but as a definite correction of his own thought. Thus in this book he did not see the specific problem of Pietism in its temptation to reach for God (which in Barth's view is generally true of any movement). Rather the problem lay in a certain understanding which in his view is characteristic of Pietism. It is at this point, and in my view only at this point, in the explicit critique of Pietism, that both Barth's understanding of Pietism as well as his objections to it become *discussable*. According to Barth, Pietism is marked by the fact that it believes it can confidently and directly lay hold of the divine by performing the "negative works" of repentance, humility, and self-denial

---

[221]Ibid., p. 357.
[222]*Ges. Vorträge* 1, pp. 99-100.

while renouncing "works." Barth's verdict on Pietism understood in these terms and thus his objection to it is that this line of thought is a "new Pharisaism" (of the tax collector).

If we restrict our discussion to this characterization and this verdict it seems to us that it is meaningful to ask the question of *whether Barth's critique of Pietism is accurate.* To answer this question would require an interpretation of Pietism and a discussion of its possible interpretation that is beyond the scope of this book, so that our response here can only take the form of a few examples and suggestions. Let us turn to the Pietistic works we know Barth was very familiar with,[223] the works of G. Tersteegen and J. Scheffler. It is apparent that his understanding of Pietism can be documented at least from them. The manner in which these authors thought of the reality of God is closely connected to the "method" they thought they could use to come into contact with it, namely, by "death," by mortification, self-denial, etc. Here are a few samples to illustrate this.

Gerhard Tersteegen:

Christian, you always want to enjoy, have, be much;
Your Savior loved scorn, poverty, suffering;
Do it the same way; for the way of peace and light
It leads (understand me correctly) through nothing, through nothing,
through nothing.[224]

You will not be afraid when all props are taken away from you
and you must hover exposed . . .
The most profound death is to me the purest life.
Let go willingly and close your eyes!
If you do not lose, you will never find.
Whoever sinks away, will find rest in God;
His life remains, your own must disappear.[225]

Whoever profoundly recognizes his nothingness,
And calls God his all in all;
Whoever does not look at himself,
And just trusts in God;
Whoever destroys himself in humility,
Will stand upright in God . . .[226]

---

[223]Compare above, chapter 1, nn. 67 and 68.
[224]G. Tersteegen, *Eine Auswahl aus seinen Schriften, Liedern und Spruchen,* ed. T. Klein, 1925, p. 287.
[225]Ibid., p. 289.
[226]Ibid., p. 291.

Die, die, as long as you live; never speak; it is enough!
Whoever believes he has done it, is already being deceived.[227]

Angelus Silesius:

Man, where you are still something, where you know, love and have something,
You are, believe me, not rid of your burden.[228]

Death is a blessed thing; the stronger it is
the more glorious the life that emerges from it.[229]

May I die and God live: I want to live eternally for him.
Therefore I must eternally give up my spirit to him.[230]

God himself, when he wants to live for you, he must die:
How do you think you can inherit his life without death.[231]

In view of these sayings we can understand why Barth in his *Epistle to the Romans* theology felt a certain closeness to the "ascetics and Pietists." We can also understand the critical point at which he separated himself from them. The critical point is where "death" according to those men is understood as people's final opportunity and a transition that can be navigated by them instead of a real end of the person and her or his opportunities. Here the knowledge of the line of death becomes a recipe, an instrument, a method to directly attain "life." In any case, Barth has good reason to see "mortification" defined in these terms as the hinge of their thought, at least as far as these two theologians are concerned. If they understand mortification as a transition making possible the visible discovery of a before and after in the existence of the same individual, then Barth has good reason to criticize them for having disregarded the *simul justus et peccator* of the doctrine of justification. As far as we can see, by interpreting Pietism in these terms, he is less sympathetic to the view espoused by C. Baur[232] and later by himself[233] that sees Pietism as a modern movement, than to the view es-

---

[227]Ibid., p. 293.
[228]Angelus Silesius, *Der Cherubinische Wandersmann,* ed. Ch. Waldemar, 1960, book 1, p. 24.
[229]Ibid., 1, p. 26.
[230]Ibid., 1, p. 31.
[231]Ibid., 1, p. 33. How close Silesius, thinking "God" from there, is to the dialectical understanding of God, thinking "God" from there, is shown by his sayings 1, pp. 43-45: "I love a single thing and do not know what it is./And because I do not know it, that is why I have chosen it." "Man, if you love something, so you truly love nothing:/God is not this or that, therefore let go of the Something." "Whoever desires nothing, has nothing, knows nothing, loves nothing, wants nothing/he still has, he knows, desires and loves much."
[232]F. C. Baur, *Kirchengeschichte der neueren Zeit,* 1863, pp. 585-86.
[233]K. Barth, *Die prot. Theologie im 19. Jahrhundert,* 1946, pp. 64-65.

poused by E. Troeltsch,[234] H. Stephan[235] and P. Wernle, who understand it as a retrogressive movement hostile to culture and the world, mainly going back to a mysticism, that "immediately before the crisis of old Christianity again manifests its paradoxical uniqueness."[236]

Now it is certainly no coincidence that the Pietists mentioned here were especially close to mysticism, just as it is also no coincidence that Barth in the *Epistle to the Romans* sees a close link between Pietism and mysticism. But there is also another form of Pietism that is more distant from mysticism, the form that is called "church-based Pietism." The influence of mystical spiritualism in this form of Pietism not only hampers the development of the thought found in the tradition of early Protestant orthodoxy but also blends with it. However, the influence of mysticism is restrained by this orthodox thought. Of course, even in church-based Pietism the idea of mortification plays a dominant role in its particular understanding of repentance as a "process," a "ways and means" to attain "true life" and "living faith" through *spiritual* "mortification."[237] I would even tend to believe that this understanding of repentance characterizes the Pietism of the eighteenth century (the church-based type as well).[238] But I must add that church-based Pietism, at least to some degree, distances itself from its mystical, "radical," "logical" side because it has maintained a knowledge of justification by faith alone through grace alone along-

---

[234]E. Troeltsch, "Leibnitz und die Anfänge des Pietismus," in *Ges. Schriften* 4, 1925 (the essay itself comes from 1902), pp. 514ff. Compare p. 531: Pietism is "the enlivening of an old possession," in a pessimistic turning against modern culture (p. 514). Compare further E. Troeltsch, "Prot. Christentum und Kirche in der Neuzeit," in *Geschichte der christlichen Religion*, 1909, 663-64.

[235]H. Stephan, *Die Neuzeit*, 1909, 27ff. For example, he stresses the "ascetic traits" in Pietism, which were "in opposition to the world culture that was growing stronger" and had alienated the wide circles that had inwardly fused with the world culture (p. 47). Moreover, the pronounced distinction between Pietism "within the established Protestant church" and "outside the church" is found in his work. He understands the latter form (he counts G. Arnold and G. Tersteegen as part of this group, for example) as the actually "consistent Pietism" (p. 38). As a young theology student Barth assisted in editing the book and thus knew its contents in more detail.

[236]P. Wernle, *Der Schweizerische Protestantismus im 18. Jahrhundert*, 1, 1923, p. 112.

[237]Compare, for example, E. Peschke, *Studien zur Theologie August Hermann Franckes*, 1, 1964, pp. 28ff.

[238]I know that the immense work of M. Schmidt (compare, for example, *RGG* 5, pp. 370ff.) is aimed at proving that the "new birth" is the center of Pietistic thought. However, I would like to say it in a more nuanced fashion and also see proof of the fruitfulness of Barth's interpretation of Pietism in reference to this: not an interest in a "new birth," but an interest in a certain *understanding* of the "new birth" characterizes Pietism; that is, the idea of the *manner* in which what they call "new birth" comes about: namely *through* "mortification." In my view E. E. Peschke saw this more carefully and more clearly than M. Schmidt.

side, with and in spite of this understanding of repentance based on the mystical idea of mortification.[239] It is a knowledge that is also associated with its greater dependence on early Protestant orthodoxy, a knowledge that made an even stronger impact in the revivalist movement.[240] If it may be said that Pietism is inconsistent in clinging to such a doctrine of justification, we could also ask with Chr. Märklin whether this contradiction is not "the actual nature of (church-based) Pietism?"[241] However that may be, a knowledge is found in church-based Pietism that resists the label given to it by Barth. In view of this discussion it can be said only with reservations that this label is an accurate description of Pietism.

Barth's stress on the Pietistic question of *individualism* was found throughout the first *Epistle to the Romans,* but in the second one this question is missing from his discussion of Pietism or takes a back seat. In the meantime Barth did not come to agree with Pietism on this point. We saw how his understanding of the new birth (in contradistinction to the understanding of this subject in the Pietistic movement) leads him to see "all people" standing under judgment but also under the promise. Once again it is evident that the author of the second *Epistle to the Romans* no longer thinks he should see the essence of this movement in its individualism. There may be two reasons for this. It was the thesis of the early, liberal Barth that the location of religion in the individual was the defining mark of the thought influenced by the spirit of modernism. And if the essence of Pietism no longer seems to lie in its individualism for the author of the *Epistle to the Romans,* this probably also has to do with the fact that he now sees this phenomenon less in conjunction with modern culture than in a certain aloofness toward it. However, the question is whether Pietism can be understood appropriately without considering the fact that its question is also a modern one especially under the spell of the Cartesian thesis that human self-consciousness is decisive for the recognition of truth. In contrast to the early Barth, the later Barth did not see clearly enough that it was not *only* under this spell. This is why in the second *Epistle to the Romans* individualism was left out of consideration in defining its essence. Now Barth obviously finds himself in such limited opposition to it that this aspect of it

---

[239]Later, in "The Protestant Theology of the 19th Century," Barth saw this very strongly. When A. H. Francke (according to Peschke, *Studien zur Theologie August Hermann Franckes,* p. 39) could say: The "matter of spiritual mortification is as necessary as the article of justification," this shows where Francke's special interest lies, but also that he knows about that article. More than that, he knows this article does not coincide with what is important to him as "mortification."

[240]Compare F. W. Kantzenbach, *die Erweckungsbewegung,* 1957, pp. 17ff.

[241]*Darstellung und Kritik des modernen Pietismus,* 1839, p. 28.

not only does not appear offensive to him but does not even seem conspicuous to him. Now the individual has become important to him, not along the lines of Cartesian individualism but of Kierkegaard's existentialism. Because he no longer sees any fundamental difference between his thought and Pietism here, he obviously no longer considers this point to be essential for defining the specific nature of Pietism. We must ask this question: Does he perhaps no longer see the difference between himself and Pietism on the question of individualism because in this regard (via Kierkegaard) he himself has become partially dependent on their tradition? And the question is whether he has made too clean a break with what he had recognized in the first *Epistle to the Romans.*

Barth's objection to the Pietists is that they saw the negation of all meritorious "works" but that they did not really follow through on this insight. Instead, they turned it into a new "meritorious work." The objection evidently is made from a position where he himself intends to really follow through on this insight. If we see this correctly, it seems to confirm the surprising thesis of A. Oepke that in Barth's struggle against mysticism (or Pietism!), ironically, without noticing it himself, "a conflict within mysticism," took place, "the struggle of a mysticism of radical observance against one less radical."[242]

Should this thesis be completely dismissed or seen "at most as a humorous read," as Barth did?[243] Oepke distinguishes two forms of mysticism, the affective one in which the self withdraws from the world and experiences the divine in heightened inwardness or even merges with it, and the radical one which results in a self-denial that radically detaches itself from such inwardness and in which the divine is no longer experienced and thought but can only be described in negations.[244] It must be admitted that Oepke, who associates Barth with the latter type, is able to draw striking, even astonishing parallels between the thought of radical mysticism and the *Epistle to the Romans.* We can at least speak of an eclectic use of that thought by the author of this book whether or

---

[242]A. Oepke, *Karl Barth und die Mystik,* 1928, p. 28. Of course, Oepke understands Barth not only as a radical mystic but thinks "that his theology bears a Janus face, half faith, half mysticism" (p. 90).

[243]Barth/Thurneysen, *Briefwechsel* 2, 1921–1930, 1974 (= *Briefwechsel* 2), p. 566. However, Barth's mockery is understandable to me in view of the "family tree" that blurs and confuses much, in which Oepke in an historical line derives many parts of the older and newer theological and philosophical thought of the West (including Kant, Hegel, Nietzsche, Overbeck, Kierkegaard, Blumhardt, Dostoyevsky, etc.) on the one hand from Hinduism and Parseeism, on the other hand reclaiming all of them as figures of mysticism as well. What is still mysticism there? What is actually not mysticism there?

[244]Oepke, *Karl Barth und die Mystik,* pp. 23-28.

not he was aware of it[245] or however he may have come to use it in such a way. His attempt to prove that Barth himself was a radical mystic does not seem to me to have been successful.[246] Oepke describes the concept of radical mysticism in such a way that not only the diversity of the surrounding world is totally eliminated, but even the soul and finally the Godhead itself is swallowed up "by the unending flood of pure, undifferentiated being."[247] But this is an idea that does not apply to the second *Epistle to the Romans*. There Barth is explicitly concerned about God's relationship to humanity with and in all the negations. And if radical mysticism calls God "not-God" as a consequence of its negations,[248] the concept appears in Barth's thought, not to describe God but the conceptual idols of human beings.[249] And when Barth sees God beyond this Not-God, he does not mean the "God above all gods" of mysticism, caught in "false transcendence" as a mere negation of this world. Rather Barth sees him in terms of a "beyond" in the world to come so that he can put himself in a definite relationship to this world.[250] And when radical mysticism makes self-denial its goal, a central idea in the *Epistle to the Romans* is that not only all positive possession but "all acts of mortification and self-denial," even the strongest negations, do not enable human beings to gain access to God. The negations of the *Epistle to the Romans* also negate such negations and in the end serve one purpose. They do not point to the hereafter but to the barrier that blocks all paths to the world to come in order to call attention to the reality, that breaks through this barrier from the other side. As informative as Oepke's thesis certainly is in its specifics, on the whole it is based on a misunderstanding. But then how is Barth's "radical" position to be understood? What comments can perhaps be made about it?

---

[245]When Barth in January 1922 describes the position he is coming from as "somehow in the corner between nominalism, Augustinianism, mysticism . . . which was not the Reformation itself, but from which it later emerged" (*Briefwechsel* 2, p. 30), one can wonder if this applies to the first or perhaps also to the second *Epistle to the Romans*.

[246]Oepke himself sees differences between the *Epistle to the Romans* and radical mysticism but explains them too quickly by claiming that in these places the other soul "in Karl Barth's breast" (p. 90) got his chance: his Calvinism on the one hand, Luther's influence on the other hand. When Oepke summarizes all opposition to mysticism in the second *Epistle to the Romans* with a word from Luther, "Where there is forgiveness of sins, there is also life and salvation" (p. 92), it becomes palpable that he does not do justice to Barth with his thesis.

[247]Oepke, *Karl Barth und die Mystik*, p. 24.

[248]Ibid.

[249]Ro 2, pp. 19-20.

[250]Barth certainly does not know a "Christ in us" in terms of affective mysticism, but in contradistinction to "radical mysticism" he knows a "Christ in us" understood as "the Word of God directed to us" (Ro 2, p. 268).

A Comparison with the Position of the Young, "Liberal" Barth

The persuasiveness of a critique of Pietism surely does not depend only on the accuracy of its description of Pietism but also on the weight of the "position" from which the criticism is made. We have sketched Barth's "position," but now we have to inquire about its soundness after discussing its implications for Pietism. Therefore let us first ask the question of where the author of the second *Epistle to the Romans* actually stands in *comparison to the position of the young, "liberal" Barth.* The young Barth had reduced his theological outline to this common denominator: "religious individualism and historical relativism."[251] The opinion he expresses in this formula is that the realm of revelation or faith (understood as "religious individualism") and the natural realm (or the historical realm) stand "in sharp contrast" to one another.[252] There is nothing definite, or absolute in the latter realm, since "all that is transitory is only a parable."[253] All that is scientifically, naturally and historically comprehensible is relative, so that all religious statements made on this basis are subject to criticism that qualifies them. In the former realm, however, there is an absolute, though not in such a way that it is "given" scientifically or historically or that it is universally comprehensible. It can be said with Schiller: "What has never and nowhere occurred,/this alone never grows old."[254] The reality of this other realm becomes comprehensible in a certain sense. But everything that becomes comprehensible in it (in "thoughts and words") is no longer absolute as such but relative once again. "Intellectual communication" of the intellectually "inaccessible act of faith" is possible as something relative (and only in this way). "Confession" is possible.[255] But we encounter this reality itself (which, as we have said, is found for the young Barth in the innermost human emotions, in the personal experience of the individual) only to the extent that it is scientifically, historically, etc., not comprehensible.

If we are clear about these basic theses, we encounter the surprising fact that the thought pattern of the second *Epistle to the Romans* is structurally related to the thought pattern of the theology of the "liberal" Barth. Here too the divine and the natural-historical realm stand in "sharp contrast": There is "no transition" between them.[256] The divine is "never and nowhere" given in the

---

[251]"Moderne Theologie und Reichsgottesarbeit," in *ZTK,* 1909, p. 319.

[252]Ibid.

[253]Ibid., p. 484. Compare p. 318: "For science . . . there is no absolute phenomenon in nature and in the intellectual world."

[254]Ibid., p. 484.

[255]Ibid., pp. 483-84. Compare p. 484: "The normative, objective, eternal is found only in the 'emotion' of this inner experience—everything that enters into thoughts and words is itself a part of the relative current of history."

[256]Ro 2, pp. 222, 116ff.

earthly-historical realm, that is, in the realm of the "visible," the comprehensible and observable.[257] All that is transitory is still always "only a parable."[258] Everything in this realm is transitory, is relative; and all phenomena in the realm of history are thus subject to qualification,[259] even this, "that God speaks, . . . is not removed from the dubious nature of all historical things, in so far as there is also a history within history."[260] Therefore we must take a stand against all attempts to make the divine comprehensible, "visible" at the level of the earthly, natural and historical. In contrast to this, the divine is the epitome of what is "invisible." Everything in this invisible realm that becomes tangible in the arena of temporal history can certainly be a "witness" and "signpost" and "parable," but only of that which "always lies beyond all historical reality" and thus is and remains as such relative itself: "By knowing something, we know it as a thing, as a relative thing . . . and we have no knowledge of that which is not created, not in time! . . . And precisely our lack of knowledge of what God knows is knowledge possessed *by God*, . . . with whom we are in time."[261] The affinity between the thought structure of the "liberal" Barth and the "dialectical" Barth is astonishing. As large and considerable as the shift and change may be that took place in Barth's thinking, it is clear that his thought structure has essentially remained the same. Therefore, on the one hand, we must expect to see the fruitfulness of the young Barth's starting point revealed in (as a result of?) that change. On the other hand, we must expect to see in the second *Epistle to the Romans* certain key lines of thought from his original starting point to which he remained closely attached in spite of his determination to distance himself from them.

Of course, the change between the position of the liberal and the dialectical Barth cannot be overlooked. It is undoubtedly far-reaching. It lies in the fact that (1) what the young Barth sought to put into "*religious individualism*" is no longer said of "religious individualism" (because it can no longer be said; see

---

[257]Ibid., p. 67; compare pp. 222, 226.

[258]Ibid., pp. 26, 52-53, 70.

[259]A few examples: "Apart from God we are in agreement with every honestly profane observation of nature and history, but not with the half-truths of theological observation of nature and history" (p. 302; examples of this, pp. 218, 296). "Even the highest, the most intellectual, the most righteous differences of opinion among human beings appear here as they are: in their natural, inner-worldly, profane, 'materialistic' significance" (p. 51). "This critical position [on history] signifies . . . an ability to see the historical in its profane, relative and ultimately meaningless context" (p. 82). Our world is the system "ultimately understandable only in terms of biological categories . . . , ultimately only from economic-materialistic viewpoints. We call this system history" (p. 260).

[260]Ibid., p. 67.

[261]Ibid., p. 294; compare p. 105.

point 2!). Instead it can be said exclusively of *God,* who as such stands in sharp contrast to all that is relative, including "religious individualism." This change thwarts the earlier idea of the "inner human emotions" in which the divine and human are closely linked—to such an extent that now the living God (as "the pure boundary and the pure beginning of all that we are") replaces "what we . . . experience as God"[262] by now recognizing that this is two different things. Thus the old dualism is overcome and exposed as thinking in terms of false, only relative, inner-worldly differences. Such dualism assumes the dissimilarity of two human dimensions (individual values/universal facts). Thus the realm of the divine is no longer seen as part of a human dimension but in its uniqueness. It is characteristic of this realm that it is "something different, unique, special, new even in contrast to all experience."[263]

Furthermore, the change lies in the fact that (2) *"historical relativism"* has now been so radicalized that it has also blown up the last bastion to which the "liberal" Barth thought he could retreat in order to safeguard the independence of the religious realm on the human level, namely, persons' inner, individual experience, described as "religious individualism." This too is now considered to be relative. This too is a "visible" event in which God is brought down to the level of the "comprehensible." Indeed, by forgetting that all temporal things are relative, religious individualism attempts to make the invisible divine being visible in the realm of relativity, but now this attempt must be subject to a critique that qualifies religious individualism itself. This critique must become a critique of religion.

The change is also found in (3) a new clarification of the *relationship* between that which stands in such "sharp contrast." For if human thought is no longer defined by the difference between two human dimensions but by the difference between God and man, then more than ever the question of the relationship between these two conflicting phenomena must be asked, and consequently this question as well: "How should we guard against . . . the charge of a gnostic dualism?"[264] Barth guards against the charge by *dialectically* reinterpreting his earlier idea of persons' inner ability to feel emotion as the relationship established between God and humanity.[265] Seen from the perspective of God, it can be said that he does not "merge" into humanity but that he limits it, at the same time establishing it as his ultimate condition so

---

[262]Ibid., p. 315.
[263]Ibid., p. 67.
[264]Ibid., p. 90.
[265]The place where he can say with certain qualifications: "The impression made by revelation *is* eternal reality" shows that Barth did not simply give up the idea (p. 65).

that he touches it in such a way that he does not touch it (like the tangent!). Seen from the perspective of man, it can be said that what he has from God is not any kind of fullness in him, but "hollow space." However, in this way and only in this way it is at the same time a "pointer" to God, a sign of being touched by him. The interface at which the divine being and human beings meet and touch is death, but "continuity" exists between the two in such radical discontinuity.

Let us say it again: The change that occurred in Barth's thought compared with his earlier position is considerable, but it does not fundamentally change the thought pattern in which even the "liberal" Barth thought. *Kant* clearly schooled him in this thought pattern, which can be easily recognized and which Barth never denied. Kant distinguished between experiential knowledge and intellectual knowledge.[266] As closely as both are linked, they are still fundamentally different. Experiential knowledge takes place as the knowledge of pure being in the unity of perception and idea. All conceptual, theoretical statements about God within the framework of such experiential knowledge are illusionary because they must lack any visual perception since God is not a being like other beings. Or rather such statements are impossible because there is no material available for us to determine supernatural ideas; we would have to get this material from the things of this material world, but it is not adequate for that object. In Kant's view God is recognizable only within the framework of that intellectual knowledge which takes place (not theoretically but) practically, as an act of practical reason and in which God is recognized (not as an object of experiential knowledge but) as a boundary, as a regulating idea. The position of the liberal Barth and the position of his second *Epistle to the Romans* coincide in adopting primarily the negative aspect of Kant's epistemology: in any case, the divine is not recognizable within the framework of what was called "experiential knowledge," or to put it the way Barth does: not within the framework of what is historically observable. Therefore it is not recognizable because it cannot be recognized according to these premises, so that all knowledge of God claimed within this framework must be illusionary. This explains the passionate preference of the young Barth but also of the author of the *Epistle to the Romans*[267] for historical relativism, on whose level there can be no knowledge or only illusionary knowledge of the "absolute"! This explains why Barth takes it for granted that all statements about the di-

---

[266]Compare here, for example, I. Kant, *Kritik der Urteilskraft*, p. 91.
[267]See n. 55. Compare also p. 184: "No being and happening . . . on this earth is protected from relativism."

vine on this level are subject to criticism!

The "liberal" Barth understood the knowledge of the divine as practical knowledge as Kant does, though in such a way that he then supplemented Kant by Schleiermacher; that is, he viewed the categorical imperative only as a propaedeutic, preliminary stage of actual religious knowledge of God, which is only real in the purely individual experience, though far from universal legitimacy. The first *Epistle to the Romans* expressed a strong feeling of unease at this solution, that is, at locating the knowledge of God in this realm (although he again made use of an interpretation of Kant's imperative as a mere demand in contrast to life filled with the divine being!). The second *Epistle to the Romans* takes issue with this solution more circumspectly. Why does Barth now find it completely inadequate? We must primarily mention that this has to do with a discovery of Scripture in his study. But in this context we are only interested in the ideas in which he expresses his discovery. As far as this is concerned, we could say that in the second *Epistle to the Romans* Barth distanced himself from Schleiermacher, or from the idea that God can be comprehended in the sphere of religious individualism by adopting a more radical interpretation and application of Kant's epistemology. He did this in such a way that he now decisively follows through on the idea that God cannot be conceived of in any other way than as the "boundary" of human knowledge, as the "regulating idea." As Barth now stresses this (in a way that was critical of Schleiermacher), his thought is being stimulated by Neo-Kantianism. This influence makes itself felt especially through *Cohen,* in whose thought the contrast between the "visible" and the "invisible" plays such a crucial role that the realm of the "visible" is the questionable one. In contrast, both "pure knowledge" and the subject of pure knowledge are not given, not visible or given, visible only as something unfinished, only as a task that remains unending.[268] The fact that Barth so strongly emphasizes an understanding of God as "boundary" also has to do with the fact that he is influenced by Feuerbach's critique of religion. In Barth's view, what Feuerbach "rightfully objected to" was that in human religion the one who prays, the pious individual does not "get beyond what he himself has thought and experienced," that all his "attempts to bridge the gap . . . take place within this world."[269] The *interpretation* that leads Barth to entertain Feuerbach's critique of religion is clearly in line with Kant's critique of the assertion that the knowledge of metaphysical

---

[268]G. Kruger, "Dialektische Methode und theologische Exegese. Logische Bemerkungen zu Barths 'Römerbrief,'" in *ZdZ,* 1927, pp. 139ff.

[269]Ro 2, p. 300.

truth is on the same level as experiential knowledge.[270] Once again it is Kant in whose thought Barth finds the intellectual possibility of *overcoming* Feuerbach's critique of religion. He does this by advancing the thesis that God is not a hypothesis (of man) only when he is conceived of per se as the "presupposition" (of man).[271] Therefore "God" is not untouched by Feuerbach's critique when he is generally understood as a metaphysical reality beyond all human hypotheses, but only when he is understood as "the origin of the crisis of all objectivity devoid of all objectivity."[272] After all this, we may assume that Barth is especially influenced by Kant, deepened by Neo-Kantianism but also by Feuerbach's critique, when he insists in his *Epistle to the Romans* that God cannot or only supposedly can be recognized as an object of experiential knowledge. And we may further assume that the same influence is in play when Barth now separates himself from Schleiermacher and his own earlier position with the thesis that God can only be "recognized" as the critical boundary of human experience.

Barth's Discovery of the Reformation and Its Problems

It is obvious that with these conceptual clarifications, carried out with the suggested conceptual means, a *change* has truly taken place in Barth's thought, in relation to his earlier "liberal" position. It could not even have been said with such clarity in the approach of the first *Epistle to the Romans*. I see the actual significance of the second *Epistle to the Romans* for historical theology in its articulation of this understanding.

1. Barth rediscovered and reinterpreted the Reformational doctrine of justification in which the sinner is simultaneously the one who is justified, and the one who is justified is simultaneously still a sinner. At the same time he also rediscovered the right to reject Pelagianism and semi-Pelagianism, stressing that

---

[270]For example, compare the following statement from Ro 2, p. 56: "There is no object without the thought of the object. There is no characteristic we observe in an object without any advance knowledge that gives us the concept of this characteristic. Thus, if God is an object in the world, there can be no statement about God . . . ,which is not derived from this superior advance knowledge. If God . . . were one object among many, he himself would be subject to this crisis, he would clearly not be God at all."

[271]Ibid., p. 90.

[272]Ibid., p. 57. Compare p. 52: God is "not a metaphysical being alongside other beings, not a second being . . . alongside that which would exist without him, but the eternal, the pure origin of all that is." He himself occasionally indicated what he owes to Kant here. For example, p. 370: "Only one thing is at issue for humanity: the recognition of God's freedom [which occurs in Kant's thought!]." Or pp. 351-52: The church should be "humble enough" not to allow itself to be surpassed by Kant in carefully maintaining the "boundaries of humanity." Compare p. 418.

God's grace is not only free but also remains free. He did this in a theological situation in which both of these truths seemed to have been largely forgotten. He interpreted both discoveries by linking them to a positive acceptance of the modern criticism of religion which served to confirm his insight that the one who is completely justified in the sight of God at the same time remains completely a sinner. In stressing this insight it must not be said that Barth did not know any ethics, but he did see its problem to be that the ethical discourse must take place in such a way that this basic insight would not be rejected retroactively in one's ethics.[273]

2. Beyond this he also *applied* the doctrine of justification to the *understanding of God* and his relationship to the world more consistently than the Reformers, forced to this consistency not least by his discussion with the modern criticism of religion. Or should we rather say that he saw the doctrine of justification understood in these terms *rooted* in a particular understanding of God? Thus he stressed that God is a *free counterpart* to humankind and not something in human beings, and that if he were something in human beings he would no longer be the counterpart of humankind. The crucial point is that God is free in his *relationship* to human beings and remains free by proving that he is beyond their control. The dialectics of the hiddenness of the revealed God and the knowledge of God as the unknowable one as well as the dialectics of the sinner who is justified yet remains a sinner obviously complement one another.

3. Finally, the significance of the second *Epistle to the Romans* can be found in the fact that its author, again more consistent than the Reformers, interpreted the *simul,* in which a sinner is the one justified and the hidden God is revealed, in a strictly eschatological fashion. In this view these two truths are not two equal possibilities that can be realized on the same basis, but the second can only be *expected* within the framework of the first one, and really only *at the end* of the first possibility. In short, the significance of the second *Epistle to the Romans* for the history of theology is its consistent and radical willingness to follow through on the Reformational *simul justus et peccator.*

Of course, we must add that certain shortcomings are inherent in the theology of the second *Epistle to the Romans,* shortcomings that cause the reader of the book to rather frequently get the impression that the author is only on the threshold of understanding what he outlined here. It is as if there were still a few open doors, each leading off in a different direction from there. The shortcomings can be explained historically. In spite of all the change from his original, liberal start-

---

[273]Compare, in the chapter on "the problem of ethics," the succinct sentence: "Grace is sufficient for ethics as well" (p. 423)!

ing point, he was still caught up in the thought structure of this starting point
and was not able to overcome it, and his overzealousness in struggling to free
himself from the concept of including the divine in humanity produced an attitude which kept him from clearly expressing what he wanted to say. It seems to
me that the shortcomings of the *Epistle to the Romans* can be found in the fact
that to a certain degree Barth kept himself from saying *what* he apparently
wanted to say by how he said it.[274] We can certainly conclude that the theology
of the *Epistle to the Romans* was in need of criticism by examining the critical
evaluations made from many sides and from many points of view, which raised
noteworthy concerns about the weak points in Barth's concept. These critical
evaluations often ran the *risk* of hitting the sack when they meant to hit the don-
key! They accused Barth of "rationalism" (W. Schmidt), "radical mysticism" (A.
Oepke), an exaggerated Calvinism (E. Dörries), but in fact they broke with the
fundamental insight of Protestant theology he rediscovered.[275] An appropriate
critique of the shortcomings of the second *Epistle to the Romans* would have to
distinguish itself by not again burying the insight that breaks through in it but by
seeking to bring this insight to real clarity if it is distorted there. I see the following shortcomings in the conception of the second *Epistle to the Romans*.

1. I see a shortcoming not in Barth's controversial thought on the separation
of God and man, but in the way he unmasks the problem of the "separation"
by assuming their original *identity*.[276] When Barth says, "God and the human being I am, do not go together,"[277] we must surely see the rightness of this statement against the position it rejects. But we have to wonder if Barth made too
clean a break and thus was not careful enough.[278] It is problematic that a boundary is crossed beyond which the legitimate and necessary separation from any
form of justifying of the *sin* absorbs the truth of the justification of the *sinner*.
Indeed, there is no divine justification of sin and thus no divine company with
it. But there is a justification of the sinner, and thus God and humanity "come
together." Of course, in saying this we cannot emphasize strongly enough the
character of the miracle, the undeserved grace of God. If this is not seen, we
are forced either to think of the person with whom God comes together as the
person whom "I am not" or to think of God's coming together with him in terms

---

[274]Compare the remark of G. Krüger ("Dialektische Methode," p. 137), who believes he can
show "how Barth's intention to express the concepts is shifted and actually thwarted by their
own tendency." Compare H. U. Von Balthasar, *Karl Barth,* p. 93.

[275]Compare P. Schempp's vicious "marginal comments on Barthianism," in *Zwischen den Zeiten,*
1928, pp. 529-30.

[276]Compare von Balthasar, *Karl Barth,* pp. 77-78, who astutely called attention to this point.

[277]Ro 2, p. 242.

[278]Compare von Balthasar, *Karl Barth,* p. 75.

of the (old mystical) principle that "birds of a feather flock together." Thus we are forced to see the person with whom God comes together as closely linked to God. The more the person "who I am" is seen only in separation from God (and the more this separation is seen in terms of human nature),[279] the more "the new man" must be moved closer together with God. And in fact Barth can unreservedly speak of an "immediate unity" (of humankind) with God as the origin from which humanity has fallen[280] as the goal of redemption, indeed, as the now valid reality of "the lost unity of God and man that is not to be lost."[281] Therefore Barth can speak of this "new man" in such a way that the distinction between him and Christ,[282] or between him and the Holy Spirit, disappears.[283] Of course, all of this is true only of the man who cannot be seen, who is not the man "who I am." Of the latter (and only of the latter) one can firmly assert that there is "no merging of God and man into one."[284] On the other hand this new man who cannot be seen is "not another, not a second person beside me."[285] Indeed, there is an "identity between him and me,"[286] a paradoxical yet unified identity which the person "who I am" encounters at his end. This is an identity whose paradoxical nature seems to be more like Hegel's, in which two contradictory members are joined together into one identity and whose paradoxical nature seems to be less than the paradox Kierkegaard affirms, for whom this paradox takes the place of the synthesis.[287] It appears to us that the more *the fellowship* (not the unity) *of God with the sinner* is seen, the wonderful coming together with him, the less danger there is of seeing the new man, who is the person with whom God comes together, as unified with God. However this danger is present in the *Epistle to the Romans* in spite of his good intentions. In this book we encounter a line of thought that we have perhaps investigated in a one-sided manner, but it shows that in spite of how Barth stresses the distinctiveness of God and man, he is kept from saying what he wants to say by the way in which he thinks of it and stresses it.

2. I see a further shortcoming in the theology of the *Epistle to the Romans* in

---

[279]Ibid., p. 77.

[280]Ro 2, pp. 146, 233.

[281]Ibid., p. 260.

[282]Ibid., p. 279: "If I call myself 'the son of God,' I mean by that in every respect the same thing as when I call Christ the Son of God . . .; for I mean by that . . . that other, the new, invisible man."

[283]The Holy Spirit "is the invisible . . . new subject, the self of man that stands and exists before God" (p. 134).

[284]Ibid., p. 127.

[285]Ibid., p. 211.

[286]Ibid., p. 125.

[287]See on this issue Krüger, "Dialektische Methode," pp. 117ff.

the *way* Barth seeks to go *beyond Christian, anthropocentric thought*. It is certainly to Barth's credit that he called attention to the problems of such thought. And we cannot deny that for his part he seriously sought to overcome it. But our question is whether he actually remains entangled in such thought or at least is not effective in opposing it by the way he objects to it.[288] Barth says God's truth comes "vertically from above,"[289] and therefore all paths from humankind to God are closed. "We cannot begin with the truth, for it is our beginning."[290] Good, but how do we recognize this truth which is our beginning, and how do we speak appropriately about it? Should not we be able to start with it, to think from its point of view and so think its thoughts? Would not humility be disobedience if it makes the assertion "I cannot" an absolute? But now Barth thinks he can speak of this truth and the fact that it is our beginning, in no other way than by asserting such an "I cannot" by dialectically neutralizing and negating all human possibilities (even the negative ones) of persons' coming to God. But does not this procedure mean that he still thinks of truth from the starting point of humanity, instead of starting with truth? By negating first the positive and then the negative possibilities, he advances to their limit from the perspective of these human possibilities. It is clear that God is to be understood as a "presupposition" (in terms of Kant) and not as a "supposition" (in terms of Feuerbach). But how does a human being recognize God as such a presupposition? Is it not Barth's view that humans assume God is such a "presupposition" because he has revealed himself as such? Or is it not in the second *Epistle to the Romans* practically a fact that persons encounter the limits of their dubious circumstances by recognizing their radically dubious nature from the perspective of these circumstances? And are these limits perhaps even the "presupposition" to critically reflect on these circumstances? And if this suspicion goes too far, we must nevertheless ask whether the truth which comes "vertically from above" is thought and recognized by negating all thought "from below"? Indeed, is it not again an all too optimistic assumption that we encounter this truth, that we have the "beginning of the new man" at the end of the old one only if this radical negation is kept up (as if the negation could also not point to a void)?[291] Where does death get the dignity of being proclaimed "an epistemological principle"?[292] Does even the most radical, dialectical negation of Christian-anthropocentric

---

[288]And not only ours; von Balthasar (*Karl Barth,* p. 92) dared to make the hard statement: "His crying out 'not I! but God!' directs everyone's attention to *him*, instead of to God."

[289]Ro 2, p. 77.

[290]Ibid., p. 270.

[291]Ibid., p. 126.

[292]Ibid., p. 148.

thought have the power to overcome this? Is the recognition that all paths from humankind to God, even the negative ones, are "dead ends,"[293] not itself a "dead end" if these paths are the way we recognize what it is, our Christian responsibility to know? Surely Barth knows that even the most radical negation cannot overcome anthropocentric thought by itself, but only the new beginning coming from God. But he still thinks he can assume that such negation has great affinity to this new beginning and is qualified to put us in front of it and lead us to it. Our question is addressed to this assumption. We think that Barth's good intention has a chance only when theological thinking seeks to correspond to the truth that begins with us, and does so in that it begins at the beginning with that truth. If it does this, the gospel would be expressed more clearly than seems to be the case in the language of the second *Epistle to the Romans,* which sounds strongly legalistic.[294]

3. A further shortcoming in the theology of this book can be seen in the rigid *structure* of his thought. It cannot be different as long as the antithesis of God and humankind is thought of in terms of the contrast between the visible and the invisible. As long as this is so, nothing moves. Although Barth interprets the concept of God by the idea of "source," he certainly does not understand God merely as otherworldly (as long as he is not a reality alongside visible realities). At the same time he is related to this world (as long as he is not a second, other being alongside the reality of this world but the presupposition that creates it).[295] Yet understood in these terms, this relationship is not an act of love and compassion but a being who has always been the presupposition of the world. When Barth understands this world as perishable, for him humanity is certainly not only enclosed in this world, for at the same time the perishable is recognized as a parable of the imperishable.[296] But precisely this relatedness of the perishable to the imperishable is clearly characteristic of him as such. Barth would not like to talk about a history in the relationship of God and humankind because he equates *Geschichte* with *Historie* and *Historie* with *relativism,* and he wants to deny historical relativism any "say in divine things."[297]

But does not relativism retain its say in a negative way when revelation is only understood as "a line of intersection which can have no extension itself,"[298]

---

[293]Ibid., p. 299.

[294]Barth himself pointed that out later: both the ultimate inability of the *Epistle to the Romans* to counter the anthropocentric thought in theology and the problematic nature of its "legalistic" thought; see "Dank und Reverenz," in *EvTh* 1963, pp. 337ff.

[295]Ro 2, p. 52.

[296]Ibid.

[297]Ibid., p. 184.

[298]Ibid., p. 35.

which touches the world "as the tangent touches a circle without touching it"?[299] The rigid structure of this theological thought is manifested precisely in its understanding of revelation. Basically there is no dynamic teleological, but only a static dialectic. There is certainly not only a no but also a yes, not only hiddenness but also openness, not only death but also life, not only the old, but also the new man. His critics were wrong to criticize him for not having these things.[300] However, there is no *movement* (or else it is hardly recognizable)[301] from here to there, but the latter (paradoxically) is considered to be the invisible *other side* of the former, visible side. By emphasizing the paradox of this state of affairs, he seeks to protect himself from the danger that is nevertheless evident when the yes is understood as the invisible other side of the visible no. The danger is that on the one hand nothing more has to happen from God's side because the visible simply has that invisible reverse side. On the other hand, since the invisible always retains that visible flip side, really nothing new *can* happen on the human level; thus the world remains left on its own. We must wonder if the conceptuality of "visible/invisible," controllable/uncontrollable is sufficient to state what could be said here about Christian responsibility. Barth is certainly right that the proper understanding of God's uncontrollability must not be corrected, not even subsequently, by a view in which he can be brought under control again. I consider it legitimate that Barth stood firm against the objection often raised with him that he must correct his insight by recognizing "God in history."[302]

But it is not clear enough in the *Epistle to the Romans* that the uncontrollability of God is the uncontrollability of the One who decrees that he himself would become human, for in doing so he has humankind under "control" and claims it for himself. Where this is seen, we can and must speak of a *history of God with human beings.* Thus a dimension comes into focus where several things can be said that did not get the attention they deserved in the *Epistle to the Romans,* yet they must be said. Then there is the "word became flesh," then the

---

[299]Ibid., p. 6.

[300]For example, this can be said of B. Dörries, *Der ferne und der nahe Gott,* 1927.

[301]We seem to not do Barth justice here when one can read on page 143 in his work: "This turbulent unity of humanity is not a balance of two conditions or even an eternal cycle . . . in death and life. The seemingly unending parallelism or polarity of differences breaks apart in so far as *this* movement is *genuine* movement." This passage shows that Barth knew about the problem envisioned by us. But it is once again the case that Barth only speaks here of "movement" to deny the equivalency of sin and grace, death and life, and that in the end the "movement" only consists in the fact that "we see through the visible conditions . . . and look into their preconditions" (p. 144).

[302]Compare W. Schmidt, *Zeit und Ewigkeit,* 1927, or W. Bruhn, *Vom Gott im Menschen,* 1926. On the latter compare Barth's "Epilogue," in *Zwischen den Zeiten,* 1927, pp. 33ff.

"cross and resurrection," the "earliest Christian history," but not earliest history detached from its roots in this and that, here and there, but only recognizable by being tied to a particular "then and there" and thus by no means removed "from *all* story telling."[303] For the divine is not merely to be understood in an Aristotelian manner as an other-worldly eternal form over against all "contents."[304] Revelation cannot merely be restricted to the fact that God is recognized there (as the unknown one). Then there is the reminder that God must not be replaced by any (human) definition of him (God is . . . love, freedom, personality, etc.), but that God is God (also by becoming man, which is not at all denied), not forgetting Barth's harsh reminder of the prohibition of images. Then we must also see that God (as God) defines himself in revelation so that the problem of *who* God reveals himself to be is not left out of consideration.

Furthermore, it is not sufficient to simply equate "Israel" with the "church" and the church only with the "world of religion."[305] Then "Israel" could come into focus as a unique phenomenon, as the "chosen people," and the church not merely as a religious club but as the place where sinners are called to be hearers and witnesses to revelation when the Word of God is proclaimed. Then theological insight and understanding would not be merely an act of an individual thinking of God, as the theological thought of the *Epistle to the Romans* could give the impression,[306] but an act of a human being listening in the community of the church and thinking for it. Then the sanctification of human beings would not be identified with their justification. Rather it would be seen that grace is grace only when it produces *two things:* a pardon through it *and* a claim on one's life for it. Thus it would have far-reaching consequences if Barth's static thought laboring under the epistemological dialectics of visible/invisible could be overcome by taking seriously the history of God with human beings.

Summarizing all these comments, it could be said that Barth's critique of Pietism was made from a position of strength because in a new way Barth radi-

---

[303]Ro 2, p. 260.

[304]Ibid., p. 105. Barth applies the separation of contents here only to "psychological, historical" contents, but it seems to me that Barth does not want to express a "content" of revelation in the *Epistle to the Romans,* since for him revelation does not indicate *as whom* God reveals himself but strictly *that* he reveals himself.

[305]Ibid., pp. 314ff.

[306]This is Schlatter's crucial objection to Barth's *Epistle to the Romans.* Of all the other objections of critics at that time it is an objection of refreshing originality: "Paul gave listeners here (in *his* Epistle to the Romans) instruction and these listeners did not sit isolated, each of them preoccupied with reading in his study; rather they were a community of faith gathered harmoniously before God. They now and later carried out their common worship time and again by letting Paul speak to them. . . . Are we . . . isolated, lonely 'readers' who have long since forgotten that we are members of the church?"

cally, very radically acted on the key insights of the evangelical-Reformational message. The fact that his objections to Pietism clearly had this theological background gave his arguments weight, an incomparably greater weight than the arguments of the first *Epistle to the Romans,* which came from a different background. Whoever had ears to hear among the Pietists found that he had to answer tough questions about how his concern related to that Reformational message. On the other hand, we have seen that the way Barth articulated this message also covered up points of view that did not allow other important biblical insights to have a chance. If this is correct, it follows that certain factors inherent in the theology of the *Epistle to the Romans* make it partially understandable why the Pietists had trouble recognizing an alternative to their own thought in Barth's theology and that this theology offered an occasion for the Pietists to raise questions and objections to it. Thus we must expect the possibility that Pietism guarded insights that it rightfully found missing there.

PART B

PIETISTIC RESPONSES TO THE CRITIQUE OF PIETISM MADE BY THE YOUNGER BARTH IN THE PERIOD UP TO 1930

I. The Pietistic Self-Interpretation

Comments on the Pietistic Barth Literature

The response of the Pietistic community, mainly in Germany, was a part of the great diversity of responses Barth's second *Epistle to the Romans* found. The response to the theology of this book was so great in this sector of church life alone that the relevant literature can hardly be seen in its entirety.[1] Although only a portion of it is dealt with in this treatise, we think it will become apparent that a representative cross-section has been chosen from the multitude of Pietistic reactions.[2] The argument that groups within the Pietistic community had with the second *Epistle to the Romans,* which came on the market at the beginning of 1922, only began around 1926 or 1927, apart from certain exceptions. But then it grew into a lively discussion in these and the following years. However, this discussion took place at a time when Barth was clearly striving to go beyond the position he took in the *Epistle to the Romans,* which was seen and taken into consideration by some but not all of the Pietistic interlocutors. The argument took place in many forms. Brochures were published which made the Pietists' position on Barth's theology their special subject, but also articles (essays, reviews) in the leading community periodicals and newsletters.

There are also passages in other Pietistic writings dealing with other subjects in which their argument with Barth takes place. The anthology *The Struggle for the Church,* published by the community people in 1930, is not on the whole directly and explicitly an answer to Barth, but it contains so many individual statements on him and the problems raised by him that we may view it implicitly

---

[1]This not only has to do with the fact that the Pietistic literature was published partially in the form of rather short commentaries, partially in quite remote locations, but also with the fact that they, especially the abundance of Pietistic periodicals cannot be found or are only rarely found in public libraries. But this is not all: It is astonishing that these works and especially the back issues of the community movement's magazines are also not available in the various headquarters and Bible schools of this movement. Would it not also be a task of this movement, precisely if it wants to be taken seriously, as it deserves to be, to somewhere make a collection of its literature and especially of its periodicals?

[2]I think I am permitted to make this claim because apart from the other literature I have mentioned I have systematically searched through all the issues of at least one of the leading community magazines of that era, the journal *Licht und Leben* published by J. Gauger.

as a Pietistic commentary on the theology of the Epistle to the Romans. But they dealt with Barth thoroughly and in detail not only in their literature but also in oral presentations and at conferences of the community circles. For example, such discussions took place at the Gnadau Pentecost Conferences in 1926 and 1927, at the gathering of representatives of the Rhenish community association in 1927 and at the Neukirchen Brethren Conferences in 1928 and 1929.

In what follows we will mainly limit ourselves to discussing the literature of such authors who expressly claimed to be Pietists in their discussion with Barth and who claimed to uphold the Pietistic heritage in opposing him. The voices of those academic theologians who were close to the community organizations or who believed these circles were close to them will be heard in separate sections. Otherwise, the Pietistic authors as a rule were not academic theologians but largely pastors or occasionally Christian laymen who were engaged in practical ministry. This is in keeping with the fact that the Pietistic community movement understood itself as a movement of the laity. However, this was always in tension with the work of theology. They took a rather aloof attitude toward it, at least toward all such theology that did not affirm them.

How did it come about that in the case of Barth they felt pressured to come to grips with a theology that did not simply affirm them? They themselves mentioned several reasons for it. (1) Barth's theses were so fundamental and at the same time of such magnitude that the discussion of them could not be limited to lecture halls and studies but had to be thrown into "the life and beliefs of the Christian community."[3] (2) In their view, Barth had declared war on Pietism as a whole[4] in such a way that they could no longer avoid responding to this declaration of war. (3) They felt Barth's critique disrupted the emerging efforts "of the church and community movement to come to terms with each other,"[5] a disruption they had to take seriously and which pushed them into the task of theological reflection because the other side declared it had to move away from Pietism "for the sake of the gospel."[6] For these reasons a lively engagement with Barth's theology began within the second half of the 1920s in the various circles of the Pietistic community movement, as they struggled, at times quite vigorously, to find a position on it.

---

[3]H. Brandenburg, in the foreword to G. F. Nagel, *Karl Barth und der heilsgewisse Glaube,* 1929, p. 3.

[4]G. F. Nagel, *Karl Barth und der heilsgewisse Glaube,* 1929, p. 10.

[5]F. Mund, "Die Gemeinschaftsbewegung eine Anklage gegen die Kirche," in *Im Kampf um die Kirche,* 1930, p. 62. Compare H. Oltmann, *Die Gemeinschaftsbewegung auf der Anklagebank,* 76.

[6]Oltmann, *Die Gemeinschaftsbewegung auf der Anklagebank,* p. 76.

As we have said, their statements were largely not of an academic nature[7] but "amateurish" and "generally accessible." This not only has to do with the fact that their authors were not actually scholars but with the fact that their work was first of all addressed to the community people themselves. It was the intention of these authors in part to inform them about Barth's theses, to reassure them in view of the unrest caused by Barth and to provide them with ammunition against the theology presented there. But it was also the intention of some of these authors to encourage the community people to examine themselves on the basis of "what was legitimate in it."[8] The fact that the discussion was primarily aimed at their own circles produced statements that ran the risk of falling into the monologue style of self-affirmation which supported their own preconceived notions instead of carrying on a tacit, inquisitive conversation with Barth. On the other hand, this discussion produced something positive. Because this lay movement had to come to grips with Barth's theology, something significant happened. The laymen partially overcame their aloofness toward theological work and suddenly began to show an interest in theology themselves. By dealing with a theology they neither could simply approve of nor simply reject, they were encouraged to embrace more sophisticated theological reflection. They found themselves pressured to pursue theological reflection because Barth's theology initially disrupted amicable and peaceful efforts to achieve reconciliation between Pietism and the church or theology, and because it claimed to be critical of Pietism "for the sake of the gospel." So in the end the *Epistle to the Romans* encouraged various attempts to resolve the tensions among the church, academic theology and the Pietistic community.[9]

The Essence of Pietism

The Pietistic camp primarily understood Barth's theology as an attack not only on something in Pietism but on Pietism itself. "He does not want to enlist us in a thoughtful discussion so that we can cut out the diseased part of the organism for the sake of a healthy Pietism. Rather Barth is putting his probe into position to strike Pietism at its roots."[10] Therefore they viewed his attack as a challenge to understand and explain themselves anew as Pietism. Let us first

---

[7] One can view what was described in note 1 as a sign of this.

[8] W. Knappe, "Karl Barth und der Pietismus," 1927, p. 13.

[9] This is the subtitle of the anthology *Im Kampf um die Kirche,* edited by L. Thimme in 1930. This is itself the document of such an attempt. Further examples of such attempts: The volume *Rechtgläubigkeit und Frömmigkeit* edited by H. Asmussen in 1938 and the anthology *Pietismus und Theologie,* edited by O. Schmitz in 1956.

[10] W. Hützen, *Biblisches Glaubensleben,* 1928, p. 4.

describe the Pietistic self-interpretation given in this context.

According to the Pietistic responses to Barth's *Epistle to the Romans*, where can the *essence*, the central concern *of Pietism* be seen? What is for them the objective criterion an observer could use to recognize Pietism as Pietism? According to G. F. Nagel, the new aspect of the New Testament compared with the Old Testament can be summarized in these two words: "in you."[11] For him Pietism is that movement which knows this central New Testament truth as an experiential certainty and which now keeps this truth alive in the church and especially defends it against moral laxity and dead orthodoxy. Therefore this is the concern of Pietism. It can be recognized by its interest in "personal fellowship with God and gaining a share in the divine life. . . . The person who is not born again and has not experienced the power of the gospel in his own heart is not a Christian."[12] It is not as if the person could do this himself, but the Holy Spirit creates such a "spiritually alive personality."[13] And it is not as if the truth of justification by grace alone through faith alone were to be violated, but to realize this truth and protect it from abuse, it requires, first, the condition "of true, heartfelt repentance" and second, the outworking of justification in "growing ethical self-presentation."[14]

Likewise W. Hützen defines the concern of Pietism as the "clearly articulated biblical doctrine of the inner life as the personal experience of the living God who really lives and works in us through his Spirit."[15] He adds that this understanding of the Pietistic concern is not controversial "among those who consciously move in the thought patterns of Pietism and approve of them."[16] According to F. Mund, it is the manifest working of the Spirit which constitutes the essence of our community movement and for whose sake we speak of the mission of the community movement.[17] Our mission is to awaken natural, "church people" from the sleep of death so that they "come to faith, are spiritually alive, born again, converted and receive in their heart the Holy Spirit who comes directly from above. All of these things are facts experienced a thousand fold and noticeable to others."[18] According to L. Thimme, an interest in a living "religious possession" is characteristic of Pietism. "The new possession of the community

---

[11]Nagel, *Karl Barth und der heilsgewisse Glaube*, p. 5. Also, Anonymous, "Kritische Ecke," in *In alle Welt, Zeitschrift für missionarische Arbeit*, ca. 1928, p. 38.
[12]Nagel, *Karl Barth und der heilsgewisse Glaube*, p. 7.
[13]Ibid.
[14]Ibid., p. 8.
[15]W. Hützen, *Biblisches Glaubensleben*, 1928, p. 5. Compare W. Hützen, "Heiligung," in *RKZ*, 1928, pp. 8ff.
[16]W. Hützen, *Biblisches Glaubensleben*, p. 3.
[17]F. Mund, "Die Gemeinschaftsbewegung eine Anklage gegen die Kirche," p. 49.
[18]Ibid., pp. 47ff.

movement was their victory in aggressively laying hold of the assurance of salvation as well as of sanctification. This led to a revival of genuine, early Christian community life as well as the spirit of evangelization."[19] And according to W. Knappe, Pietism is at the same time concerned to emphasize the whole Bible and activate a practical life of faith. The latter is clearly not a second concern alongside the former. Knappe sees Pietism's emphasis on the whole Scriptures in the way it rediscovered and advocated the "forgotten truths of Scripture: the personal laying hold of salvation, the assurance of salvation and sanctification."[20] This is the central concern of the community people in their own view.

It is important to notice that as a rule this *understanding* of its concern is linked to a particular *evaluation* of the movement. On the one hand, this concern is claimed as a special gift of Pietism in contrast to other manifestations of the church. This gift identifies it *as* Pietism. On the other hand, at the same time they resist an interpretation of this special insight as a special find made by Pietism. Rather they are inclined to identify it with the whole Bible, with mere biblical Christianity.[21] Pietism's representatives boldly conclude from the fact that it has faithfully upheld the concern described above not only that it is not just any "school of thought" but that "the community movement is . . . a work of God,"[22] not made by human beings "but accomplished by God."[23] And they further conclude from this that it not only has a right to exist in the church but that it is absolutely "essential" for the "health" of the church.[24] Pietism is basically God's action, Christ's offer of grace to the modern church, and fighting against it is tantamount to "fighting against God."[25] Therefore the history of Pietism can be depicted in correspondingly vivid colors. The older Pietism emerged against the dark background of the eighteenth century, for which "the dissolute spirit of the French in fashion and morals and the dead orthodoxy of the church" were typical.[26] In Pietism "the spring water of the apostolic and Reformational witness

---

[19]L. Thimme, *Kirche, Sekte und Gemeinschaftsbewegung,* 1925, p. 250.

[20]Knappe, "Karl Barth und der Pietismus," 1927, p. 12.

[21]Compare Nagel, *Karl Barth und der heilsgewisse Glaube,* p. 7: " Here the living sources of the gospel are rushing clearly in a powerful spiritual torrent."

[22]Mund, "Die Gemeinschaftsbewegung eine Anklage gegen die Kirche," p. 46.

[23]A. Essen, "Kirche und Gemeinschaftsbewegung," in *Licht und Leben,* 1929, p. 179.

[24]Ibid., p. 180. Also compare the sentence: "It was . . . indispensable for the church, that the inner life was cultivated in Pietistic circles." The community movement of more recent times also thinks and speaks in these terms, for example, F. Mund: "There is no living community of faith without that which Pietism wants" (*Pietismus-eine Schicksalsfrage an die Kirche heute,* 1936, p. 13), or G. Bergmann: "The church has become sick because it is missing Pietism" (*Die Aufgabe des Volkes Gottes heute,* 1963, p. 67).

[25]Mund, "Die Gemeinschaftsbewegung eine Anklage gegen die Kirche," pp. 70-71.

[26]Nagel, *Die Gemeinschaftsbewegung,* p. 6.

suddenly bubbled up again in a barren time."[27] In the view of G. F. Nagel, the names of Francke, Bengel, Zinzendorf, Tersteegen as well as Spener shine "on the tablets of history in a light that has its source in Jesus' abundant light."[28] Likewise, "streams of light and salvation flowed into the believing church" from "the men of the revivalist movement in the 19th century."[29] And in the same way, vital spiritual power is pouring into human lives from the community movement of the present day which again is a time of "decadent laxity" and "moral decline."[30] In short, "time and again the waves of the Pietistic movement have carried death-overcoming life into the world."[31]

Drawing Distinctions

Certainly the community people did not lack an appreciation for making distinctions in their self-portrayal as they interacted with Barth's theology. First of all, they saw the *historical differences* between Pietism in the eighteenth, nineteenth and twentieth centuries. For example, we can hear from the Pietists that the Pietism of the eighteenth century thought in strongly individualistic terms. Indeed "they lacked a focus on the whole nation and an appreciation for the value of the natural tasks of life and the cultural mission of Christianity."[32] L. Thimme describes Spener's and Francke's intention like this: "We need a new Reformation, not of doctrine, but of life." What is praiseworthy about this intention is that it was "basically concerned to develop a new version of the inner possession of biblical truth."[33] What is dubious about it is that it was (unnecessarily) impaired by "scrupulous self-examination, ascetic legalism as well as timid escapism."[34] The revivalist movement of the early nineteenth century was different. Such dubious features diminished; instead it took a special interest in "Christian charitable activities and mission to the heathens."[35] The community

---

[27]Ibid., p. 7.

[28]Ibid., p. 10.

[29]Ibid., p. 34.

[30]Ibid., p. 40.

[31]Ibid., p. 10. Also compare the bold words of Mund, *Die Gemeinschaftsbewegung eine Anklage,* pp. 46-47: The community movement "is a spiritual movement," the Pietistic communities are "places favored by the Spirit of God," "in which the conditions of the New Testament church . . . prevail."

[32]Essen, "Kirche und Gemeinschaftsbewegung," p. 180. Compare E. G. Ruppel, *Die Gemeinschaftsbewegung im Dritten Reich,* 1969, p. 11: He sees "what was actually new" in the community movement in comparison with the older Pietism as its willingness "to publically assume responsibility for the proclamation of the gospel."

[33]Thimme, *Kirche, Sekte und Gemeinschaftsbewegung,* 1925, p. 137.

[34]Ibid., p. 145.

[35]Essen, "Kirche und Gemeinschaftsbewegung," p. 181. Compare L. Thimme, *Kirche, Sekte und Gemeinschaftsbewegung,* 1925, pp. 165, 188.

movement from the end of the nineteenth and the beginning of the twentieth century was also different. It was not only shaped by the older Pietism, but beyond that by the American-English evangelical and holiness movement in the mid-nineteenth century.[36] They stress that its thought was more nationalistic than the revivalist movement, and thus they were primarily concerned about "rescuing their own people."[37] They actually thought in such nationalistic terms that the English influence could appear suspicious to them.[38] They also stress that the more recent community movement has distinguished itself by creating a tighter organization that has made it more effective in comparison with the earlier forms of Pietism.[39] Therefore we find in these Pietistic self-descriptions that they have the ability to take a *more discriminating* view of the history of Pietism, and they have done this in a way that leaves room for them to occasionally even see this history self-critically. The latter is most strongly developed in the work of G. Kerz. He still assumes that there is "much light" in Pietism, but in view of its history he takes this statement seriously: "Where there is much light, there are also many shadows."[40] On the other hand, the attention they give to the differences between the three movements does not basically change their conviction that they are basically defined by the same concern and thus closely linked together. So the more recent community movement presents itself in this self-understanding: "In the community movement God has given the church a

---

[36]Compare Ruppel, *Die Gemeinschaftsbewegung im Dritten Reich,* 1969, p. 12. Further compare H. von Sauberzweig, *Er der Meister-wir die Brüder: Geschichte der Gnadauer Gemeinschaftsbewegung 1888–1958,* 1959, p. 68.

[37]Essen, "Kirche und Gemeinschaftsbewegung," p. 181.

[38]Compare Mund, *Die Gemeinschaftsbewegung eine Anklage,* p. 66.

[39]Compare Essen, "Kirche und Gemeinschaftsbewegung," p. 181: Pietism in the community movement "has now become a great, organized association to which almost all of the circles in the Pietistic church community belong." He means the so-called Gnadau Association of Pietistic Communities, or more precisely: the German Association for the Promotion of Community and Evangelization, in which some national and some regional Pietistic community associations joined together in 1897 under the initiative of E. Schrenk, Count Puckler, J. von Oertzen, and Th. Christlieb among others (compare Ruppel, *Die Gemeinschaftsbewegung im Dritten Reich,* 1969, pp. 17ff).

[40]G. Kertz, "Pietismus und Kirche im Kampf um die Jugend," in *Im Kampf um die Kirche,* p. 268. Kertz has an astonishingly critical view of the history of Pietism on condition that we realize the debt of gratitude we owe to the Pietists: "we know enough about the power and the current of blessing, about the eternal and about the temporal to quite confidently and joyfully thank God for these fathers and to assume their legacy" (p. 255). He charges that rationalism has its roots in Pietism (p. 258). Francke "brought up Pharisees" (p. 266). His conversion is not a conversion "in the biblical sense of the word." "Religious experience was often stressed in a manner that is not biblical." "One can not guard against the impression in many, but not all Pietists that the powerful, pious self has taken the place of the justified sinner." "A . . . non-Reformational concept of humility is prevalent in Pietism" (pp. 266-67). This critique is so radical that one must assume that Kertz stood on the boundary of Pietism.

new revival, after the old Pietistic movement in the 18th century and the revivalist movement of the first half of the 19th century. It is clear that the community movement is carrying on the tradition of the earlier movements."[41]

When the community people described themselves as they interacted with Barth's theology, they also had a definite appreciation for more *sophisticated thinking* when it came to advocating the *cause* they represented. Their circles were in fact ready to concede that Pietism did have its questionable aspects as well. "By joyfully affirming Pietism, we are by no means covering up its excesses."[42] They conceded that Pietism also had its problematic side since in principle they distinguished between a "healthy" and a "sick" (unhealthy) Pietism, or between its essence and certain "excesses." But then they claimed that the discovery of questionable features in Pietism (and thus the legitimacy of possible objections to it) basically applies to this latter form of Pietism, not to itself but only to a distorted form of it. "What is healthy in it, its spirit, must definitely be held on to, whereas its unhealthy aspects as fleshly aberrations can not detract from its truth."[43] Thus they conceded that the charges against Pietism must not only stem from "hostility to the gospel." They laid themselves open to attack because of occasional "eccentricities and imbalances" in it.[44] But it is only a matter of "excesses" in a cause that is healthy in itself. Thus the community people gave themselves credit for developing the critical capacity to point out these excesses time and again in the service of a healthy life of sanctification.[45] Indeed, one voice even believed, not without consequences, that a Pietist only had to submit to those objections that emerged from the community movement itself.[46]

What then did they mean by the "unhealthy" features of Pietism that the community people could recognize or reject as "aberrations" in their own ranks? In part they simply mean a certain degree of failure in their serious effort at sanc-

---

[41]Mund, *Die Gemeinschaftsbewegung eine Anklage*, p. 47. Compare H. von Sauberzweig, *Er der Meister-wir die Brüder*, p. 67.

[42]Knappe, "Karl Barth und der Pietismus," 1927, p. 12.

[43]Hützen, *Biblisches Glaubensleben*, p. 4.

[44]Nagel, *Die Gemeinschaftsbewegung*, pp. 9-10. Later a remarkable situation could occur when W. Michaelis applied this distinction between a healthy and an unhealthy Pietism to Barth's treatment of it. Michaelis stressed that Barth had a caricature of Pietism defined by certain blunders whereas Pietism distanced itself from the blunders made, for example, by the Herrnhut community—all this just at the time when, conversely, Barth did not take offense at these Herrnhut "blunders" at all. Rather he discovered in them an element of true christocentric theology. This illuminates the problematic nature of this whole distinction from a new angle. Compare W. Michaelis, "Zum Problem Pietismus und Theologie," in *Pietisms und Theologie*, 1956, p. 121, and K. Barth, KD 4/1 (1953!), p. 763.

[45]Hützen, *Biblisches Glaubensleben*, p. 4.

[46]Pfr. Eckardt, "Der Geist fuhrt in die Freiheit . . . Lecture at the Gnadau Pentecost Conference 1927," in *Licht und Leben*, 1927, p. 414.

tification, and they mention vices such as judgmentalism, gossip, pettiness, superficiality and unmanliness, all of which should be put away.[47] In part they also mean the influence of "Anglo-Saxon Christianity,"[48] of evolution, perfectionism, enthusiasm for glossolalia. They were all rejected in a polite way as too superficial,[49] occasionally also "alien to our German nature."[50] At any rate it is clear in all this that the distinction they drew between healthy and unhealthy Pietism did not mean that any distinctions were made within the framework of what was previously described as the concern of Pietism. Rather those "excesses" only describe an aberration from this concern, and their separation from those excesses served to solidify their concern in an even purer form. Indeed, we must wonder if this theory could not in practice assume the function of making a Pietist inaccessible to critical objections. From the outset it was a foregone conclusion for him that these objections were based on a misunderstanding. The critics were confusing the "excesses" with the "essence" of the cause. The "essence" of his cause could only appear more untouchable to him than ever. It is unmistakable that on the part of some the awareness of a difference between "healthy Pietism" and its "excesses," on the part of others a feeling for the *difficulty* of *drawing a boundary* between them, signaled a certain degree of uncertainty in the self-understanding of Pietism in the 1920s, and this could also be viewed as a subtle effort of Barth's *Epistle to the Romans*. The contrasting vision of two Pietistic works is typical of this uncertainty: H. Dallmeyer's "The Community Movement: What It Must Do Away With" (1924) and P. Fabianke's "What Must the German Community Movement Hold On To?" (1925).[51] But it is also unmistakable that this uncertainty did not shake the inner bastion of the idea that there is a "real," experiential "in you" of the divine in humanity.

In the self-understanding of Pietism shown here the outlines of its *relation-*

---

[47]H. Dallmeyer, *Die Gemeinschaftsbewegung: Womit sie aufräumen muss,* 2nd ed., 1924; compare Essen, "Kirche und Gemeinschaftsbewegung," p. 243, and Oltmann, *Die Gemeinschaftsbewegung auf der Anklagebank,* p. 77.

[48]Compare *Licht und Leben,* 1925, pp. 118-19.

[49]Compare the review of W. Knappe on L. Thimme, "Kirche, Sekte und Gemeinschaftsbewegung," in *Licht und Leben,* 1927, pp. 31-32. Further, A. Essen, "Kirche und Gemeinschaftsbewegung," pp. 183-84, and P. Fabianke, *Was muss die Deutsche Gemeinschaftsbewegung festhalten?* 1925, p. 113.

[50]Mund, *Die Gemeinschaftsbewegung eine Anklage,* p. 66. In his work *Pietismus-eine Schicksalsfrage an die Kirche von heute,* which was published in 1936, his belief in the leading role of the Nordic race and the belief of the Pietists got badly mixed up in his mind. It is remarkable that a man such as Erich Schick could recommend this work to get to know the true Pietism! (E. Schick, *Die Botschaft des Pietismus in den theolog. Kämpfen der Gegenwart,* 2nd ed., 39ff.).

[51]Compare Hützen, *Biblisches Glaubensleben,* p. 4: "It is the question of what can be recognized in the older and newer Pietism and what part of it can be discarded."

ship to other phenomena in church history have already been sketched out. First of all, let us turn our attention to the question of how it saw its relationship to the Reformation! The community movement obviously attached great importance to its agreement with the Reformation, especially with Luther. It is "a genuine child of the German Reformation,"[52] "a genuine, healthy child of the Reformation."[53] G. F. Nagel, for example, appealed to the Reformers for the following ideas in his position: Faith has to be a heartfelt faith, not an intellectual faith; such faith boasts of the presence of the Holy Spirit; it signifies a rebirth in terms of an ethical change of course at the heart of one's personality; where such faith is robbed of its assurance, Christ's act of grace is destroyed.[54] The Pietist may certainly believe he is a "genuine, healthy child of the Reformation" when he takes this, and only this, from the Reformers. Of course, the community people did not totally lack of sense that there were at least certain differences between it and the Reformation. But they found two different ways to process the discovery of such differences. On the one hand, many tended to count the fact of such differences as a plus for Pietism in terms of the old thesis of Pietism that it was the true completion of the Reformation by bringing about "the reformation of life after the reformation of doctrine."[55] Or they claimed Pietism was the true interpreter of the Reformation by first bringing to light the true opinion of the Reformation that "Christ in us must be brought out of the darkness and once again be placed in the light alongside Christ for us."[56] On the other hand there were also a few community people who viewed the fact of those differences not only as a plus but also as a minus for their movement. They pointed to the priority of the Word before faith, the *simul justus et pecca-*

---

[52]Essen, "Kirche und Gemeinschaftsbewegung," p. 212. And conversely: the Reformation was a great "revivalist movement" (p. 179). "What the [community] movement wants . . . and what . . . the old Pietists strived for, are things whose necessity the German Reformers recognized and left behind as a task for the church in the future" (p. 211).

[53]P. Fabianke, *Was muss die Deutsche Gemeinschaftsbewegung festhalten?* 1925, p. 115.

[54]Nagel, *Die Gemeinschaftsbewegung,* pp. 25, 18, 19, 30, 44. With the exception of a passage from Calvin in which he talked of God's holiness, all the passages are listed in which Nagel appeals to Luther and Calvin. Consider what aspects of Reformational teaching Nagel conceals!

[55]Ibid., p. 5. They always liked to quote Luther's somewhat ambiguous talk of those "who seriously want to be Christians" in his foreword to the German mass in this sense, thus as a reference to the reformation of life in Pietism; for example, P. Fabianke, *Was muss die Deutsche Gemeinschaftsbewegung festhalten?* 1925, p. 103. It is hard to imagine, though, that for Luther this "vision" of a reformation of life was linked with disrespectful talk about those who merely get stuck in the "views" "that sinful man can take hold of the forgiveness of his sins by the blood of Jesus Christ and may comfort himself with God's great grace, which accepts sinners"—as this is the case, however, in Fabianke (p. 12).

[56]Nagel, *Die Gemeinschaftsbewegung,* pp 5-6.

tor, the warning against security,[57] and thought "they recognized a defect in the community movement here."[58] Thus they saw grounds for a "Reformational cleansing of Pietism" (Thimme). Notice at this point how much was set in motion among the community people of that time.

Second, we gain a similar impression when we see how they define the relationship between *Pietism* and *mysticism*. The notably strong interest in making a sharp distinction between them along the lines of a "healthy" Pietism and an unhealthy degeneration may possibly be an effect of Barth's critique.[59] This interest is even more remarkable because they could concede that this difference had sometimes been blurred in Pietism.[60] However, they did not use it as an opportunity to further ask how such blurring could have occurred. Instead, they claimed an "essential difference between the ideal of piety found in mysticism and the New Testament life of faith" (Pietism).[61] Although an inward, hidden and supernatural life gifted by God is important to Pietism, mysticism means something quite different because it does not know the seriousness either of sin nor "the fear of a holy God" nor the problem of the atonement.[62] Of course, we must wonder if an "essential difference" between Pietism and mysticism can actually be claimed in this way. On the one hand, we must ask whether they have an inadequate understanding of mysticism when the mystics are denied any knowledge of sin and the fear of God. On the other hand, we must ask whether the point where Pietism agrees with mysticism, claiming a "God in us" in a realistic, experiential sense, is not also a point in Pietism where a person finds himself beyond "sin" and "fear of a holy God." Is this danger in mysticism sufficiently averted, and are they separated enough from mysticism when they declare, vaguely enough, that the "God in us" that can really be experienced does not signify any mixing with God (in contrast to mysticism) but just means that we "are drawn into his sphere of influence"?[63] Nevertheless, whether this attempt was successful or not, the community movement's interest in clearly separating from mysticism remains a fact.

Third, the community movement also saw itself on the frontlines in sharply

---

[57]W. Knappe, "Heilsgewissheit und Heilsunsicherheit," in *Im Kampf um die Kirche,* pp. 135ff. L. Thimme, "Kirche, Sekte und Gemeinschaftsbewegung," pp. 68ff. Even more strongly: L. Thimme, "Das Problem der Kirche und die reformatorische Lösung," in *Im Kampf um die Kirche,* pp. 33-34.

[58]Thimme, "Das Problem," p. 33.

[59]Hützen, *Bibl. Glaubensleben,* p. 16.

[60]Nagel, *Die Gemeinschaftsbewegung,* p. 32.

[61]Ibid.

[62]Ibid., pp. 32-33.

[63]Hützen, *Bibl. Glaubensleben,* pp. 14-15.

opposing the *Enlightenment, Rationalism and Liberalism,* although this battle
had first become important in the revivalist movement whereas an occasionally
quite relaxed relationship to the Enlightenment could be observed in the Pietism
of the eighteenth century, for example in A. H. Franke and J. Lange, in J. A. Bengel, and, in a different way, in N. von Zinzendorf as well.[64] Now however Pietism was defined "as a reaction to rationalism" and its supporters were judged
to be "trailblazers in overcoming the ruling rationalism."[65] What then was rejected in this battle against rationalism? They rejected the "whole flight of fancy
called evolution that idolized humanity and also had an impact on theology,"[66]
"evolutionism in theology in which man wants to reach up to God and thus
pulls God down into humanity."[67] "What does all this have to do with Pietism?"[68]
Nothing at all!

Why not? What arguments can it use against rationalism to "overcome" it? It
can argue that it knows about "true spiritual life that God has planted and still
wants to plant in man by his Spirit."[69] This is an experiential reality that does not
idolize humankind but on the contrary overcomes idolatry because it is experienced as a divine reality placed in human beings by God. But how did it come
about that the Pietism of the eighteenth century historically did not "overcome"
the Enlightenment but was so quickly and so thoroughly replaced by it? It was
a critical friend of Pietism who could ask on the occasion of the Gnadau Pentecost Conference in 1927 whether this was not due in part to shortcomings in
Francke's theology.[70] Instead, with regard to this problem they preferred to be
content with the information given to them by Fritz Mund. The counteracting
force of Pietism unleashed against the Enlightenment could not become effective in the church because the pastors rebuffed the revival given by God in Pietism, motivated by their desire to maintain the hierarchical status quo.[71] Nev-

---

[64]I am thinking of Lange's appeal to Cartesius, of Francke's appeal for empirical realism, of Zinzendorf's dependence on Pierre Bayle, of the relationship of the later Bengel (for example in
his *Cyclus*) to the natural theology of the Enlightenment.

[65]L. Thimme, "Kirche, Sekte und Gemeinschaftsbewegung," pp. 164-65.

[66]Nagel, *Die Gemeinschaftsbewegung,* p. 11.

[67]Hützen, *Bibl. Glaubensleben,* p. 36. Compare also L. Thimme, "Das Problem," p. 34.

[68]Nagel, *Die Gemeinschaftsbewegung,* p. 33.

[69]Hützen, *Bibl. Glaubensleben,* p. 36.

[70]"Why did even Francke's student go over to the opposite camp of the Enlightenment with
flying colors? Was not it due to the fact that in Francke's thought . . . a real reduction in essential parts of the Christian message accompanied "the legitimate one-sidedness?" (*Licht und
Leben,* 1927, p. 491). The person asking this question can therefore at best be understood as
a critical crossover theologian of Pietism because this question runs counter to the typical Pietistic view of history, which describes the situation at that time in these terms: When human
beings lay captive in Rationalism and the Enlightenment, God caused the dawning of Pietism.

[71]Mund, *Die Gemeinschaftsbewegung eine Anklage,* pp. 59-70.

ertheless we must ask whether the Pietists have seriously grasped the concern of the Enlightenment by subsuming it under the labels "human idolatry" and "the enthronement of the autonomous individual"? Is not the uniqueness of the Enlightenment simply that it elevates "experience," making it a criterion for the credibility of theological statements?[72] With regard to this point is not Pietism in its own way related to the Enlightenment? And is there not a parallel to the evolutionism it abhors in its idea of a growth in sanctification? But these are questions it did not ask itself apart from that one exception.

Questions About the Self-Understanding of Pietism

Now that the picture the community movement had of itself as Pietism has been sketched in outline, we will move on from this portrait to ask some critical questions. Let us ask: What is the relationship of the Pietists' self-understanding to the interpretation of this phenomenon in Barth's *Epistle to the Romans*? Could W. Knappe rightfully accuse Barth of misjudging Pietism?[73] "He has only a caricature of Pietism in view."[74] Let us first of all notice that the idea of the "negative way" which Barth regarded as a characteristic of Pietism in the *Epistle to the Romans* is certainly included in the self-understanding of the community movement and its concern. This "negative way" plays a role here as the prerequisite for Christian experience, the experiential indwelling of God in us.[75] The "collapse of egocentrism," "repentance" and "self-examination" are indeed considered the way to achieve the goal of a "biblical life of faith."[76] Following this path evidently also serves the function of distinguishing such a life of faith from one's own human product and of proving that it is a divine work in man. This idea rather precisely corresponds to Barth's interpretation. Thus it would be hard to say that he had only a caricature in view when he clashed with the Pietists. They said his critique only affected certain "excesses" of an "unhealthy" Pietism, whereas he knew nothing of "healthy Pietism." Thus they could think that they were unaffected by it. We sense that the Pietistic statements felt embarrassed when they realized Barth actually could have meant the "healthy" Pietism. Because they apparently could not imagine that "healthy Pietism" could even be criticized, they all tend to posit the idea that Barth *must* have had a caricature of Pietism when he thought he had found something to criticize about it. We

---

[72]This is the thesis advocated then by E. Hirsch in his *Geschichte der neuern evang. Theologie* (1949ff).

[73]Knappe, "Karl Barth und der Pietismus," p. 37.

[74]Ibid., p. 13.

[75]Nagel, *Die Gemeinschaftsbewegung*, p. 21.

[76]Ibid., pp. 21, 23.

must respond by first making a general comment. It was characteristic of this theologian's critique of Pietism at all times that he did not indulge in cheap ridicule or stoop to a condescending smile or to nitpicking on any peripheral abuses or tangible weaknesses. Rather he took this opponent seriously and tackled it at its strongest points. To move from the general to the specific, why should his interpretation of Pietism in the *Epistle to the Romans* and its understanding of repentance be a caricature when it practically coincides with how its supporters explicitly understand themselves in relation to this theology? However, we must add that the crucial interest of Pietism as it is articulated in relationship to this theology does not seem to focus on the idea we have just mentioned but on what follows from that "prerequisite": the positive fact of a biblical life of faith,[77] the presence of the Spirit of God in us as "our personal possession,"[78] as "an event in the heart of man," in the "inner sphere of experience,"[79] the real, experiential indwelling of God in man, "not in a dialectical sense, but in an actual sense,"[80] "God in the hands of human beings,"[81] so that there are in fact Christians who have this possession.[82] We could say: negation in terms of a "negative way" clearly does not play such a weighty role as Barth assumed in the *Epistle to the Romans* (in praise of Pietism), although this was the case with Tersteegen and Angelus Silesius! The community movement places itself much closer to the position of a pious "possession" Barth criticized than he had thought in his interpretation. When he praises the "ascetics and Pietists" for being closer to true Christianity than the "healthy evangelical folk piety," the community movement now suddenly settles in the neighborhood of such a "healthy folk piety."[83] To this extent we can say that he misjudges Pietism, perhaps not necessarily the older Pietism but the more recent community movement. However, he misjudged it less in the sense that he caricatured it than in the sense that he seems to have overestimated it (viewed from his perspective).

A further question: How does the understanding of the community movement as Pietism relate to the *Pietism of the eighteenth and early nineteenth centuries?* Does its understanding of the Pietistic concern agree with what the earlier Pietism meant and wanted, and if so, does it agree to the extent that it thinks it

---

[77]Hützen, *Bibl. Glaubensleben,* p. 3.

[78]Ibid., pp. 5-6.

[79]Nagel, *Die Gemeinschaftsbewegung,* p. 21.

[80]Hützen, *Bibl. Glaubensleben,* pp. 5-6.

[81]Ibid., p. 15.

[82]L. Thimme, "Kirche, Sekte und Gemeinschaftsbewegung," p. 253. Compare p. 73.

[83]This observation is confirmed by the fact that the community movement clearly wanted to especially separate itself from the ascetic aspect of the older Pietism; see above notes 32 and 34.

does? Of course when we distinguish between the image the community movement has of Pietism and the "real" older Pietism, we possess only an image of the older Pietism which requires historical verification just like any other image. Nevertheless, after comparing Barth's interpretation of Pietism with sample texts from older Pietists we could ask whether his view does not have advantages compared to the community movement's view of the older Pietism. But our concern now is not to compare different images of it but to reach a methodical clarification of how the community movement arrived at its "image" of the older Pietism. Has it verified this image historically? Their thesis is that the concern of Pietism, including the older Pietism, can be reduced to the common denominator of the "inner life," the experiential indwelling of God in us. Have they examined this thesis in a thorough study of the writings of Spener, Francke, Bengel, Zinzendorf, Tersteegen and then of a Hofacker, Tholuck, etc.? Such a study may have been made. But in its explanations of "Pietism" it is hardly evident that it has been made. It seems symptomatic to me that even in works that refer to the history of Pietism, practically no quotations from its writings can be encountered. But how then did the community people come to believe possibly without having studied their writings that they are actually following the tradition of those older figures and that they agree with them that the "inner life" is of dominant significance in Christianity? It is clearly the case that what those older figures taught them is relatively unimportant compared to what they have "lived" and "experienced." "Revivalist movements are carried by men of action, by people of great dedication. Spener's contemporaries had the impression of Spener that he was really a perfect Christian."[84] This is the way they argue here. The material the community people used to construct their image of the older Pietism was not gathered from what those older Pietists taught, for example, about the inner life. Rather their image of the older Pietists was based on the impression they gained that such an inner life was present in them and that "streams of light and salvation" flowed from them. On this basis they claimed to be in essential agreement with them. The question is only whether they can make a historical case by arguing this way. Can they really do justice to those men and their views, views that have been documented in their extensive writings? To mention an especially glaring example, can they even remotely do justice to what a Zinzendorf said, preached and composed when they examine him from the point of view that he was a "very determined person,"[85] that he was "blessed" and had a "strong faith," that he "lived" and "experienced" what he taught? And a further question is

---

[84]Kertz, "Pietismus und Kirche im Kampf um die Jugend," p. 261.
[85]Ibid., p. 260.

whether they can argue theologically in this way. When such an "inner life" in certain persons is seen as a given, is something not simply being claimed, something that from the outset eludes any critical reflection or must dismiss any critical question as "unbelieving doubt"? Is not this claim in fact only a particular "teaching" which must not and cannot be exempt from critical theological examination just as any orthodox teaching is not?

A further question: How does Pietism's understanding of itself and its concern relate to the *biblical* witness? Does what it confesses to be its concern agree with the Scriptures? To what extent do both agree with each other? This question too cannot be quickly and easily answered because what can be said about the Pietistic view of the biblical witness is itself only a "view" about the biblical witness which requires thorough exegetical examination just as any other view does. Here we will also limit ourselves to a methodical comment on the problem of answering this question in the ranks of the community movement. First of all, this question is not at all unimportant to it. "We know that Pietism, if it is to retain its vitality, must always prove itself by conforming to the Scripture and to the interpretation imparted to us afresh by the Reformation."[86] They have such a strong interest in upholding biblical authority that the community movement proves the reality of Christian experience not by declaring "I have experienced it this way" but by providing this surprising information, "It is written this way in the Bible."[87] This is how they handle criticism of their experiential possession of faith, which they view as a denial of all Christian experience. We can see that this question is important to the Pietists, but a long time ago they basically gave a positive answer. "We have never resisted Scriptural regulations."[88] It is striking to see in the Pietistic writings we have before us how the biblical witness and the Pietistic concern are merged, analogous to the claim of a real divine presence "in us." The adjectives *biblical* and *pietistic* are also joined together in such a way that we gain the impression that Pietistic statements no longer require any further examination by the biblical text.[89] Do they really need no further examination? When they say that "repentance and rebirth," the heart of Pietistic concerns and understood in their terms, is also the heart of the biblical message, is this assertion actually exempt from all further discussion? Is this really the message of

---

[86]Knappe, "Karl Barth und der Pietismus," p. 12.

[87]Compare Nagel, *Die Gemeinschaftsbewegung,* p. 27.

[88]Hützen, *Bibl. Glaubensleben,* p. 4.

[89]The distinction between a "healthy" and a "sick" Pietism enhances this situation even more by making it possible to ascribe all legitimate objections quickly to the "sick" Pietism in order to keep the "healthy" one free from all criticism.

the whole Old Testament? Is it the message of the exodus from Egypt and the covenant on Mt. Sinai? Is it the message of the psalms and prophets? Is it the message of Good Friday and Easter as it is viewed by the Synoptic Gospels and Paul? Good, we can believe this assertion, although good reasons can be advanced against it. But we dare not believe it without making a fundamental distinction between what we believe and what the Bible says. For example, when we hear them say, "what is at stake is certainly not Pietism as such," it only seems as if Pietism is being portrayed in relative terms because what it considers the central "biblical teaching" is by definition equated with what is central in "biblical teaching." We further heard them say, "Instead, what is at stake is the biblical teaching about the inner life that comes to clear expression in Pietism."[90] Wherever their own teaching is seen to be in such close proximity to the "biblical teaching," they invariably tend to be uncritical toward their own position and to dismiss objections raised against their own position from the outside as unbiblical. Among the Pietistic authors there are voices that warn against this tendency.[91] But even a W. Knappe, who has given such a warning more clearly than the others, does not escape the danger of equating Pietism with biblical Christianity or criticism of Pietism with criticism of the Bible. For he can say, "What is Pietism other than a necessary emphasis of Scriptural truths . . . because Barth fights against Pietism, he overlooks important truths of Scripture."[92] Such thinking can be found even more strongly in other supporters of the community movement. Let us remember the forceful words of F. Mund. In his view Pietism equals God's work of grace in the church of the modern era, and "fighting against Pietism means fighting against God, therefore it is sin."[93] It is clear that the more it uncritically equates its

---

[90]Hützen, *Bibl. Glaubensleben,* p. 5.

[91]For example, Oltmann, *Die Gemeinschaftsbewegung auf der Anklagebank,* p. 75, and Knappe, "Karl Barth und der Pietismus," p. 7. Knappe even dares to admonish his fellow Pietists: "Woe to us when we are not prepared to listen to the voice of truth, because it may be blowing against us as a strong east wind! . . . Woe to us, when we are only intent on saving our language, our theology, our piety, and refuse to pay attention to anything that deviates from it!"

[92]Knappe, "Karl Barth und der Pietismus," p. 37.

[93]F. Mund, *Die Gemeinschaftsbewegung, eine Anklage gegen die Kirche,* pp. 68ff. In his work *Pietismus-eine Schicksalsfrage . . .,* 1936, Pietism is given a downright messianic quality when it can be called in the language of Galatians 4: What happened when the world was laid low with sin, dead belief, and trust in reason? "Then God sent Pietism!" (p. 15). Compare this to the glorious heights from which Pietism looks down on the sinful church in the view of J. Gubler: "As long ago the elderly patriarch Jacob in his encounter with the Egyptian monarch raised his hands to bless Pharaoh, Pietism desires to give the church a blessing today" (*Kirche und Pietismus: Ein Gang durch die neuere evangelische Kirchengeschichte der Schweiz,* 1959, p. 198).

cause with the cause of the Bible, the more it is bound to lose its ability to listen and learn from other biblical insights and especially from biblically based objections to its teachings. Therefore we must assume from the outset that Pietism's confrontation with Barth's theology ran the risk of bearing little fruit, at least as long as it took its stand on this ground and wanted to continue standing there.

II. The Pietistic Interpretation of Barth

Whether the community people had something serious to *say* to the author of the *Epistle to the Romans* decisively depends on whether it had properly *listened* to him and how it had *understood* him. For he could feel motivated to make corrections in his thought as a result of their responses only when he felt that he was affected by their objections. And he could only feel that he was affected by them if they really applied to his ideas and not merely to a caricature of them. Therefore let us now enquire about the Pietistic interpretation of Barth in these terms.

The Negations of the Epistle to the Romans

What was mainly seen and understood, outweighing everything else, are Barth's negations. His theology is a "theology of collapse."[1] Its intention is to "crush us."[2] L. Thimme was therefore able to describe the theology of the *Epistle to the Romans* far too dramatically as a terrible act of war: "An onslaught with a broadly based attack is taking place there." "Columns are being led into battle and batteries are being moved. Their jaws are spewing out ruin against all of liberalism, against orthodoxy and against a Pietistic and experiential theology."[3] "Romanists, mystics, perfectionists lay mutilated on the battlefield until finally everything that seemed to stand firm in church and Pietism is shot to pieces,"[4] until "only fragments, only smoking ruins, only memories are left of it all!"[5] What is it that the Swiss pastor had to say to a perishing world? It is God's judgment on all human endeavors and hopes.[6] This is the concern of this school. "It vigorously crusades against all conceited ecclesiastical, scientific and civic possessions by negating of all that man is, can, has and knows."[7]

---

[1] W. Knappe, "Karl Barth und der Pietismus," 1927, p. 5.
[2] L. Thimme, "Das Problem 'Karl Barth,'" in *Gnadauer Gemeinschaftsblatt*, 1929, p. 97.
[3] Ibid., p. 95.
[4] Ibid., p. 96.
[5] Ibid., p. 95.
[6] Ibid., p. 94. P. le Seur thinks that is why Barth's book is such a "torment to read" ("K. Barth Der Römerbrief," in *Hochweg*, 1924, pp. 47-48).
[7] L. Thimme, *Kirche, Sekt und Gemeinschaftsbewegung*, 1925, pp. 72-73. He writes in his review of Barth's *Epistle to the Romans* in the *Deutschen Gemeinschaftsblatt*, 1923, Barth's theology is primarily about "denying all of what is from man." "Apart from Luther, Spurgeon (!) and

What is negated in particular? All heights, all human standpoints![8] Not only egocentrism but the ego itself, not only sinful man but the human being himself must "collapse and be overcome" in Barth's view.[9] And further: "In Barth's thought the historical date of rebirth as an experience in the life of the individual is negated."[10] "Such an experience could only be an illusion, self-experience."[11] What is at issue for Barth is a "passionate resistance to any kind of testimony to a present, inner spiritual possession."[12] "All certainties, securities, tangible experiences and comforts should be abandoned."[13] "His denial of the assurance of salvation is a logical consequence of such negation."[14] Indeed, he "fights against any kind of experience . . . in any sense." And "all ethical events are to be detached from the concept of faith."[15] But this is not yet enough of the negations! "Barth denied that man is able to be a covenant partner with God for now."[16] "The teaching of Karl Barth lined up against every attempt to mediate between then and now. There can be no relationship between what we are invisibly before God and what we are visibly in ourselves."[17] And even more: "In his thought the finite is incapable of grasping the infinite."[18] "There is to be no talk of the transcendental God coming near to man."[19] "In a real sense . . . God has not given us his Spirit."[20] "Barth thinks it is contrary to Scripture to say that God is present."[21] "Barth's polemics vehemently object to all syntheses, to all 'artificial' immanence, where God and man are brought together as one."[22] This means "he objects to the idea of God's immanence."[23] In short, "So that God is all in all, man must be nothing in Barth's view."[24]

---

perhaps (!) Kierkegaard I have never read such a devastating critique of all that man is and can do." In similar fashion H. von Sauberzweig summarizes in retrospect the understanding of Barth's theology in the community movement of the 1920s: "He is the Master—We are the Brothers." *Geschichte der Gnadauer Gemeinschaftsbewegung 1888–1958,* 1959, p. 291.
[8]Knappe, "Karl Barth und der Pietismus," pp. 7, 13.
[9]G. F. Nagel, *K. Barth und der heilsgewisse Glaube,* 1929, pp. 14, 24.
[10]W. Hützen, *Biblisches Glaubensleben,* 1928, p. 8.
[11]Ibid., p. 9.
[12]Nagel, *K. Barth und der heilsgewisse Glaube,* pp. 17-18.
[13]Ibid., p. 20.
[14]Ibid., p. 26.
[15]Ibid., p. 22.
[16]Ibid., p. 29.
[17]Ibid., p. 30.
[18]Ibid., p. 18.
[19]Ibid., p. 19.
[20]Hützen, *Biblisches Glaubensleben,* p. 14.
[21]Ibid., p. 12.
[22]Nagel, *K. Barth und der heilsgewisse Glaube,* p. 12.
[23]L. Thimme, "Das Problem 'Karl Barth,'" p. 95.
[24]Nagel, *K. Barth und der heilsgewisse Glaube,* p. 19.

Did they accurately describe Barth's opinion here? Not always! We cannot resist the impression that the Pietists are *exaggerating* when they describe Barth's negations. What they have done is somewhat comparable to the suspicious exaggeration of Eve in paradise when she said that not only eating the food but also touching the fruit of any tree was forbidden! The statement, for example, that God is everything and humankind is nothing, and even more that ultimate definition of human beings' loss of selfhood (so that God might be all in all!), are opinions that can be found in the older Pietists, for example, in Tersteegen,[25] but it cannot be documented in the second *Epistle to the Romans* and is even refuted by it.[26] When Nagel cites Barth's polemics against "artificial immanence" or against "the assurance of salvation in terms of more recent Protestantism," he is about to overlook the predicates attached to these themes here that indicate that Barth obviously does not want to speak against God's immanence as such or against the assurance of salvation as such.[27] When they allege that Barth is fighting against any kind of experience, their assertion is simply incorrect when it is measured by what is written in the *Epistle to the Romans*. Instead, he sharply objects to a particular meaning that is attributed to "experience."[28] When it is claimed that in Barth's thought there is no relationship between the invisible man and the visible one, they have falsified Barth's view that the new man is certainly invisible and the old man is visible, but now a relationship of paradoxical *identity* exists between the two in faith.[29] When they say it is Barth's view that God is always "beyond this world" and never comes near to man, they believe he could be easily refuted by quoting Acts 17:27.[30] However, they overlook the fact that for him God is actually never "simply" beyond this world but is very near, so he can also quote Acts 17:27 in his own way.[31] When Hützen portrays Barth's view on the Pietists' claim about what "we possess," it is striking that he

---

[25]Compare G. Tersteegen, *Eine Auswahl aus seinen Schriften . . .* , ed. T. Klein, 1925, p. 289: "In the ocean of the Godhead lose yourself . . . /His life remains, your own must vanish"; p. 291: "Whoever deeply recognizes his nothing/And calls God his all . . ."

[26]Römerbrief, 2nd ed., 1922 (= Ro 2), pp. 263-64.

[27]Ibid., p. 91: Here Barth speaks positively about God's immanence. On page 396 Barth separates himself only from what the assurance of salvation "is not in any case," which was at least seen and understood by Oltmann ("Die Gemeinschaftsbewegung auf der Anklagebank") and by Knappe ("Heilsgewissheit und Heilsunsicherheit") in *Im Kampf um die Kirche,* pp. 81-82, 141.

[28]In the *Epistle to the Romans* 2 Barth speaks positively about the "experience of God" on page 352; his criticism is only targeted at "experiences . . .which *as such* desire and claim to be important, great and divine in some sense without submitting to the judgment of *God,* without waiting for the *divine* justification" (p. 82).

[29]For example, ibid., p. 179.

[30]For example, Nagel, *K. Barth und der heilsgewisse Glaube,* p. 16.

[31]Ro 2, p. 69.

quotes from the *Epistle to the Romans* to document his interpretation of Barth only to the point where the quotation negates this Pietistic claim. But the quotation breaks off exactly at the spot where Barth goes on to explain under what conditions "a qualified 'we' and a qualified 'possess'" can be stated in positive terms.[32] It is clear that Barth's negations are presented in a greatly exaggerated form in the Pietistic literature that deals with his *Epistle to the Romans*. Thus we can already ask here whether the Pietists intend to put him in the corner by overinterpreting his negations so that it would then be easy to finish him off. However, he is not in that corner at all, so that at least in part the objections raised against him cannot touch his position. On the other hand, it cannot be denied that the negations mentioned above actually can be documented to a not insignificant extent in Barth's book. Indeed, they have accurately taken aim at a crucial line of thought in the book by referring to these negations. However, not much is gained by doing so. Although they understood that Barth has made certain negations in the *Epistle to the Romans,* they have not yet understood them. This can happen only when they have understood *in what sense* he has made them. For if they were understood as pure negations, they could simply be viewed as a direct, undialectical, unbelieving denial of the reality of revelation and the Christian faith, which of course Barth does not mean. Have his negations been properly understood? This question will only be decided by submitting these negations to a closer examination.

Their Understanding of Barth's Dialectics in the Epistle to the Romans

Therefore, we ask, In what manner does Barth make these negations? The answer must be that he makes them in the form of dialectics, by referring to the paradoxical character of a particular theological fact. For example, these negations do not deny the presence of God, the gift and communication of the divine to man. It only denies that all of this is given to us in this world directly, concretely, undialectically and unparadoxically. Barth does not deny, and it is not the purpose of his negations to deny, that the "positive relationship between God and man *exists,*" but he does deny that this relationship exists in any other way than as an "absolute paradox."[33] In his view there are "divine-human or human-divine" encounters, but never as something that could be directly seen so that human beings could boast of it, but only as a paradox,[34] only "against ap-

---

[32]Hützen, *Biblisches Glaubensleben,* p. 131. see Barth on this, Ro 2, p. 257.
[33]Ro 2, pp. 69, 75.
[34]Ibid., p. 94.

pearances (para-dox)."[35] These negations also do not deny that "the spiritual event" has something to do with God, but they serve this statement: "If the spiritual event is focused on God, is defined by God and accepts the form of faith, the impossibility, the miracle, the paradox occurs."[36] The category of paradox, in the language of Paul it would be called "mystery,"[37] is intended by Barth to safeguard the theological insight that what faith recognizes, the reality of God, especially as it is turned toward man, is "wonder" and "grace."[38] Such paradoxical dialectical thinking claims to be a form of thought that is appropriate to the theological content to be thought. This form seeks to clarify how what is to be thought can be thought.

Is this seen and understood correctly by the Pietistic authors? It can be said that they have trouble or do not try very hard to understand what Barth means by "paradox" or "dialectics." There is a group of them for whom a reality is "dissolved" and "denied" when it is viewed as a paradox. W. Hützen thinks that in Barth the divine realities are denied "in this dialectical way"[39] or are dialectically dissolved into a "vacuum."[40] In G. F. Nagel's opinion, who would prefer to dismiss Barth's dialectical thoughts as splitting hairs,[41] the problem with the category of paradox is that "things are ripped apart" that once were bound together in an essential, inner and indissoluble unity.[42] Even for the open-minded W. Knappe, Barth's dialectics are finally nothing but a "game with ideas and concepts that are no longer tied to reality."[43] He expressed this view in a section of his book significantly titled "faith or dialectics?"[44] In contrast to this position, we must again be reminded that to state that a fact is paradoxical and can be understood dialectically does not deny this fact but only makes a statement about the *way* it is given: it is not given directly, not visibly, it is not controllable, it is

---

[35]Ibid., p. 98.
[36]Ibid., p. 96.
[37]Ibid., p. 398.
[38]Ibid., p. 83.
[39]Hützen, *Biblisches Glaubensleben,* p. 17.
[40]Ibid., p. 28.
[41]Nagel, *K. Barth und der heilsgewisse Glaube,* p. 31. In L. Thimme's view ("Das Problem 'Karl Barth,'" pp. 94-95) "dialectic" or better "paradox" is simply a "somewhat muddled" concept, and it cannot be otherwise since he translates the concepts with the phrase "seemingly absurd" (Knappe is similar, "Karl Barth und der Pietismus," p. 44). By believing that Barth intends to assert the absurdity of faith, which is again only "apparent" for him, Barth's talk of the paradoxical character of faith could in fact seem to be a truly superfluous intellectual game.
[42]Nagel, *K. Barth und der heilsgewisse Glaube,* p. 20.
[43]Ibid., p. 45. There is also found: "Barth's dialectics" = "a theory out of touch with real life."
[44]Knappe, "Karl Barth und der Pietismus," pp. 44ff.

not given as a conceptual human possibility.[45] For another group Barth's dialectics simply seem to express no truth without asserting the opposite truth. In practice this means that he always seeks to insert a "both-and" in all his theological insights.[46] Based on dialectics understood in such terms they boldly conclude that Barth should be "more dialectic, more dialectical in the Barthian sense." Indeed, he even thinks "undialectically."[47] For in Barth "the other side" of the truth is actually lacking, which is that the reality of God is not only given indirectly but also directly, not only invisibly but also visibly, as a possession. However, this objection is based on a misunderstanding of Barth's dialectics and signifies, in Barthian terms, the nonsensical idea that according to true dialectics the reality of God is theologically expressed not only dialectically but also undialectically, not only as "miracle" and "grace" but is also given as a human possibility, something that is self-evident.

An appropriate understanding of the category of paradox in Barth by these Pietistic authors cannot even be remotely recognized. They pay dearly for this by continually taking his statements out of the context of paradox in which Barth dared to frame them and by placing them on the level of a (naive) realism where they are now not only misunderstood but often must appear absurd.[48] Here are a few examples. Barth states: "By being born again by his Holy Spirit, we can only recognize ourselves as we are, only as lost sinners." This sentence obviously means something different when they interpret it "realistically." Then it is given the meaning that there is a direct equation of being lost and being renewed and so it could be concluded that in Barth being renewed means "not being renewed

---

[45]A. Schlatter too apparently has trouble understanding Barth's talk of the paradox of faith when he thinks he can finish Barth off with the statement: "Paul did not jump into a void, but followed Jesus" (Karl Barth's "Epistle to the Romans," in *Furche,* 1922, p. 232). This is not an objection to Barth that can be taken seriously because in his thesis he does not even call into question that Paul "followed Jesus"; rather it seeks to understand *how* such following takes place on the part of man (as a quiet possession and self-enrichment or as a leap into the void).

[46]L. Thimme, "Das Problem 'Karl Barth,'" p. 97.

[47]Ibid., p. 98. W. Knappe, "Heilsgewissheit und Heilsunsicherheit," in *Im Kampf um die Kirche,* p. 142. Also, Bucherschau, in *Licht und Leben,* 1927, pp. 670ff, also Nachrichten, in *Licht und Leben,* 1928, p. 187. In the same vein, A. Koberele, *Rechtfertigung und Heiligung,* 3rd ed., 1930, pp. 130ff.

[48]The anonymous, typewritten argument of a Pietist in 1929 especially with Nagel's work on Barth (preserved in the Karl Barth archives in Basel) considers this work to be just as useless as dangerous because, disregarding its "dialectical structure," it transfers all of Barth's statements to the level of an "unparadoxical, simple" logic without reflection and because it is in reality fighting only "against windmills instead of against the *Epistle to the Romans* and considers the windmills to be giants" (pp. 1-2). "Barth's elements of method are very sensitive instruments of thought . . . Nagel runs over them with the fist of his thinking and smashes them to pieces."

in any way"[49] instead of being understood (as he intends) as a description of the paradoxical relationship between the renewing Spirit and the lost sinner. When Barth sees "the good works" of persons as God's justifying their sinful actions, this is again meant paradoxically. But it leads the Pietists to make the nonsensical claim that Barth teaches "sin = good works."[50] This is only possible if Barth's understanding is disregarded and it is understood on the basis of such realism. Barth occasionally says that the statement "we have the Spirit" can only be said if "we" only means "not we" and if "have" only means "not have,"[51] a statement which is meant paradoxically and which must be misunderstood if understood undialectically, meaning that in Barth's view God "has not given us his Spirit."[52] Or when Barth says that Jesus, "who can be understood only as a problem, only as a myth within historical concreteness," is "the Christ" only paradoxically,[53] the Pietists could only become incensed over this sentence. To find it objectionable they had to disregard its paradoxical meaning and insist that Barth teaches that the person of Jesus is only a myth.[54] We conclude from all this that a defect is inherent in the Pietistic understanding of Barth's negations because they largely disregard the paradoxical character of his statements.

To what extent are these negations in Barth limited by *positive* statements? These negations cannot be understood without seeing that there is also a limit to them in his thought. In a reversal of what has just been explained, we must now stress that for Barth, the paradoxical includes the following: There is a negation that "remains side by side with the position it negates";[55] "the positive relationship between God and man," "the eternal as an event," "God's righteousness breaking into history,"[56] in fact "God's most genuine immanence."[57] There is the human who is more than "flesh"[58] who is even "a possessor, one who has peace,"[59] who "is aware of his ultimate strength and comfort and pride,"[60] for whom the power of God and the resurrection are the focal point of his life.[61] Of

---

[49]Hützen, *Biblisches Glaubensleben,* pp. 18-19.
[50]Ibid., p. 26.
[51]Ro 2, pp. 256-57.
[52]Hützen, *Biblisches Glaubensleben,* p. 14.
[53]Ro 2, pp. 5-6.
[54]Nagel, *K. Barth und der heilsgewisse Glaube,* p. 38. Compare Knappe, "Karl Barth," pp. 34-35, and Thimme, "Das Problem 'Karl Barth,'" p. 97.
[55]Ro 2, p. 90.
[56]Ibid., p. 69.
[57]Ibid., p. 91.
[58]Ibid., p. 69.
[59]Ibid., p. 129.
[60]Ibid., p. 130.
[61]Ibid., p. 143.

course, in Barth all this is not directly but only paradoxically true, as an impossibility among and in contrast to all human possibilities in this world. This is the reason why in relationship to that truth they are described by negations which are now limited by a positive. And Barth goes further. To the extent that these problematic human possibilities are related to the divine, they receive a positive value. So on the one hand they are signs, witnesses, pointers; on the other hand they indicate our need to "wait" as far as the divine is concerned.

Let us ask again: Have the Pietistic authors seen and understood that Barth's negations are limited in this way? The positive things Barth wants to say and says are at least in part seen by them.[62] "Barth also speaks of rebirth, the new man, life from God and in God."[63] They notice Barth's statement "The change that has taken place in Christ Jesus . . . is yours"[64] and also his recognition "that man finds God's salvation through Christ and in Christ alone."[65] And W. Knappe believes he is correct in making this statement: "Barth is not fighting against the assurance of salvation, but only against unbiblical reasons for it."[66] And when he says: "Of course not even Barth totally succeeds in denying the condescension of God,"[67] this statement suggests to the reader that such a denial was actually his intention but still concedes that Barth does not actually speak only of God's otherworldliness. Finally, the Pietists do not overlook the fact that Barth does not simply judge all human possibilities to be "negative" but that they can be a sign that "we have understood God in his love"[68] and that in Barth there is a "life of faith lived in the hope of its being fulfilled in the age to come."[69] At least some of the Pietistic authors see the positive aspect Barth points out in spite of and in his negations.

However, it is obviously difficult for them to understand his statements as "positive"; at least they are not "positive" enough for them. For example, Barth's positive theses that there are in this eon "signs" of the kingdom of God that enable us to "hope" and "wait" for it, is not assessed by them as positive but as much too "stunted."[70] All of these statements about "salvation in Christ" and "the

---

[62]How difficult it is for the community people to see this in Barth is apparent in the fact that even Thimme, who is so open to Barth, sees him completely blinded by the "one-sidedness" of negating everything man is, can do, has and knows so that he totally lacks "the positive side of Luther" (*Kirche, Sekte und Gemeinschaftsbewegung,* 1925, pp. 72ff.).

[63]Hützen, *Biblisches Glaubensleben,* p. 8.

[64]Ibid., p. 8.

[65]Oltmann, "Die Gemeinschaftsbewegung auf der Anklagebank," p. 81.

[66]Knappe, "Heilsgewissheit," p. 141.

[67]Knappe, "Karl Barth," in *Licht und Leben,* 1927, p. 500.

[68]Hützen, *Biblisches Glaubensleben,* p. 28.

[69]Ibid., p. 31. Compare Nagel, *K. Barth und der heilsgewisse Glaube,* p. 20.

[70]Hützen, *Biblisches Glaubensleben,* p. 28; Nagel, *K. Barth und der heilsgewisse Glaube,* p. 20.

new life" would clearly be positive in their terms only if they were descriptions of an experiential reality given directly and tangibly. Because for Barth these positive things only exist paradoxically, he must deny that they are direct, undialectical givens. Because the Pietists claim these positive things are direct, undialectical givens, Barth's positive statements do not seem to them to be positive or at least not "positive enough." Instead they are basically only seen as further negations. Of course, the difficulty of communication at this point has to do with the different language used here and there, but it also has to do with differences in their basic positions. The Pietists made it their concern to come to grips with Barth's theology, but it was not enough for them to say his negations were limited by positive statements, although in any case he is not speaking "positively enough." Rather it would have been necessary to at least understand why Barth in his view could not speak more positively, why for him every "more" in positiveness had to be a "less,"[71] to understand that the actual difference was not whether such positive statement were possible but whether these positive aspects could be ascertained unparadoxically and undialectically, indeed, whether undialectically stated reality could be seen in a "completely" positive light or not. It would have been really helpful to notice that the difference was not whether there may be "positive" statements alongside these negations, but how these positive statements could be appropriately advocated. Since the discussion did not advance to this point, as far as I can see, the Pietists' understanding of Barth's concern remained too superficial.

What theological motives are defining for Barth when he formulates these negations? By asking these questions we are by no means denying that there are also motives in Barth's thought from outside theology (for example, the "crisis of culture" after the war, or how the culture was influenced by the "critique of religion" made by a Feuerbach or Overbeck). But we assume that he also had theological motives. Beginning with what we described above, we especially see three theological motives which are closely connected in his thought: an understanding of God as the free counterpart of humanity and therefore not as a "component" of human beings, which is why he denies all attempts to claim God as an element of humanity; an understanding of the justification of the sinner by grace alone in which not only something in a human but the person himself is and remains in need of justification, so that all

---

[71]Compare K. Barth, *Christliche Dogmatik im Entwurf,* 1927, p. 207: "Precisely in this way God gives himself to man directly . . . so that he is and remains himself —hidden in him and, that means, for us in hope. . . . Woe to him who precisely here . . . would perhaps not want to see the highest positive, but 'only negation.'"

"works," even persons' pious and negative "works," are ruled out; and the discovery of the "last things" not merely as the final chapter of dogmatics or salvation history but as a fundamental dimension of divine reality in its relation to human reality in which all human existence and possessions, all human action and experience are basically subject to the "not yet."

Have the Pietistic authors seen and understood that these negations of Barth are also rooted in these theological motives? By asking this question we encounter a particular shortcoming in the Pietists' effort to understand. A few authors have at least asked questions about Barth's motives in making such strong negations concerning a human possession of God. However, many more are largely content to observe the existence of the negations and ask questions about their effects (for example, do they have a "morally paralyzing" effect?). H. Oltmann asked these questions most clearly of all, with the following result. In his view, Barth criticized the human, pious "possession" of the divine because "man is robbing God of what is God's";[72] while upholding the sovereignty of God, he is at the same time concerned to uphold the truth that "grace remains grace," and in making the charge of "religious subjectivism" Barth wants us to "remember biblical Reformational objectivity on the question of Christ and his salvation."[73] Even if the motive of eschatology is overlooked, a not insignificant understanding of the reasons for Barth's negations cannot be disputed. W. Knappe sees the reason for them mainly in his recognition of God's holiness before whom unholy human beings must not insist on their faith. He also refers to Barth's theological thinking in light of the resurrection of the dead and to his view of "the absurdity of faith."[74] Of course, Knappe does not see clearly enough that Barth's concern is not to emphasize the gap between the holy God and unholy humanity in merely abstract terms but rather to stress the insight that "grace remains grace." L. Thimme focuses more on this when he sees Barth's motive for his negations in safeguarding the Reformational insight on justification by stressing human inability and by objecting to any attempt to confuse the giver with the gift.[75]

However, the other Pietistic authors have little or no appreciation for the theological motives guiding Barth in his radical negations. W. Hützen and G. Nagel, for example, think they see Barth opposing the "delusions of grandeur cultivated by an arrogant culture that has forgotten God,"[76] "the insanity of idolizing

---

[72]Oltmann, "Die Gemeinschaftsbewegung auf der Anklagebank," p. 77.
[73]Ibid., pp. 80, 85.
[74]Knappe, "Karl Barth," pp. 8ff.
[75]Hützen, *Biblisches Glaubensleben*, p. 36.
[76]Nagel, *K. Barth und der heilsgewisse Glaube*, p. 11.

the self,"[77] human "egotism"[78] and every attempt to "get to God from a human starting point"[79] when he makes his negations. Although they think he was right to negate these things, they do not think he had to carry the principle so far that all human possessing and experience are negated. But they do not ask if Barth could have serious theological reasons for so radically and fundamentally criticizing all human possibilities. They notice that in his view sin is not only something in human beings, but the person herself as a sinner is in need of justification, and they notice that Barth distinguished between God and "experience," between faith and "the life of faith." But the fact that he could have "biblical" reasons for making these distinctions is not seriously asked by most of the Pietistic authors. Barth's idea that the Christian is one who waits in this life is linked to Barth's eschatological insight, but why he advocates such a radical form of eschatology is not discussed further. Because the motives for Barth's sharp negations suggested here are overlooked or their meaning and intention is not understood, personal suspicions take the place of factual arguments. Harboring these suspicions, they try to explain why he is so one-sided in "dissolving" and "destroying" the truth that human beings can possess faith. Nagel presumes the reason for it is his inclination to play intellectual games in which he prefers to balance things "on a pinhead" instead of wanting to ground them "on the eternal rock."[80] Knappe sees the reason for it in a "rationalism scantily clad in biblical garments" that prevents him from coming to true faith.[81] Hützen sees a simple reason for it. He believes that Barth himself is not born again and "knows nothing about being equipped with the power of God."[82] "One person has experienced it, the other has not."[83] Of course, this is said "in all humility and humbleness of heart." In E. Schick's view, Barth lacks true Christian love.[84] In Henrich's view he lacks a true repentant spirit.[85] H. Dannert misses "in his life the moment that Luther had in his monastery cell in Erfurt. Only in this way can we understand why he is fighting Pietism as well as the man of piety in his teaching."[86] The discussion stops where personal suspicion takes the place of a

---

[77]Ibid., p. 16.

[78]Ibid., p. 24.

[79]Hützen, *Biblisches Glaubensleben*, p. 36.

[80]Nagel, *K. Barth und der heilsgewisse Glaube*, p. 31.

[81]Knappe, "Karl Barth," p. 49.

[82]Hützen, *Biblisches Glaubensleben*, p. 28.

[83]Ibid., p. 17.

[84]E. Schick, "Offener Brief an Herrn Prof. D. K. B.," in *Kirchlicher Anzeiger für Württemberg*, 1931, p. 8.

[85]According to *Licht und Leben*, 1928, p. 357.

[86]H. Dannert, "Die Evangelisation," in *Licht und Leben*, 1928, p. 357.

factual argument, where his criticism of the man of piety and his pious "possession" is simply seen as an expression of his own "unbelief." Since his critique is really based on theological motives, their critiques do not in the least do him justice, and in their encounter with his questions they must come away empty-handed and uninstructed. Indeed, we must wonder if the allegation that the questioner is unconverted and their claim to be converted serves the function of making themselves "unconvertible" concerning all the questions addressed to their own position, questions that could at least be reasonable.

Their Understanding of the Critique of Pietism Found in the Epistle to the Romans

The impression that the Pietistic authors had a limited understanding of Barth's concern in the second *Epistle to the Romans* is confirmed and strengthened when we specifically enquire about their understanding of Barth's *position on Pietism*. First of all, what is striking is that the Pietistic authors only briefly go into his *explicit critique* of Pietism and sometimes not at all. They prefer to quote two places in which he talks about Pietism in the *Epistle to the Romans,* two places where he takes a critical position on it. Let us first of all turn to page 84, where he distances himself from the "new Pharisaism" which wants to take hold of God's grace not by self-righteousness but by humility. But in quoting this passage the Pietistic authors do not deal with the problem of the "negative works" that Barth discusses here. Rather they view the passage as evidence for Barth's deficient understanding of "real experience" in Pietism.[87] The other frequently quoted passage is page 321, in which Barth would prefer to be with the church in hell than with the Pietists in a heaven that does not exist, a passage in which those authors completely ignore what Barth meant here (that the one who has the right to criticize the church must have his place in the church he criticizes). From this passage they turn the mere fact of his criticism into a rejection of "all Pietism."[88] Of the passages favorable to Pietism Hützen mentions those in which "Tersteegen and his followers are proven right" when they recognize that the possibility of God is hidden in crying out to God from the depths. Hützen then adds the pious wish that this possibility of God which is still hidden from Barth may one day "illuminate" and actually "revive" him. "Then he would be standing where Tersteegen stands."[89] But Hützen clearly

---

[87]Hützen, *Biblisches Glaubensleben,* pp. 6-7; Nagel, *K. Barth und der heilsgewisse Glaube,* p. 24.

[88]Nagel, *K. Barth und der heilsgewisse Glaube,* p. 12; Hützen, *Biblisches Glaubensleben,* p. 5; Knappe, "Karl Barth," p. 13.

[89]Hützen, *Biblisches Glaubensleben,* pp. 5-6.

misunderstands that passage by disregarding why Barth is talking so positively of Tersteegen or by acting as if Barth means by "the possibility of God" the life of faith as a present given. Knappe quotes the statement where true Christianity is more sympathetic to the efforts of the ascetics and Pietists than to a healthy evangelical folk piety. But he too does not explore the reasons for Barth's praise of Pietism but only notes, "On page 448 we find the first reasonably appreciative word about Pietism."[90] Moreover, this observation is not factually correct because Barth spoke appreciatively of Pietism earlier in the book.[91] It is also problematic to the extent that it falsely suggests that he spoke negatively of Pietism on the preceding 447 pages.

We conclude from all this that Barth's explicit position on Pietism in the second *Epistle to the Romans* is only partially described by the Pietistic authors. As a rule when they quote the relevant passages they do not ask about the meaning of the quotation in greater detail but generally derive from it Barth's rejection of Pietistic experiential Christianity. The crucial point in his critique of Pietism, his claim that the view of the "negative way" to salvation is characteristic of Pietism, and his critique of this view, is hardly seen at all.[92] The fact that in the second *Epistle to the Romans* he has a somewhat positive relationship to Pietism is occasionally seen, but not why he can also speak so positively about it because he learned to appreciate the "ascetic streak" found at least in the older Pietism. Finally, they overlook the fact that he would like to see a certain view of Pietism corrected, that he would like to argue for a corrective to Pietism as a whole, but that he does not want to "eliminate" it as Pietism.[93] On the contrary! Yet the Pietistic authors are largely of the opinion that the critical thrust of the second *Epistle to the Romans* is targeted at Pietism. Barth's theology is understood as "this theology that is fighting against Pietism."[94] They think he intends to brutally finish off the Pietists[95] or "strike Pietism at its roots"[96] or "reject Pietism lock, stock and barrel."[97] We see in these opinions further evidence for their misunderstanding of Barth's critique of Pietism in the *Epistle to the Romans*. The explicit Pietism passages in this book do not in any way justify this view.

The authors derive least of all from these explicit passages the idea that for

---

[90]Knappe, "Karl Barth," p. 13.

[91]For example, Ro 2, p. 281.

[92]Somewhat of a promising beginning on this can perhaps be found in Knappe, "Karl Barth," pp. 13-14.

[93]At least Knappe has not completely overlooked this; see ibid., pp. 5, 13, 59.

[94]Nagel, *K. Barth und der heilsgewisse Glaube*, p. 12.

[95]Hützen, *Biblisches Glaubensleben*, p. 35.

[96]Ibid., p. 4.

[97]A. Köberle, *Rechtfertigung und Heiligung*, p. xix.

Barth Pietism is *the* opponent and essentially *only* an opponent. Rather they derive this idea from other passages in which an *implicit* argument with Pietism is
presumed. They proceed in such a way that a number of concepts which are
seen as central concepts in Pietism, such as rebirth, sanctification, inner life, experience and assurance of salvation, are compared with the pertinent statements
in the second *Epistle to the Romans*. Since they find all kinds of things in these
statements that do not harmonize with the Pietistic understanding of these concepts, they conclude that Barth wants to "finish off Pietism." This procedure is
not impossible, and they have in fact seen many examples of where he went a
different way than the Pietists. Nevertheless, by using this procedure they could
easily miss his actual position and especially his position on Pietism. On the one
hand, there is an obvious danger, one to which many Pietists succumbed in my
opinion, of ascribing a particular meaning to Barth's statements which is completely inappropriate, by merely *assuming* a position against Pietism in a large
number of citations. Only if the Pietists are right in detecting an implicit barb
targeted at Pietism in all kinds of possible remarks can the *Epistle to the Romans*
assume the form of an anti-Pietistic polemic, can it be alleged that the actual
intention of the book is to eliminate Pietism. By viewing every critical comment
about Christian "experience" as a direct vote against Pietism, its supporters gain
the impression that they are the main victims of Barth's theology. On the other
hand, they run the risk of missing his actual view of Christian experience. What
is at issue for Barth is not a denial but a critical interpretation of "experience."
Indeed, Knappe can turn things on their head with his thesis that Barth's antip-
athy to Pietism is the father of the thought in his critical examination of those
concepts we mentioned above. In other words, he assumes that this critique
would be invalid if he only had a more accurate picture of Pietism.[98]

On the other hand, their procedure of deducing a direct argument against
Pietism from his treatment of certain concepts runs the risk of missing his actual
view in another way. It can lead to a situation where they feel they are being
addressed and attacked in such passages where he possibly did not target Pietism. And we can certainly conclude from his explicit position on Pietism that
he did not target it. Nevertheless, by seeing themselves under attack there, they
defined themselves in a particular way and took a position Barth perhaps did
not even originally see as Pietism. Yet now they shift the criticism Barth made

---

[98]W. Knappe, "Karl Barth," in *Licht und Leben,* 1927, p. 531: "Because of a fear of Pietism (!)
Barth comes to the point where he almost eliminates faith as a event in life that takes place
inwardly, as an experience." Compare a similar statement in Bucherschau, in *Licht und Leben,*
1927, p. 671.

against it to themselves after consciously placing themselves in that position. For example, when he rejected "the assurance of salvation" in terms of "more recent Protestantism" and when those authors see Pietism thereby "rejected in the harshest form,"[99] then they profess solidarity with Neo-Protestantism and declare that they want to ensure that the assurance of salvation is understood in Neo-Protestant terms. Or when Barth distanced himself from the "splendid garment of human experience" in "Neo-Protestantism" following his thesis that God is Lord even when we receive his gift, and when those authors see Pietism thereby condemned again,[100] then they do with this criticism what Barth did not at all intend in the *Epistle to the Romans*. They line up with Schleiermacher, idealism and liberalism.

However, the Pietists did not intentionally line up there. They could muster no appreciation for the thesis that there is a certain degree of affinity between Pietism and liberalism or "Neo-Protestantism" as the common denominator of both movements. However they did not explicitly encounter this thesis in the second *Epistle to the Romans,* but they did explicitly encounter it in Barth's subsequent lectures and essays.[101] Yet a crucial presupposition of this thesis is obvious here, for Barth believed he knew of a position where he neither could nor should follow either a "liberal" or a Pietistic path. The Pietistic authors clearly saw the criticism he made against "liberalism" from this position and heartily, too heartily agreed with it. "Everything that can be useful in the struggle against evolutionism's flight of fancy that idolizes humanity remains unquestioned." Liberalism in theology is meant here.[102] Of course, we wonder if they are right in thinking they agree with Barth when they distance themselves from liberalism in this way. For his critique of liberalism would only be understood if they would see the *location* where this criticism was made. It is reasonable to doubt that this was seen by the community people since the acceptance of such a lo-

---

[99]Ro 2, p. 396; Nagel, *K. Barth und der heilsgewisse Glaube,* p. 27.

[100]Barth, *Christ: Dogmatik im Entwurf,* pp. 206-7; Knappe, "Heilsgewissheit," p. 141; Nagel, *K. Barth und der heilsgewisse Glaube,* p. 26; Hützen, *Biblisches Glaubensleben,* p. 14. The reaction of Barth to the thesis that the Schleiermacherian man does not need to listen because "the Word" is superfluous where one claims direct fellowship with God inwardly, is also remarkable. Nagel expresses this opinion: "But what does this have to do with Pietism?" (*K. Barth und der heilsgewisse Glaube,* p. 33). According to Hützen this definitely has something to do with Pietism in that he see Pietism under attack in this way (*Biblisches Glaubensleben,* p. 13). And Thimme even admits self-critically that Pietism is in danger of seeing the Word of God not as foundational for Christian existence but as an additional prop for experience ("Das Problem der Kirche," in *Im Kampf um die Kirche,* p. 33).

[101]K. Barth, *Ges. Vorträge* 1, p. 197; *Ges. Vorträge* 2, pp. 100, 197, 200, 211, 350.

[102]Nagel, *K. Barth und der heilsgewisse Glaube,* p. 11; compare Hützen, *Biblisches Glaubensleben,* p. 36.

cation was problematic for them because it was the same location from which
he also addressed questions to Pietism (in *Romans* in another way). Their self-
understanding was decisively affected here. In their own eyes they are the cus-
todians of true, biblical Christianity,[103] who take God seriously and know sin and
grace. In contrast all of their critics are basically open or hidden rationalists, followers of the Enlightenment or liberals who are "dissolving" true Christianity.
Barth's theology, especially his critique of Pietism, had to seem confusing to
them, almost incomprehensible, because its claims could not be consigned to
that exclusive corner where the community people felt their opposition must be
found. Barth's critique instead emerged at the very point which Pietism had long
regarded as their own property—truly taking God seriously, focusing on the
knowledge of sin and grace. Thus Barth's theology raised for them the unsettling question whether they really stood where they thought they stood. It
would be good to consider whether Barth's theology met the requirements of
their claim.

But an understanding both of his critique of liberalism and his critique of Pietism first depends on our willingness to see from where he at least claimed to
make this criticism. It may seem understandable that the Pietist had a hard time
noticing the position from which Barth made his critique, but it is a fact. Still H.
Oltmann could ask his supporters to observe that Pietism was being challenged
by its present accusers from a point of view that was not alien to the Bible. "Our
situation is different today because it is now being contested from the vantage
point of the Bible."[104] The Pietists hardly paid attention to his request. To a great
extent they were still trying to understand Barth by interpreting him into the
only corner from which criticism of Pietism can come. Such criticism is discredited from the outset as far as they are concerned when it comes from this corner.
Then they only have to understand him as a "rationalist" whose work it is to
"destroy the positions of our faith."[105] Certainly we cannot in principle deny that
such an opinion is legitimate; however, it could only be considered to be proven
by providing explicit evidence that would show that his theology's claim had
been seen and then indicate to what extent his theology did not fulfill that claim.
As far as I can see, this has not happened. Thus we are not mistaken in attrib-
uting to the community people a deficient understanding of the position from
where Barth made his critique of Pietism.

---

[103]Compare pp. 149-50 above.
[104]H. Oltmann, "Die Gemeinschaftsbewegung auf der Anklagebank," pp. 76-77.
[105]Nagel, *K. Barth und der heilsgewisse Glaube,* p. 44., similar to Hützen. Even Knappe accuses
  Barth of rationalism ("Karl Barth," p. 49).

The Limits of the Pietists' Understanding of Barth

Looking at the Pietists' interpretation of Barth we can say in summary that it understood one particularly prominent aspect of the theology of *Epistle to the Romans* more or less profoundly (and this aspect is not felt to be prominent without reason!). But on the whole it only understood this one aspect while leaving others out of consideration (which would make this aspect truly understandable). And on the whole it only understood this aspect in a somewhat superficial way. Furthermore, looking at the Pietistic understanding especially of Barth's critique of Pietism we can say that it generally felt it was being attacked by it, above all its self-understanding as "experiential Christianity." However the actual point of Barth's critique of Pietism, "the Pharisaism of the tax collector," was not grasped at all as far as I can see. The sarcastic comment by P. Schempp on the secondary literature dealing with the *Epistle to the Romans* does not seem to be far-fetched, at least as far as the Pietistic secondary literature is concerned. "It would be a miracle if everyone could not read his own enemy into Barth."[106] In a similar way Otto Weber, who was sympathetic to the community circles at that time, remarked, "With regard to Barth these circles often said 'No' and discovered 'differences' before they listened to what was being said to us."[107] Still, Otto Weber was one voice in these circles, the voice of a maverick, who critically discussed the Pietistic literature on Barth, especially the work on Barth by G. F. Nagel. He made the "demand" that when we intend to criticize a thinker, "we must first faithfully reproduce his teaching."[108] If we measure the secondary literature by this demand, then a good portion of it could be disqualified as "spiritual junk," representing "amateurish thinking" and working with a "caricature" of Barth's theology.[109] We can assume from the outset that the arguments the Pietists presented against the "Barth" they saw and fashioned would have little immediate persuasiveness for Barth based on the way the Pietistic authors understood him and did not understand him. In the following section we will speak of the Pietists' argumentation against the author of the *Epistle to the Romans*.

---

[106]P. Schempp, "Randglossen zum Barthianismus," in *ZdZ,* 1928, p. 531.Compare p. 530: "Barth and the Barthian literature are mutually exclusive, though not in principle. . . . This statement is . . . merely a statement of experience."

[107]Weber, on Karl Barth's "Dogmatics," in *RKZ,* 1928, p. 349.

[108]Ibid., p. 16.

[109]Ibid., pp. 3, 9.

III. The Pietists' Counter-Position on the Theology of the Epistle to the Romans

1. THEIR AGREEMENT WITH BARTH'S THEOLOGY

Reasons for Their Conditional Agreement

A. Köberle thought he could say that a "lively renewal movement was growing against the anti-pietism of Barth."[1] What arguments did they have to counter Barth? What position did the Pietists take on Barth? What did they object to in his theology of the epistle to the Romans and what did they not object to? What was the position to which they were committed in relation to him? First of all, we can make a general statement. They certainly did not want to simply condemn his theology. They did not only feel as though they were being attacked and "crushed" (L. Thimme) by it. They also felt that his theology spoke to them, stimulated their thinking and even called them to repentance. There was also no shortage of voices that warned against "holding a heresy trial" against Barth and taking a position on his theology based only on a feeling of being offended and misunderstood.[2] It is obvious that this warning was necessary, but it is also obvious that this warning was expressed by representatives of these same circles. Nevertheless, as far as we can see, the position the Pietists took against Karl Barth was basically to repeat and affirm what they posited as their essential concern based on their own interpretation of themselves. On the one hand, they defended this concern as a central biblical teaching. On the other hand, by focusing on this biblical teaching, they discovered a serious deficiency in Barth's theology.

Of course this doesn't mean that they exclusively and in every respect said no to it. In fact, they not only noticed shortcomings in it but also merits to varying degrees which we will discuss in the final chapter. First of all it must be emphasized that they did not merely challenge and reject the theses of this theol-

---

[1]A. Köberle, *Rechtfertigung und Heiligung*, 3rd ed., 1930, p. 5.
[2]W. Knappe, "Karl Barth und der Pietismus," in *Licht und Leben*, 1927, pp. 535-36.

ogy but also *recognized* and *affirmed* them. Within which limits this recognition of Barth's theology took place is already indicated by the general statement we made at the outset. However much they affirmed it, the Pietists' decisive issue was not shaken by Barth; rather they reaffirmed it in reaction to him. And what they welcomed in this theology were on the whole only "pieces" they could build or believe they had already built into the position they upheld against it. And even though there were great differences among the Pietists over the degree to which they should or must make concessions to Barth, they were united in their belief that his theology lacked something important that was both taught in the Bible and held on to in Pietism.

As great as their differences among themselves were in their position on Barth, all Pietistic responses to his theses followed the same pattern. They were all in agreement that their position consisted neither in a mere yes nor in a mere no but in a yes-but. They have this in common with a large part of the secondary literature on the second *Epistle to the Romans*.[3] Even the most critical responses stressed that certain insights of Barth should remain untouched[4] and that there was much they liked seeing.[5] On the other hand, even the most open-minded responses that "welcome the appearance of this school" inserted a clear "but" and pointed out the dangerous imbalance of Barth's reaction and its destructive effect on local churches.[6] It is certain that few of these responses reflected this yes-but so circumspectly as W. Knappe, who carefully listed the merits of Barth's theology and then juxtaposed them with its dangers,[7] clearly aware that "only a greater One can claim (Mt 12:30) to answer the question 'Yes or no?' 'For or against Barth'? As human beings we can only take a more cautious line of questioning I call yes-but. Therefore in this case we have to try to accept the powerful truths of his theology for ourselves . . . without espousing it, also aware of its biases, shortcomings and dangers."[8]

Where did the Pietistic side believe they could agree with the author of the *Epistle to the Romans?* Essentially in three points. (1) He correctly reemphasized God's holiness.[9] "The fact that he so forcefully stressed God's holiness was a necessary reaction to a generation that in part had forgotten the fear of God."[10]

---

[3]Compare O. Weber, "On Karl Barth's 'Dogmatics,'" *RKZ*, 1928, p. 348.
[4]G. F. Nagel, *K. Barth und der heilsgewisse Glaube*, 1929, p. 11.
[5]W. Hützen, *Biblisches Glaubensleben*, 1928, p. 36.
[6]L. Thimme, *Kirche, Sekte und Gemeinschaftsbewegung*, 1925, pp. 73, 259.
[7]Knappe, "Karl Barth," pp. 6, 27.
[8]Ibid., p. 3.
[9]H. Dannert ("Die Evangelisation," in *Licht und Leben*, 1928, p. 357) seems to doubt that Barth truly rediscovered this.
[10]Knappe, "Karl Barth," p. 483.

"Although we have many reservations toward him from the standpoint of the New Testament, with great prophetic seriousness Barth shows the generation of our day the holy God before whom all people have to sink into the dust."[11] "In his whole theology Barth shows us the burning bush, the landmark of God's holiness and we again hear the call, 'Take off your shoes . . . the place where you stand is holy ground.'"[12] In contrast to others, Knappe was prepared to see a corrective to Pietism in this insight.[13] However, he understood it like the others as "one-sided" since it needed to be augmented by an understanding of God's love. Yet bearing in mind this reservation they intended to concede to Barth that he had the "mission" of sharply "distinguishing God's holiness from the world's justice with passion and paradox."[14] "This is why we first of all like to hear about barriers that have been torn down by this theology that also fights against Pietism. We like to hear his strong and often used terms such as 'respect,' and a feeling of reverence 'toward God,' as well as man's 'distance' from him."[15]

(2) Barth is right in his criticism of "*Pharisaism.*" "With an iron broom this theology is sweeping all of man's boasting away and shows man's unholiness when human beings fend for themselves."[16] "Indeed, Barth is right when he endeavors to keep the doors closed to even the most secret self-confidence."[17] "Barth is largely right when he opposes a self-made assurance of salvation and an impudent claim of having been adopted into the family of God."[18] "We urgently need disarmament before a holy God, disarmament of a moral and also of a religious nature."[19] And certainly it was also necessary that "under Barth's blows all our imagined possessions collapsed and the bottled experience of allegedly pious souls vanished into nothing."[20] Yet even on this point approval was given to Barth only under the reservation that this insight was one-sided

---

[11]H. Oltmann, "Was fordert die neue Zeit von unserm Dienst am Evangelium?" in *Licht und Leben*, 1926, p. 409.

[12]Knappe, "Karl Barth," pp. 483-84.

[13]Ibid.

[14]Hützen, *Biblisches Glaubensleben*, p. 35.

[15]Nagel, *K. Barth und der heilsgewisse Glaube*, p. 24.

[16]Knappe, "Karl Barth," p. 470.

[17]Nagel, *K. Barth und der heilsgewisse Glaube*, p. 24.

[18]Eckardt, according to *Licht und Leben*, 1927, p. 414. One can see this sentence as an example of the insufficient way, even on the linguistic level, that Pietistic authors often took issue with Barth: The sentence says, as it is written, something that the author surely did not mean (that "a self-made assurance of salvation" and an "impudent claim to being children of God" is at least somewhat justified).

[19]Nagel, *K. Barth und der heilsgewisse Glaube*, p. 29. A. Köberle also stresses this (*Rechtfertigung und Heiligung*, p. 63).

[20]L. Thimme, "Das Problem der Kirche un die reformatorische Lösung," in *Kampf um die Kirche*, 1930, pp. 34-35.

and had to be augmented by positive statements because of its negativity.[21] Within the framework of this reservation W. Knappe was able once again to venture out the farthest and praise Barth for fighting against *all* the "high places," not only against the obvious ones of liberal self-confidence but also the "secret high places" of the converted who "gird themselves with the appearance of biblical piety."[22]

(3) Barth is right in his rejection of *liberalism.* We like to see his polemics against "all evolutionism in theology."[23] "Therefore may everything in his thinking that can be of use in our struggle against the whole idolatrous flight of fantasy known as evolutionism remain untouched by criticism, for this human idolatry is often reflected in theology."[24] In fact many claimed to see the main thrust of Barth's theology in repulsing this liberal trend. "At first his attack was targeted at liberal theology."[25] Yet at the same time its decisive merit is "that a generation that had largely sunken to the depths of the most pale liberalism once again learned to listen to God's Word."[26] However, even on this point Barth found no undivided approval, since they were determined to agree with him only on the condition that his critique had to stay focused on the battle against liberalism instead of overshooting the mark and hitting Pietism as well.[27]

An Examination of the Reasons for Pietism's Approval

At first glance the community people's approval of Barth may seem substantial. But now we must examine more closely how far their approval actually reached.

1. By praising him for his emphasis on God's holiness and the necessity of fearing God, it was already clear where their criticism of him would start. His one-sided insight must be augmented by an understanding of the much more important love of God. It cannot simply be denied that his opinion on this point is correctly reported both positively (God's holiness) as well as negatively (humankind's unholiness). And yet this report is so "one-sided" on its part that it hardly does justice to Barth's intention as such and taken by itself. It was not Barth's intention regarding the knowledge of God to stress a certain divine *attribute,* "holiness," at the expense of others.[28] If this were the case, it would be

---

[21]Ibid., p. 73.
[22]Knappe, "Karl Barth," pp. 467-68.
[23]Hützen, *Biblisches Glaubensleben,* p. 36.
[24]Nagel, *K. Barth und der heilsgewisse Glaube,* p. 11.
[25]Thimme, "Das Problem der Kirche," p. 33.
[26]Knappe, "Karl Barth," p. 483.
[27]Compare Nagel, *K. Barth und der heilsgewisse Glaube,* p. 27.
[28]Although Barth occasionally can talk in such an abbreviated fashion, as if that were his concern!

easy to agree with this understanding and then to augment it with God's love because it would otherwise be too "one-sided." The Pietists seem not to have seen Barth's typical phrase "God is God" correctly. They probably understood it as a reference to God's holiness whereas Barth did not intend to offer a definition of God which could then be completed by adding such definitions as "God is human," "God is love," etc. Rather by stressing God's holiness it was Barth's intention to assert a *hermeneutical principle* for all knowledge of God in the phrase "God is God." The sentence "God is God" thus does not at all rule out the statements "God is human, God is love etc."[29] and consequently cannot be augmented by these definitions. Rather this statement indicated in what sense these other statements may be ventured: only by remaining conscious of a dual truth. In all that he is, God *is identical* not with one of our definitions of God (and not with what we already know as "man," as "love," etc.) but only with his own self-definition. God is not the prisoner but the Lord who remains free in his self-definition. Of course this thesis could be made problematic and then be discussed. In any case, the Pietists did not do this because they did not quite see that this thesis was at stake for Barth. They were largely not clear about the purpose and magnitude of what they were praising here when they praised Barth on this point.

2. More obvious is the Pietistic misunderstanding of Barth's concern when they approved of his *critique of Pharisaism*. Did the Pietists themselves seriously believe that they concurred with his opinion on this point? When they praised him for his criticism of Pharisaism, they understood the phenomenon criticized here differently from Barth (this understanding had been in continuity with the Pietistic tradition since the eighteenth century). It was not the attitude of *pious possessing* but the attitude of a hypocritical piety, only a *putative* possessing.[30]

By agreeing with him they turned his critical statement that all possessing is "putative" into a different statement that all merely putative, only imagined possessing is inadmissible. Their intention in this process of rearranging the view of the *Epistle to the Romans* to fit their own understanding is clear. On the one hand, while they could now agree with his critical thesis (understood in this reinterpreted sense), they could also portray it as "one-sided," in need of positive augmentation. There is indeed not a putative but an actual pious possession!

---

[29]Opinions differ on the question not of *whether* "God's love can be felt" (Ro 2, p. 73) but of *how* this is to be understood.

[30]In other places they too strongly rejected Barth's critique of "pious possession"! Compare also W. Knappe's review of L. Thimme, "Kirche, Sekte und Gemeinschaftsbewegung," in *Licht und Leben,* 1927, pp. 31-32. Further compare P. le Seur's review of the *Epistle to the Romans* 2 in Hochweg (1924?), pp. 47-48.

And G. F. Nagel could boldly say from this perspective that Barth was right in criticizing Pharisaism, but he could not overcome it in contrast to Pietism. Thus he got stuck in Pharisaism himself since he eliminated this positive augmentation, that is, the divine as a "power experienced anew each day."[31] We may consider this idea and their criticism worthy of discussion, but we cannot say that the Pietistic authors had really agreed with Barth's thesis on this point and not just repeated an old Pietistic idea.

3. The problematic nature of the Pietists' agreement with Barth's theology is also evident in their overly self-confident praise of his *criticism* of *liberalism*. This praise has something of a fatal lack of self-criticism about it ("Spare our homes."). It is certainly correct that the *Epistle to the Romans* criticized liberalism. When they agreed with his criticism of this movement, they referred to the insanity of its idolatry of the self.[32] This characterization expressed what the Pietists felt in their hearts against liberalism but was less of an issue for Barth. The crucial point of his criticism of liberalism was overlooked. He did not say (as the Pietists did) that the distance between God and humankind must not be overcome *by way of* an idolatry of the self, but the reverse. The "denial of the distance" between God and humanity is idolatry of the self. His critique of Romanticism, liberalism, and rationalism involves not simply accusing them of "hubris," arrogance and idolatry of the self, but it includes his judgment of their view of the direct *immediacy* between God and man.[33] However it comes about, their attempt to take God's standpoint and want to be "something with God and do something with God,"[34] even if in the finest, most noble sense is hubris, arrogance and idolatry of the self, as is their claim that something human *in* this world would not also be *of* this world.[35] Therefore one could not really concede that this criticism of liberalism is right without at least being open to asking a critical question about the Pietists' position. By largely not being prepared to respond to it, they showed they had not at all understood *his* thesis when they agreed with Barth's opinion on this point but repeated their own criticism of this interlocutor.

The impression is not mistaken that the Pietistic authors agreed with the the-

---

[31]Nagel, *K. Barth und der heilsgewisse Glaube*, p. 25. Compare Henrichs in *Licht und Leben*, 1928, p. 357: "Repentance and humility is also fitting for the theologians of a Barthian persuasion, the repentance and humility they preach to others. If both were more abundantly present among them, then it would be impossible for them to so arrogantly and sarcastically pass judgment on what is the unmerited grace of God for us."

[32]Compare Nagel, *K. Barth und der heilsgewisse Glaube*, p. 16.

[33]Ro 2, p. 32.

[34]Ibid., p. 48.

[35]Ibid., p. 49.

ology of the second *Epistle to the Romans* only in a somewhat superficial way or only with an interpretation that recast it in a certain way. Nevertheless, we must not ignore the fact that these authors at least *intended* to say yes to Karl Barth on several important points and that they did not simply say no to him. And we will demonstrate that this approach did not remain without influence on their thinking after all. Through this dialogue they were led to make certain emphases which would perhaps not have occurred without their encounter with the theology of the *Epistle to the Romans*. But it must again be stated that there was at least a strong inclination among the community people to welcome this theology only to the extent that its theses could be seamlessly built into their already existing concepts and used for their own purposes.

The Theory That the Theology of the Epistle to the Romans Could Be Supplemented

The Pietists understood their approval of Barth only as a limited approval, and they expressed their reservations by adding a but to their yes. The opinion that led them to assert a but in relation to his theses is basically the same in all the Pietistic authors. In their view, he overlooked not only certain important aspects but the most important aspect of the biblical witness! The insights of Barth they affirmed were not wrong and not superfluous compared to this shortcoming. They perhaps even had a special claim to be heard "in a time like ours," but essentially they were more of a *propaedeutic nature*. Furthermore, they were of the opinion that by asserting the but, they could *complete* Barth's correct and promising start that they had (supposedly) affirmed. By not just saying the one thing that Barth says, but on the other hand also what the Pietists stress in their but, they are even more dialectic, whereas Barth "becomes undialectic at certain points, expressing a truth without allowing for an opposite truth."[36] Did not Barth himself characterize his theology as a "little cinnamon to go with our food"? See, our but provides the needed "food!"[37] And did he not understand himself as one who is only in a process of development? Look here at the Pietists, who have already reached the goal of this development because they also know the other side of the truth![38]

Perhaps A. Köberle followed such a yes-but pattern most insistently. He said yes to faith as hope, but also yes to faith as a present possession.[39] He said no

---

[36]L. Thimme, "Das Problem 'Karl Barth,'" in *Gnadauer Gemeinschaftsblatt*, 1929, pp. 97-98.
[37]See K. Barth, *Ges. Vorträge*, 1924, p. 100. For the opinion of Knappe on this, see "Karl Barth," p. 536.
[38]Compare Nagel, *K. Barth und der heilsgewisse Glaube*, p. 11.
[39]Köberle, *Rechtfertigung und Heiligung*, p. 292.

to Pharisaism, but also no to sinning after receiving grace.[40] He said yes to God's transcendence but also to his immanence,[41] yes to an "empty space" but also yes to its being filled with the riches of the Spirit.[42] Similar remarks can also be heard among the others. What counts is that "we hold on to what is biblical and correct in Pietism (i.e., against Barth) and then combine it with the correct, biblical teaching he has given us."[43] "We hold on to what Barth has made great for us, God's holiness." At the same time we know that Barth has not opened up all the riches of Scripture for us. Indeed, "we miss in his theology what is most important of all," the testimony of the experience of God's love.[44] On the one hand, he is right; on the other hand, he is wrong, for the "condescension of God which is the subject of the whole Bible and the incomprehensible object of worship for redeemed souls is completely ignored or denied by Barth."[45] He is "right as long as he lifts up God's glory. He is not right as long as he exaggerates this truth in a one-sided fashion and in so doing suppresses or keeps quiet about the opposite truth."[46] His knowledge is "truth" but not "the whole truth," just as he has also not "fully understood" Luther.[47] But what he especially lacks is "the innermost heart" of both the biblical, Reformational and Pietistic understanding.[48] We know "something that is greater still than Karl Barth . . . the child-like attitude of faith that marks a child of God."[49] Thus Hützen could describe the relationship between Barth's insight which is to be affirmed and the "other" insight which must be asserted against him and guarded by Pietism, by using the image of Elijah's vision at Horeb. "Barth's thought may cleanse the theological world as a thunderstorm cleanses the air," but "after the stormy wind that sweeps away all the falsely famous art in theology comes the whistling of the wind in which the Lord speaks to us today as he once did with Elijah."[50] Thus Knappe could give his companions a simple piece of advice for handling Barth:

---

[40]Ibid., p. 283. Compare also p. 184: Yes to the sole efficacy of God, but also yes to synergism.
[41]Ibid., pp. 130ff.
[42]Ibid., p. 138.
[43]Knappe, "Karl Barth," p. 536.
[44]Ibid.
[45]Ibid., p. 500.
[46]Thimme, "Das Problem 'Karl Barth,'" p. 97. H.v. Sauberzweig, *Er der Meister-wir die Brüder. Geschichte der Gnadauer Gemeinschaftsbewegung 1888–1958,* 1959, p. 292, summarizes the position of the community people on Barth in the 1920s in similar fashion: On the one hand, what is good about him and to the liking of Pietism: "the dethronement (1) of liberal theology. On the other hand, it would have meant self-abandonment if they had followed Barthian theology in its attitude toward sanctification."
[47]Thimme, "Das Problem 'Karl Barth,'" pp. 97-98.
[48]Thimme, *Kirche, Sekte,* p. 252.
[49]Thimme, "Das Problem 'Karl Barth,'" p. 99.
[50]Hützen, *Biblisches Glaubensleben,* p. 36.

"Simply leave off those parts of Barth's theology which are only burdened by resignation, skepticism and brooding and take from it what is biblical."[51]

Now we will specifically deal what they miss in this theology, what objections they raised and how they believe they could effortlessly supplement it. But first we must critically reflect on the Pietists' theory that this theology could be supplemented as such, the theory that they could take up its concerns, but had to "biblically" complete them or simply scrap certain negative statements to preserve "biblical doctrine." The theory that they could and should deal with this theology in such a way is not an originally Pietistic idea since it was, in general, a feature of the secondary literature on the *Epistle to the Romans*. In this literature the *Epistle to the Romans* was "everywhere framed in a more or less happy photo" but then was "corrected, improved or worsened."[52] We consider this theory problematic, even if it seems understandable to us since it somehow expresses the idea that the theology of the *Epistle to the Romans* is indeed in need of criticism. This is not only so for the general reason that it is not a timeless truth but a truth bound to and defined by its time, but also for the concrete reason that the thought structures with which it expresses its truth are too little formed by the biblical thought structure (as we sought to suggest in a few examples above). But that thesis fails to adequately express this well-founded discomfort because it disregards the fact that the theology of the *Epistle to the Romans* is a *whole* in its main statements, in spite of the mixture of diverse influences and elements that are found in it, even in spite of certain inconsistencies where the author ventured to make certain statements he really could not justify in the total context of his theology at that time.[53] His whole theology was certainly in need of criticism, and it was only capable of critique in that one thought through the "entire thing" in a fundamentally new way in order then to say "the same thing differently," to use Barth's words. It was only theologically meaningful to criticize this theology in such a way. It could not be done by treating it as a "half-truth" only to add to it another, "better half." Even less could one simply cut the parts weighed down "by resignation, skepticism and brooding" so that we could learn the remaining part as biblical understanding from Barth. The theology of the *Epistle to the Romans* is too much a whole for such simple additions or subtractions to be made in it. It would have to lose its face in such a proce-

---

[51]Knappe, "Karl Barth," p. 672.

[52]P. Schempp, "Randglossen zum Barthianismus," in *ZdZ*, 1928, p. 530.

[53]For example, one can think here of "strangely gnostic-like sayings" with which Barth sometimes ruins the plan for himself, which J. Fangmeier pointed out: *Erziehung in Zeugenschaft-Karl Barth und die Pädagogik*, 1964, p. 44.

dure, or to put it another way, we would lose "our face," our understanding of it. Seen in these terms, it was not "half" of the truth or a "one-sided" truth so that the critics could add to it because they believed it had a hole that could have been easily filled with what was missing. Rather it was a whole because it contained reasoned statements about those things seen as missing, statements that for their part blocked such attempts to "fill the hole."[54] It was not so easy to reduce it to an acceptable "half" by eliminating those statements that were resistant to being filled in, only to complete the acceptable "half" by drawing upon other insights. And if they believed they could "supplement" Barth's theology in such a way, they could not think that they had really understood or even partially affirmed his theology by wanting to add to it. They had little warrant to think they had actually said yes to his theology when they said yes to it while subtracting all those negative parts.

What is at stake here can be illustrated by examining this statement written by A. Köberle: "Wanting to be with God without God having spoken is just as arrogant and disobedient as denying God's presence *after* God has spoken."[55] In the first part of the statement he wanted to reiterate Barth's thesis and thought he was saying yes to it. In the second part of the statement he believed he had mentioned what was missing in it and thought he should assert a but to complete it. We consider this statement insufficient to accept Barth's concern and unsuitable for a discussion with him. For it was not merely his intention to analyze the situation apart from the fact that "God has spoken" but to really analyze it *after* God has spoken." It was not his intention to deny "God's presence" but only to deny a certain interpretation of God's presence. Our conclusion is that their yes to Barth was a yes to a Barth who was understood in an abbreviated, biased fashion, a yes with which he was not seriously understood or affirmed because an important aspect of his theology was not taken into account. The but with which they thought they could supplement Barth could not simply fill a gap that existed in his theology since it was already occupied by another idea in his theology. We do not imply that Barth meant to say the same thing the Pietists did, but that what he meant was neither properly understood with their yes nor properly criticized with their but. This is why Köberle could not complain about the "contemptuous, dismissive gesture" with which Barth re-

---

[54] The aforementioned anonymous Pietistic author rightfully stresses this in his treatise against G. F. Nagel: he and his kind see only *one* "radical" side in Barth; it would have been just as necessary to show the radicalism dialectically supplementing (these radical sides) of Barth's teaching as to show these radical sides themselves" (p. 8 of the manuscript in the Karl Barth archives in Basel).

[55] Köberle, *Rechtfertigung und Heiligung,* p. 132.

acted to his objection.[56] "He [Köberle] should not really think he has completed
the statements of dialectical theology at a point where it seems that dialectical
theology itself has not yet done so to this day."[57]

Excursus: The Pietist Understanding of Barth's Theology Since the 1930s

For a moment we will go beyond the temporal framework of our study and ask
what position the community people took on the later form of Barth's theology.
The question is interesting because in his theological concept since the 1930s,
especially in his *Church Dogmatics,* he has explicitly taken up some of the
themes the Pietists wanted to see completed in his theology of the *Epistle to the
Romans.* Now they could no longer miss a discussion of God's "condescension,"
his love and the life of the children of God because he dealt with these issues
in a weighty fashion.[58] Now he was saying yes to the condescension of God
more strongly than to the transcendence of God. Indeed, now it becomes clear
in his thinking that the "God is God" of the *Epistle to the Romans* in fact could
be understood only as a hermeneutical principal that was meant to stress God's
sovereignty in his incarnation, revelation, love and presence. Therefore the deity of God most certainly did not rule out his incarnation, and his otherworldliness did not rule out his revelation. With this definite change in his theological
thinking Barth at least generally agreed with the feeling the community people
expressed during the 1920s when they asserted their but and their thesis that
the *Epistle to the Romans* could be supplemented.

The important question for us to ask here is whether the desire of the community people during the 1920s with regard to the theology of the *Epistle to the
Romans* was fulfilled with the change we indicated in Barth's theology. The answer is by no means! Their criticism of his theology changed as well so that they
no longer had to make the charge that Barth should also speak of the love of the
living God and not only of his holiness and otherworldliness. Now the charge
they leveled against him monotonously for decades was one thesis. What Barth
says about God's revelation and grace is correct but one-sided because it only
emphasizes the "objective" aspect of faith. But this must be supplemented by
what Pietism still guards as its special insight, by solemnly considering the "sub-

---

[56]Ibid., p. xvi.

[57]K. Barth, *Zur Lehre von Heiligen Geist,* 1930, p. 80 (n. 82a).

[58]For example, I refer here to volume 1/2 with its big chapter comprising five hundred pages
on "the revelation of God" with its subtitles, "The Incarnation of the Word" and "The Outpouring of the Holy Spirit," in which the latter section deals with "the Life of the children of
God."

jective" element of faith. E. Schick said Pietism is concerned about maintaining the "biblical, organic unity of the subjective and objective aspects of the faith"[59] whereas Barth is only concerned about the latter. On the one hand, this is proper; on the other hand, in its one-sidedness it is a "crucial mistake" he made in laying the "foundation for this whole theology."[60] W. Busch said it was the incomparable merit of Karl Barth to have shown the objective nature of salvation, but this is only "a half truth," which as such would lead to the "corruption of the church" and become "opium for the sleeping conscience" if this objective salvation is not taken hold of "subjectively and very personally in a clear conversion."[61] F. Rienecker said the Bible and Pietism demand both "the gospel of objective salvation *and* the personal, subjective acceptance of salvation through repentance, conversion and faith." The latter "gets a raw deal in Professor Karl Barth's theology."[62] P. LeSeur said that he (Barth) "forcefully set objectivism over against a wrongheaded subjectivism and this was necessary. He helped many to get out of liberal subjectivism." Again, for a Pietist this was not earthshakingly new because he has always known that Barth's concern leads to dead orthodoxy if one does not take seriously what is missing there. "The objective aspect only becomes salvation for us when we appropriate it subjectively."[63]

We will make two remarks about this Pietistic position on the later form of Barth's theology. First, as far as this position as such is concerned, the situation is at first glance confusing to some degree because it is really palpable that stressing the objective side of revelation is by no means the only thing of importance in this theology. The objective and subjective implementation of revelation and the question of "divine spontaneity and human receptivity in revelation" are equally important.[64] This is so openly there for all to see that we must shake our heads and ask ourselves how the Pietists came to accuse Barth of getting stuck in an "objectivism" that is in need of being completed by subjectivism. We are warranted in doubting whether his concern is properly expressed in this way. However, it is simply not the case that the Pietists' sense of a difference between them and this theology merely rests on a misunderstanding and that in fact both were concerned about paying attention to and linking those two sides of revelation in the same sense. We could put it in slightly exaggerated terms.

---

[59] *Die Botschaft des Pietismus in den theologischen Kämpfen der Gegenwart,* 2nd ed. (1939?), pp. 45, 57.
[60] Ibid., p. 22.
[61] "Die innere Bedrohung der evangelischen Kirche," in *Licht und Leben,* 1950, pp. 132ff.
[62] "Biblische Kritik am Pietismus alter und neuer Zeit," in *Badener Konferenz,* 1952, pp. 15-16.
[63] *Aus meines Lebens Bilderbuch,* 1957, pp. 95-96.
[64] KD 1/2, pp. 1-2. In keeping with this, Barth speaks in detail about *both* sides in this book.

The community people were not totally wrong when they labeled the way in which Barth linked those two sides as "objectivism." Conversely Barth was partially right in seeing the way they wanted to link those two sides as "subjectivist."[65] It was obvious that when Barth mentioned "the objective implementation" of revelation he meant something different from what they understood by it. For him revelation was most certainly not characterized as a completed "object" now awaiting human action, but (as strange as this may sound) it is essential to revelation's objectivity that the *revealer* continues to be subject (i.e., his being Lord) who resists the transformation of its objectivity into being such an "object."[66] Moreover, for him it is characteristic of revelation understood in this way that it is not a mere possibility only turned into reality by its subjective appropriation but an authentic reality before all "subjective acceptance." It would be wrong to deduce from this that there would thus be no "subjective acceptance," "repentance, conversion and faith." However, he clearly emphasizes that the *understanding* of such subjective acceptance must be shaped by the objectivity of the revelation understood in such terms. This is why such acceptance never means that salvation is then realized. It is only an answer to the reality of salvation that reaches out to us. But when we say as the community people do that the "objective" aspect only "becomes salvation" for us by our subjective appropriation of it, a "subjectivism" does in fact exist that only seems to rely on the objectivity of revelation. On the one hand, revelation is understood here as an "object" available to human action. On the other hand, it is understood as a pure possibility in itself. A "subjectivism" exists here since the realization of salvation depends on human action and thus occurs only by a subjective act.

The second remark refers to the relationship of the Pietists' criticism of the *Church Dogmatics* to their criticism of the theology found in the *Epistle to the Romans*. The externally most conspicuous difference between both was that they have silently discontinued their objection that the *Epistle to the Romans* only knew an otherworldly God. What is most amazing about the later Pietistic critique of Barth's theology is that it did not become milder even though the desire of the community people during the 1920s was fulfilled. They had stressed that the recognition of an otherworldly, holy God must be "supplemented" by recognizing his condescension, his revelation, his love and his presence. It is actually the case that Pietism's critique of its counterpart has basically kept the identical structure. Then as now it had the form of a yes-but by conceding that this theology was right, but of course its "one-sided" understanding

---

[65]Compare ibid., pp. 275ff.
[66]Compare on this subject *Die Christliche Dogmatik im Entwurf,* 1927, pp. 95ff.

revealed a dangerous imbalance in its one-sidedness and thus was in need of being supplemented by other, actually more important and truly "biblical" insights (that have been guarded by Pietism for a long time). But if it is correct that the structure of the Pietistic critique of this theology remained the same, even their critique of the *Church Dogmatics,* this means that their later critique reveals even more how their yes-but on the *Epistle to the Romans* was meant (and this makes our look ahead at the Pietists' later critique of Barth so important in this context). It reveals that already at that time they were evidently not really concerned about emphasizing the revelation, condescension, incarnation and love of God in contrast to a "one-sided" talk of his transcendence and holiness. For as soon as Barth talked about these things, it became apparent that the but they announced to him was not yet taken into account. Not just a christocentric understanding of revelation, but also the idea of an immediate tangibility of God through subjective acts such as those they called "repentance," "conversion" and "rebirth" and the idea that the reality of faith depended on such tangibility (which will be confirmed in what follows) are the ideas they believed would "supplement" the phrase "God is God" found in the *Epistle to the Romans.* Therefore we may ask this question again. Is the whole Pietistic thesis that the *Epistle to the Romans* can be supplemented based on a deception and is it thus unworkable? Did they not in fact mean something different from the beginning, not only where they wanted to supplement it, but already where they thought they agreed with it?

2. THEIR ALTERNATIVE TO BARTH'S THEOLOGY

The Central Concept of Experience
We could summarize what the Pietists found crucially lacking in Barth, what they found that he basically denied, with the concept of *experience*. This is the truth they had to value on the basis of their understanding of Scripture. What they meant is an event in a human being where he inwardly but really participates and shares in the divine reality that is immediately present to him. W. Knappe, more cautious than most of the others, wanted to make the distinction that what counts is not "*our* experience"[67] but only an "experience granted to him by grace";[68] it is not about a "human experience" but a "divine experience effected in us human beings."[69] In a similar fashion Köberle also

---

[67]W. Knappe, "Karl Barth und der Pietismus," 1927, p. 39.
[68]Ibid., p. 43.
[69]"Heilsgewissheit und Heilsunsicherheit," in *Im Kampt um die Kirche,* p. 141.

wanted to distinguish between an "arrogant" and a "purely receptive experience," between an experience produced by oneself and one produced by God.[70] This distinction testifies to a certain difficulty which they had begun to foresee while still insisting on the necessity of "experience." It was probably caused by their encounter with Barth's theology. It also testifies to their good will in showing that the "experience" of God must be something quite special compared to what a person can otherwise experience. But this doesn't change the fact that this distinction is pretty vague, especially since the larger context does not illuminate what it is actually dealing with. What does a "divine experience" look like in contrast to a "human" one? Does the former differ from the latter merely by being receptive? But is this not by definition the characteristic of every experience? What kind of significance does this have for the experience itself when it is a "divine" one and not a "human" one? At any rate, why is there the common denominator of "experience" for both? It is clear that several Pietists have sensed a certain degree of difficulty on this point. But it is also clear that this feeling has not kept these few individuals in the least from seeing the main objection to Barth's theology here and seeing it as the main concern of the Pietists. Indeed, the suspicion cannot be dispelled that this distinction was only introduced to rescue this disputed phenomenon from criticism and defend it against its critics. Thus Knappe as well saw this concern as the crucial charge they leveled against Barth. "The most important thing we miss" in his theology is "a radiant testimony" to God's love and that "this love can be experienced by a human heart in faith,"[71] indeed must be experienced if one wants to be "saved." And so in the end his distinction amounts to what the other Pietists stressed without making such a distinction. Wherever Christian faith is lacking experience, it becomes untenable. "Biblical faith cannot be detached from the inner sphere of experience. Rather it is the most inward, the most personal and the most radical event in the human heart."[72] "It is obvious that it is of decisive significance for our life of faith whether *we* have in reality received the power of the Holy Spirit or not," but we have received it only when it is a "real experience of God's presence" for us.[73] If the presence of God, the "personal communication of God to man," the reality of the new man does not strictly, directly and undialectically have the solid form of experiences, then the "reality" of all this

---

[70]Köberle, *Rechtfertigung und Heiligung,* pp. 107-8.

[71]Knappe, "Karl Barth und der Pietismus," p. 57.

[72]Nagel, *Karl Barth und der heilsgewisse Glaube,* p. 21.

[73]Hützen, *Biblisches Glaubensleben,* p. 17.

is denied, then there is no presence of God, no personal communication of God, no new man."[74] In short, this is the central "biblical" position of the Pietists, and this is their main objection to Barth: "We are not going to change our mind that we can have God in no other way than in the experience of the pious human being."[75]

In the view of the Pietists the "experience" to which they attach such great value has an objective side to a certain extent (*what* you experience in it) and a subjective side (the fact *that* you consciously experience that What). First of all, let us consider the objective side of the experience. In all that the believer can "experience" in the opinion of the Pietists (here the "facts of salvation" have their place, what they later called the "objective" nature of salvation) it was important to them that this experience in the life of the believer results in a "having" and a "possessing." In fact, in view of Barth's criticism of the idea of "happy are those who possess" *(beati possidentes)* the Pietists committed themselves even more firmly to the truth that there is a Christian "having." So it is true: the finite has the capacity to hold the infinite *(finitum capax infiniti)*. "Barth should feel free to let the philosophers have the statement: the finite does not have the capacity to hold the infinite *(finitum non capax infiniti)*, as if the opposite statement would automatically be a biblical one! "To this day no one has ever managed to live on his hunger. We must have him [God]. Jesus says, 'I have come that they may have life, and have it to the full.' There is no mention of a problem here. Rather there is a blessed possession."[76] Again, Barth is "not dialectical enough." The true dialectic upholds "the capacity of the finite to receive the infinite."[77] This is true not only in view of the revelation in Jesus Christ but understood and asserted in view of the "finite." So they objected to Barth's understanding of faith as a "hollow space." This is an "emptying of the concept of faith."[78] In saying this, they did not understand Barth. For him it was not a question of "emptying" but of faith's irrevocable relatedness to the "outside of us" *(extra nos)*; however this also expresses what was at stake for the Pietists themselves. So they protested Barth's "rejection of any testimony to a living, inner,

---

[74]Ibid., pp. 12ff.

[75]Knevel's review of the *Epistle to the Romans* 2 (location unknown), 1924, p. 215. Compare also W. G. in his review of Barth's *Christliche Dogmatik im Entwurf*, in *Der Hilfsbote*, 1928, p. 168: "Barth is adverse to all experience of grace, and certainly an imaginary experience can lead to smug satisfaction and lethargy; but . . . did not Paul and Peter, the Ethiopian treasurer and others *experience* grace?"

[76]P. Kuhlmann, "Die Problematik und ihre Gefahren," in *Licht und Leben*, 1929, p. 355.

[77]W. Knappe, "Nachrichten," in *Licht und Leben*, 1928, p. 187. The same in Bücherschau, in *Licht und Leben*, 1927, p. 672. Compare A. Köberle, *Rechtfertigung und Heiligung*, pp. 130ff.

[78]Nagel, *Karl Barth und der heilsgewisse Glaube*, p. 26.

spiritual possession."[79] For "there are in fact Christians who have attained the possession of salvation through a personal experience of judgment and grace. We accept this as a fact that has been proven by history and experience. In doing so, we are clearly aware of our definite opposition to Barth."[80] L. Thimme, who said this, thought he had recognized the innermost heart of the Reformers in this idea of a Christian "having."[81] He had seen in the existence of such "possessors" the innermost, living core of the church "without which every local Christian congregation is very much up in the air."[82] "Faith" and "taking possession" are "inseparable."[83] Once again it was W. Knappe who considered such possession legitimate only when certain distinctions are made. "*We* have nothing. Christ has us, and therefore we have him. So it is true that we *have,* but we have *him,* and with him we also *have* grace, refuge, peace, happiness, etc."[84] From this vantage point Knappe was able to criticize those who anchor their possession of Christ "more in their subjective experiences than in the objective fact of redemption."[85] Nevertheless, from this perspective such a possession is not subject to criticism but anchored even more firmly. Yet if a degree of uncertainty or restraint can be noticed in Knappe on this point, the others are even more certain. If "possessing grace" as an "experience of the heart and conscience" is called into question, this "carries a question mark up to the solid rock that supports people of faith."[86] Notice that primarily faith is meant by this "possessing," not the solid rock itself, the objectivity of salvation in Christ *extra nos,* not what is true before all experience on our part and, above all, what happens to us and in us"; rather such a "possession" signifies that what God decided about us from all eternity. What Christ accomplished for us becomes a reality in us through "our historical experience."[87]

As far as the subjective side of experience is concerned, it was supremely important to the Pietists that *however* the experience of believers turns out, salvation, the reality of God, the new creation, etc., is something that the believer can *experience,* that he in fact *consciously* experiences, in such a way that on

---

[79]Ibid., p.18.

[80]L. Thimme, *Kirche, Sekte und Gemeinschaftsbewegung,* 1925, p. 253.

[81]Ibid., p. 74.

[82]Ibid., p. 253. Compare L. Thimme, "Das Problem der Kirche und die reformatorische Lösung," in *Im Kampf um die Kirche,* pp. 34-35: If "amidst all of Barth's cutting all imagined possessing collapsed. . . . Barth could not shake the fortress of *those* who spoke in view of the living Christ: In Christ we *have* redemption."

[83]"Das Problem 'Karl Barth,'" in *Gnadauer Gemeinschaftsblatt,* 1929, p. 98.

[84]Knappe, "Karl Barth," pp. 38-39.

[85]Ibid., p. 37.

[86]Nagel, *Karl Barth und der heilsgewisse Glaube,* pp. 26-27.

[87]Hützen, *Biblisches Glaubensleben,* p. 10.

the basis of this experience a *"clear assurance of salvation"* develops in him. It is striking how this concept was defended by the community people against Barth almost as if it were their last bastion. "Barth's struggle against the assurance of salvation is mainly a struggle against Pietism. For it was this movement that again brought to light the assurance of salvation, that forgotten treasure of the faith."[88] Or to put it differently, "It is probably not saying too much to claim that the theology of Karl Barth fails here because with his one-sided emphasis on the holiness of God he leads people only to despair and not to the assurance of salvation."[89] The Pietists' spiritual well-being seems to depend on a consciously experienced "assurance of salvation." "The very foundation of the whole Christian life is in jeopardy here."[90] If it is contested, "we as a people of Christian life and work must say that our solid ground is made shaky here . . . the very truth that gives our gospel ministry power and meaning is being put in jeopardy here. In the shadow of these efforts we could no longer provide pastoral care."[91] In contradiction to Barth the Pietists affirmed that a Christian must necessarily be certain of his salvation. For a true Christian is the "devout Christian who is certain of his salvation and experiences his state of peace as an inner possession."[92] "Christians must be people who by faith have gained assurance of their state of grace with God."[93] It is notable that the passage in the Romans commentary which was especially attacked in this regard was in no sense an apodictic rejection of this concern: "An assurance of salvation *without* the most exclusive double predestination, an assurance of salvation as defined by more recent Protestantism is worse than paganism!"[94] "Assurance of salvation" in itself was not being denied here at all but only a particular interpretation of it: an assurance that calmly oscillates within itself, apart from its strict, indissoluble relationship to God's free severity and kindness which is "new every morning."[95] When Nagel commented on the incriminating passage he asserted that "the validity of Jesus' and the apostles' words was being rejected in the harshest form."[96] This means that Jesus and the apos-

---

[88]Knappe, "Karl Barth," p. 36. It is worth noticing that Knappe rejects the distinction between assurance of salvation and the lack of assurance of salvation. In *Im Kampf um die Kirche,* p. 141, and in *Licht und Leben,* 1927, p. 517.

[89]H. Dannert, "Geschenkweise gerecht!" in *Licht und Leben,* 1929, p. 239.

[90]Nagel, *Karl Barth und der heilsgewisse Glaube,* p. 27.

[91]Ibid.

[92]H. Dannert, "Die Evangelisation," in *Licht und Leben,* 1928, p. 357.

[93]L. Thimme, *Kirche, Sekte,* pp. 253-54.

[94]Ro 2, 2nd ed., p. 396.

[95]Ibid.

[96]Nagel, *Karl Barth und der heilsgewisse Glaube.*

tles would have taught assurance of salvation without referring to "God's free severity and kindness" and in line with "more recent Protestantism." In short, Barth deserves "only sharp condemnation" for this statement. "Belief in the possession of salvation, the assurance of salvation, binding us all together in a community of faith, these are the essential pillars on which the community movement is based."[97]

Their Understanding of the New Birth

You may have noticed that we have not yet mentioned the concept some would expect to see mentioned first since the whole tradition of Pietism is based on it: *new birth* or *conversion*.[98] It certainly turned up in their controversy with Barth in important ways.[99] Yet it is remarkable that it did not play a dominant role in it. We surmise that the community people deliberately put it on the back burner. Putting what has been said into specific terms, it must be said that in attaching great importance to experience, they were little or not at all interested in a way of life generally attuned to intense experience as defined, for example, by Romanticism. Rather their interest in experiencing something focused especially on *one* point (and this is probably what Knappe meant by his distinction between a "human" and "divine" experience). Everything that made the concept of experience important to them was centered around it to a certain extent. We are referring to the point of change in which a "natural," dead human being turns into a new, spiritually alive one. In their terminology this change is his rebirth, his conversion and spiritual awakening. In F. Mund's opinion, when this change takes place, he experiences a "divine" awakening from the "natural man's sleep of death and his habitual religion expressed in an external churchliness."[100] In W. Hützen's opinion an intrinsic impartation of God to human beings occurs in this change,[101] and something of God's essence is "born" in them[102]; if it were not real in them, they would remain the old human beings they were

---

[97]Pfr. Eckardt, "Gnadau," in *Licht und Leben,* 1927, p. 414.

[98]Both terms are not terminologically delineated from each other in the literature available to us as far as I see, and they are clearly used as quasi-synonyms.

[99]As an example I will refer to the outline in Knappe's objections to the theology of the *Epistle to the Romans:* (1) His insufficient stress on the love of God. (2) His problematic christology. (3) His lack of understanding for the assurance of salvation. (4) His replacement of "faith" by "dialectics." And under point (4) Knappe then specifically rejects Barth's understanding of the law, of conversion and of predestination. Therefore the problem of conversion is brought up only as a very subordinate factor (W. Knappe, "Karl Barth und der Pietismus," pp. 27ff.).

[100]Mund, "Die Gemeinschaftsbewegung eine Anklage gegen die Kirche," in *Im Kampf um die Kirche,* p. 47.

[101]W. Hützen, "Heiligung," in *RKZ,* 1928, p.10.

[102]Hützen, *Bibl. Glaubensleben,* p. 14.

before.[103] In this change they become different, receive "a new self"; "the reality of man changes."[104] *This* is the decisive experience in the life of a human being. Without a doubt we can say that this concept of experience was so important to the Pietists in their discussions with Barth because it was so vitally important to them that *this* decisive event takes place in human life. And they were in agreement that this is indeed the decisive event.[105] As Nagel said, in "repentance and rebirth" the central core of the gospel is at stake. And the community people understood a Christianity focused on this central content of the gospel as an alternative to the theology of the *Epistle to the Romans.*

But we must immediately add that their interest in "experience" not only aimed at such change in a human life, but conversely the concept of "experience" seemed to clarify what they actually understood by "rebirth." They saw and openly admitted that in his own way Barth also spoke of repentance, conversion, rebirth, renewal and turnaround.[106] And this made them aware that these terms in themselves were ambiguous. As they saw and rejected the interpretation of these terms found in Barth,[107] it had become clear to them that the Pietistic concern is not at all characterized by these terms as such, but only by a certain *interpretation* of these terms. And this is where the other term, "experience," emerged in their thinking. Only in their interpretation of "rebirth" as an *experience* did it become apparent what they actually meant by rebirth. Therefore what they found fault with in Barth was not generally that Barth failed to consider the change from the old to the new self, but more specifically that he denied this change as an experience of the individual and understood it as a promise instead of an experiential event in man. Their opinion on this view was that in this case a human being is really not converted.[108] Thus the true concern of the Pietists, as they understood themselves in comparison with the theology of the *Epistle to the Romans,* was not their insight into the necessity of a new birth, but their insistence that this new birth is "real" only when it is *experienced.* This was their concern: "In a real sense, eternal life is given to us in the rebirth," as "an experiential reality in the historical person."[109] "Through this personal ex-

---

[103]Ibid., p. 17.

[104]Compare note 34.

[105]Nagel, *Karl Barth und der heilsgewisse Glaube,* p. 28.

[106]Compare, for example, Knappe, "Karl Barth," p. 48, and W. Hützen, *Bibl. Glaubensleben,* p. 9.

[107]Compare Knappe, "Karl Barth," p. 50.

[108]Hützen, *Bibl. Glaubensleben,* pp. 8ff. Compare L. Thimme, "Die Frage der personlichen Bekehrung um die Wende des 20. Jahrhunderts," in *Rechtglaubigkeit und Frommigkeit 2,* 1938, p. 48. In Barth's view man is converted only platonice, not realiter.

[109]W. Hützen, "Heiligung," in *RKZ,* p. 10. Compare Nagel, *Karl Barth und der heilsgewisse Glaube,* p. 21: the new birth is an experience in man's heart.

perience" we gain "possession of salvation,"[110] and as a result we can and must insist on the fundamental difference between "converted" and "unconverted," "born again" and "not born again."[111]

We would like to assume that the preoccupation of the community people with the theology of the *Epistle to the Romans* led them to become so specific in expressing their concern. This would make it understandable why the idea of a change from the old to the new self which had traditionally been so important to them became somewhat less important as they came to grips with this theology. Moreover, this would justify our treatment of the term *experience* before dealing with this idea in our portrayal of Pietistic theology. The concession that the Pietists made in distancing themselves from this theology is a significant fact. Their actual concern was not "the rebirth" in itself but its interpretation as an experience. On the one hand, at least theoretically (although they opposed it), they could expect another non-Pietistic understanding of rebirth. On the other hand, they allowed themselves to be defined in their understanding of rebirth by an external, previously formulated, overarching concept that predetermines what their view will be: experience.

Excursus: The Objections of Adolf Schlatter, Karl Heim and Adolf Köberle

At this point in our study it is instructive and meaningful to compare what was most important to the community people in Barth's theology with what the representatives of academic theology whom the Pietists felt were sympathetic to their own position had to say about Barth. We will first mention the name of Adolf Köberle, but just in passing, because his objections to Barth found in his book *Justification and Sanctification,* first published in 1929, so largely coincide with the Pietistic objections we have described here. Thus we feel justified in citing his opinions in the same breath with the community people in the preceding and following discussions. Like the Pietists, he understands Barth as one who merely teaches the holiness and transcendence of God but nothing of his immanence. Like them, he believes he can and must complete Barth's theology

---

[110]Thimme, *Kirche, Sekte,* p. 253.

[111]Thimme, "Das Problem der Kirche und die reformatorische Lösung," in *Im Kampf um die Kirche,* p. 31: "The nucleus of the church is the community of saints, i.e. of . . . those who have been born again. With regard to the question of the church this is the article by which the church stands or falls *(articulus stantis et cadentis ecclesiae),* the *rocher de bronze,* from which one must not deviate or fall away if one does not want to fall into the labyrinth of bizarre ideas and philosophies. Compared to this, all attempts to abandon the fundamental difference between 'converted' and 'unconverted' . . . signify only a helpless reaction to which . . . Barth succumbs."

by speaking of God's immanence, our possession of the Spirit, the nearness of God and ethics. Like them he believes he is actually speaking *of these things* when he speaks of the believer's experiences,[112] of God who is "inward,"[113] and of our possession of faith.[114] Consequently Köberle's book met with the complete, undivided approval of the community people.[115]

The second scholar who must be mentioned in this regard is Adolf Schlatter, who paid tribute to Barth's *Epistle to the Romans* in 1922.[116] In its second part, the review contains much that the community people said in more or less the same way: "The forceful no" to all that we are is not "Paul's whole discussion on God," indeed it only reflects the "pre-Christian state of the God-consciousness."[117] Christianity is not only about waiting but about something that is given to the believer in the present;[118] a "hollow space" is not yet faith but only a place that must first be filled with faith.[119] Schlatter is neither original nor profound in these points. But the main emphasis of his arguments does not lie here but in the first part of the review where he makes the criticism that Barth in his *Epistle to the Romans* theology abstracts from the concrete situation in which Paul is speaking. He is not addressing human beings "who were each sitting in their own study in isolation from one another, preoccupied with reading," but "the congregation gathered before God in a spirit of harmony, members of the church."[120] A sign that Barth is overlooking this truth is that in his thought, "the particular contours of Israel disappear!"[121] The danger of this procedure that abstracts from the concrete situation of the congregation—this is Schlatter's most surprising objection—is that the interpreter of the Bible becomes "the expositor of his own life and the interpreter of his own heart"![122] We can recognize in this argument of Schlatter a distant echo of the Pietistic objection to Barth that the divine reality must be "experienced." In fact, Schlatter's argument is also critical of this concern. This point confirms the originality of Schlatter's theology as well as his critical freedom in relation to the theology of the Pietists. His argument also touches a sore spot in the theology of the *Epistle to the Romans*. It was per-

---

[112]Köberle, *Rechtfertigung und Heiligung*, pp. 107-8.
[113]Ibid., pp. 130ff., 137.
[114]Ibid., p. 292.
[115]See W. Knappe's review of Köberle's "Justification and Sanctification" in *Licht und Leben*, 1929, pp. 623-24.
[116]A. Schlatter, "K. Barth's Römerbrief," in *Furche*, 1922, pp. 228ff.
[117]Ibid., p. 231.
[118]Ibid., pp. 231-32.
[119]Ibid., pp. 232-33.
[120]Ibid., p. 229.
[121]Ibid., p. 230.
[122]Ibid.

haps even one of the most weighty arguments that Barth had to listen to then, and he certainly did listen to it![123]

In conclusion we refer to Karl Heim, who expressed his views on Barth's theology in 1925 in his introduction to "Faith and Life,"[124] in 1928 in his "Open Letter"[125] and in 1931 in the final chapter of "Faith and Thought,"[126] each time in the same terms. Barth responded to him three times.[127] Heim's objection to Barth emerges most clearly in his last statement, although it is also most clearly fraught with somewhat conflicting ideas. On the one hand, he makes the crucial point that Barth's theological teachings must not be completed or corrected. Rather their material content and existence had to be fully recognized and retained all the truths dialectical theology has rediscovered, including "the relativity of all human values, the boundary of death between God and his creatures, the impossibility of directly speaking about God, the incapacity of the finite to receive the infinite *(finitum non est capax infiniti)*."[128] Barth's theology must therefore not be supplemented by a doctrine of sanctification that could later heal the rupture that emerged between the Creator and the creature and that could help us to acquire a religious possession. The "alien righteousness" can "only be either fully recognized or fully rejected. The smallest plus sign that is smuggled in afterwards and is credited to our account destroys the whole structure of this basic Reformational insight."[129] Therefore Barth's critique of all "human religiosity, its own pious possession, the *habitus infuses,* which we owe to grace but which we later 'possess as a gift' is correct. Nothing can be changed or added to all these insights from Barth. There is no shortcoming in any of these theological statements as such."[130] It is amazing to what a great degree Heim moves toward Barth and seems to be in agreement with him. And it is quite obvious that Heim distances himself from the objections of the Pietists to Barth or from the position they defended against him. Nevertheless, the position that Heim holds in relation to Barth could be called the position of a Pietism that understands itself more consistently. For

---

[123]Compare Ro 2, foreword to the 3rd ed., pp. xx: "I have attentively and gratefully took notice of the reservations and concerns reported by Schlatter."

[124]Ibid., pp. 29ff.

[125]In *Furche,* 1929, pp. 28ff.

[126]Ibid., p. 407.

[127]"Offener Brief an K. Heim," from June 12, 1928, in *Furche,* 1928. Further, in the footnotes to "Der romische Katholizismus als Frage an die prot. Kirche," in *Ges. Vorträge* 2, 1928, pp. 330ff. Further, "Karl Barth an Karl Heim," in *ZdZ,* 1931, pp. 451ff.

[128]K. Heim, *Glauben und Denken,* 1931, p. 409.

[129]Ibid., p. 424.

[130]Ibid., p. 425.

the Pietists' opposing thesis is that the divine is not only transcendent but immanent to such an extent that a person actually experiences this reality in a vivid and clear way and at the same time experiences transformation into a new self through this reality. In Heim's thought this Pietistic thesis is intensified and reinterpreted into the thesis that Christian truth is disclosed only through existential involvement. Therefore his objection to Barth is not intended to be a "material" but only a "methodological" one in terms of an inquiry into whether he is clear that all of his theoretically unobjectionable sentences are a "serious danger" as mere theory, as abstraction, as general statements because as such they are nonsense. They are all only true as "existential statements, true only when the individual is personally affected by their truth."[131] This objection is meaningful. It is actually not an objection as such but the focusing of a question that "must be behind every genuinely theological statement." Barth definitely welcomed Heim's ideas expressed in these terms. But Heim means more and something different than only the focusing of such a question. This idea subtly gains a material filling in his thought by which the "truths dialectical theology has rediscovered" are actually "supplemented" as well as corrected. This is the other side of Heim's argumentation, which somewhat contradicts the first side. When Heim holds against Barth that for dogmatic reasons he wants to "forbid God from concretely speaking to me,"[132] this is no longer the focusing of that question but the direct discovery of a gap or a mistake in the material content of his theological doctrine, apart from the fact that Heim either thoroughly misunderstands him here or understands something else by the word *concrete* than he.[133] Put in different terms, by judging this teaching to be an outright prohibition of God's specific address "to me," indeed as a "safeguard" against God,[134] including what can clearly be heard in this teaching about God's concrete speech "to me," he documents that he actually intends to materially complete and correct Barth's teaching. In fact, the idea he wants to use to see this teaching materially supplemented and corrected is the idea "divine election," through which something that is relative, "something occurring in my consciousness," becomes something new and special and clearly different from

---

[131]Ibid., pp. 409-10. Therefore what Barth, for example, says about the judgment of God, is true, but true "only under *one* condition": if the statements about it are "the outcry of a human being who collapses like Christopherus."

[132]"Karl Barth an Karl Heim," in *ZdZ,* 1931, p. 452.

[133]Compare Ro 2, p. 258, the strong emphasis on the "You, existentially!" or p. 220, the description of the "imperative of sanctification" in the image of an "arrow from the other shore, . . . which has nonetheless hit us."

[134]Heim, *Glauben und Denken,* p. 423.

all else that is relative and receives the unmistakable "assurance" of being a child of God.[135] Here Heim's objection to Barth strongly approaches the Pietists' objection. It is not surprising that Barth also took it this way.[136]

In summary, looking at the support given by these theologians to the Pietists' position against the theology of the *Epistle to the Romans,* it can be said that they could definitely appeal to Köberle, only partially to Heim, but the least to Schlatter. Of course, Heim's more carefully considered position on Barth's theology compared with the Pietistic objections could be viewed as a key that unlocks the ineptly phrased but actual concern of the Pietists in asserting the importance of "experience" over against this theology. Basically only a "marginal note" on theological method would have been at issue for them: a reminder that theological truth is not a general, "abstract" truth but concrete truth that can only be heard, thought and told when one is existentially involved. It cannot be denied that this aspect *also* mattered to them when they stressed "experience." There is no need for further discussion on their right to give us such a reminder. However, it seems certain to me that giving such a reminder was not their only concern. Indeed, it looks as if by insisting on the necessity of pious experience they intended to materially supplement and correct Barth's theology even more strongly and decisively than Karl Heim. From the perspective of their main objection described above they in fact disputed certain "teachings" of Barth and replaced them by other "teachings" which we will describe in detail in the next section. When we discuss the Pietistic assertion of pious experience over against Barth in what follows, this concept is understood in terms of our aforementioned discussion. So let us now come back again to the main thing the Pietists missed and wanted to supplement in his theology!

The Problematic Nature of the Pietistic Alternative

1. First of all, let us make it clear once again—and the Pietists could have known about this, because at that time at least a portion of the relevant texts were available—that Barth originally came from a position that was incredibly sympathetic to the concern that was turned against the author of the *Epistle to the Romans* by the community people. What the Pietists meant when they stressed the necessity of "experience," "assurance of salvation," etc., against him was at one time his own concern: "Faith is an experience of God, an immediate awareness

---

[135]Ibid., pp. 417-19.
[136]Compare "Karl Barth an Karl Heim," in *ZdZ,* 1931, pp. 451-52: Heim's theology is "the newest form of . . . the humility of modern Pietism."

of the presence and effectiveness of the divine life force."[137] "In faith trans-individual life descends into the individual." Calvin was the chief witness for the young Barth as he was for the Pietists[138] in making the case for the "assurance of salvation" that flowed from this event.[139] To be sure, then he was a liberal in speech and thought, and yet the "Christ in us" that was his concern did not at all mean that he advocated the idea of a "Christ in us" who is inherent in our nature.[140] By understanding faith as being deeply moved by God, "seeing something outside ourselves," "a work of God in us,"[141] he considered the idea of grace and the rejection of synergism to be sufficiently safeguarded, just as the Pietists did.[142] To be sure, for him Christ as "the Christ who affects us" was simultaneously and essentially "Christ in us,"[143] in relation to whom the issue was "appropriate him as one's own."[144] Underlying this view is an understanding of revelation which emphatically states that "in the finite there is an eternal absolute."[145] And like the Pietists Barth referred to the Word to support his view: "In him we live and move and have our being."[146] Like them he could label this view as a "paradox."[147] Barth drew the same consequences from this as the Pietists did, as we will soon see. "Justification" and "election" become a fact in no other way than "in contemplation, in faith, in moral obedience."[148] So defined in this way there is "assurance of salvation."[149] Indeed, by virtue of this divine descent into a human being there is a new being that is "qualitatively equal to the inner life of Jesus."[150] Thus "sanctification simply becomes the content of justification."[151] So we see emerging what is also important to the Pietists as a believer's church. "The devout individuals who have become alive in their faith are the rock on which the church is built again and again."[152] It brooks no doubt that Barth himself in his early years at least in the basics said what a decade later

---

[137]K. Barth, "Der christliche Glaube und die Geschichte," in *Schweizer Theologische Zeitschrift,* 1912, p. 5.
[138]Compare Nagel, *Karl Barth und der heilsgewisse Glaube,* pp. 30-31, 44.
[139]Barth, "Der christliche Glaube und die Geschichte," pp. 57-58.
[140]Ibid., p. 55.
[141]Ibid., p. 56.
[142]Ibid., p. 63.
[143]Ibid., p. 58.
[144]Ibid., p. 62.
[145]Ibid., p. 51.
[146]Ibid., p. 50.
[147]Ibid., p. 6.
[148]Ibid., p. 53.
[149]Ibid., p. 57.
[150]Ibid., pp. 59-60.
[151]Ibid., p. 63.
[152]Ibid., p. 66.

was claimed as the Pietists' concern over against his *Epistle to the Romans*. Unfortunately, the Pietistic authors did not see this parallel. They probably would have been more cautious in their opinion that they were advancing an argument that he was rash not to consider, so that the theology of the *Epistle to the Romans* could thus simply be supplemented or even overcome by using this argument. But even without a knowledge of Barth's origin they could have and should have gone to work more cautiously. Before raising their objection they could have been more thorough by asking themselves what compelling reasons he may have had to be critical on this point, a point on which they were not critical.

2. A more careful analysis of Barth's remarks in the *Epistle to the Romans* should have preceded their attempt to raise an objection to the theology of that book. Here the demonstrable superficiality of the Pietists' Barth interpretation took its revenge. What was overlooked by the Pietistic authors, and this made their argumentation "crooked" at the outset, is that the phenomenon of "experience" in the *Epistle to the Romans* was by no means denied, as they alleged. On the contrary, they could for example, see the whole interpretation of Romans 7 as an explicit discussion of just this phenomenon. He really did see that "grace is not grace without an *experience* of grace."[153] It was not Barth's intention to dispute but to *interpret* this phenomenon. Surely, it was a *critical* interpretation, but again, "critique" did not mean a denial but a critical, dialectical, illumination of the phenomenon. It meant inquiring about what role the phenomenon of "experience" may play in the Christian life. By almost totally overlooking this, by understanding Barth's criticism as a denial of the phenomenon, the Pietists' objection operated on a different, "deeper" level than Barth's discussion. He asked *how* the "experience" of the Christian is to be understood and what role it should play in our theological thinking. And their counter-position was to affirm that there *is* "experience," assurance of salvation, etc.! Their argument was the answer to a question he did not ask or the wrong answer to the problem that was on his mind, falling under the level of the question asked by him. They claimed against him what he had not disputed at all. And by claiming it, they should not have thought they had overcome him or corrected him. Their objection could only have been meaningful if they had meant that "experience" had to play a different role than he thought. Of course, this was in fact part of what they meant when they raised their objection. They clearly believed that once the legitimacy of the "assurance of salvation" and pious "experience" is affirmed, the question of what meaning and value these phenomena should have is already decided on the terms of their position. Clearly, their position on Barth

---

[153]Ro 2, p. 218.

was neither refined enough nor well founded.

3. When the Pietists posited the phenomenon of "experience" to oppose his theology, they were not willing or able to reflect critically on their own position. This is the point where their position and the position of the young Barth differ. Why did *this* phenomenon appear to them to be the central concern of the Bible, and why then was it claimed to be the solid rock that had to be unconditionally defended? The young Barth saw that the decisive reason for necessarily associating faith so closely with the phenomenon of "experience" was the fact of *modern thought* as defined by relativism and autonomy. However, the Pietists did not see in the least, let alone admit, that their insistence on this phenomenon could have had anything to do with the fact that it was determined by modern thought. Rather for them it was the most obvious thing in the world to pass off this idea "of the inner life as the personal experience of the living God" as a "clearly expressed biblical doctrine."[154] It is remarkable that they were not taken aback when they could not prove at all that the decisive concepts of their "biblical" concern are found in the Bible, not just the linguistic terms but the central biblical concepts! At any rate, they failed to provide the evidence. They evidently derived the necessity of these concepts from their inability to explain the biblical references to the working of the Holy Spirit in any other way than that the Bible was talking about the human experience of God's reality and the new man. But again it is strange that they did not all reflect self-critically that they had *interpreted* this biblical language in a particular way and perhaps even falsely attributed a meaning to it that was not there! And it is strange that they did not reflect on or at least did not furnish any evidence why this biblical language must *necessarily* be interpreted along these lines! They should have noticed that they were acknowledging the right to ask a thoroughly modern question when they insisted on pious "experience": Is Christian truth *real?* Although their theology was biblically based, they gave an answer to this question that was also determined by modern thought: It is real because *"I"* have *experienced* it!155 Then they should have noticed that their interest in this matter was not so *automatically* biblical as they simply assumed. Their emphasis on "experience" in comparison with Barth's theology was an unthinking enterprise to the extent that they did not make this state of affairs clear to themselves.

154Compare Hützen, "Heiligung," p. 5.

155It is possible that the Pietists of the eighteenth century more strongly knew about the historical conditionality of their concern. At any rate, one gets this impression when one, for example, sees how the theorist of Halle's Pietism, J. Lange, in his *"Medicina mentis"* (1708) could agree with Cartsius and could relate its method of gaining assurance with the "penitential struggle" of Halle (compare p. 395, for example).

4. It cannot be denied that in his own way Barth himself was also a theologian determined by modern thought in his critical position on the phenomenon of "experience" found in his *Epistle to the Romans*. For the discovery of the modern critique of religion was also one of the reasons for his critique of religion and especially for the fact that the evidential value of experience to counter doubts about the truth and reality of the divine world had become dubious to him. It was, for example, Ludwig Feuerbach who taught him that an understanding of faith as "experience" was unsuitable to refute the suspicion that such experience is an illusion, that a person could only be dealing with himself when his consciousness is expanded, deepened and transformed by such experience. "How completely the bravest leaps and the boldest bridge-building activities of so-called 'piety' occur within the sphere of this world, and have in themselves nothing whatever to do with the incomprehensible and unexperienced but living God . . . the objection Feuerbach brought against all religion is justified."[156] We can also question whether Barth adequately tackled the problem of the illusory nature of religious experience with *his* solution. In any case, it is evident that the Pietistic authors did not make the slightest attempt to come to grips with the accusation that they could not escape this suspicion of illusion by pointing to certain "experiences" that prove the reality of the divine. The logic, "it is not an illusion because I experienced it," does not have evidential value. And all the distinctions Pietists made between a "putative" and "genuine" experience, "a human" and "divine" experience, an "arrogant" and "receptive" experience were incapable of making this logic more compelling. The fact that "I have experienced this" was not under dispute, but the actual question was what this could actually *prove* in matters of faith. This question was not answered by repeating this sentence.

5. But now it must also be said that Barth thought he had yielded to the modern critique of religion only to the extent that he believed its critique was in harmony with "biblical" insights, especially with the "critique of religion" found there. This was one of the reasons, at last this was what he claimed, why he critically examined pious "experience" and no longer treated it with the dignity he once attributed to it. He asked the question whether the individual who "experiences" the reality of God has had experiences of the life to come that are any different from enhanced experiences of life in this world, and thus only in-

---

[156]Ro 2, p. 300. Must one also not question the Pietists in this way: Do you not notice that not only can all experience be an illusion, but also that you practically portray salvation in Christ (apart from your experience) as uncertain, as unreal, thus precisely as an illusion by asserting that salvation is realized only in experience?

authentic immanent experiences.[157] The prophetic critique of idolatry and the prohibition of images made this question a real issue for him. From this perspective he corrected the thesis of the modern critique of religion with his theological insight that we dare not have the desire to furnish any proof on the issue of knowing God because a God that could be *proven* would no longer be *God*. But it was also his understanding of grace that drove him to critique the pious experience. Questions arose in his mind as he reflected on this issue. If we identify faith with certain pious experiences as defined by the Pietists, don't we cease to "wait upon divine justification"?[158] Doesn't this mean that we are no longer saved "by grace alone" but by something that is in the hands of man?[159] Doesn't this mean that we no longer live by faith alone, which does not yet live by sight, but also by "works and thus by what we can see"?[160] Therefore doesn't this also mean that "we ourselves can forgive our sins under the authority of our own personal experience"?[161] Doesn't this mean that a pharisaic spirit is brought into Christianity, a spirit in which faith basically evades the necessity of being "confronted with pagans and tax collectors who are justified in God's sight"?[162] Is this not a spirit in which certain pious people contrast favorably to others by something given in themselves?[163] Thus Barth made the logical application of the insight that justification is not by works but by grace alone, when he critically examined pious experience and distanced himself from a particular meaning they wanted to ascribe to such experience. It is an open question whether he applied this insight properly and consistently. But the Pietists could not merely refute him by referring to their opposing argument that there are experiences of grace, we have experienced it, etc. They can only refute him by demonstrating how he failed to properly and consistently apply this insight or by demonstrating in what sense language about pious experience is *possible* that does not contradict the insight that the sinners' justification is by grace alone and faith alone, and in what sense speaking about pious experience is *necessary* on the basis of this insight. Here too we see a shortcoming of the Pietistic alternative because they did not demonstrate the validity of their position.

6. Of course, we must see that by insisting on the importance of Christian experience the Pietists have called attention to a definite problem that at least in

---

[157]Ibid., p. 82. Compare p. 222.

[158]Ibid., p. 82.

[159]Ibid., p. 83.

[160]Ibid., p. 352.

[161]Ibid., p. 101.

[162]Ibid., p. 352.

[163]As far as I can see, the fact that Barth based his critique of experiential Christianity on the idea of "grace" was not perceived by the Pietistic authors.

the *Epistle to the Romans* clearly stays in the background. This fact makes their opinion on the problem appear relatively understandable, that they believe they can and must supplement and correct this theology on this point. We are referring to the problem of *mediating* the divine to man. By believing that the divine is mediated to us "by our historical experience,"[164] they have reminded us that a problem exists here that we have to take seriously. "The finite is not capable of holding the infinite" *(finitum non capax infiniti)*—Barth indeed said this in his attack on experiential Christianity.[165] Although this statement may have its place in challenging the assumption that there is a universally existing "capacity" of the finite to hold the infinite, it runs the risk of not seeing that problem with the care it deserves and of paying too little attention to the events in which the "mediation" of the divine to human beings actually occurs, in which there is a specific "capacity of the finite to hold the infinite" *(finitum capax infiniti):* the incarnation and the testimony of the Holy Spirit. The question is only whether the weak point in this theology can be adequately overcome by focusing on pious experience as the Pietists maintain. Instead, would not the Reformers' solution of correlating the word in relation to the promise of faith be the more biblically appropriate way to resolve it? And was not the *Epistle to the Romans* at least more open to an expansion and correction in this direction than the Pietists' experiential Christianity which confidently assumes that a universal human capacity *(capax)* can be simply and directly deduced "from Christ" and "the Holy Spirit"?[166] Don't we close our mind to an understanding of the "capability of the finite to hold the infinite" *(finitum capax infiniti)* in *Christ* and in the Spirit when we assume that at least in certain people the "non-capax" is simply and undialectically suspended? Indeed, the question is whether it was not more promising to temporarily say too little than to be rash in saying too much. Would it not be wiser to temporarily accept this weakness in order to reach an adequate understanding

---

[164]See note 21 above.

[165]Ro 2, p. 193. It seems to be that this sentence, though, is not typical of the *Epistle to the Romans theology,* but that it should and could read in its own dialectics: Finitum *non* capax infiniti; only in this way is the finitum *capax* infiniti by being its *non* capax!

[166]It took its toll here too that the Pietists largely overlooked the fact that Barth talked not only about God's transcendence but also about his immanence. If they had seen it, they could not have taken their opinion for granted: if only the immanence of God is asserted, then the rightness of their experiential Christianity is already proven. But Barth thought that precisely the *immanent,* the "God with us," is the *hidden* God who remains free. Strictly understood this must mean that the non capax is not just limited but simultaneously affirmed and truly put into effect by the incarnation and the testimony of the Holy Spirit so that precisely the "capax infiniti is and remains *simultaneously* incapax." In this insight laid out in the *Epistle to the Romans* we see an open door to the Reformational understanding of how the divine reality is mediated to man in the correlation of promise/word and faith.

of how the divine is mediated to humanity based on an adequate understanding of the "non capax infiniti" than to be satisfied with a problematic solution on this point? Whether pious experience can have the capacity and purpose of serving as a channel of mediation between God and humankind could in fact appear problematic in light of the arguments we previously discussed. We may say that by insisting on the phenomenon of experience, the Pietists pointed out an open question, even an unsolved problem in the *Epistle to the Romans* without solving it themselves with their opposing thesis.

3. DOGMATIC OBJECTIONS TO BARTH'S THEOLOGY

"Doctrine" in Pietism
The Pietistic emphasis on experience, in contrast to Barth's "doctrine," can be clearly understood as an application of an old Pietistic phrase: not merely doctrine, but also life! In the course of its history, Pietism has demonstrated a certain degree of mobility in understanding this phrase. It could at times almost understand it in a disjunctive sense. Then "orthodoxy" appeared to be its decisive opponent in battle. What counts is not doctrine, but "life," not intellectual knowledge but "heartfelt faith."[167] But it could also understand the phrase in a comprehensive sense. Then rationalism became its decisive opponent (occasionally to such a great extent that it thought it could agree to an alliance with orthodoxy). What counts is both "right doctrine" and true "life." Indeed, Pietism could be the advocate of a proper linkage between both, between the "objective" and "subjective" aspect of faith.[168] Among the Pietists there have been mainly advocates of a mediating position between both extremes. They are not indifferent to the question of right doctrine, but what is ultimately crucial is not what you believe, but that you live what you believe.[169] Clearly the yes-but that the Pietists asserted against Barth represents a variation of that phrase "not

---

[167]One can say in an abbreviated form: this view can primarily be found in the early Pietism of the eighteenth century, especially in spiritualistic Pietism. *Pars pro toto:* There is really salvation for man only when the "head is brought into the heart" (Ph. J. Spener, *Theologische Bedenken* 2, p. 383).

[168]One can say in an abbreviated form: this view can primarily be found in the more recent community movement. *Pars pro toto:* Pietism's concern is the "genuine biblical unity of the subjective and objective" (E. Schick, *Die Botschaft des Pietismus in den theologischen Kämpfen der Gegenwart*, p. 45).

[169]We may say, "not doctrine, but life." Not this formula as such is characteristic of Pietism, but its more detailed *interpretation*. On the other hand, one can get straight in one's own mind the fact that Pietism is a diffuse phenomenon that cannot be easily reduced to a common denominator by seeing that this formula has been interpreted in *different* ways in Pietism.

merely doctrine, but also life." To be sure, on the one hand Barth might be right about this or that doctrine (for example, the holiness of God), but on the other hand it would be necessary that doctrine leads us to a certain kind of life. Or they might prefer to say that doctrine leads us to a certain kind of "experience" (this exhibits something of a change in their thinking compared to baroque Pietism). And as we will still see, this objection to Barth was also articulated in different interpretations in which some of these various possibilities for interpreting this phrase were reflected.

In this phrase the first phenomenon called "life" does not seem to touch the other phenomenon called "doctrine." Their interest in the first phenomenon apparently does not make an issue of doctrinally supplementing or even correcting the second phenomenon. Their concern is, however, to supplement their doctrine to the extent that they want to indicate the medium in which their teaching is real or is put into practice. We think, though, that looks are deceiving. Rather we believe that this formula, with the alternative it assumes, represents a certain "doctrine," a specific dogmatic thesis, as Martin Schmidt in particular never tires of stressing in our day.[170] It is a "dogmatic" thesis that true doctrine is dead, unfruitful doctrine without the dimension the Pietists call "life." Thus it is in need of being supplemented by this second dimension. And it is a dogmatic thesis that only through this dimension the Pietists call "life" is faith real or can be put into practice. Such "life" actually has the power to give reality to faith.[171] The thesis they advocated against Barth is that it is not enough to say that God is God and that he is holy but that his reality must also be "experienced." We think that especially this thesis is not merely a practical application or supplement of his doctrine of God but is itself of a dogmatic nature and as a whole implies a doctrine of God that is different from the one found in the *Epistle to the Romans*. We see evidence for our opinion in the fact that the Pietists did not actually limit themselves to this statement that what was taught must also be "experienced" and lived. Rather on a number of issues they taught different things from Barth. These other doctrines they espoused against him and to which they expressly committed themselves flowed logically, as we see it, from the fact that in contrast to Barth they were mainly concerned to assert that the reality of God can be expe-

---

[170]Compare, for example, Martin Schmidt, "Spener und Luther," in *Luther-Jahrbuch*, 1957, pp. 109-10.

[171]What the Pietists say about "doctrine" they can also say about "faith": it is dead and unfruitful without such "life." The first person who saw the problematic nature of the assumption that there is a "dead" Christian doctrine as such or a "dead" faith as such was Count Zinzendorf. In his view the Pietists should have shifted to "doctrine": the people "believed enough, only now they should learn" (compare S. Eberhard, *Kreuzes-theologie*, 1937, pp. 130-31). And in his view this teaching is the beginning of the corruption of Christianity.

rienced in the specific terms described above. This concern found its expression in the articulation and formation of their theological doctrines to such a degree that as a result they taught a theology that differed from Barth on important points. We will point out several of these significant points in what follows.

The Question of Humanity's Capacity for Revelation

First of all, we will discuss the question of *humankind's capacity* to become the recipient of the divine truth and revelation. Both Barth as well as his Pietistic opponents were in agreement that this capacity is problematic because of human *"sin."* But they clearly diverged in their judgment of the *extent* to which our human capacity has become problematic because of sin. According to G. F. Nagel, their difference of opinion on this point can be portrayed in this way: In Barth (the crucial quotation Nagel refers to comes from Thurneysen)[172] humankind is seen to be under sin to such a great extent that not only something in the person and her ego must be overcome but the person herself, her ego itself, must be overcome. But this makes too much of the evil in human beings. For the Pietists this idea is unacceptable because in this view sin is no longer "guilt caused by personal transgression" but a "natural condition" that is identical with "human existence itself," thus making God's "incarnation" no longer appear "possible."[173] It is curious that Nagel referred to Oepke in rejecting this view and the Pietist accused Barth of being captive to mystical thoughts![174] How strange it is to think that Barth's criticism of the assumption that humanity has the capacity to be receptive to God could only be explained by Barth's dependence on a "mysticism that answers in the negative"! How strange it is to think that the self-renunciation of mysticism from which Barth repeatedly distances himself in the *Epistle to the Romans* (as Nagel seems to have overlooked) could actually amount to declaring humanity once again capable of becoming the recipient of revelation! (This is the opinion of the *Epistle to the Romans*.) In contrast to Barth, in the opinion of the Pietists the rule of sin extends only so far that not the self, but only all the "arrogance"[175] and "idolatry of the self"[176] must be overcome. In

---

[172]G. F. Nagel, *Karl Barth und der heilsgewisse Glaube*, 1929, p. 13. The quotation is found in K. Barth/E. Thurneysen, *Komm Schöpfer Geist!* 1924, p. 117. The authorship of Thurneysen is not indicated there, which is why Nagel could believe in good faith that he was quoting Barth. But it is important to remind ourselves that this quotation did not stem from Barth since we can see more clearly today that Barth and Thurneysen even then did not simply say the same thing.

[173]Nagel, *Karl Barth und der heilsgewisse Glaube*, pp. 15, 17.

[174]Ibid., p. 15.

[175]Ibid., p. 14.

[176]Ibid., p. 12.

W. Hützen's opinion, the "body of death" Paul speaks of is "not the totality of his 'I am,' as Barth says."[177]

It seems as if the fight between Flacius and Strigel was being repeated in this difference of opinion between Barth and the Pietists. It is true, we have already noted, that Barth (and to this extent he followed in the footsteps of Flacius) occasionally flirted with the idea of equating our existence as human beings with our existence as sinners. Of course Nagel derived his charge from the section in the *Epistle to the Romans* where Barth stated that sin is a "natural condition."[178] He was clearly attempting to go beyond Strigel and Flacius by wanting to understand actual sin neither as an "event" nor as a "condition" of humanity but as the presupposition which underlies every human event and conditions every human status.[179] Therefore sin is neither merely the accidental individual sin we could possibly stop doing, nor something that necessarily follows from being human because of the sinful state that is inherent in him, but at its root it is "the condition of the possibility" of sinning. When Barth stressed the fact that humankind is radically controlled by sin, he did this with the intention of rejecting any human capacity for God. He did it because he wanted to rule out the necessity of a point of contact for revelation that is already found in persons without it. He also wanted to rule out the assumption that there is continuity between the "old" and the "new" self that would legitimize the idea that we are entitled to grace. When Barth in this context picked up the not unproblematic idea of "the finite not being capable of holding the infinite" *(finitum non capax infiniti)*, he did it only because he expressly understood by "finitum" humankind outside of grace.[180]

Although Nagel probably did not understand Barth's doctrine of sin correctly, he was nevertheless not of one mind with him. On the key point that really counted, he was clearly of a different view from Barth. It was his conscious intention to maintain a continuity between the old and new self. It was important to him to see the "collapse of egocentricity,"[181] but not of the "self" because this self is clearly to be "rescued," unchallenged by God's judgment, as a point of reference and vessel for the reception of grace. Thus the equation of grace with the experience of grace is to be guaranteed. Therefore it is only logical that for him as well as for the other Pietists the finite is indeed capable of holding the

---

[177]W. Hützen, *Biblisches Glaubensleben*, 1928, p. 16.
[178]Nagel, *Karl Barth und der heilsgewisse Glaube*, p. 14.
[179]Ro 2, p. 151.
[180]Ibid., p. 193.
[181]Nagel, *Karl Barth und der heilsgewisse Glaube*, p. 24.

infinite.[182] Their statement that the incarnation is possible was not deduced from the historical reality of the incarnation but from the fact that the contrast between deity and humanity is by no means a "natural" one.[183] Thus humanity does indeed possess a suitability for God. Because sin is essentially individual sin and because the root that preconditions it is lacking, a person is not so controlled by it that he has to go before the judgment seat of God, as Barth thought he had to say. At least he is left with the negative ability to escape this judgment by repentance, which was consciously understood as a "judgment on oneself" and thus to open himself to grace on his part.[184] Indeed, for that reason a universal human "ability to covenant with God" could be affirmed against Barth.[185] However one evaluates it, it is obvious that while insisting on the necessity of repentance and grace and surely doing so in a sublime form the Pietists committed themselves to a bit of "natural theology" in contradistinction to Barth. Although they could talk persuasively about the Holy Spirit and especially about the effects of his working that they themselves had experienced, he apparently did not have the significance of being the event of "man's capacity for God" and thus strictly speaking, also not the negative significance of ruling out every other human capacity for God ("I believe that I can *not* with my own reason and strength"). Although they also spoke so persuasively about grace, they could basically no longer understand it as free grace because they counted on grace's dependence on something other than grace already given in man, and thus on a certain claim to it.

Their Understanding of Grace

The crucial difference between Barth's doctrine and the Pietists is found precisely in their different understanding of God's *grace*. Of course, the fact that the Pietists wanted to see his key insight only in his emphasis on God's holiness (which they considered to be correct but one-sided) has an adverse effect here. From that perspective they had trouble even seeing his doctrine of grace, let alone its not insignificant function in the whole of this theology. Because of what they understood grace to be, it could only remain mysterious to them that what he understood by the term was actually "grace"! "The God who talks to us in this theology is the God of Sinai, the God of Moses, but not the Father of our

---

[182]Ibid., p. 18. Hützen, *Biblisches Glaubensleben,* p. 9; Knappe, "Karl Barth und der Pietismus," p. 29.

[183]Nagel, *Karl Barth und der heilsgewisse Glaube,* p. 17.

[184]Ibid., p. 23. Repentence is considered to be a "way" to faith that *precedes* the reception of grace and therefore can be mastered with the natural capabilities of man (also pp. 8, 21, 23).

[185]Ibid., p. 29.

Lord Jesus Christ."[186] We cannot only see the Pietist reviewer's lack of understanding of Barth's doctrine of grace in such an opinion but also a certain, not
unfounded intuition of a shortcoming in this doctrine of grace which they could
at first express only in emotional terms. If he is really concerned about grace,
why doesn't he talk more graciously about it?[187] Their impression is not far-
fetched. The problem with Barth's doctrine of grace was not found where Pietistic critics and others at that time thought. For them Barth's God was simply
otherworldly, distant, only holy and for that reason not present, not kind or gracious, but this objection is discredited by many explicit references in the *Epistle
to the Romans*. However, the problem with his doctrine of grace actually found
in his theology is that the concept of "grace" moves into such close proximity
to the general "principle" of its unavailability that the biblical idea of freedom
"for . . ." became less important for him in the interest of stressing the undeserved nature of grace.

We can gather from the Pietists' objection to this doctrine of grace more that
it is in need of correction, but less that it is in need of correction in *this* sense.
For they wanted to see it corrected in another sense so that the rightness of this
doctrine of grace, its stress on the radical undeserved nature of divine grace,
was no longer seen correctly. The Reformational feature of Barth's doctrine of
grace was the discovery that God's grace is not an alternative to his judgment,
but is itself God's judgment because it rules out all human claims and merit *as*
grace. Thus God's grace is at the same time *free* grace, and it is free not only
until it is bestowed on human beings but also in that it is bestowed on human
beings. "Grace is only grace when it is recognized as being incomprehensible."[188] The Pietists could also say this in their own way. Barth said it differently
and more consistently than they because for him the gift of grace is simply "incomprehensible" because there is nothing in human beings themselves that
would merit it. And there is nothing found in human beings to merit it not only
before but also *during* and *after* their reception of grace.[189] This teaching rules

---

[186]W. Knappe, "Karl Barth," in *Licht und Leben*, 1927, p. 500. Compare also L. Thimme, "Das
Problem 'Karl Barth,'" in *Gnadauer Gemeinschaftsblatt*, 1929, p. 98: for Barth "law . . . is like
grace," and that is why he has a legal understanding of grace.
[187]Compare Barth's self-criticism in "Die Menschlichkeit Gottes," 1956 (in *Theologische Studien*,
nr. 48), in which he criticizes precisely this in his earlier theology.
[188]Ro 2, p. 7.
[189]For example, compare Ro 2, p. 35: "How did *I* deserve this . . . ? Nothing, nothing at all can
be brought forward to substantiate and explain this 'I'; it hangs completely in the air, it is a
pure, absolute miracle. . . . What becomes true in man from God and only from God can
never be anything other than a new call to God, a new call to conversion, to reverence and
humility, a new summons to abandon all security and all fame. . . . Any claim, any right of
ownership that is derived from this is a misunderstanding."

out not only synergism but also the Augustinian teaching of the *gratia infusa*. Like synergism, it can basically talk about a directly observable reality of new obedience, a noticeable transformation of the sinner into a nonsinner; and an ability to desire and accomplish the good that is inherent in man. This teaching differs from synergism only by placing this (synergistic) reality under a different presupposition and attributes this new reality to a divine rather than a human influence. Synergism is given up here only to be put into effect once again, now sanctioned by God's grace. Evidently the Pietists were now inclined to understand the concept of grace precisely in terms of such a *gratia infusa*. When they wanted to correct Barth on this point, they did so precisely in these terms. Hützen expressed this difference of opinion between Barth and the Pietists in a remarkably clear way: "Grace is [in Barth] not [as in the Pietists] the power of God present in us, by which we alone are equipped to do good works, but grace in its fullness means [in Barth] that God forgives man his sin."[190] This definition is remarkable both with regard to what grace should not be "in its fullness" as well as with regard to what it positively is in the view of the Pietists. The character of grace as a gift could also be strongly emphasized in this view. "*All* that we have is *a gift of God.*"[191] But the grace meant here differs from Barth's view of the phenomenon because it is not also judgment as such and thus as grace does not permanently rule out all claims to it. Instead, judgment here has the form of "repentance and judgment of oneself" and is thus a preliminary stage of grace, a passing moment on "the way to it."[192] Since for the Pietists judgment was not a dimension of grace itself but a factor in the events preceding it, something they have put behind them in receiving grace, the Reformational understanding of the simultaneity of "sinner" *(peccator)* and "justified" *(justus)* was no longer comprehensible to them, at least not in its radicalness. Instead, the simultaneity was broken down into successive stages, with the result that the vivid distinction between believers and unbelievers they were so interested in could be made.

Barth for his part radicalized the Reformational phrase *simul justus et peccator* by logically interpreting the doctrine of predestination from this standpoint. "Damned" and "saved" were no longer understood as a divine but somehow also as a humanly ascertainable verdict on two fixed groups of human beings, but as two sides of the one divine verdict on one and the same human beings.[193]

---

[190]Hützen, *Biblisches Glaubensleben,* p. 24.
[191]Ibid., p. 29.
[192]Nagel, *Karl Barth und der heilsgewisse Glaube,* p. 23.
[193]Ro 2, pp. 308-9.

Here the Pietists objected most energetically, and they had to object because they were terribly serious about making a clear, tangible separation between believers and unbelievers.[194] Such a separation could only be made by asserting an earthly existence as *justus* that has essentially left the *peccator* existence behind. By maintaining this stance, though more or less persuasively adding that the recipient of grace was not yet completely perfect, they had to talk about a directly observable, renewing effect of grace in the most emphatic terms. By maintaining this stance, grace that merely resulted in sinful persons' grasping the forgiveness of their sins by the blood of Jesus Christ, grace that resulted in God's accepting the sinner, was by far not grace enough for them. Rather, beyond that it had to be a "blissful experience" that made real change possible and established a new way of life![195][196] Grace is "tangible power."[196] For by grace divine empowerment enters certain people. By grace a human being becomes a born-again, new man, by grace an "ethical change of course takes place at the heart of the personality,"[197] by grace a step-by-step release from poisonous, self-centered instincts is achieved and the new self "puts on the Lord Jesus Christ."[198] All of this is not as "images that would first have to be interpreted to us on the basis of philosophical assumptions," not in a dialectical sense, but in an actual sense; all of this is an "experiential reality."[199] They said in this sense Paul and Peter, the Ethiopian treasurer and others *experienced* grace.[200] Grace is "an *essential impartation* of God" to man.[201] Thus the divine descends into us in such a way that "this becomes a reality in us through our historical experience so that the line of death runs here (within this experience), separating our former life from our new life in the present."[202] It works in us a "rebirth" defined as a "change of reality that takes place in our present life,"[203] by virtue of which "*we* have really become new men and women"[204] and by virtue of which we can talk about a state of being in sin that is now in the past for certain human beings.[205]

In short, we can say that for the Pietists grace can be experienced, and they insist on this because it is understood by them to be an infused grace (*gratia*

---

[194]A. Köberle, *Rechtfertigung und Heiligung,* 3rd ed., 1930, pp. 93-94.
[195]P. Fabianke, *Was muss die Deutsche Gemeinschaftsbewegung festhalten?* 1925, p. 12.
[196]Nagel, *Karl Barth und der heilsgewisse Glaube,* p. 25.
[197]Ibid., p. 21.
[198]Ibid., p. 25.
[199]Hützen, *Biblisches Glaubensleben,* p. 6, and "Heiligung," in *RKZ,* 1928, p. 10.
[200]W. G. in *Der Hilfsbote,* 1928, issue 7, p. 168.
[201]Hützen, "Heiligung," p. 10.
[202]Hützen, *Biblisches Glaubensleben,* p. 10.
[203]Ibid., p. 11.
[204]Ibid., p. 17.
[205]Ibid., p. 20.

infusa). At once we can comprehend how they missed any mention of God's presence, love and immanence in this theology of the *Epistle to the Romans*[206] and why they could not recognize what Barth said about it as a real discussion of it. Using these concepts, they sought to understand the presence of God in terms of the *gratia infusa,* as the "eternal God's presence in historical human beings."[207] Once again, not their own power but the Holy Spirit who has made his dwelling in them and through whom they have come to share in the divine nature, produces in them and through them good works that are pleasing to God."[208] But in a situation of grace and legitimized by it, synergism had an even greater effect on the theological thinking of the Pietists.[209] In contrast to Barth, they committed themselves to a variety of the Augustinian-medieval doctrine of the *gratia infusa* in their understanding of divine grace. In so doing, the problems associated with this teaching have placed a strain on their thought.[210]

Their Doctrine of Sanctification

Furthermore, the Pietists made a conscious effort to offer an alternative to Barth's teaching on the topic of life under grace, in other words, *sanctification* or *ethics*. As the Pietistic authors saw and said themselves, the difference was that in their opinion human beings under grace have only *been* lost sinners, whereas for Barth they *are* always "lost sinners."[211] In this case as well it can be said that the Pietists' protest against Barth's view of sanctification was a legitimate concern. They remind us that "justification" and "sanctification" belong together but must be distinguished. A strong inclination to equate "justification"

---

[206]Compare W. Knappe, *Karl Barth,* 1927, p. 27. W. Hützen, *Bibl. Glaubensleben,* p. 12. L. Thimme, "Das Problem 'Karl Barth,'" p. 97. Also "Das Problem der Kirche und die reformatorische Lösung," in *Im Kampf um die Kirche,* 1930, p. 35.

[207]W. Hützen, "Heiligung," p. 10. K. Reuber, who is sympathetic to the community movement, basically says the same thing in a more refined way. Compare his remark in his book *Mystik in der Heiligungsfrömmigkeit der Gemeinschaftsbewegung,* 1938, 4: "It is an inner congeniality created by the Spirit, to which alone access is given to transcendence in immanence" ("Wort, Offenbarung und Geschichte," in *RKZ,* 1926, p. 387).

[208]Hützen, *Bibl. Glaubensleben,* p. 28.

[209]In the view of Nagel, *Karl Barth und der heilsgewisse Glaube,* p. 23, the action of the believer has "salvific value," though it is not said to be "the cause of salvation." For a similar view, see Köberle, *Rechtfertigung und Heiligung,* p. 183.

[210]In his position on Barth, O. Weber expressly declared his allegiance to the "Christianity of the community movement" at that time. But by just as expressly understanding the Christian as "a pardoned *sinner*" and rejecting the *"gratia infusa,"* in fact approving of Barth's "fight for the invisibility" of our relationship to God ("K. Barth's 'Dogmatik,'" in *RKZ,* 1928, p. 349), he practically no longer truly stood on the same ground on which the rest of the community movement stood by its own definition.

[211]Hützen, *Bibl. Glaubensleben,* p. 18.

and "sanctification" can be observed in Barth's *Epistle to the Romans*. In fact, he is inclined to merge "sanctification" into "justification."[212] Where this happens, the danger of allowing human beings to become autonomous moral agents often occurs, a danger the author of the second *Epistle to the Romans* at least saw.[213] Nevertheless, we must say that the theology of this book is weak on this point. Once again, while making an appropriate critique of this weak spot, we should guard against the danger of losing sight of the legitimate points he made about life under grace and sanctification. The second *Epistle to the Romans* simply says, "Grace is sufficient, for ethics as well!"[214] This is what is legitimate, what cannot be given up in a Protestant understanding of sanctification. Barth stressed this point and saw it in a new light. If his statement is true, then it follows that what has been said previously under the heading of "justification" may not be retracted later under the heading of "sanctification" or "ethics."[215] Then we must take a stand against "the guidelines those newly converted Christians establish who are far too eager to jump into the Christian life and shout for ethics" which basically amounts to "casting suspicion on grace," as if it made things too comfortable for sinners and as if it were a "cozy bed" for lazy people. These guidelines make an attempt to turn the pardon the person receives and the action he or she takes into two separate functions and then proceed to live the Christian life beyond grace.[216] With regard to sanctification Barth recognized how important it was in any case to never talk about "something beyond grace." Now the question is whether the Pietists broke with this important and correct aspect of the doctrine of sanctification found in the *Epistle to the Romans* because they felt it needed to be corrected. At least they appeared to understand what was at stake here: As Hützen observed, Barth wanted to understand sanctification as "sanctification of the impious," as forgiveness that is granted to us evildoers.[217] According to Hützen, he interprets the "growth of the inner man in such a peculiar way that sanctification means an increase in God's mercy."[218] His use of the adjective *peculiar* calls attention

---

[212]Compare the later implied self-criticism of Barth in KD 4/2, pp. 570-71.

[213]Compare Ro 2, p. 416, where we read, "There is no more terrible misunderstanding than to hope or fear that grace could become a bed for 'theorists' and mystics."

[214]Ibid., p. 423. Of course, justification must not be devoured by sanctification so that this grace does not turn into a manageable principle (see p. 294).

[215]Weber ("K. Barth's 'Dogmatik,'" p. 349) sought at that time to move the community movement and its concern forward in this direction: How one could do justice "to the fact of the man of action who has died to sin and who is invisible, but . . . at work in eminently practical ways" without falling back behind the knowledge of the doctrine of justification?

[216]Ro 2, p. 416.

[217]Hützen, *Bibl. Glaubensleben,* pp. 22-23.

[218]Ibid., p. 30.

to the fact that for Hützen this view was surprising and probably even bizarre.

Let us therefore ask what the Pietists wanted to understand by "sanctification"! We will especially follow W. Hützen's presentation, which was the most comprehensive one on this issue. In short, his counter-argument goes like this: There is really a life from God that turns us into actual new creations. Therefore the name "lost sinners" no longer applies to them. This life is really produced in us by the Holy Spirit in our historical life.[219] Surely Barth too knew the reality of the new man. The difference of opinion is not found there. It can definitely be found in Barth's statement that "the new man" cannot be seen but can only be believed, whereas the Pietistic side insisted that "these new creations are surely not to be found in the invisibility of heaven, but quite visibly here on earth."[220] The accusation made against Barth's concept was that in Barth's view there was practically no difference between the person outside of grace and the person inside of grace.[221] Nothing in his condition has changed. Indeed, one Pietist even thought that Barth's theology was "a protective wall . . . against a real change in man that takes place here in this life."[222] And thus it was his intention that "every ethical event" should be separated "from the concept of faith!"[223] In the end, "it leads human beings to put their hands in their lap in despair."[224] Barth knew how to talk about a "turnaround, a reversal" and thus a change in man, although not all Pietistic authors saw this.[225] He even talked about this change in such radical terms that for Knappe such talk was too radical.[226] Thus it is not correct when they allege that in his view "nothing at all" changes for man, that he is finally indifferent about whether men live under grace or not. And the allegation that "all" ethics are separated from faith can surely not be verified from the *Epistle to the Romans.*[227] However, the deep-seated difference between Barth and the Pietists on this point is, to say it again, that this turnaround and change in the person is invisible in Barth's view, "visible" only in rendering all visible givens as problematic, as an "attack" on the visible; whereas for them this turnaround and change is seen as a positive

---

[219]Ibid., p. 22.

[220]Ibid., p. 20.

[221]Ibid., p. 18. Compare also Hützen, "Heiligung," p. 9.

[222]N. N., "Kritische Ecke," in *In alle Welt. Zeitschrift für missionarische Arbeit,* 1928 (?), p. 37.

[223]Nagel, *Karl Barth und der heilsgewisse Glaube,* p. 22.

[224]P. Le Seur, "Rezension zu Barths Römerbrief," in *Hochweg,* 1924 (?), p. 48. Compare also the review of the *Epistle to the Romans,* in *Missionsblatt der Brudergemeine,* nr. 5, May, 88th year.

[225]Ro 2, p. 258.

[226]W. Knappe, "Karl Barth," p. 51.

[227]Compare, for example, Ro 2, p. 415, where Barth stresses "that grace . . . leaves us no other choice than to render obedience with our 'members.'" The whole section 410ff deals with the "problem of ethics."

given fact that is visible, experiential and directly noticeable. In confronting Barth, the Pietists did not in fact plead for the necessity of paying attention to "*sanctification*" in general terms but only for a certain *understanding* of "sanctification." What makes the discussion so difficult on this point is that of course, they thought "sanctification" was only being discussed when the discussion about it was carried on in terms of *this* particular understanding.

Now we must see *what* in their view is proven to be "real" in their "experience." It is nothing less than the existence of "really new men and women" to whom the *simul justus et peccator,* the name "lost sinner" no longer applies.[228] Great things can be said about this existence. It is "capable of doing good."[229] What it does is a work of those who "have come to share in the divine nature,"[230] in whom "the new creation has become . . . personality."[231] So what they do is "a work that does not fully lack the character of eternity."[232] Thus they can speak of the "salvific value"[233] or of the "eternal value of our works."[234] In this context it is also remarkable that for the Pietists those who are not engaged in such a struggle for sanctification are understood to be "Pharisees," but not those who boast before God. So in their view Pharisaism is not overcome by renouncing all the glory of works (both positive and negative works as Barth stressed) but rather by "good works" that lead to a "step-by-step separation from poisonous, self-centered instincts."[235]

What they said of the new man as a visible, noticeable given was so great that they dared to express it only with certain modifications. On the one side, they stressed that a person does not actually do the new and good works in the life of such a new man, but it is God who works in him. "If our heart is frightened by the invitation to fly so high, then we should consider that God gives us the desire and the performance and works in us."[236] They seem to have

---

[228]Compare note 53.

[229]Hützen, *Bibl. Glaubensleben,* p. 23. Compare P. Fabianke, *Was muss die Deutsche Gemeinschaftsbewegung festhalten?* 1925, pp. 11-12. In his view the essence of the community movement lies in its emphasis on a "life of holiness" that on the one hand consists in the fact that God "sanctifies a heart devoted to him by his divine power"; on the other hand it consists in the fact that "a holy man does holy works."

[230]Hützen, *Bibl. Glaubensleben,* p. 28. Compare H. Dallmeyer, *Die Gemeinschaftsbewegung: Womit sie aufräumen muss,* 2nd ed., 1924, p. 41: "Every truly born again individual is a saint on the basis of the Scripture, because God has made his dwelling in him through His Spirit."

[231]Hützen, *Bibl. Glaubensleben,* p. 30.

[232]Ibid., p. 26.

[233]Nagel, *Karl Barth und der heilsgewisse Glaube,* p. 23.

[234]Hützen, *Bibl. Glaubensleben,* p. 29.

[235]Nagel, *Karl Barth und der heilsgewisse Glaube,* p. 25.

[236]Hützen, *Bibl. Glaubensleben,* p. 28.

given themselves little or no account of how a particular human behavior was identified with God's will and action in this way. On the other side when looking at humankind they stressed that "shortcomings can still remain in his works."[237] "The fragmentary nature of our good works is not hidden from us."[238] And they dared to utter this truly "peculiar" expression: the "good works" of believers are still "imperfect good works" for the time being.[239] How "good" is a good work that is "imperfectly" (not totally) *good?* Be that as it may, they believed they had sufficiently distanced themselves from "the false extreme of sinlessness" by adding this tentative explanation.[240] As far as the temporary or passing imperfection of the "good works" is concerned, good works the new man visibly performs, they were able to comfort themselves with these two truths: God also "graciously accepts the imperfect good work"[241] and there is time and latitude for "real growth" in the new man,[242] for a "continuous and growing renewal of these sons and daughters of God."[243] However, this dual idea signifies an attack on grace by understanding grace as a "stopgap" for what the pious man achieves or does not quite achieve, and by understanding the new man as a person who is only partially dependent on grace (or less and less dependent on it to a "growing" extent).

Whatever position one takes on this Pietistic doctrine of sanctification, the fact is that they are advocating a doctrine that actually takes back what is asserted in the doctrine of justification with its realization that a person is saved by grace alone and faith alone and thus is *simul justus et peccator.* The fact is that this doctrine of sanctification not only contradicts the Epistle to the Romans but also the Reformational understanding of this issue. Rather it is clearly in keeping with the medieval, Catholic and especially Franciscan view. Thus it is semi-Pelagian to the core. The fact is that Pietists expressly committed themselves to this teaching against Karl Barth, so they must answer for it.

The Relevance of Eschatology

The question of the relevance of eschatology for an understanding of Christian faith was also in dispute between Barth and the Pietists. The Pietistic side at least partially saw that one of the reasons for Barth's critique of all notions that the

---

[237]Ibid., p. 26.
[238]Ibid., p. 25.
[239]Ibid.
[240]Ibid., p. 19.
[241]Ibid., p. 25.
[242]Ibid., p. 31.
[243]Ibid., p. 30.

pious "possess" and "enjoy salvation" was found in his understanding of eschatology and in his realization that eschatology has far-reaching implications for all
of Christian theology and fundamental significance especially for Christian existence in this eon. On the one hand, it places this eon under the fundamental reservation of the "not yet"; on the other hand, it places it under the authority of the
"promise." This statement from the *Epistle to the Romans* was quoted repeatedly:
"Christianity that is not totally eschatological has absolutely nothing to do with
Christ. Whatever is not hope is a millstone around our neck."[244] Or take this statement: "This hoping is possessing."[245] The context of such appreciation for eschatology is seen in Barth's understanding of Christ's resurrection as the "turning
point of all time and eternity."[246] Because it is not a contingent "historical" fact
we can at the same time approach it in hope. The following statement can be
understood from this perspective: "In Barth's teaching the believer is merely said
to be one who waits and hopes. He must never make use of his faith to gain an
experience. He should abandon all certainty and security, all visions and comforts."[247] It was nonetheless W. Knappe who could see a positive side to this insight. He wanted to make sure that the "genuine biblical aspect of these ideas
was powerfully underscored," but he too discovered "an essential shortcoming
in Barth's view."[248] His friends were more critical than he. They could surely not
be uncritical here because in his understanding of eschatology Barth ran the risk
of linking the eschaton to the transcendental limitation of all temporal moments
and thus minimizing the importance of knowing that the kingdom of God has
already drawn near while stressing the importance of knowing that God's kingdom is otherworldly.[249] They were certainly justified in criticizing this. But whoever does so must beware of losing sight of the positive discovery in Barth's eschatology. (1) The Christian hope is not merely the final part of dogmatics or
history, but it is part of the center and structure of Christian revelation. It especially characterizes the existence of the Christian in the present age as a time of
waiting and journeying in light of the promise. (2) The eschaton also marks a
definite boundary between now and then, according to which all existence on
this side of the boundary is given the character of "not yet."

In criticizing Barth's eschatology, the Pietists apparently did not want to go
along with this dual understanding. The main reason for their opposition was

---

[244]Ro 2, p. 298; for example, in Hützen, *Bibl. Glaubensleben,* p. 14.
[245]Ro 2, p. 141; for example, in Knappe, "Karl Barth," p .41.
[246]Ro 2, p. 44.
[247]Nagel, *Karl Barth und der heilsgewisse Glaube,* p. 20.
[248]Knappe, "Karl Barth," p. 24.
[249]Compare Barth's later self-criticism in KD 2/1, pp. 715ff.

that they believed they had to assert that the believer is not merely "someone who waits, but who already possesses, who is sure of a present inner spiritual possession."[250] "The highest stage that we human beings can reach in our age (in Barth's view) is the expectation of being adopted as sons and daughters, but not adoption as a possession."[251] However, this is much too little; indeed, it is an "emptying" of faith. If "faith is hoping, never having," then you do not reach what is so central for the Pietists, "the experience of salvation and the possession of salvation."[252] Therefore they expressly rejected Barth's view that "the new life only becomes a reality in what we hope for."[253] Rather this is already a "reality" in our present "visible" life. "In the new birth eternal life is really given to us."[254] That is why there is already such a thing as Christian "experience" in the present age. That is why "we can have a certainty and assurance and see visible change."[255] So Barth "does not get it right when he relates redemption only to the resurrection of the flesh." Therefore Hützen interpreted 1 Peter 1:3 in such a way that this verse does not say "that new birth in this life is only a hope, rather the new birth realized in individual lives has a hope."[256] This verse certainly does not say that the *new birth* is merely a future event, but it does say that being born again is about the *hope* we have for a fulfilled life in the eschaton. In that Hützen appears to have overlooked this point, his formulation clarifies what the difference was between Barth and the Pietists with regard to eschatology. For him the whole nature of Christian existence "in time" is characterized by hope; on the other hand for them hope is a knowledge of future things that is linked to our present possession of salvation, but which is not definitive of this possession. In another place Hützen interpreted the same verse from Peter in such a way that the phrase "he has given us new birth into a living hope through the resurrection of Jesus Christ" means that the precondition for persons' new birth is found only in Christ's resurrection that makes it possible, but it only becomes real in the new birth that is experienced in the present.[257]

---

[250]Nagel, *Karl Barth und der heilsgewisse Glaube,* pp. 17-18.

[251]H. Dannert, "Die Evangelisation," in *Licht und Leben,* 1928, p. 357.

[252]H. Dannert, "Geschenkweise gerecht!" in *Licht und Leben,* 1929, p. 239.

[253]Hützen, *Bibl. Glaubensleben,* p. 32.

[254]Hützen, "Heiligung," in *RKZ,* 1928, p. 10.

[255]Hützen, *Bibl. Glaubensleben,* p. 33.

[256]Ibid., p. 21.

[257]Ibid., pp. 11-12. On the other hand, Knappe could take this present experience as "the experience of eternity" as "proof" for the reality of the "fact of the resurrection" (as a historical event), which he found denied by Barth's definition of the resurrection of Christ as "an unhistorical event *kat' exochen*" (Ro 2, p. 185) ("Karl Barth und der Pietismus," pp. 33-34), though without understanding that Barth did not at all intend to assert its unreality, but wanted to describe it as the reality of something totally new.

Therefore the new life's "hour of birth" is not Easter but takes place in my present experience, and Easter is only the precondition that makes it possible. We can see how the Pietists consciously and consistently attempted to hold on to their thesis that the Christian is not primarily one who waits but one who possesses. The Christian did not have new life *already* because Christ has "objectively" risen from the dead; he has it only since new life was created in him.

The price they paid for this statement was high: for the most part they lost what had been hidden from theology for a rather long period of time but which they could now learn anew from Barth and others:[258] their insight into the eschatological structure of the Christian message. This statement from Nagel reveals how little they were prepared to learn. "The eschatological character of that theology results from the misguided anthropological thesis that underlies it. Since our rebellion has to do with our creatureliness, the new creation cannot possibly come within the framework of this age and on the basis of the present creation."[259] Two things about this are problematic: (1) The assertion they make about the derivation of eschatology, allowing them to excuse themselves from paying attention to it in this way. Should they not at least have asked whether conversely eschatology could be the reason for the thesis that the new age cannot come "within the framework of this age" and "on the basis of the present creation"? Could it not be due to the newness of this new creation that it goes beyond this "framework" and that this "basis" is shaken as Barth claimed? (2) We could conclude from this statement as it stands: Wherever theology does not advocate a misguided anthropology, as the Pietists claim theirs does not, the eschatological character of theology can and will become superfluous. This statement is hardly a mistake. It is basically meant to be taken as it reads. Certainly the Pietists also have eschatological views that revolve around events at the end of the historical age. The Pietistic fathers could even be lauded for having discovered eschatology anew.[260] Yet in their view what will then occur is not so far-reaching that it will result in serious change. The actual change for them is the one that takes place in their personal experience of the new reality called the new birth. Their assumption of a direct continuity between "what we now have" and the eschaton automatically results from this teaching that there is a "direct relationship between our life of faith and our circumstances in eternity."[261]

---

[258]It was at that time not merely Barth's merit to have rediscovered the decisive significance of eschatology for biblical faith. We must remember Johannes Weiss, but also Christoph Blumhardt as well as Albert Schweitzer.

[259]Nagel, *Karl Barth und der heilsgewisse Glaube*, p. 17.

[260]Ibid., p. 9.

[261]Hützen, *Bibl. Glaubensleben*, p. 28.

Is this assumption based on a concept of "realized eschatology" for which the difference between "life by faith" and a future "life by sight" is already in principle abolished in the present? Perhaps Pietistic eschatology can be interpreted "so charitably." Only then the foundation for such "realized eschatology" must be seen more strongly in the "objective" Christ event and especially in his Easter resurrection. However, this does not seem to be the case for the Pietists, who mean by the present above all the "present" of their pious experience. Indeed, it is to be feared that there is reason to ask (we are reminded of what was said under the first point!) whether their assumption is not also based on an "anthropological thesis" in which the "framework" and "basis" of this age is not at all so bad that it would need such a complete renewal. Be that as it may, in any case there is such a "direct relationship" between the present age and the eschaton in their thought, at least for those who are born again. Our "good works, therefore, reach into eternity."[262] God will "perfect" in eternity what is already taking place in their "growth" in sanctification that is being experientially realized here, in the "growing renewal of the people of God," in their gradual separation from their "poisonous selfish instincts."[263] There will certainly be a judgment when we pass from time to eternity.[264] But it is a judgment "of works" in which born-again Christians who have grown in sanctification are rewarded "because they are worthy of it."[265] So there is a Pietistic eschatology. But we cannot see an appreciation of the fact that the eschaton is something new compared with all that exists on the earth and that the idea of grace must retain a clear and dominant position in a proper understanding of this matter. So we can also not find an appreciation of the fact that the Christian message itself has a thoroughly "eschatological character," nor can we find the closely related idea that Christian existence in the present era is fundamentally an existence lived in hope, in waiting and taking hold of the promise. The Pietists explicitly distanced themselves from this idea when they took their position on the *Epistle to the Romans*.

On the Theological Position of the Pietists

The following points should have become clear from what has been presented. (1) The Pietists defended not just a methodological concern when they took their position on the *Epistle to the Romans* (the Christian must live and experience what he or she teaches). They also presented their concern in the form of

---

[262]Ibid., p. 29.
[263]See note 69.
[264]Knappe, "Karl Barth," p. 56.
[265]Hützen, *Bibl. Glaubensleben,* p. 29.

particular *doctrines.* (2) It must surely be conceded that in contrast to Barth the
doctrines they advocated are in fact clearly grouped around their basic concern,
a direct, tangible *experience* of God's reality and the new man, and they are
shaped by this concern. (3) It is also clear that at several points the Pietistic doctrines shaped by this basic concern present a *different* teaching from the one
found in Barth. Thus they take a reasonably clear position in opposition to the
second *Epistle to the Romans.* (They have not merely misunderstood him only
to actually mean the same thing on these issues.)

But in addition several other statements can be made. We indicated that
Barth's teaching on each point is also in need of criticism and correction. But
we think that the Pietistic doctrines not only intended to "correct" Barth where
his doctrines are in need of correction, but also where he reemphasized important aspects of biblical, Reformational thought! And not only "intended"! In distancing themselves from the theology of the *Epistle to the Romans,* the Pietistic
authors explicitly committed themselves to doctrines which cannot easily be
harmonized with the Reformers' fresh understanding of the biblical message at
several not insignificant points: the Reformational concentration on salvation in
Christ given for us while at the same time remaining outside of us, the understanding of free grace bestowed on sinners, the justification of the impious, etc.
The assertion that Pietism is a "genuine, healthy child of the Reformation"[266] is
of little help here. It was the concern of the community people to emphasize
Christian "experience" in contrast to Barth. From this perspective they maintained that humanity has a "natural ability" to enter into covenant with God,
transformed grace into an inward human condition, replaced the idea that the
Christian is simultaneously both a sinner and justified with the idea that the sinner is supplanted by the new man and abolished the eschatological boundary.
Pietism should not have understood its concern in these terms if it were serious
about wanting to be "a genuine, healthy child of the Reformation."

4. THE CONSEQUENCES OF THE PIETISTS' COUNTER-POSITION ON BARTH'S THEOLOGY

We have seen what the Pietistic authors advocated in opposition to the theology
of the *Epistle to the Romans.* We must add that the Pietists were obviously very
certain of their cause, so certain that they leveled two significant accusations
against Barth in so far as he did not move along the lines of their counter-
position. He did not agree with the "full" testimony of *Holy Scripture,* which had

---

[266]Fabianke, *Was muss die Deutsche Gemeinschaftsbewegung festhalten?* p. 115.

to do with the fact that the Scripture did not truly have binding authority for him. He not only did not promote but even inhibited, indeed "destroyed," the existence of a *spiritually alive church*. This had to do partially with his intellectualism and partially with the weakness of his moral fervor. We will now more closely examine both of these accusations.

Their Accusation That Barth Was Not Sufficiently Faithful to Scripture

H. Oltmann made this charge in a cautious form when he stated that the *Epistle to the Romans* "could not communicate the full ring of truth found in the New Testament."[267] W. Knappe became even more direct when he voiced the opinion that "Barth has not opened up for us the full riches of Scripture; indeed, we miss in his theology what is most important in Scripture."[268] In fact, Knappe could occasionally even remark: What Barth says about Christ and the resurrection is "a slap in the face of the New Testament's witness."[269] In his view Barth only "seemed to have a positive position on Scripture" since he actually "went beyond it whenever the demands of his philosophy called for it."[270] Others rendered even more severe judgments. One of them shook his head after reading the *Epistle to the Romans*. "And all these assertions that contradict the witness of the Bible come from an acclaimed professor of theology. I cannot believe my eyes!"[271] W. Hützen accused Barth of "essentially emptying Scripture of its truth content"[272] and once expressed the opinion that "Scripture will undoubtedly say something quite different from Barth."[273] Therefore "we [Pietists] intend to continue to read the Bible in terms of how we have read it up to now," unmoved by what Barth has said.[274] And G. F. Nagel asked the question, "Can Barth be called a proclaimer of the unadulterated biblical gospel?" He elaborated, "Hundreds of scholars have taught and worked, and answering this question about their theology is not difficult. Although their teaching may show a confessional bias or some other imbalance, although at certain points erroneous views may be mixed in with their core teaching, their message had solid biblical

---

[267]H. Oltmann, "Was fordert die neue Zeit von unserem Dienst am Evangelium?" in *Licht und Leben,* 1926, p. 409.

[268]Knappe, "Karl Barth," p. 57.

[269]Ibid., p. 33.

[270]Ibid., p. 56.

[271]"Kritische Ecke," in *In alle Welt: Zeitschrift für missionarische Arbeit,* 1928 (?), p. 38.

[272]Hützen, *Bibl. Glaubensleben,* 1928, p. 17.

[273]Ibid., p. 30.

[274]Ibid., p. 35.

content."[275] For Nagel, answering this question about Barth was actually not difficult because he was certain that Barth could not be associated with those scholars since in his theology "the basic doctrines of the Word are dealt with in a critical and doubting fashion."[276] In his theology not only a "weakening" but "an obliteration of faith positions" takes place.[277] These authors also thought they knew why Barth had such a broken relationship to Holy Scripture. Thimme believed it was because he "was still flirting with liberal theology"[278] or as Knappe believed, "the roots of his thought lie in philosophy."[279] How did they know about this bias in his thought? His theology was "not simple enough" and *therefore* "not biblical enough"; thus "the word of philosophy emerged from it more than the word of the Bible."[280] His theology as well as his language lacked "simplicity" and thus removed itself from "Christianity" that is "so simple at its core."[281] For this reason the Pietistic circles of that time felt justified in creating the impression that "Barth was a despiser of the Bible."[282]

What can be said in response to this charge? Surely it does call attention to a genuine problem. Barth's exegesis in the second *Epistle to the Romans* has its difficulties, not only with regard to the particular results of the interpretation but also and mainly with regard to the manner in which he handled the biblical text. Of course, the crucial difficulty was not that his language as well as his thought was in fact philosophically loaded, although we could make some further remarks on this issue. Rather the problem lies in the fact that Barth tended to identify Pauline statements with his own, which was demonstrated by his well-known boldness in titling his book simply *Epistle to the Romans* without any further addition. The obvious danger was that submissive listening to the text by the exegete turned into the direct speech of a confidant without any explanation of how the one who was listening turned into the one who was doing the talking. Primarily there, further clarifications in Barth's thought were imperative, and from there he certainly needed to clarify his ex-

---

[275]Nagel, *K. Barth und der heilsgewisse Glaube*, 1927, pp. 27-28.

[276]Ibid., p. 38.

[277]Ibid., p. 44.

[278]L. Thimme, "Das Problem 'Karl Barth,'" in *Gnadauer Gemeinschaftsblatt*, 1929, p. 97.

[279]Knappe, "Karl Barth," p. 44.

[280]W. Knappe, "Nachrichten," in *Licht und Leben*, 1928, p. 187.

[281]"Rezension zum 2 Römerbrief," in *Missionsblatt der Brudergemeine*, 88. Jahrgang, nr. 5. On the other hand, a critic of the *Epistle to the Romans* in the Ebing "Alb-Boten" (January 24, 1925) nicely remarks, in view of the "difficulties that the structure and the depth of the book's intellectual world causes," "It is astonishing how community people, who, for example, are coming from Oetinger, Brastberger, Ph. M. Hahn and Roos, get into the book so quickly."

[282]This is the anonymous author of the response to Nagel's work. Manuscript in the Karl Barth archives, Basel, 4.

egesis of particular texts as well.[283] Therefore his position on Scripture could in fact be made into a problem, and his exegesis in particular could be critically examined.

Nagel pointed out Acts 27:11 and Galatians 1:6ff. as "proof texts" for the necessity of this task. Of course both verses do not talk about what was so important to the Pietists when they made their accusation against Barth. They believed a theological doctrine must not be one-sided but must "completely" take all relevant Bible verses into consideration. However, to a certain extent in both texts he cites talk about a "canon in the canon." The one talks about whether Paul's preaching of Christ can be recognized as the fulfillment of the Old Testament promise. The other talks about the "gospel of Christ" proclaimed by Paul as being the standard for all proclamation and teaching in the church. If the Pietists felt encouraged to examine Barth's "teaching" by quoting these verses, they only proceed properly when they are not merely contented to list a series of Bible verses that apparently do not harmonize well with this teaching, but when they advance to the question of whether the (Pauline!) "gospel of Christ" is expressed here or not. However, we have the impression that to a large extent the Pietistic authors got bogged down in trying to list Bible verses to prove their point.

Their Criteria for Discovering a Lack of Biblical Faithfulness

As I have demonstrated, these authors reached a verdict—more or less cautiously presented—that the author of the *Epistle to the Romans* did not have a correct, positive relationship to Holy Scripture. This verdict cannot be rejected out of hand. Of course, in our opinion it can only be called a responsible position when the following conditions are met.

1. As a working hypothesis they would have to take seriously Barth's claim that he dared to make his undoubtedly bold, "extreme" statements not as a "philosopher," also not merely as a dogmatician, but as *an interpreter of the biblical text.* A verdict on this issue would first have to take proper notice of the fact that he did not write a general treatise about "an otherworldly" God, or the problematic nature of religious experience, etc., at least judging by its literary form. Rather he made statements relating to these issues verse by verse, follow-

---

[283]Compare Barth's self-critical remark in the foreword to his "Explanation of the Epistle to the Philippians" (1927), which is deliberately not titled *The Epistle to the Philippians,* that "I . . . did not commit myself to the procedure I followed at that time with the Epistle to the Romans." Compare also the similar self-critical remark in the foreword to Barth's "Brief Explanation of the Epistle to the Romans" (1956): "No interpreter gets past this added reservation: 'just as I understand it,' and I do not get past it either." And further: "One never stops learning from the Epistle to the Romans. In this sense it is still waiting for me as well (as I had expressed it somewhat cheerfully)!"

ing a rather lengthy biblical text. Taking this factor into account does not automatically legitimize his statements as being shaped by the Bible. But taking this factor into account should have noticeably defined the terms of their discussion with him. Then they could have openly asked at problematic points whether he possibly could have arrived at the statements under discussion *as an exegete*. The fact that he used a language shaped by "philosophical" concepts, that he had a complicated way of thinking does not really prove in itself that he did not also talk as an exegete at the same time. Conversely, a language and a simple way of thinking that dispenses with Kantian terminology does not in itself furnish any evidence that the language and way of thinking are shaped by the Bible. For example, when Barth used the term *ineffable,* a term obviously defined by Kant and Neo-Kantianism, or when he criticized the concept of religion, a concept clearly shaped by Feuerbach, this state of affairs does not prove by a long shot that his statements relating to these matters are "philosophical" and not "biblical." Even if they held such a suspicion, they could have at least examined his claim that in using these concepts and ideas, he thought he was interpreting the Pauline "grace alone" *(sola gratia)* and "faith alone" *(sola fide)* (*the* grace that is *free* and *remains* free of all human claims and *the* faith that does not yet live "by sight"). By not advancing to this level of questioning, they have simply made it too easy for themselves to reach their verdict on his lack of biblical faithfulness.

2. A further condition would have to be met to make this accusation and to make it appear credible. The presentation of this concern would have to reveal something of their willingness to at least hypothetically expect that when they accuse Barth of mixing a "biblical" understanding with contemporary ideas, with "philosophy," etc., such mixing could also have occurred in their own case or could at least pose a danger. Only those who know that they themselves remain under serious scrutiny in this matter can convincingly make such an accusation. After all, Barth had made a particular critique of Pietism in the course of his biblical exegesis. The Pietists saw themselves put in the same category as mysticism, and their concern was characterized in such a way that in the end it boiled down to a variety of rationalism and Romanticism, although its starting point was understood as being different. Barth's interpretation and critique could be certainly mistaken, but when they responded to it and rejected it, they referred to the fact that the position of the critic was itself not ("fully") biblical but also philosophically conditioned. They acted as if they knew they were immune to the danger they detected here, simply portraying their own concern as "biblical." This naive matter-of-factness had to appear suspicious. Their response to the *Epistle to the Romans* should at least have given rise to a serious

examination of the question whether the thinking of the Pietists was not also conditioned by contemporary history. If they could understand their own concern as the clear, central "biblical teaching on the inner life as a personal experience of the living God,"[284] we can realize with the help of the terminology used here that this did not just happen to be first espoused in a particular era, continuing on to the present day (Enlightenment! Romanticism!), at least in the form and language presented by the Pietists. When Hützen considered his interest in a "real experience of God's presence" to be a central biblical truth, he could not "literally" prove that this was biblically based. At best this could be a conclusion drawn from certain Bible verses which he could not explain any other way. ("When we are spoken of as a new creation, then it must mean a real, experiential fact").[285] However, he had to be clear that this was a conclusion, an interpretation, and he had to be prepared to answer the question posed to him: How did he arrive at *this* interpretation? And when Nagel said "repentance and new birth" are the "heart" of every message of "healthy biblical content,"[286] or when he opined, "God's revelation" is "according to Scripture" the event that "perceptibly and impressively moves the inward man,"[287] he did not cite any biblical support for this view. What then must have been the reason why he nevertheless committed himself to an interpretation of the Bible and revelation using this wording? Of course, what we commented on in Barth's teaching applies to the Pietists as well. The fact that their language and way of thinking is also conditioned by contemporary history does not by itself say anything for or against the truth and legitimacy of their concern. But it does say something against prematurely identifying their own concern with the biblical witness. Only by *giving up* such an identity does the *freedom* of the biblical witness to overcome all the limitations of its interpreters come into focus. If the historical conditionality of the interpreter does not have to be made into a principle, a methodological requirement for the interpretation of Scripture, it does not have to be a disadvantage if the Bible is actually read through the lens of a worldview conditioned by its time. Perhaps no other way is possible. At any rate, it has always happened this way in the church. The Pietists have also done it. If they were not willing to admit *to what extent* they did it, they still could have known *that* even they were and are not protected from it. The knowledge of this fact would have prevented them from so irresponsibly making the

---

[284]Hützen, *Bibl. Glaubensleben,* p. 5.
[285]Ibid., p. 17.
[286]Nagel, *K. Barth und der heilsgewisse Glaube,* p. 28.
[287]Ibid., p. 19.

sweeping accusation that the exegete Barth was guilty of "essentially emptying the truth of Scripture."

3. A further condition is necessary to make this accusation first appear credible. To back it up, a particular, more convincing exegesis would have to be juxtaposed to a particular exegesis of Barth, assuming that his remarks claimed to be an exegesis. As far as we can see, this has not even remotely happened in any Pietistic statement. As a rule the procedure of their authors looks like this: One of Barth's assertions is reported on, and then another assertion is set over against it, and this is occasionally supported by a quotation from Scripture that actually or apparently says something different from what can be found in Barth. Finally, his assertion is considered "unbiblical" and their own assertion is shown to be "biblical." Here is an example. "In Barth's view, God is said to be the One who is unreachable and unapproachable. In contrast to this view, the word of the Apostle retains its validity, 'He is not far from each one of us'"[288] (Acts 17:27). The way he reports on Barth's assertion is not precise. This is apparent from the fact that he was able to come back to Acts 17:27 and use it constructively to lay out his understanding of God in his second *Epistle to the Romans*.[289] Yet the reader of the Pietistic writing finds out nothing about it. However he did interpret that verse in a different way from his critic. The Pietists have not tackled the task of grappling with him by simply quoting Acts 17:27, although this task is still possible and perhaps more necessary now than ever. This would only be true if a different, better interpretation were set over against his *interpretation,* which however is not the case. By limiting themselves to occasionally quoting a biblical statement to refute an assertion made by Barth, the Pietistic authors evidently assumed that the *meaning* of the quoted verse is a *foregone conclusion.* To be more precise, they assumed that the quoted verse can of course only be understood in terms of the opinion that in *their* view is supported by the verse. But this view would have been problematic for them if they had gained a clear understanding that Barth on his part referred to a good number of the same verses (not only in the Pauline Epistle to the Romans but also in other biblical books).[290] Yet the Pietists believed they could refute him merely by quoting those same verses. This does not mean that Barth was right when he referred to these verses and the Pietists were wrong. But it does not follow that by merely quoting a verse the correctness of their own reference to that verse or the incorrectness of Barth's interpretation is proven. What follows is that his assertion can be refuted only by

---

[288]Ibid., p. 16.
[289]Ro 2, 2nd ed., pp. 23, 69-70.
[290]Compare the index of Bible verses by G. Merz in the 3rd edition of the *Epistle to the Romans.*

recognizing that one interpretation stands against another and by trying to overcome one interpretation by making a better one. By dispensing with both, the Pietists' condemnation of Barth as a "despiser of the Bible" seems superficial. Might they have thought that by refraining from probing into the depths of exegesis where competition between different interpretations is inevitable, they would not get entangled in the thicket of merely "human opinions"? But then they would truly be in danger of practically equating "God's Word" with a particular, namely, their own, "interpretation"! Or might their decision to refrain from interpreting these Bible verses be attributed to their desire to prop up and confirm a fixed opinion when quoting these verses? But then their appeal to Scripture would have to be made at best out of reverence for it and not because the witness of Scripture was their binding authority!

4. A further condition must be met if the Pietists want to claim that Barth's thinking is "unbiblical." The Bible verses that they cited against his thinking, assuming that the Pietists contented themselves with quoting Bible verses against him, would have to *prove* what they wanted to prove. But in this regard we have the impression that this condition was met by the Pietists at best in a very limited way. Here are two examples that are typical of what we mean: "According to Barth's teaching the believer should merely be one who waits and hopes."[291] But this is not reported exactly because in his view the believer who waits is at the same time the "one who possesses."[292] However, Barth did not understand by "faith" what Nagel understood by it. He saw faith as "a psychic, historical phenomenon of trust."[293] Because Nagel considered this view biblical in contradistinction to Barth, it would have been his task to quote Bible verses that suggest an understanding of "faith" in these terms, instead of merely in terms of a waiting faith that does not yet live by sight. But when Nagel quoted nothing more than Acts 17:31 ("He has given proof of this to all men by raising him from the dead") and Jeremiah 5:3 ("O LORD, do not your eyes look for truth?") and Jesus' words about helping faith, he certainly emphasized the importance of faith, but he did not show by any means that such faith can be understood in terms of that "psychic, historical phenomenon of trust." What was to be proven was not proven with the Bible verses he quoted. Here is another example. One of the Bible verses frequently used

---

[291]Nagel, *K. Barth und der heilsgewisse Glaube,* p. 20.

[292]Ro 2, p. 129. Compare pp. 181-82: "Faith is the turning point, the act of turning around, of conversion in the full paradox of its concept as human hollow space, no, divine content . . . as the last human, no, the first divine possibility . . . 'If you believe, you have!' If we believe, we *have* turned away from sin."

[293]Nagel, *K. Barth und der heilsgewisse Glaube,* p. 20.

against Barth is Romans 5:5 ("God has poured out his love into our hearts by
the Holy Spirit, whom he has given us"). Nagel declared: "Barth cannot accept
all this."[294] This is not correct, as Barth's exegesis of this verse shows. He understood it in this way: "The Holy Spirit is God's work in faith that touches
man and his world in faith." It touches him so deeply that it is not assimilated
by "this" world and not by "this" person but constitutes a *new* subject beyond
the tangible human being. "In the grace given by God that lifts us up to establish us in God, it is a fact that the invisibility of God turns into the vision of
God."[295] Therefore Nagel should not have said that Barth did not want to accept this verse, Romans 5:5, but only that Barth understood it differently than
he. He himself wanted to understand it *as* proof that we can really experience
a "present inner spiritual possession"[296] in which "God palpably and impressively touches the inner man." Nagel may have had his reasons to insist on
this view. But he undoubtedly did not prove the correctness of his view by
simply quoting Romans 5:5, which should have been clear to him because he
at least had the possibility of another interpretation in view in the *Epistle to
the Romans*. Here too what actually had to be proven was consequently not
proven by quoting the Bible. These two examples could easily be supplemented by others. Thus we can say that this further condition was not met by
the Pietistic authors. Their accusation that Barth was thinking "unbiblically"
whereas the assertion made against Barth was "biblical" seems unjustified.

And there is yet one more condition that would legitimize such an accusation. As extensively as possible, they would have to avoid the impression that
they were arbitrary in *selecting* the quotations if they limited themselves to an
occasional Bible quotation in distancing themselves from Barth. A large percentage of the Bible verses the Pietistic authors quoted sought to demonstrate that
the Bible actually talks about God, Christ and the Spirit being "in us."[297] The se-
lection of Bible quotations was made in the interests of a particular "dogmatic"
stance. This was done in a way that they not only refrained from exegeting biblical passages but also refrained from considering as broad a spectrum as possible of various biblical statements on a particular point (for example, on the
subject of "grace" or "faith"). They also refrained from drawing on complementary biblical concepts (for example, biblical references to an "outside of us," "be-

---

[294]Ibid., p. 18.
[295]Ro 2, pp. 134-35.
[296]Nagel, *K. Barth und der heilsgewisse Glaube*, pp. 17ff.
[297]This is the case, for example, with Nagel, for whom most Bible verses serve as proof of this.
See p. 5, Col 1:26ff.; p. 18, Rom 5:5, 1 Cor 3:16, 6:19, Gal 3:2ff., Rom 8:5, 2 Tim 1:7, 1 Jn 4:2;
p. 32, 1 Cor 2:9, Eph 3:17; p. 37, 1 Cor 6:19, Gal 3:3, Heb 10:32, Rev 3:3; p. 44, Eph 3:16.

cause of us," " for us") during their discussion of certain basic biblical concepts (such as the Bible's talk of an "in us"). Thus they refrained from referring to those Bible verses that could complement their own statements or possibly correct them and put them in the proper perspective. Instead, the authors confined themselves to merely mentioning those Bible verses that in their view affirmed their "dogmatic" assertions and especially their view of an experiential reality of God in us. It may well be that in so doing they pointed out verses that were not considered in the theology of the *Epistle to the Romans* or were given short shrift. Yet it must be remembered that Barth believed he was able to appeal to a not inconsiderable number of these verses, even if in a different sense, and he did indeed appeal to them. However, if this is accepted, the exact opposite must also be affirmed. By concentrating on the quotation of Bible verses supporting the Pietistic concern (the experiential reality of God in certain individuals), other Bible verses were left out of consideration which could conversely be lacking in Pietistic theology. And this must be added: What happened to the claim of the Pietists that they could "communicate the total chorus of New Testament truth" and open up "the full riches of Scripture"? Was not this claim compromised by in fact concentrating on letting the Bible speak so selectively that their own primary concern, the experiential nature of God's reality and the pious possession of eternal life appeared to be legitimized? We could concede to the community people that they believed they could supplement the theology of the *Epistle to the Romans* by adding their but. In quoting Scripture, they believed they could content themselves with a procedure that was by its very nature one-sided, so that the way they used Scripture should not be seen as a problem. However, if this is conceded, the suspicion that they used the Bible arbitrarily could arise again in a much more profound way. The way they backed up their counterargument with Bible verses seems to be rooted in an understanding of Scripture that assumes faithfulness to Scripture is guaranteed by merely adding up Bible quotations and by stringing together proof texts. The problem with such an understanding of Scripture is that the danger of distorting the meaning of the Bible verses in question by taking them out of context is always lurking in the background. In addition, the never-ending but always essential issue of what is really crucial in the biblical witness is left out of consideration. Then we run the risk of making certain details the most important thing, even if those details may well be significant as such.

In summary, it may be said that the Pietistic authors have not furnished convincing evidence for their accusation against Barth, and we are still waiting for it because only in a very limited way have they met the conditions for charging Barth with a lack of biblical faithfulness and then making it credible.

Their Accusation That Barth's Theology Destroys the Christian Life

The second accusation the Pietists made against Barth, to the extent that he was
not in line with their counterargument, is as follows: His theology exerted a
"paralyzing influence" on church life and Christian action today. Of course, their
accusation presupposes that there is "flourishing church life" and moral action
only where real experience of God, the religious possession of eternal life and
the assurance of salvation are both theoretically "taught" and are actually existent. Because Barth objected to this, L. Thimme believed, "we cannot help but
call his critique of religious possession destructive for the church."[298] Köberle
made a similar judgment. Because of his ("one-sided") criticism of Pharisaism
Barth tends to be "morally indifferent."[299] Nagel understood by a Pharisee a person lacking the ethical "fruit of the Spirit." Thus he maintained that the author
of the *Epistle to the Romans* runs the risk of "Pharisaism," which paralyzes the
life of the "believers' church."[300] Because such Pharisaism not only "fights
against" the unconverted but also the believing Christian, H. Dannert concluded
that Barth himself is evidently unconverted and this explains why his theology
prevents "any kind of flourishing church life."[301] Hützen also feared that "Barth's
train of thought" amounted to "destroying the harvest like a thunderstorm,"
"casting suspicion on, attacking or even destroying the true spiritual life that
God has planted in man through his Spirit and still wants to plant."[302] Indeed,
he leveled this rather poorly phrased accusation against Barth: "Since he knows
nothing about what it means to be equipped with God's power, he cannot lift
an inch above the misery of a pitiful 'I want to, but cannot.'"[303] Nagel believed
the same thing. "For years we have been witnesses of the partly confusing,
partly morally and spiritually paralyzing effects of these teachings in the church
of the Lord."[304] With Köberle[305] he held against this theologian that "in times of
decadent laxity" it does no good to "scorn moral fervor wherever it may come
from." "Such a time is here again today" (when was it ever not here for the Pietists?).[306] "More than ever we need such holy forces," but in those dialectic
teachings "they are being virtually eliminated."[307] "Here the decadently lax are

---

[298]L. Thimme, *Kirche, Sekte und Gemeinschaftsbewegung,* 1925, pp. 258ff.

[299]A. Köberle, *Rechtfertigung und Heiligung,* 3rd ed., 1930, p. 283.

[300]Nagel, *K. Barth und der heilsgewisse Glaube,* pp. 37ff., 24ff.

[301]H. Dannert, "Die Evangelisation," in *Licht und Leben,* 1928, p. 357.

[302]Hützen, *Bibl. Glaubensleben,* p. 36.

[303]Ibid., p. 28.

[304]Nagel, *K. Barth und der heilsgewisse Glaube,* p. 31.

[305]Köberle, *Rechtfertigung und Heiligung,* p. 278.

[306]Compare Zinzendorf's word in the previous chapter, note 5.

[307]Nagel, *K. Barth und der heilsgewisse Glaube,* p. 40.

given an instructive dispensation from all probing questions about their possession of salvation, their struggles and their spiritual growth."[308] Knappe basically
phrased the same accusation somewhat more cautiously: He saw Barth caught
up in "intellectualism," badly listing to the side of "playing with ideas and concepts . . . that no longer have any connection to reality."[309] Totally superfluously,
he was preoccupied "with making useless speculations from the standpoint of
our intellect," asking, for example, whether and how it "is compatible with
God's majesty to enter into the finite although he is the eternal, the wholly
other."[310] In the process he totally overlooks the fact that our actual need is not
this speculative thought, but "ethical and religious" renewal.[311] Nagel was of the
same opinion. Barth transformed the "whole faith into a sand pile of problems."
"In his hyper astuteness" he balanced "the sanctuary on a pinhead . . . instead
of basing it on the eternal Rock." This is why "the spiritually paralyzing effects"
of his teachings are not surprising.[312]

Reflections on the Accusation That Barth's Theology Is Destructive
What can be said about this accusation? (1) Presumably something is surfacing
here that more *subconsciously* than consciously has defined the whole confrontation between the author of the *Epistle to the Romans* and the community people. To a certain extent different levels of thought encountered each other in
this conflict. In the preface to the second edition of his book Barth declared,
"This book claims to be nothing other than a part of the conversation of a theologian with theologians."[313] However, in this confrontation it was not simply
theologians who were facing each other but a theologian and representatives of
an avowedly lay movement, "men of the Christian working world," as Nagel
characterized himself and his own.[314] Although Barth admitted to "some theological and philosophical bombast" in his book, he expected many such lay
people to "understand him better than many theologians"[315] Yet it is unmistakable that a number of Pietistic readers had some trouble understanding both his
ideas and his language. Some of the "brothers" were clearly not up to the intellectual challenge of this book, and it was a representative of the Pietistic movement who gave those brothers the advice of refraining from the discussion of it

---

[308]Ibid., p. 41.
[309]Knappe, "Nachrichten," pp. 44ff.
[310]Ibid., pp. 28ff.
[311]Ibid., p. 44.
[312]Nagel, *K. Barth und der heilsgewisse Glaube,* p. 31.
[313]Ro 2, p. ix.
[314]Nagel, *K. Barth und der heilsgewisse Glaube,* p.27.
[315]Ro 2, p. ix.

rather than allowing intellectual incompetence that would prevent the "typical member of a congregation from receiving the gift of spiritual growth God has given him in Barth by intellectual incompetence."[316] Was this good advice? Perhaps it was a hopeful sign that representatives of this lay movement saw themselves challenged to take a position on explicitly theological problems and thus to participate in the theological conversation. But the advice is understandable because it reminded them of the high degree of intellectual concentration required to take issue with the assertions of this book. In that same preface Barth responded to the objection that the book was too complicated: "Neither Paul's epistle to the Romans, nor the present theological situation, nor today's world situation, nor the situation of man in relation to God is simple for *us:* Whoever is concerned about the truth in this situation must summon the courage to also *not* be simple."[317] The difficult situation in Barth's communication with his Pietistic critics was that some of them discovered a theology that was "not simple," while it was their natural tendency to see the "simple" truth of the gospel at stake here.[318] In reading Barth they were moved to ask the question, What can I get out of this? yet they could not find any satisfactory answer to this question. We can also venture to make the assumption that two thought patterns also clashed in this encounter, one naive and the other reflective. From the perspective of their different presuppositions and questions they were bound to have trouble making themselves understood to each other. Humanly speaking, we can understand to some extent that they would try to dismiss Barth's questions on the one hand as "useless" and on the other hand as "paralyzing" because their naive approach was jeopardized by the reflective one and they saw their faith threatened. But I believe this whole aspect can only be considered to be a secondary factor in evaluating this second accusation, and this is also the view of the Pietistic authors.

(2) We must seriously ask what is legitimate about this accusation. On May 18, 1923, Barth wrote these words in a letter about a successful preacher: "If the many people there *probably* do not hear what they need to hear, their absence from our pews is *probably* a sign that they don't hear much at all. If we would say the right thing in the *totally* right way, then it should definitely not look the way it did in the Safenwil church on Sunday. This can only be a transitional stage. I only want to say: My situation is just as problematic for me as his situation should be for him [the preacher mentioned above]."[319] Barth could

---

[316]"Erwiderung an G. F. Nagel," manuscript in the Karl Barth archives, p. 9.
[317]Ro 2, p. x.
[318]Compare note 15 above.
[319]K. Barth/E. Thurneyson, *Briefwechsel 1921–1930,* 1974, p. 167.

not claim and certainly did not even want to claim in this self-critical reflection that "success" defined as the exact opposite of the repugnant "paralyzing influences" is a criterion for the health of "congregational life." The Christian church should be warned against relying on this standard by looking at the life and message of a Jeremiah, let alone One who is even higher than he. A key part of the mission of the *Epistle to the Romans* theology was to assert the relevance of Jeremiah's message in an age that believed this standard was of decisive importance. But the question remains, How can the church preach, teach and provide pastoral care on the basis of the theology advocated in the *Epistle to the Romans?* What does the ministry of a congregation and ministry in and to the congregation look like when it is done on the basis of this theology? Perhaps the *Epistle to the Romans* could not have and should not have touched on this question in the situation in which it was written. Perhaps the postponement of this question was actually necessary as a transitional stage. But it remains legitimate even more so because Barth himself understood his theology at that time "in one sense as an illumination approaching theology from the outside, in fact an illumination right from where you are standing as pastors."[320] In fact, it became apparent in his theology after the second *Epistle to the Romans* that the gap Barth sensed after reflecting on this question was only a "transitional stage" and not meant to be a principle of his theology. But looking at what still had to come, one thing was decided on the basis of the *Epistle to the Romans*. In answering this question, the proper understanding of the deity of God, the justification of the sinner and the eschatological dimension of Christian truth must not be declared as such to be a "useless intellectual game" ("What can I get out of it?") or portrayed as "morally and spiritually paralyzing" and thus practically abolished for the sake of a "flourishing congregational life." Instead, the church faces the task of looking for preaching, instruction, pastoral care and ministry that are performed in such a way that these insights are honored and begin to have an impact. Or was the charge the Pietists brought against Barth supposed to imply that the proper understanding of Romans 5:20, "where sin increased, grace increased all the more," is "morally paralyzing" as such and "destructive of congregational life"?[321] This objection would not be new. It seems to have been raised against Paul in Romans 6:1 and is the objection the Pelagians raised against Augustine and the objection the "enthusiasts" raised against the Reformers. They charged that the Reformers' teaching made "people lazy." We cannot dispel the suspicion that a trace of these old objec-

---

[320]K. Barth, "Das Wort Gottes und die Theologie," *Ges. Vorträge* 1, 1924, p. 103.
[321]W. Knappe seems to think so. Compare Ro 2, p. 386.

tions that "paralyze" and "destroy" the message of *free grace* can be detected
in the misgivings the Pietists had about the theology of the *Epistle to the Romans,* namely, that it was "a dispensation . . . from every concerned question
about the possession of salvation, the spiritual struggle and spiritual growth."[322]
Indeed, the suspicion lingers that in pushing aside the crucial issue of how
God's revelation is consistent with his majesty as "useless reflection," they have
repeated the same kind of attempts once made within the church to cut off the
branch on which they were sitting.

(3) Finally, we must notice in this second accusation what is also true of the
first accusation. Whoever makes such a weighty accusation must also be asked if
he cannot be accused of something similar. In this respect, the Pietists thought
they had an especially clear conscience. Their accusation is clearly so vehement
on this point because it was made in the certainty that their own movement was
laboring under the Lord's blessing and thus espoused doctrines that neither paralyze nor destroy congregations. On the contrary, it carries "death-overcoming life
into the world."[323] By pointing out the blessed effectiveness of the community
movement, they believed they had simultaneously proven the rightness of Pietism's concern and its specific doctrines, now defended anew against Barth. Let
us remember what was emphasized by its representatives as its basic concern:
God in us, the new man, sanctification, the ability to do good as an experiential,
discernable, "real" fact in human beings at the present time! Let us make this statement: By claiming that this is true of particular human beings at whom you can
point your finger, they were making an incredibly *bold* claim, to put it mildly. This
claim is even bolder because Pietist circles believed they could affirm these "facts"
as givens. Thus F. Mund could say "the community movement is a work of God"
and "is the divine reaction against the natural man's sleep of death."[324] H. Dallmeyer said, "The community movement is a movement of the sun because it is a
movement of the Spirit" and to top it off, a "movement of truth."[325] Pastor Gauger
said that it is a "historical fact" that the Pietistic communities are places favored by
the Spirit of God."[326] Pastor Michaelis said that the "eternal" significance of the
community movement is that through it "many thousands have gained salvation

---

[322]See note 44 above.

[323]Nagel, *K. Barth und der heilsgewisse Glaube,* p. 10.

[324]F. Mund, "Die Gemeinschaftsbewegung eine Anklage gegen die Kirche," in *Im Kampf um die
Kirche,* 1930, pp. 46-47.

[325]H. Dallmeyer, *Die Gemeinschaftsbewegung: Womit sie aufräumen muss,* 2nd ed., 1924, pp.
6, 37. Dallmeyer once says the following unheard-of sentence, which in one go outlines the
problematic nature of Pietistic identifications: "We have among us solid Christians, who let
the spirit of Pastor Engels rule in them, which was the Spirit of Christ" (p. 21).

[326]According to Mund, "Die Gemeinschaftsbewegung," p. 46.

as blessed children of God."[327] This claim was not only bold because an unbearable personal insinuation was slipped into the issue-oriented discussion between Barth and Pietism, which if it was not always verbalized was clearly in the air: You deny the "religious possession" only because you do not truly believe.[328] Of course, the claim was more than bold primarily because of the way they identified God's work and Spirit with the empirical fact of the community movement. But in the final analysis, it was bold because it invariably had to stimulate the further inquiry: If the new man in you is existent in a "real" and "discernible" way as a personal possession and in moral efficacy, where are your fruits? In looking at the new Pietism, F. Mund courageously invited others to examine the movement, "By their fruit you will recognize them." He then pointed out what fruit the movement can boast of, the "'visible grace' that many thousands" have "gained life from God" through it and "have been preserved in such a life even in the fiery trial of the World War and inflation, . . . this is the divine legitimation of the movement."[329] At this point the community people could cheerfully go on to point out all the historical achievements their movement had produced. Did they not notice that by making their bold claim they came dangerously close to confusing God's blessing with external, measurable success, embracing a works righteousness and an inflated opinion of themselves that made them unable to critically and contritely reflect on themselves and all those achievements?[330]

Excursus: The Socioethical and Political Views of the Community People During the 1920s

If so many gained "life" in "visible grace" through the community movement, we could once again ask, By *what* fruits could the "many thousands" who received

---

[327]D. Michaelis, in *Gnadauer Gemeinschaftsblatt,* 1928, no . 7.

[328]See notes 37 and 39 above. A. Essen, "Kirche und Gemeinschaftsbewegung," in *Licht und Leben,* 1929, pp. 201ff.: "The primary cause of Pietism's rejection . . . lies in the fact that only one who is himself touched by this movement of the Spirit . . . has an understanding of spiritual movements."

[329]Mund, "Die Gemeinschaftsbewegung," p. 46.

[330]For example, let me point out that the Pietists took it for granted that their movement was justified because they promoted *mission* in such a special way. As if the way in which mission work was done under their influence were so totally unproblematic! Was it not also burdened with the features of an expansionist, if not to say, imperialist (pious) self-commendation? But as long as the community people saw God's cause and their cause as so closely linked, it must have been difficult for them to even understand the *spiritual* dimension of this critical reference. In 1928 K. Hartstein (who was also coming from Pietism) demonstrated in his work: "What Does Karl Barth's Theology Have to Say to Missions?" that from the perspective of the *Epistle to the Romans* theology only a certain understanding of mission but not mission itself was "impeded, that instead it was made possible and promoted" from this perspective, but in a new way.

"life from God" be recognized? Basically this question could only be asked if one were a Pietist himself or at least recognized the principle that the position of humanity before God can be detected in its historical, visible form. Only then could one volunteer to definitively answer this question either positively or negatively. Nevertheless, in order to focus this question *as* a question and to at least put a dent in the matter-of-fact way the Pietists answered their own question in the affirmative from the outset, we have compiled several socioethical and political opinions that are found in one of the leading magazines of the community people in Germany, *Light and Life*. In these same issues we can also find their ongoing, truly intense treatment of Barth's theology. At any rate, the Pietists as they understood themselves wanted to be held to these opinions which followed a very definite line[331] and took up considerable space.[332] Our overview of these opinions is only intended to point out the problematic nature of the Pietists' *certainty* in claiming that the "new man" in the community movement is a recognizable given, recognizable right down to his social and political behavior!

First of all, in the articles found in these magazines the Pietists were busy propagating their insights on all kinds of issues having to do with private morality. They expressed their aversion to "indecent movie theaters"[333] and came out against Mardi Gras, dancing, theater going[334] and the opera[335] and addressed the problem of alcoholism.[336] With regard to sexuality, they said, "It is the duty

---

[331]E. G. Ruppel, *Die Gemeinschaftsbewegung im Dritten Reich,* 1969, pp. 28ff., demonstrated that the political posture of the Pietistic communities in Germany during the 1920s was somewhat more subtle than the line that was espoused in *Licht und Leben*. But Ruppel also showed that the magazine *Heilig dem Herrn,* which was more widely distributed in community circles, espoused a political posture that essentially corresponded to the line we will present now in this excursus (compare pp. 45ff.).

[332]*Licht und Leben* answered a reader's question whether "a Christian magazine" should even express an opinion on political issues: "Yes! For our relationship to God has to have an impact in life, in the world and among human beings." It is therefore "an important task to also apply the principles, the judgment and the strength of Christianity to the life of this world and economy" (1924, p. 69). "Every believer has an obligation . . . to the larger circle of the nation and the fatherland" (1926, p. 27). Note the following on the technical aspect of documenting the sources of the quotations: We will limit ourselves to providing the year and page number in *Licht und Leben* without indicating the respective author and the heading of the article. In this context we consider the latter to be unnecessary because our concern is only to stress a certain line on the issues.

[333]1927, p. 667.

[334]1924, p. 318.

[335]1927, 543.

[336]1927, p. 488. We lost the World War because of alcohol (1924, p. 370), and workers in the Ford Motor Company are not working productively enough (1929, p. 559). In the *Gnadauer Gemeinschaftsblatt* (1929, p. 99) the question was also raised: "whether it is a sin to buy oneself chocolate?"

of a Christian state to prohibit and punish sexual immorality of any kind and put a stop to it."[337] With regard to hairstyles, they said, "The bobbed haircut is . . . un-German since it is not in keeping with the nature of the German woman and mother,"[338] but "we really do not have enough strength to become indignant at everything that is taking place in the world."[339] But much more was at stake for the Pietists in the public arena. They vigorously fought against the abolition of confessional schools: "A secular school is a criminal school!"[340] They also vehemently fought against the "destruction of parental authority"[341] today and against the emancipation of women, referring to the "natural, divine order of creation,"[342] the lack of "talent" and the natural "disposition" of women.[343] They also lamented how a witch hunt was being conducted against the death penalty, because "whoever sheds human blood, his blood should also be shed."[344] They took the same position against pacifism. It is a "national indignity";[345] "every kind of pacifism is misleading"[346] because it completely misjudges "God's intention . . . God's Word never demands that sociopolitical conditions must be changed first, but conversion is always and everywhere the first priority."[347] Such statements were no coincidence. There was a system behind them.

We can clearly notice this by looking at the following points. (1) The *folkish* element was given a positive interpretation in their thought. "We are all only human beings through the medium of a particular nation. . . . We are not human beings in and of ourselves, we are Germans."[348] "Loyalty to our nation and loyalty to our faith go hand in hand." "Whoever cannot make sacrifices for the nation can also make no sacrifices for God. . . . The struggle against foreign influences must be taken up, the struggle against Jewish intellectual thought and influence."[349] "*One* church, *one* fatherland."[350]

(2) *Their destructive criticism of democracy.* The German people were suffering from the hypnosis of "parliamentary government." "This horrible and for Ger-

---

[337]1929, p. 616.
[338]1927, p. 664. Also, "the majority of those getting bob cuts are Jews!"
[339]1927, p. 221.
[340]1927, p. 777.
[341]Ibid., p. 709.
[342]Ibid.
[343]1927, p. 106.
[344]1928, p. 663.
[345]1926, p. 26.
[346]1928, p. 204.
[347]1926, p. 168.
[348]1928, p. 202.
[349]1927, p. 476; here it has to do with a approving repetition of ideas expressed by Paul Althaus.
[350]1927, p. 488.

many totally unsuitable parliamentary system is perhaps the greatest of the many great defects that mar the Weimar constitution. We feel that we have been betrayed and sold out when we even remotely think of these things."[351] It was proven "that in fact democracy turns into plutocracy."[352] A journalist fined by a court was applauded for his statement that parliamentary government appeals to the lowest instincts of human personality."[353] In the same vein they complained loudly about the changing times. "No longer does any power stand *above* the people, rather the people themselves have the power."[354] "No! No!" was the response to this change: "We want and need a uniform state authority as before."[355]

(3) *Their disinterest in the labor issue.* In response to a letter to the editor, stating that the interests of the working population get short shrift in *Light and Life*, to put it mildly, this reader was informed that his "class egoism" was deeply "shocking." (He ought to be looking at "the nation as a whole.") "There must always be higher and lower classes," which is why the "envy of the lower classes"[356] is prohibited. These laborers only focus on "bread and butter issues."[357] And socialism meant only acting "according to the motto . . . everything that is yours is mine and it says, 'Make your life here good and beautiful.'"[358] This is what conclusively refutes it: "Selfishness is the great engine . . . in economic life, and since sinful humanity just acts this way, this engine cannot be replaced by anything else." Human beings cannot "rule the world with the Sermon on the Mount,"[359] let alone in the "polluted atmosphere of the socialist sewer!"[360]

(4) *Its pronounced anti-Semitism.* "How unthinkable is this Social Democratic Party which is influenced by international Jewry."[361] "Moscow and Jewry"![362] And how unlikable is the daily press, these "Jewish newspapers"![363] "Generally speaking, we too consider the Jews to be a detrimental influence, and we are convinced that a curse rests on the Jewish people . . . and that they also carry this curse into the host nation in which they have settled."[364] "This is

---

[351]1926, pp. 471-72.
[352]1929, p. 822.
[353]1927, p. 121.
[354]1924, p. 239.
[355]1928, p. 314.
[356]1928, p. 302.
[357]1926, p. 471.
[358]1929, p. 312.
[359]1926, p. 471.
[360]1924, p. 201.
[361]1926, p. 471.
[362]1926, p. 539.
[363]1926, p. 79. Compare 1924, p. 538.
[364]1929, p. 253.

also our opinion. A Jew remains a Jew, and his blood is not changed by baptism's washing with water. . . . Therefore, we can also be a friend of the mission to the Jews and nevertheless be an anti-Semite. . . . As everybody knows there is also a biblically proven Anti-Semitism in the New Testament."[365]

Their numerous statements on the political issues of the day were in the same vein. There was a volley of attacks on the "shameful Treaty of Versailles," "the lie about German war guilt," "the slavery of the German people." The signing of the Dawes Plan was lamented in an article framed by black edging that covered several pages.[366] It referred to the League of Nations only in derisive terms. The French interests are "exclusively guided by selfish ambition," and the will of the French nation "is always a will to destroy."[367] "The Englishman is marked by an unscrupulous brutality and immense hypocrisy."[368] Stresemann was a national pest,[369] Erzberger was a "little Matthew,"[370] K. Eisner was "this Galician Jew."[371] On the other hand, Hugenberg was an admirable, "strong personality."[372] And Ludendorff and Hitler were called "the Anointed Ones of the Nation" after the Munich Putsch, although the "Jacobines, that is, the Socialists, the Jews and the Jesuits rail at them, complain about them and revile them."[373] Before every election, detailed election recommendations were monotonously given for the same reasons. "Communism is insanity";[374] the Social Democratic Party is "quite simply unpatriotic and infiltrated by Jews,"[375] and it was "quite intentionally godless"; the Democratic Party was unelectable because it was democratic[376] and "more heavily influenced by the Jews than any other";[377] "the Center Party must be rejected! The party itself is as unprincipled as its name is nondescript."[378] To top it off, it was also "hostile to Germany."[379] The only remaining choice was between Hugenberg's German National Party and Ludendorff's national bloc. Both could be recommended. Why? Both "find the continuous hu-

---

[365]1926, p. 493.
[366]1924, pp. 568ff.
[367]1924, p. 67.
[368]1926, p. 472.
[369]1929, p. 793.
[370]1924, p. 239.
[371]1924, p. 203, among others.
[372]1929, pp. 505, 823.
[373]1924, p. 202.
[374]1928, p. 31.
[375]1926, p. 471.
[376]1928, pp. 313-14.
[377]1924, 241-42.
[378]Ibid.
[379]Ibid.

miliation of Germany by its enemies unbearable."[380] And both did not cooperate with the Weimer Republic. Their opposition was "based not on the issues but on principle."[381] Finally, "what I especially like about the national parties is that they seek to ward off the spirit of Jewish corruption from the German people."[382]

The political comments of the Pietistic magazine *Light and Life* were more than a little noticed. In 1928 even the *Frankfurter Zeitung (Frankfurt News)* took a position on them, asking the church what position it took on this movement in its midst in which the "most reactionary clerics" engage in the most "spiteful polemics" imaginable against the Weimar Republic, amounting to a call for its destruction.[383] How did *Light and Life* respond to this? It was new evidence that Germany was being undermined and ruled "by international Jewry"![384]

We must keep in mind that the Pietistic authors of this periodical attached great importance to this fact: "We are so seriously concerned about public affairs for the sake of the gospel."[385] Undoubtedly they *wanted* to be recognized by *this* fruit. However, with this fruit they obviously dug a riverbed for the things that were to come, and they did it as forcefully as possible with the means at their disposal.[386]

But in this context our interest is not focused on this point, but on a different one. The Pietists emphasized that Barth's theology and especially his understanding that the reality of God and the new creation in Christ cannot be seen was destructive to the church and morally paralyzing. On the other hand, the

---

[380]1924, p. 242.

[381]1929, p. 505.

[382]1928, p. 316.

[383]*Frankfurter Zeitung*, 1928, nr. 287.

[384]*Licht und Leben*, 1928, pp. 299-300.

[385]1924, p. 313.

[386]Therefore we must contradict the slant in H. von Sauberzweig's portrayal of the history of the Gnadau community movement (*He Is the Master, We Are His Brothers: The History of the Gnadau Community Movement from 1888-1958*). He seeks to excuse the undisputed fact that many Pietists went along with the leaders of the Third Reich by asserting that they slid into it gullibly and were completely unsuspecting and innocent. This view is at variance with what we have just shown. Still, the excellent report by Ruppel on "the Community Movement in the Third Reich" shows that in fact many Pietists became followers of National Socialism, but it also shows that others in the movement were reluctant to embrace the "national uprising," and still others even resisted it. Many who at first were favorably inclined finally changed their ways and separated from the supporters of National Socialism. Barth clearly saw this as well. To be sure, he could say at the Free Reformed Synod on January 3 and 4, 1934, "What was not good about Pietism has woken up with the German Christians." But the statement did not at all imply that everything was "not good" in it. Not all of its representatives "woke up" there. And in 1936 Barth declared that he came to greatly appreciate certain Pietists "in the hour of danger" (in *Lebenszeichen aus dem Kreis der Evangelischen Predigerschule Basel*, 1936, p. 26).

reality of the "new creation" is clearly seen not only in its teaching but also in the Pietistic movement itself. This is why their movement is under God's "blessing" and is "God's work." However, based on what we have just described here, we must say that what they claimed in this area including the "fruit" by which they wanted to be recognized could be had equally well without "the new birth," "the assurance of salvation" or the "religious possession." What they claimed for themselves as "the new birth" and the reality of the new creation had no greater weight, at least in the area just shown, than simply saying the same thing that the "old creation" also said in the garb of the right-wing extremists of the 1920s. Their claim that the "new man" was clearly a given, especially in Pietism, their claim that "God's work" could be equated with the community movement and that the "faith" of its supporters could be recognized by "these fruits" is simply challenged by all this. They would have had good reason to handle their criticism of Barth much more cautiously and put their own house in order before accusing him of destroying the church and morally paralyzing it.

PART C

A FURTHER EXPLORATION OF THE ENCOUNTER BETWEEN THE YOUNGER BARTH AND PIETISM

I. The Learning Process on the Part of the Pietists

We will now inquire whether both sides learned something from one another when the author of the *Epistle to the Romans* and the Pietists encountered each other in the 1920s. Or to ask the question more cautiously, were both sides motivated by this encounter to learn something new? We believe that we can actually speak in such terms and that their encounter was actually not exhausted by defending and affirming the position they had first taken. First of all, we will deal with the question to what extent the *Pietists* might have been led a little further through their engagement with Barth's theology. After the discussion in the second chapter, it should be clear that this could have happened only within narrow limits; they could have gone just "a bit further." But to what extent did their confrontation with the *Epistle to the Romans* initiate at least a modest "learning process" among the Pietists?

The Difference of Opinion Within Pietism over Their Position on Barth's Theology

In answering this question we start with the fact that Pietism did indeed react to Barth's theology and saw itself under pressure to take a position on a number of occasions.[1] These statements were not all merely addressed to Barth but also to their own Pietistic movement. On the one hand, they wanted to inform their own supporters about Barth's theology. On the other hand, they wanted to reach an understanding on how they should relate to it. In this context we must especially stress the fact that Pietism revealed a conspicuous *disunity* in its position on Barth's theology. We have mentioned this in passing time and again and must now explicitly turn our attention to it. When Pietism voiced its opinion on Barth's theology, it presented itself not as a uniform but as a pluralistic bloc which led to more than just a little tension among its adherents. At that time Karl Müller from Erlangen correctly stated, "It makes you think when you realize that

---

[1] A. Köberle, *Rechtfertigung und Heiligung*, 3rd ed., 1930, p. 7, remarked: "In the circles . . . influenced by Pietism . . . 'the crisis theology' has shaken many and caused many to shift their thinking."

Karl Barth not only found rejection, but also wide recognition in precisely these circles although he is constantly engaging in polemics against the Pietists' emphasis on the believer's new qualities."[2] We must expect that these tensions among the community people were not first caused by their confrontation with the second *Epistle to the Romans,* but they were at least intensified by it and erupted in public. And so we must expect that on the one hand different positions taken by Pietists on the theology of this book triggered such tensions, but on the other hand these tensions in turn forced them to deal with Barth's theology in greater detail. Roughly speaking we can divide the Pietists into two camps as far as their position on Barth is concerned, without denying all kinds of crossovers between both camps and without overlooking the fact that a good number of the differences between both camps seem to be only nuances. Nevertheless, the difference between both Pietistic positions was not only quantitative (they were more or less willing to make concessions to Barth's theology of the *Epistle to the Romans*) but also qualitative (they took a different approach on the issues).

We can picture this difference of opinion within Pietism by focusing on the question raised by the Pietists, Does the author of the *Epistle to the Romans* deserve to be seriously heard as a teacher of the church and in Pietism as well? On one side, this was energetically affirmed by L Thimme. "Barth had to be heard."[3] In his view "the community movement owes a great debt of gratitude to a friend, even if an often uncomfortable one."[4] "When we want to understand Barth, we can understand him in no other way than as a preacher in the wilderness. God sent him, when the time was fulfilled, when the tower of Babel was almost finished."[5] In a similar vein W. Knappe also wanted to see Pietism pay attention to what "in our view will remain valuable, what is divinely necessary in this theology."[6] Indeed, "here we stand firmly on the foundation of the Reformation."[7] And he added, addressing his friends in Pietism, "Woe on us if we are not prepared to listen to the voice of truth because it blows in our faces like a strong east wind."[8] And P. Kuhlmann also believed, albeit with great reservations,[9] "Barth's message has something to say to us. This is evi-

---

[2]K. Müller, "Rechtfertigung oder Heiligung?" in *Im Kampf um die Kirche,* 1930, p. 110.

[3]L. Thimme, "Das Problem der Kirche und die reformatorische Losung," in *Im Kampf um die Kirche,* p. 34.

[4]Ibid., p. 33.

[5]L. Thimme, "Das Problem 'Karl Barth,'" in *Gnadauer Gemeinschaftsblatt,* 1929, p. 94.

[6]W. Knappe, "Karl Barth und der Pietismus," in *Licht und Leben,* 1927, p. 499.

[7]Ibid.

[8]Ibid., p. 467.

[9]P. Kuhlmann, "Die Problematik und ihre Gefahren," in *Licht und Leben,* 1929, p. 355.

dently the will of the Lord of the church."[10] On the other side, there is a group that primarily warns against Barth's theology and doubts that Barth deserves a hearing as a teacher of the church. For example, Henrichs said, "We take the matter very seriously." In this "sarcastic theology we see a totally illegitimate attack on our most holy possessions, revealing a lack of respect for what is holy."[11] W. Hützen sharply disputed that "the apostles wanted to tell us what Barth finds in their words. I can do nothing else, I must confess that I find an essential emptying of Scriptural truth in his presentation."[12] In examining Barth's theories he came to the conclusion time and again that "fidelity to Scripture makes it impossible for us to agree with these ideas of Barth."[13] With holy earnestness and with heart and soul we resist his radical demolition on the fairgrounds of religions and world-views because we must in principle make a fundamentally different judgment based on Scripture and experience."[14] G. F. Nagel contradicted Barth just as resolutely. "Through his dialectic approach Barth wants to twist the foundational biblical gospel to mean just the opposite."[15] He offers the "Word" in "an attenuated and skeptical form" instead of in perfect clarity and in the unbroken power of the Spirit."[16] His theology is a "practical devaluation of biblical watchwords."[17] "Here dangers loom for the believing church, which demand the most strenuous objection and the most decisive resistance."[18]

We can elucidate this difference of opinion within Pietism by examining the following circumstances. As we said, if the Pietistic responses to Karl

---

[10]P. Kuhlmann, "Søren Kierkegaard und die Pietisten," in *Licht und Leben,* 1929, p. 790.

[11]Quoted in a lecture by H. Dannert, "Die Evangelisation," in *Licht und Leben,* 1928, p. 357. Dannert thinks in a similarly critical fashion with regard to Barth. Compare *Licht und Leben,* 1929, p. 355.

[12]Hützen, *Biblisches Glaubensleben,* 1928, p. 17.

[13]Ibid., p. 28.

[14]Ibid., p. 35.

[15]Nagel, *Karl Barth und der heilsgewisse Glaube,* 1929, p. 36.

[16]Ibid., p. 39.

[17]Ibid., p. 41.

[18]Ibid., p. 44. Compare here the casual way J. Gubler, *Kirche und Pietismus: Ein Gang durch die neuere ev. Kirchengeschichte der Schweiz,* 1959, copes with this object in his position on the "dialectical theology" of the 1920s (including the theology of the *Epistle to the Romans:* Whereas Pietism espoused "the true and always same biblical teaching," "dialectical theology" is an example of the "numerous doctrinal systems that replace each other" (p. 209), in short: a fashionable phenomenon (fashionable foolishness?!) to which "Gellert's fable of the old hat is applicable. This old hat could be adapted to contemporary fashions and tastes in form and ornamentation. And "when it was at times especially difficult to find one's way in the labyrinth of the competing teachings, the Pietists were given the privilege of offering many a seeker the staff in the form of God's Word to get to the secure mountain top" (pp. 209-10). They did not learn anything? No, nothing at all!

Barth agreed by taking the form of a yes-but position on his theology, they diverged considerably in the way they specifically filled the yes and the but with content. For the latter group their yes basically reached only as far as they thought Barth's theology affirmed their own concern.[19] Here they welcomed his theses only to the extent that they object to liberalism but not to Pietism. "We like to see" his separation from liberalism.[20] It should remain "untouched."[21] "But we resist his tactic of heading for us with a harsh hand and wanting to finish off the "'men about town', as Barth once called the Pietists."[22] All this means that they could agree with Barth's theology to a certain degree or at least they thought they could. In this respect there was nothing at all for the Pietists to hear, learn or correct because what Barth said "correctly" was nothing other than "what we have always thought."[23] However, for the other group their yes meant that they were more willing to allow an opponent to tell them the truth, "even if it may be one-sided or painful for us."[24] Here they were not concerned "to save *our* language, *our* theology, *our* piety." They were not necessarily prepared to defend Pietism, but on the basis of its theology they tried to obey the "voice of truth."[25] Here they knew or at least suspected that the voice of truth and the voice of Pietism were two different things. Here they could concede that Barth had seen a truth afresh that even Pietism had forgotten, that his criticism of Pietism was justified at

---

[19]Fortunately the process of "co-opting" one's opponent that now and then has not been unpopular with the Pietists was undertaken at that time only by F. Mund with regard to Barth. Mund simply claimed him more than boldly as the chief witness for an unbroken revivalist Pietism not in the least touched by Barth's critique. "What Karl Barth . . . calls the outpouring of the Holy Spirit is the crucial factor in every revival" in which the Holy Spirit, "ascertainably" and "experientially" creating those who are born again, does not just visit individuals, "but also whole communities and regions" ("Die Gemeinschaftsbewegung eine Anklage gegen die Kirche," in *Kampf um die Kirche,* p. 48). Here he was clearly not affirming a seriously understood theological insight of Barth. Instead, he was only being co-opted by Mund, who completely obscured Barth's actual statements. Mund later gave up this procedure and conversely vehemently accused Barth of being incapable of "really perceiving the powerful effects of His Holy Spirit" (who for F. Mund not only manifested himself in Spener, etc., but also in the "Fuhrer" of the "Nordic race"). See *Pietismus-eine Schicksalsfrage an die Kirche heute,* 1936, pp. 14ff.

[20]Hützen, *Biblisches Glaubensleben,* p. 36.

[21]Nagel, *Karl Barth und der heilsgewisse Glaube,* p. 11.

[22]Hützen, *Biblisches Glaubensleben,* p. 35.

[23]Ibid., p. 15. Compare also the repetition of the Pietistic view of the 1920s in H. von Sauberzweig: "We wholeheartedly rejoiced that the divine Word was taken seriously and liberal theology was dethroned [in Barth's theology]. Those were things the community movement had supported from its beginnings" (*He Is the Master, We Are His Brothers,* p. 292).

[24]Knappe, "Karl Barth und der Pietismus," p. 467.

[25]Ibid.

least to a certain degree and actually pointed out "an essential danger in Pietism."[26] It easily forgets that before God not only the "mountain top experience" of Idealism's self-redemption does not count for much, but also the "pious" mountaintop experience of the converted.[27] In other words, Barth "rightly" pointed out the danger of Pharisaism, which is more concerned with "possessing" than with the Giver.[28] H. Oltmann even spoke of the imminent danger of "betraying the secret of Christ's church."[29] Knappe admonished his friends "not to make themselves guilty of ignoring this huge call to repentance which certainly does not occur without God's will and decree, by always remaining impenitent. We of all people should heed this call because we talk a lot about repentance."[30] Their yes to the theology of the *Epistle to the Romans* did not extend only as far as it proved them right, rather it was coupled with their willingness to admit that it was right and could possibly correct their theology. Thus their yes was coupled with their openness to learning new things and changing their approach.

Furthermore, this difference of opinion within Pietism becomes apparent in the way in which they raised objections, the but, to Barth's theology. The question that was controversial among the Pietists related to whether the essence of Barth's theology could be spoken of as *"biblical"* or not. On this question an often very fine but clear line was drawn between two distinct camps within the community movement. The one group, led by G. F. Nagel and W. Hützen, flatly denied that the essence of Barth's message was biblical. Here they ascertained with "holy sensitivity" that "it treats the basic doctrines of the Word in a critical and doubting manner,[31] indeed, they are practically eliminated."[32] And this preemptory demand was made: These skeptical theses "had to be deleted if the Christian church could ever listen to his message with real confidence. A 'clarification' could only take place if such words were unambiguously dropped. Nothing but this demand could be derived from the New Testament with its verdict on doctrines that differed from its own."[33] And W. Hützen concluded from his understanding that Barth "emptied" the Scripture of its meaning at essential points that community people should be asked to treat Barth as if he were not

---

[26]Ibid., p. 483.

[27]Ibid., pp. 467ff.

[28]L. Thimme, *Kirche, Sekte und Gemeinschaftsbewegung,* 1925, pp. 258, 276.

[29]H. Oltmann, "Die Gemeinschaftsbewegung auf der Anklagebank," in *Im Kampf um die Kirche,* p. 89.

[30]Knappe, "Karl Barth und der Pietismus," p. 483.

[31]Nagel, *Karl Barth und der heilsgewisse Glaube,* p. 38.

[32]Ibid., p. 40.

[33]Ibid., pp. 38-39.

there and simply continue to read the Bible the way we had read it before, as if there had been no *Epistle to the Romans*.[34] At this point even the other group shared these strong reservations about Barth and spoke of the "not unfounded charge of spiritualism and intellectualism[35] or rationalism that had been brought against him."[36] Yet on this side they saw and recognized Barth as an interpreter of Scripture. Indeed, "Barth's theology is ruthless with itself. It does not allow us to rest on any human standpoint, even if it were a pious one, even if it were Barth's."[37] Indeed, "it is due to Barth's theology that a generation has once again learned to listen attentively to *God's Word*."[38] Of course, he presented his understanding "in an unbalanced radicalism."[39] But even that is not *only* problematic because "the truth has something radical about it."[40] However it is *also* problematic. Barth's message is biblical, but biblical "in an unbalanced way." Therefore it must be supplemental by many other "biblical truths" which he "ignores."[41] The theory of Barth's "unbalanced theology" which was in need of and capable of being supplemented by other insights guarded by Pietism was strongly advocated by this second group. Still, they believed they could couple their Pietistic critique of his theology with a recognition of its at least partial fidelity to Scripture.

We can see from these juxtapositions that Pietism, at least in the way it related to Barth, did not simply speak with *one* voice. We can conclude from this that when the representatives and leaders of the community movement dealt with the theology of the *Epistle to the Romans,* it had a devastating effect in two ways: At least some of them felt motivated to begin a process of critical *self-reflection,* and certain *tensions* emerged among them as a result.

Excursus: The Gnadau Pentecost Conference of 1927

To what extent the engagement of the community people with this theology in the aforementioned terms shook them up and how they then (sharing common ground amid certain tensions) sought to cope with this "shock" will be illustrated by the example of the Gnadau Pentecost Conference, which took place

---

[34]Hützen, *Biblisches Glaubensleben,* p. 35.
[35]Thimme, "Das Problem der Kirche," p. 35.
[36]Knappe, "Karl Barth und der Pietismus," p. 533.
[37]Ibid., p. 470. Compare also Bucherschau, in *Licht und Leben,* 1927, p. 671: "Barth's theology . . . is a struggle to understand the Word of God."
[38]Knappe, "Karl Barth und der Pietismus," p. 483.
[39]Ibid., p. 499.
[40]Ibid., p. 470.
[41]Ibid., p. 499.

in Halberstadt on June 7-10, 1927.[42] It was a meeting of the "German Federation for the Promotion of Fellowship and Evangelization." To this day representatives of the communities affiliated with this federation come together every year for such common discussions. The Halberstadt Conference of 1927[43] had chosen the self-critical topic: "Is the Community Movement Finished?" This is typical of the unrest that had come into Pietism at that time. However, it had already anticipated the reassuring answer in the theme of the conference, and this is also typical. "No, if the Spirit moves us!" Even if there were some conference participants who condemned this additional phrase because from the outset it "prevents us from taking seriously the question that has been raised,"[44] it must be stated that even the question in the theme of the conference did not intend to voice any fundamental self-criticism as such since it only put the current relevance of Pietism on the agenda, not the appropriateness of its cause. The first speaker, E. Modersohn, observed that the question was really meant for discussion only within the narrow confines in which it was phrased: "Many people are grateful that they have been blessed by the community movement. And yet this question is being raised when the present is compared to the past: Are we as a

---

[42]Further examples could be mentioned here. A. Köberle (*Rechtfertigung und Heiligung*, pp. 7-8) points out similar negotiations in the DCSV. A preoccupation and discussion with Barth had already taken place at the Pentecost Conference of the Gnadau Community Movement in 1926 (compare N. N., "Gnadau," in *Licht und Leben*, 1926, pp. 407, 409). Especially the meeting of representatives of the Rhineland Community Federation on February 16, 1928, in Cologne is worth mentioning. They discussed Barth's theology, and similar tensions erupted here as well (compare the report of W. Knappe, "Nachrichten," in *Licht und Leben*, 1928, pp. 186-88). In two lectures (by Schinelin and Knappe) Barth's theology was portrayed "just as positively as negatively." When Schindelin said that Barth was right in criticizing the "pious Pharisee in us" and that Pietism could ignore his critique only to its own detriment," he was vigorously opposed, for example by Henrichs: this is not the danger; the actual danger is not Pietism at all but Barth's theology, his "elimination of the earnestness of personal repentance and the striving for sanctification." In short, "the discussion . . . was very animated. Some expressed opinions that fully championed Barth's cause, but others . . . sounded a tone of rejection." They whitewashed the differences of opinion more than they tackled and overcame them by finally agreeing on the vague compromise: "We want to heed Barth's call; but Barth's theology does not yet have the final word." How vague, indeed, untenable the compromise was can be seen when immediately following the discussion the barely concealed differences of opinion came to the surface just as vehemently as before over the issue of whether the community movement should get involved in church politics to assert its interests. Here and in what follows the differences of opinion within Pietism are not simply interesting to me because of the way they evaluated *Barth's* theology but primarily because of the differences in the *Pietists' own self-understanding* that appear in them.

[43]Two extensive (both not uncritical) reports on the conference are available: W. Knappe, "Gnadau 1927," in *Gnadauer Gemeinschaftsblatt*, 1927, pp. 169-80 (quoted in what follows as GG); "Gnadau," in *Licht und Leben*, 1927, pp. 412ff., 426ff., 442ff., 457ff., 490ff. (quoted in what follows as LL).

[44]GG, p. 170.

movement still the blessing we have been?"[45] The second speaker, Pastor Oehlkers, did his part in declaring too much self-criticism superfluous by expressing
his joy that in the community movement "brothers" have always "allowed themselves to be judged by God."[46] Another speaker, the Chrischona man Eckardt,
remarked that a possible self-critique could not apply to the question of whether
the community movement's theology of conversion is right, but only to the
question of "why so few clear, lasting conversions are taking place in our
ranks?"[47] Thus from the beginning they did not have in mind a *fundamental,*
self-critical reflection. They certainly did intend to make corrections in the system but not corrections *of the* system.

But now the other aspect must be stressed. They actually had come together
with the intention of reflecting *self-critically* on their movement. "Evidently there
is such a desire for inward reflection in large parts of the community movement
and this is the deeper reason for the strong attendance this year's Pentecost conference enjoyed."[48] As they convened the conference, they were aware that this
critical "inward reflection" they had in mind represented somewhat of a novelty
in the history of the movement. And even later this conference was remembered
as a special one in the history of the movement because they dared to see the
"judgment of God" on themselves. Their powerful talk of submitting "to the judgment of God" in "a spirit of repentance" shows how much they were willing to
allow God to question them and "shake them up."[49] "Even if God desires to break
up our movement, we want to submit to him."[50] "May God give us grace to place
ourselves on a foundation of judgment, for only a conference of judgment can
turn into a conference of grace."[51] Indeed, "Blessed are those who are unfinished!"[52] They also spoke in detail about the danger of high-handedness that is
even a threat to Pietism. It is basically just "legalism and self-righteousness." Some
have acted on their own authority in the interpretation of Scripture, sanctification,
"soul winning and the care of souls."[53] Finally, one participant complained that
these points were not "dealt with in greater detail," and even the chairman of the
conference (W. Michaelis) called attention to this problem in the discussion.[54]

---

[45]LL, p. 421.
[46]LL, p. 413.
[47]LL, p. 414.
[48]LL, p. 412.
[49]GG, p. 170.
[50]Ibid.
[51]GG, p. 171.
[52]GG, p. 178.
[53]GG, p. 178.
[54]Ibid.

The conference participants themselves saw in all these questions an effect of Barth's theology, and Barth's influence was also seen in their willingness to ask questions. "The influence of this man could be clearly felt in several persons who spoke at this conference."[55] In fact, when one speaker separated himself from Barth, a heckler cried out: "The man has gotten much more from Barth than he knows,"[56] and it was reported that Barth clearly left his mark on the lectures. "For example, consciously or unconsciously, they frequently linked judgment and grace."[57] And there was even more. In the lectures and in comments made during the discussion many participants explicitly took a position on him and went into detail. "Karl Barth is attacking the community movement from the viewpoint of Pauline theology, which is actually its foundation." Therefore they had to seriously ask themselves at this conference "whether the time of the community movement is past."[58] So we may say that the peculiar intention of the conference to "place itself on the foundation of judgment" was evidently caused in part by the publication of the *Epistle to the Romans*.

But now we must also point out that the differences of opinion between the community people that we mentioned earlier became apparent and led to several clashes when the conference attempted to place itself "on the foundation of judgment" and discussed the question of whether and to what extent this was even necessary. There was dissension in the meeting over the issue of whether there actually could be a legitimate, serious critique of the community movement. Right at the beginning of his lecture Eckert denied the right of non-Pietists to make a reasoned, fundamental critique of Pietism: "If the question had emerged from the community movement itself, then the answer would be 'Yes.' But it has not emerged from it, rather it has been brought to it from the outside," for example, by Barth. Consequently the question must be denied.[59] One participant in the discussion immediately thanked Eckert for exonerating the community movement. He "literally breathed a sigh of relief" when he heard that statement. On the other hand, W. Knappe felt the statement was a big disappointment; he was "flabbergasted" when the "the question posed by the conference" was treated "in such a reassuring way from the outset."[60] Another commentator supported him. "It does not matter if it [this question] comes from the outside or from the inside"; in any case, we should "let the question do its

---

[55]GG, p. 173.
[56]Ibid.
[57]Ibid.
[58]LL, p. 414.
[59]GG, p. 172.
[60]Ibid.

work in[61] us with unrelenting and holy earnestness." But opinions were divided precisely on this question. On one side Michaelis asked the participants to make a serious self-critique. "Do we really preach the gospel? . . . We resort to all kinds of substitutes."[62] Another participant thought, "If the community movement takes itself to task today, it will not be able to avoid an examination of its foundation, especially since such a serious admonisher in the person of Karl Barth has risen up to confront it. . . . Do we really have the full gospel? . . . Not only a few barren branches must be broken off, a treatment of the roots is necessary."[63] H. Dannenbaum intensified the criticism with a "trumpet blast" that revealed him to be a student of Barth: "Is the time of the community movement past? If only it were past! If only we would finally learn to look over the fence at the body of Christ."[64] This was too much even for Knappe.[65] It was mainly the preacher Stolpmann who objected to Dannenbaum's attack in which he called Stolpmann an unkind word. But Stolpmann implored "brotherly love" and explained, "We cannot . . . leave . . . our truth."[66] Then they organized the opposition of those who more or less disputed the necessity of such a "treatment of the roots" and "such an examination of the foundation." Then it became apparent that "the question posed by the conference had clearly been too pointed for many." Thus new testimonies about the blessing of the community movement and its strength for the future were heard again and again in the discussion time.[67]

The tensions that surfaced were also personalized and developed into a controversy about the figure of L. Thimme, the undoubtedly Pietistic man who to no small degree recognized Barth's critique as justified. Eckhardt wanted to act decisively and expel him "from the fellowship." Oehlkers opposed him just as decisively: It was not right to "show someone the door who pointed out the fellowship's defects and threats to its spiritual health from inside the fellowship."[68] This difference of opinion was also apparent in their position on Barth. One participant expressed the opinion that we "must take this prophet seriously when he inquires into the foundations of our movement."[69] He was contradicted by others. In their view such questions about the foundations of the community movement were not necessary, but Barth himself would benefit if

---

[61]Ibid.
[62]LL, p. 491.
[63]GG, pp. 177-78.
[64]Ibid.
[65]Ibid.
[66]GG, p. 178.
[67]LL, p. 429.
[68]GG, p.173.
[69]LL, p. 491.

such questions were asked about his own foundations since he lacked the decisive foundation: "faith in a possession of salvation."[70] We can only wish that one day he would find his way to the biblical assurance of salvation."[71] In fact, the example of the Gnadau Pentecost Conference of 1927 confirms how much (but also within what limits) the Pietism of that time entered a period of somewhat self-critical uneasiness through its encounter with Barth. At the same time it also confirms the fact that in spite of all the "brotherly love" found in these circles their encounter with Barth resulted in tensions that for the time being were not overcome.[72]

The Merits and Limits of the Positions Taken by the Opposing Sides Within Pietism

We have discovered a certain difference of opinion within Pietism which became especially noticeable in its position on Barth's theology. I believe the fact of such disunity is significant in itself. For Pietism has always understood itself as a uniform block even up to the Confessing Church movement of our day. It believes it has a mission within the church to preserve it from a "pluralism in doctrine."[73] This is why it could occasionally even admire "the courage of the Pope's infallible teaching office to make clear decisions on doctrine."[74] In view of this it is significant that in its own house Pietism was evidently not able to maintain the "unified line"[75] it demanded of others. At least in its position on Barth's theology it clearly presented itself as a complex movement in which different ways of thinking are not only possible but also obviously unavoidable even if they are in tension with one another. Even if the statements of the different groups correspond to a large degree, it can still be said in viewing their agreement on the issues: it is the tone that makes the music, and further: *faciunt duo idem, non est idem*. In this movement there evidently were and still are different kinds of supporters of the group's common concern as there probably are in all Christian groupings: close-minded and open-minded, unrepentant and

---

[70]LL, p. 414.

[71]GG, p. 174.

[72]The paper in response to Nagel's work on Barth provides an example of how Pietists in the community movement could downright scold one another: Nagel "himself does not know how mistaken he is" (manuscript in the Barth archives in Basel, 2). "You did not honor the name of our Lord [with your treatise against Barth!], brother Nagel! No one would have held it against you if you had refrained from making such a thorough critique of Barth, knowing that you lack the necessary intellectual qualifications for this task" (p. 10).

[73]G. Bergmann, *Kirche am Scheideweg,* 1967, p. 278.

[74]Ibid., p. 274.

[75]Ibid., p. 272.

repentant, those who are in the know and those who are willing to learn, "conservative" and "self-critical."

Looking at both camps in this conflict within Pietism,[76] let us now inquire about the merits as well as the limits of the positions advocated by both sides. First of all, we believe that the representatives of the camp that largely rejected Barth's theology had at least within Pietism an important, even essential function. By insisting on the differences between the message of this theology and Pietism, they reminded their more open-minded companions that two views of the Christian faith were facing each other here, and it was actually not as easy to bridge these differences and combine these positions as the latter were inclined to imagine. By largely objecting to this theology, they kept alive the understanding that more serious, more fundamental differences were at issue between it and Pietistic theology than could be overcome by taking "something" from that theology while retaining something from Pietism. By objecting they in fact asked the question, Can a Pietism that seriously affirms Barth's basic theses still be called Pietism? Or they asked the opposite question: Has a Pietism that only wants to adopt "something" from Barth's basic theses seriously learned from him? Clearly the more open-minded Pietists ran the risk of overlooking or covering up the fundamental differences of opinion that were on the agenda and thus ultimately trivializing the necessary learning process. This is shown by the fact that two theses were favored by them that we mentioned earlier. (1) Barth's theology was correct but *unbalanced* and thus could be supplemented by the insights of Pietism. (2) Barth *misunderstood* Pietism in his critique of Pietism and had a "caricature" in view. We believe we have said what needed to be said about both theses. To us they appear to be problematic. Perhaps they also had the significance of serving as "crutches" for the progres-

---

[76]It appears that the tradition of the various camps which were present in Pietism as we have presented it has been especially cultivated at different locations and schools. Whereas, for example, the school St. Chrischona, as far as I can see, has always steered at least a very reserved course with regard to Barth's theology, one could label the similar school of the Bahnau Brotherhood as a Pietistic school that is almost defined by Barth (compare M. Fischer, *50 Jahre Bahnau. Das tat Gott,* 1956, pp. 95, 175, 154: "What inspiration came from reading the works of Karl Barth!"). This school, primarily its leader Max Fischer, took the initiative for continuing Pietism's conversation with Barth's theology in the 1950s (compare E. Busch, *Karl Barths Lebenslauf,* 1975, p. 461; further M. Fischer, "Eine erfreuliche Aussprache," in *21. Freundesbriefe der Bahnauer Bruderschaft,* 1959, pp. 16-17). Concerning the school St. Chrischona, compare the remark of E. Thurneysen in his letter from March 30, 1928: "Reports are arriving that at St. Chrischona, for example, they are contemplating serious measures to counter the spreading 'Barthian danger.' . . . In spite of all their assurances that they are thanking dear God for the fact that justification is again being so faithfully proclaimed, this proclamation should not go so far as to hurt Basel Pietism. 'Please, dear pastor, spare our faithful, believing circles!'" (K. Barth/E. Thurneysen, *Briefwechsel 2, 1921–1930,* 1974, p. 568).

sive Pietists in order to justify their openness to the message of the *Epistle to the Romans* "pro-domo." Nevertheless, it is the case that both theses proved to be obstacles to a thorough discussion of the differences between Barth and Pietism, preventing them from even seeing the depth and the fundamental nature of those differences, even if both theses were augmented by the thesis that those other Pietists had misunderstood Barth when they rejected him. At any rate, in the camp of the more open-minded Pietists, it more or less continued to be the case that they were able in principle to strongly confess Pietism's need for correction and their own willingness to listen to the message of the *Epistle to the Romans*. Yet the final result of their fundamental openness did not prove to be so successful because it was able to provide them with a clear conscience as they sought to rescue the crucial concerns of Pietism unscathed from the *Epistle to the Romans* fire of criticism. However, we certainly do not think that the group that primarily disapproves of this book would have actually tackled the challenge of carrying on such a necessary, more thorough conversation about the basic issues dividing them. On the contrary, for all intents and purposes it rejected such a conversation. But we do think that by its rejection it called attention to the fact that the conversation between the author of the *Epistle to the Romans* and Pietism would necessarily *have to* be one that focused on the basic issues in contention.

However, on the other side, the advantage of the more open-minded group over the other cannot be denied. As we said earlier, a yes-but in response to Barth's theology was expressed in both camps. However, it makes a considerable difference whether they say yes to it in so far as it affirms Pietism, or yes even in the sense of being open to the possibility that in certain respects it could be right in its opposition to Pietism. Likewise, it makes a considerable difference whether they say no to it simply where it deviates from the scheme of Pietism or no where they presume there is a gap or a lack of consistency in it. In the first case, and this did in fact happen in the former group, the yes-but they asserted was profoundly *unfruitful*. For their whole yes referred here only to what "we have always said." And their whole no here meant only that they objected to an encroachment on their theology that violated what had always been dear to the Pietists' hearts. This stance was unfruitful because what they affirmed was basically their own theology and as a rule only a caricature of Barth's theology. Furthermore, it was unfruitful because in saying no to Barth's theology they were obviously concerned about protecting their own position from critical inquiries. This attitude was so questionable because in the yes-but they articulated they only pretended that they were willing to have a dialogue. In reality they were not at all willing to do so because they basically only wanted to confirm their own position and were not prepared to listen or learn something new or possibly have to change their own ideas. In the second case, and that was actually a given in the latter group, the situation was basically hopeful. The yes-but they asserted here was *fruitful.* For the yes they expressed here was not said in self-affirmation but repentantly; they were prepared to agree with insights that could signal their willingness to learn something new and possibly even change their own ideas. Although the but expressed here was in effect filled with an emphasis on special Pietistic concerns, it was an open-minded but because they did not simply want to foist an alien element on Barth's theology. Rather they believed (in subjective honesty) they should "supplement" it with something the theology itself was asking for, and this would be the positive meaning of their thesis that the *Epistle to the Romans* was capable of being supplemented. As I indicated earlier, we can and even must ask whether in this case as well they said yes to a Barth they partially misunderstood and largely affirmed their own position in expressing this but. Nevertheless, the situation here was at least fruitful *in principle:* fruitful because at least in principle they expressed a willingness to listen, learn and even "repent." As a result their desire to make corrections in the *Epistle to the Romans* gained in importance and could be taken seriously.

But let us say it again: We do not think that only the latter group would have contributed to a "learning process on the part of the Pietists." For as we have said, the former group, probably more unintentionally than intentionally, made their contribution to such a "learning process" by voicing their persistent reservations about the theology of the *Epistle to the Romans* and by thus pointing out the need for a dialogue on the fundamental issues in contention. Beyond this we must also consider the fact that the *tension* in their own camp between two different attitudes was able to serve as a stimulus that pushed the representatives of this "more conservative" group beyond merely protecting the viewpoint they had already taken. We will shortly further discuss the fact that in this group as well, the process did not remain one of mere preservation.

The Possibility of an "Optimal" Pietistic Interpretation of Barth

At this point I would like to first of all point out that in the community movement a different approach to the theology of the *Epistle to the Romans* was possible from the two we have introduced. I am thinking of the one that an unknown Pietist of the 1920s demonstrated in a statement on Nagel's work about Barth. It went quite a bit beyond the polemical atmosphere that usually prevailed between Barth and the supporters of Pietism in those days and beyond the atmosphere in which they could say "the final word" on the problem of "pietas" raised by Barth, as Otto Weber put it.[77] This unknown Pietist by no means ruled out a "critique" of Barth, but he also did not want to "supplement," improve or correct him right away. We cannot say that he *learned* from the theology of the *Epistle to the Romans* because his typewritten manuscript is too short to judge that. But we can say that *as a Pietist* he openly *wanted to learn* from this theology *as a Pietist!* This is apparent not only in his language but above all in the way his interests centered around the same points as did the rest of the Pietists: the human need for redemption without saying that sin is human nature,[78] experience,[79] sanctification,[80] assurance of salvation[81] and even the possession of salvation.[82] Those were also his concerns. But as a Pietist he did not want to hold onto these concerns in opposition to Barth or "carry on" Barth's theology with them. Instead he wanted to calmly "sit at Barth's feet to learn from him what he can learn in this context."[83] And he did it with the working hypothesis that this theology was not merely a theoretical intellectual game but that what "can be learned" there could be of use pastorally for the "ministry of the local church,"[84] for our "approach to evangelization,"[85] even "in the most personal area of the struggle against sin."[86]

What did this anonymous author learn from Barth? Was it Barth's critique of any suitability of humankind for God? Yes, but this does not imply any contempt for human beings (God is everything, humanity is nothing); "Barth may be interpreted in such a way that man must be overcome so that the new man may come,"[87] or "so that he may be redeemed."[88] Was it Barth's critique of Pietism's insistence that the new, redeemed self was a tangible given? Yes, "as soon as we make an object out of this here and now of *God* through a corrupt act of appropriation, as soon as we make an independent realm, as isolated sphere out of it, we have turned this new self into a very pious person, but a pious person in need of being overcome." But in saying this, he does not deny that the new self as such is a given. "We may interpret Barth in this way: True redemption is

---

[77]O. Weber, "Zu Karl Barths 'Dogmatik,'" in *RKZ*, 1928, p. 348.
[78]*Erwiderung auf Nagels Barth Schrift.* Typewritten manuscript in the Karl Barth archives, Basel, pp. 4ff.
[79]Ibid., pp. 10-11.
[80]Ibid., p. 11.
[81]Ibid., p. 14.
[82]Ibid., p. 15.
[83]Ibid., p. 13.
[84]Ibid., p. 11.
[85]Ibid.
[86]Ibid., p. 18.
[87]Ibid., p. 6.
[88]Ibid., p. 7.

present in its bearers as a light emits its rays without knowing much about it."[89]
How about Barth's critique of the idea that the believer must depend on his
Christian experience"? Yes, "but he is not denying what he does not emphasize,
he is only saying that it is not emphasized."[90] Christian "experience" could be lik-
ened to the brush Grunewald used to paint his masterpiece. "While observing
the painting, we will completely forget the brush even if it could not have been
painted without it."[91] How about his critique of the "assurance of salvation"? Yes,
indeed, but "Barth does not teach that there is no assurance of salvation, rather
without double predestination there is no assurance of salvation" and put in
these terms he does not rule it out as such.[92] How about his critique of a "possession of salvation"? Indeed, "consider the fact that there is only one kind of
grace, one that remains free!" But again this only signifies a correction but not an
absolute denial of this matter.[93] How about Barth's assertion of a discontinuity
between the work of humans and the work of God? Good, but this insight includes another: "through this discontinuity God acts on us."[94] "In a similar vein
teaching on sanctification and the Christian walk have to take this path again and
again." "This can only strengthen and encourage us in the struggle of faith."[95]

By not confronting Barth with Pietism or supplementing him with the Pietist's
concerns, but instead, as a Pietist, interpreting Barth with Barth himself, he
reached this conclusion in the end: "Barth is in fact much closer to a biblically
purified Pietism than Nagel" (the most diligent Pietistic opponent of Barth)![96] Although this statement was probably an exaggeration, we can say more cautiously: With this procedure this Pietist showed a way in which both sides, irre-
spective of their different perceptions, could be led forward in their encounter
and at the same time brought more closely together. This is a much more hopeful path than the one followed by the other Pietists who argue according to the
pattern of yes-but. Indeed, we believe that this procedure is basically the only
sensible and appropriate one in the encounter that is of special concern to us
here (as well as in interdenominational discussions in general). It leads neither
to a hardening of one's own position nor to compromise but to the freedom in

---

[89]Ibid.
[90]Ibid., p. 10.
[91]Ibid., p. 12. Compare p. 13: "Nagel is like a man who stubbornly insists: And Grunewald did
   really paint! In this way one can be wrong although he is asserting something that is undeniable."
[92]Ibid., p. 14.
[93]Ibid., p. 15.
[94]Ibid.
[95]Ibid., p. 11.
[96]Ibid., p. 15.

which each side moves forward on its path and allows the other side to move forward on its path. This is the procedure in which "separated brothers" are led closer together without compromising themselves.

The Trend Toward a "Pietism Purified by the Reformation"

Finally, we would like to add a remark to all that has been said. In our opinion we can on the whole talk about a definite positive effect this theology has exercised on Pietism, an effect which basically can be detected in both Pietistic camps, even if it is certainly stronger among the more open-minded Pietists. This is true even apart from the differences between those Pietistic camps and their approach to Barth's theology or perhaps even produced by the tension between those camps. It is not easy to put this effect into words because it did not consist of an explicit correction of Pietistic views, and it certainly did not change the basic framework of Pietistic theology. Thus this effect was certainly a very limited one, but it was there. It became apparent as the Pietists made a small but clear *shift* of *emphasis* in espousing their views within the untouched framework of their thought.

K. Müller described this shift of emphasis in these terms: "The more recent community movement has surprisingly turned in a new direction . . . the pendulum must swing left for a change instead of stressing the necessity of 'sanctification' as they traditionally do, they are now suddenly also strongly emphasizing 'justification.'"[97] This seems to me to be a correct observation. Even in the most critical Pietistic responses to Barth a shift of emphasis can be seen in this sense. Even Nagel never grew tired of emphasizing that repentance, faith and the life of holiness must not be asserted as "something meritorious," as "the foundation of salvation" or as "the cause of salvation."[98] Grace "puts a stop to the deceit of Pharisaism," leads us into the "destitute poverty of the spirit" and contradicts "the most subtle self-confidence and the most hidden self-righteousness."[99] And even Hützen could not contradict Barth without at the same time somewhat shifting the emphasis of the Pietistic approach: "It is not we who have God in our hand, but God has us in his hand. It is not we who possess the truth, but the truth possesses us. It is not we who direct the Spirit, but the Spirit directs us." "This relationship" can absolutely "never be reversed."[100] A similar conspicuous shift of emphasis compared to what is traditionally dear to the Pietists'

---

[97]Müller, "Rechtfertigung oder Heiligung?" p. 110.
[98]Nagel, *Karl Barth und der heilsgewisse Glaube,* p. 23.
[99]Ibid., p. 24.
[100]W. Hützen, *Biblisches Glaubensleben,* p. 15.

heart can be noticed in the responses of the other community people to Barth. For example, looking at what they wanted to affirm in the believer, they now conspicuously emphasized that this is not true and real as something originating in human beings but only as it originated in God.[101] Or they could now emphatically say that justification and sanctification are not two acts, the latter following upon the former, rather sanctification is contained within justification.[102] Knappe attached great importance to the fact that "everything we human beings, even we believers, think, feel, speak, or do as human beings is continuously in need of the forgiveness of sins."[103] Even L. Thimme several times professed an interpretation of Romans 7 and 8 not in terms of a temporal succession but an objective interconnectedness.[104] If he had not in the same breath defended the "fundamental difference between those who are born again" and those who are not born again, one could wonder if he had not even taken a step beyond Pietism.[105] He too did not go beyond the scope of Pietistic thought. Nevertheless his view can be seen as a striking symptom of a general shift of emphasis in Pietism (which otherwise would certainly be expressed in a much more reserved manner) that presented itself in its antithesis to Barth.

Such a shift of emphasis can be detected not merely in literature that focused on this theologian, but also in other Pietistic writings of this era. In this respect it is remarkable to see how openly and attentively they advertised Luther's rediscovered lecture on the Epistle to the Romans in their magazine *Light and Life*. "The book seems destined to cleanse the movement." The "simultaneously justified and a sinner" was especially quoted from it as well as the statement, "the saints are always sinners before Him."[106] In so doing, they were aware that this

---

[101]W. Knappe, "Wie wird man ein lebendiger Christ?" in *Licht und Leben,* 1925, pp. 154ff., 204ff. Knappe wrote this, though, before his answer to Barth.

[102]Ibid., p. 206.

[103]W. Knappe, "Karl Barth und der Pietismus," in *Licht und Leben,* 1927, p. 499.

[104]L. Thimme, "Das Problem der Kirche," p. 34; "Das Problem 'Karl Barth,'" p. 96; "Was ist Evangelium?" in *Im Kampf um die Kirche,* p. 239.

[105]Thimme, "Was ist Evangelium?" p. 239.

[106]In *Licht und Leben,* 1924, pp. 628ff. If Köberle's information is correct that P. Sprenger, the author of the work *Selig die Armen im Geist* (1928), was also a community man, one would have in it an extremely remarkable example of how strongly individual Pietists at that time, without Barth's name being mentioned, could learn from the Reformers and also from Barth, as the quotation from Luther shows that is used as a motto: "No one is more holy than a sinner who has grace." Here the real and complete poverty of man before God is stressed most pointedly, for man has no virtue and no salvation in himself (p. 6), contains no claim to salvation within himself (p. 9), as well as no possibility of progress beyond this poverty (p. 10). Human beings have the kingdom of heaven precisely in such poverty and only in it: "no, they do not yet 'have' the Kingdom of Heaven, but it 'belongs' to them ("We are truly saved, but in hope"). It is their property if not yet their possession" (p. 15).

teaching of Luther was especially taken up by "the Barthian school."[107] And it was certainly a sign of the times when twice a rather lengthy section from Barth's second *Epistle to the Romans*—one about faith as "a leap in the dark" and one about the righteousness of God that cannot be seen but is "credited to our account"—was reprinted in the same magazine in 1928 without commentary.[108] Its clear purpose was to edify the community people. It was also certainly a promising sign when Knappe demanded "What we need is a Pietism purified by the Reformation," promising both in his penitent recognition that Pietism had not yet achieved this, and his clear insight that it was in need of such purification. Beyond this Knappe asked Barth to take back his critique of Pietism in view of the fact that nowadays in the ranks of Pietism "there is a vigorous reflection on the fundamental insights of the Reformation and a strong desire to carry on where the Reformation left off."[109] Undoubtedly this request was expressed too strongly considering the fact that the community people had committed themselves to a stance so clearly in opposition to this theologian. Yet we may take this statement as an indication that in the 1920s there were certain promising signs of a fruitful reorientation of Pietistic thought in spite of all that it had clearly advocated for so long.

These promising signs had probably not only emerged because Pietism dealt with Karl Barth. The encouragement needed for these seeds of change to take root was perhaps in the air at that time (the crisis mood of the postwar period, the Luther and Kierkegaard renaissance, the emergence of existentialism, etc.). But it should be clear that this encouragement was given to the community people in part precisely from these sources, especially from their extensive and intensive engagement with the theology of the *Epistle to the Romans*. Whether these first signs really represented a fruitful and promising reorientation could justifiably be made an object of discussion. The profound word of Paul Schempp (from 1928) gives us food for thought. "That which is enduring is supported today much more effectively by way of self-accusation than by mere piety. . . . Barth is setting a precedent because his theology is more in keeping with today's intellectual climate than other theologies, because the sacrifice of one's intellect is a pleasure for those who have little to sacrifice because paradox

---

[107] *Licht und Leben,* 1924, p. 629. Compare *Licht und Leben,* 1927, pp. 796-97.

[108] Under the title "Dennoch," put in by W. Knappe: "Römerbrief," 2nd ed., pp. 73-74 = *Licht und Leben,* 1928, pp. 114ff.; and under the title "Gottliche und menschliche Beurteilung," put in by E. Schreiner: "Römerbrief," 2nd ed., pp. 97-99 = *Licht und Leben,* 1928, pp. 77-78.

[109] W. Knappe, "Rezension zu J. Albani, Das Wesen des ev. Christentums," in *Licht und Leben,* 1928, p. 656. Compare also "Heilsgewissheit und Heilsunsicherheit," in *Kampf um die Kirche,* p. 142: "The *Reformational Purification of Pietism*—we see in this the task, but also the promise that is given to Pietism in the present day."

appears profound, because criticism of degeneracy is a great feat for weak-lings."[110] Nevertheless, we believe that the situation of Pietism in the twenties also revealed the first signs of a *fruitful* biblical-Reformational reorientation along the lives of the shift of emphasis in Pietistic thought indicated above. Yet it is still an open question whether this new beginning was subsequently real-ized or did not get beyond its early stages.

---

[110]P. Schempp, "Randglossen zum Barthianismus," in *ZdZ*, 1928, p. 351.

II. The Learning Process on the Part of Barth

Barth's Position on the Pietistic Responses

We will now inquire about the other side. Did Barth learn something from the community people, especially from their responses to his *Epistle to the Romans?* Or to put the question more cautiously and generally: Can a change and correction of his position on Pietism or its historical phenomenon or its objective concern be observed in his writings in the period after the publication of the *Epistle to the Romans* until the end of the decade? From the period in question there is an abundance of texts from his pen on the basis of which this question can be answered. However, no favorable answer to our question seems to come from them, to the extent that the texts have been published by now. *No extensive direct treatment of Pietism* can be found in his writings of this era, with the minor exception yet to be discussed, that he once devoted somewhat more attention to the revivalist movement of the nineteenth century. This movement was only very rarely touched on by him and if he did, then in passing, frequently together with other significant events in church history. We must not necessarily conclude from these meager references that he was indifferent to the subject of Pietism. On the one hand, it is clear that his discussion with it was not one of his chief concerns. On the other hand it can be noted that *no expressly self-critical retraction* of his critique of Pietism in the *Epistle to the Romans* can be found in his writings of this era. Indeed, it seems that his views on this matter became much more critical since he distanced himself from Pietism at almost every relevant point. Of course, the meagerness of these references as well as their character as passing remarks on what separated him from Pietism prevent us from drawing premature conclusions from it. It cannot be assumed that these references give an exhaustive account of Barth's whole position on this complex. Thus the possibility cannot be ruled out that his position was different and more positive than those references would make us think and that in his position a view was perhaps emerging that was new in comparison with the *Epistle to the Romans.* But by keeping an open mind on this, we of course have no reason to minimize the importance of these references.

Especially as far as his position on the *Pietistic responses* is concerned, the somewhat dark picture we've described only seems to be confirmed. It can be verified that he at least took notice of a portion of this literature.[1] On the other hand, apart from one minor exception, as far as I can see, he did not react to any of these writings with a public statement, let alone agree to an intensive discussion or a direct conversation with representatives of Pietism because he was moved by what he read. Rather the exception I just mentioned was a defensive gesture. He issued a curt statement that he had no interest in a conversation with the community people who articulated those responses. G. F. Nagel dedicated his polemical treatise against Barth's theology to him in the fall of 1929, confessing "a biblically purified Pietism" and stressing that he had objectively engaged Barth's "attack on Pietism in spite of its virulence" but also with the request for a "verbal exchange of views."[2] Barth's answer was harsh. He held against Nagel (1) that he contented himself in his treatise with simply restating the thesis which had just been contested by Barth. "At any rate, I cannot be overcome so easily." (2) In stating his concerns, Nagel limited himself to "mere assertions" which he made in place of "solid reasons." Barth would only allow Nagel to set him right if Nagel were willing to make a "precise, contextual examination" of the pertinent exegetical or dogmatic passages. (3) He could hardly recognize himself in the mirror of Nagel's account. Indeed, "again and again I must make the observation that it is precisely my honored Pietist opponents who play so remarkably fast and loose with the truth that I have to complain about misleading quotations from my books nowhere as often as in the adversarial writings of this side." (Barth cited an example of this here.) (4) This latter practice is all the more questionable since Nagel does not talk "to me" at all, but "about me" "for simple listeners" "who will probably never see *my* writings." His conclusion: "As long as the Pietists do not to some extent prove their holiness in this area as well, I will only half listen to their teaching about me and their objections to my teaching."[3]

This was an unambiguous rejection of a conversation with the Pietists and a refusal to get involved in a discussion of their issues and assertions. But we have

---

[1]The fact that Barth possessed the works of G. F. Nagel (*Karl Barth und der heilsgewisse Glaube*), W. Hützen (*Bibl. Glaubensleben*) and W. Knappe ("Karl Barth und der Pietismus") can be inferred from his collection of books in the Karl Barth archives in Basel. The fact that he was familiar with them is evident from his pencil marks that are found on some of the margins of these works.

[2]Letter by G. F. Nagel, the chairman of the German Evangelical Alliance, to K. Barth from August (?) 12, 1929, in the Karl Barth archives, Basel.

[3]Letter from K. Barth to G. F. Nagel, from October 14, 1929, handwritten, in the Karl Barth archives, Basel.

to keep two things in mind. First, what we saw above in our analysis of the Pietistic literature on Barth[4] illuminates the fact that in this respect Barth truly had reason to complain about a lack of understanding from their authors. And second, the purpose of that reaction was surely not to definitely refuse a conversation but to state the conditions under which he would consider such a conversation fruitful; the decisive condition in his view was clearly that the Pietists must thoroughly and conscientiously engage his theses even if they disputed them. In his answer to Barth's letter, Nagel himself furnished evidence of how difficult, almost hopelessly difficult it was to enter into a meaningful conversation in this regard. He had the letter published in the magazine of the Evangelical Alliance, yet in such a way that he quoted Barth's opinion yet left out his key statements. Thus Nagel created the impression in his readers that Barth rejected Nagel's whole position and all of his Pietism only because of the irregularity of that one false quotation. In his reply, Nagel concentrated exclusively on this point by first citing Pastor Brandenburg's expert opinion on Barth's misleading, unclear and complicated style and then by easily dispatching his opponent. "Of course, one quotation incorrectly made does not alter the overall result of my explanations."[5] Of course, in so doing, Nagel carelessly passed over the key point of Barth's view. For Barth that quotation was merely a symptom of a much more deep-seated complaint, yet Nagel acted as if the complaint once expressed by Barth was removed with the elimination of that one symptom. And once again Nagel's readers found out nothing about the true circumstances of this matter. They did not know that his opponent (Barth) was not at all concerned about that one symptom, as Nagel made them believe by abridging Barth's letter.[6] Under these circumstances a direct fruitful conversation was in fact not really possible for the time being.

We can illustrate Barth's lack of interest in such a conversation by citing the curt remarks he made in response to the objections of Köberle and Heim,[7] whom he felt were basically Pietistic.[8] Köberle complained that "all statements about sanctification" constantly "come under the fire of dialectical theology." In a footnote Barth responded laconically, "In attempting to get through the line

---

[4]See pp. 166ff., 174ff.
[5]*Ev. Allianzblatt,* January 5, 1930, nr. 1, pp. 9-10.
[6]In so doing, Nagel extensively emphasized his great love of truth!
[7]See pp. 191, 205-6.
[8]In his "Letter to K. Heim," in *ZdZ,* 1931, p. 451, Barth also called Karl Heim "a modern Pietist." Compare Thurneysen's report to Barth from June 28, 1928, on his impressions during a meeting with Heim: "He is definitely swimming along in the warm Gulf Stream of Pietism of Swabian origin and knows superbly how *not* to give the pious public a shock (K. Barth/E. Thurneysen, *Briefwechsel* 2, 1974, p. 592).

of fire, Köberle unfortunately had to pay with his life."[9] For Köberle's intention
of supplementing this theology with a doctrine of sanctification rests on a misunderstanding of this theology since Barth did not at all deny that he should talk
about sanctification but only the way in which he would talk about it. Köberle
"must not think" that he could supplement the statements of Barth's theology,
because he did not understand them at all.[10] Barth did not rebuff K. Heim in a
similar way, but he shook his head at Heim's objection.[11] On the one hand,
Barth felt he was misunderstood by Heim and was surprised "by all the unkind
things" Heim attributed to him. God must not become uncomfortable or specific
to man, ethics are a matter of indifference; on the other hand, Heim's own idea
remained "totally obscure to him": in his ears it sounds like "works righteousness" and like he is tying salvation to "biographical circumstances," etc. His answer to Heim was also brief, only a "description of the insurmountable barriers"
to understanding.[12] Here too he saw no real responsibility of a statement on the
issues in contention because he neither recognized himself in the objection
raised against him nor did he understand their claim to "supplement" his view.
This was basically the same explanation as the one he made to Nagel, which
actually only gave the reasons why for the time being he could not consider the
objections raised by the Pietists and only "half listen." But did all this not mean
that he was hardening the position of the *Epistle to the Romans* and its critique
of Pietism by rightfully (we believe) pointing out their misunderstanding of his
assertions in those objections? And did he not neglect to notice and consider the
elements of truth which can be hidden even in great misunderstandings? Therefore is it not true that the subsequent period of Barth's theology did not result
in any "learning process"?

His Position on Pietism in the Period After the Second Epistle to the Romans

Now let us first more closely examine his general position on Pietism in this subsequent period. There were essentially two contexts in which his thought
touched on Pietism from time to time in the further course of the 1920s. In each
context he distanced himself from it. In the first context (1) *the proper under-*

---

[9] *Zur Lehre vom Heiligen Geist,* 1930, p. 80.
[10] Ibid., p. 81.
[11] On the further point Barth mentioned in the same context in response to Heim—the question
of the personal conversion of the systematic theologian—Barth by no means considered this
question to be problematic as such, rather he did not want to see it asked where objective
argumentation was called for (see above, p. 205).
[12] "Brief an Karl Heim," pp. 452-53.

standing of God's revelation was at stake. And the charge he made against Pietism was that "a latent or open conjuring away of revelation" took place in it.[13] The divine revelation is decisively explained with the category of God's Word. Consequently, Christian theology is the "presentation of the reality of God's Word addressed to man."[14] From that point of view, but only from that point of view, theology not only has to do with God but at the same time with man. "But man to whom the Word of God is addressed can never become the subject theology talks about . . . for the reality of a man whom the Word of God addresses is by no means on the same level with the reality of God's Word although theology must certainly not lose sight of man's reality for one moment." The former reality relates to the latter "as the predicate relates to the subject; it is never and in no way *this* reality by itself, but only as a part of the latter."[15] This illuminates in more detail what is meant by the charge that Pietism conjures away revelation. Pietism should not be contradicted because it takes up the important and necessary problem of the believing individual, but it must be contradicted even more decisively because of its "independent interest in man," by which it paves the way for "Schleiermacher's reversal of theology into anthropology" in the form of centering theology around the "statements of pious man's experience."[16] In Barth's view this reversal, this understanding of revelation "as a predicate of *man*" already begins in Pietism so that the theology of the last two centuries has been dominated "by the ascent of a high-handed and self-satisfied humanity from Pietism via the Enlightenment to Romanticism."[17] Once again, not their interest "in man" or "the believing individual" is denied, but their "independent" interest in him. Their interest as such is legitimate because the Word of God is in fact addressed to *man*. This includes the idea that the Word can become "accessible and possible for human beings," "that we can expect a work of God in us as a reality that has happened and continues to happen," that human beings are involved in the revelation not "as spectators but as direct partners of God," "that I can come to the point where I give myself such confidence that I risk trusting in the reality of the outpouring of the Holy Spirit, and with regard to me, trusting in the reality of the grace that has been bestowed on me." I can expect that it is true that the recognition of my own sin is not a "pessimistic human wisdom" and "holiness" is not a "religious phantasmagoria" but "I know all this with ultimate confidence only when I do not say it to myself, only if it *is said to me* and I only

---

[13] *Ges. Vorträge* 1, 1924, p. 197 (the lecture stems from the year 1923).
[14] *Ethik* 1, 1928, published in 1973, p. 18.
[15] Ibid., pp. 19-20.
[16] *Christliche Dogmatik im Entwurf,* 1927, p. 86.
[17] *Ges. Vorträge* 2, 1928, p. 226 (the lecture was held in 1926).

repeat what has been said to me first."[18] From his vantage point his objection to Pietism ("only too closely related to Cartesianism intellectually") is specifically this: it does not decisively put its confidence in the Word of God understood as such but in the *"autopistia"* of my self-confidence as the "ground and measure of all certainty."[19] In this sense Pietism in Barth's view can be understood as a link in the chain of the story in which "faith loses its object."[20]

In the other context (2) in which Barth distanced himself from Pietism from time to time, *a proper understanding* of *God's grace* is at stake. He himself wanted to understand it in these terms: "God's grace which makes the Christian a Christian is free grace, and in fact, grace that *remains* free. Everything depends on this. It is grace from which the Christian cannot derive any claim, any security or any possession. No matter how you look at it, it is, in every respect, grace as justification and as sanctification, objectively and subjectively, and *remains* grace." If grace is understood in these terms, then it follows "that there is no Christianity but the Christianity of the lost sinner."[21] The objection Barth raised to Pietism from this understanding of grace is, in short, that it abandoned this insight from the Reformation. "It has ceased to be Protestant."[22] This objection has two sides. First, he doubts Pietism has done careful work in its *understanding of sin*. To be sure, it "often developed a deeply moving earnestness about sin. But is it essentially any different from Catholic earnestness about sin that can likewise not be underestimated? Has Pietism reached the understanding that fallen man is a rebel in his *existence* and is therefore not able to see himself judged as anything but a rebel in spite of a conversion that may have occurred? And he is also not able to walk over from Romans 7 into Romans 8 as if he were walking from one house into another, as he likes to portray it?" Barth doubted this! And the fact that he had reasons for this doubt was confirmed for him when "man tries to handle sin on his own."[23] Second, he doubted whether Pietism had a thoroughly thought through *understanding of grace*. For in their view "grace is perhaps free and the theologians of that era knew how to talk nicely about it, but at any rate it did not remain free, but became a claim, a security, a possession of the Christian, of the so-called devout Christian." This is "Semi-Pelagi-

---

[18] *Christliche Dogmatik im Entwurf,* pp. 297-98.
[19] Ibid., p. 298.
[20] Ibid., p. 198.
[21] *Ges. Vorträge* 2, p. 211 (the lecture was held in 1927).
[22] *Ges. Vorträge* 2, p. 350 (the lecture was held in 1928).
[23] Ibid., p. 356. Compare Barth's lecture on W. Hermann from 1925 (in *Ges. Vorträge* 2, p. 273), in which he repeats the argument from the second and primarily the first *Epistle to the Romans:* Because Pietism only wants to know the forgiveness of sins in their experience, the "seesaw ride of Sic et Non" is basically Pietism's last word.

anism which entered Protestant theology in the 18th century through the doubly opened gate of Rationalism and Pietism, achieving a triumph in Schleiermacher, the likes of which had hardly been experienced in the Middle Ages."[24]

The arguments Barth availed himself of in both of these reservations about Pietism are clearly related to those he presented in the *Epistle to the Romans,* and yet they are no longer quite the same, as we will demonstrate shortly in greater detail. Let us first observe one thing: it would seem that the *view* of *Pietism* is also no longer quite the same as it is in the *Epistle to the Romans.* We must not say that it is a completely *different* view. For the dual thesis the Barth of the late twenties defended—in Pietism *God* becomes something about *humankind* (first point) and *grace* gives the believer a reason to claim it (second point)—unmistakably points back to the second *Epistle to the Romans.* As we have attempted to show, he saw and judged Pietism there in such a way that in the end its thought and its procedure amounted to taking control of God and his grace and making it a concrete possession. And yet Barth's view of Pietism is no longer quite *the same* in the subsequent period. We saw that his understanding and opinion of Pietism in the *Epistle to the Romans,* as we discussed it, only appears on the margins and in the sense that the intentions of Pietism were *ultimately* going to end up here. At the heart of his understanding of Pietism in the *Epistle to the Romans* is the thesis that Pietism, in close affinity with the mystics and ascetics, is mainly characterized by the view of the "negative" work that justifies or the *"negative"* way that leads to God. And as we have seen, if Barth found Pietism's *negation* of these works and ways praiseworthy, he found their attempt to then view these negations as *"works"* and "ways" questionable because "in the end" they lead again to the control that they initially wanted to deny. And now, after all that we have just seen, this special view and interpretation of Pietism in the Barth of the late 1920s is practically no longer present.[25] Its chief characteristic was evidently not seen any longer in terms of that idea of the negative way and work, but only (which follows from the second *Epistle to the Romans*) the idea of the Divine and his grace as a *positive given related to and in man.* What was characteristic of Pietism was no longer seen in terms of the way one arrives at control in Pietism but rather that in it, in a certain way, one arrives at a place of

---

[24] *Ges. Vorträge* 2, p. 211.

[25] One could possibly see the phrase about the "unpleasant humility of modern Pietism" in the "Letter to Karl Heim," in *ZdZ,* 1931, p. 451, as a little exception. And a memory of the interpretation of *Epistle to the Romans* 2 mainly appears once in *Ethics,* 1928/29 (1978, pp. 406ff.), in which Barth sees the concern of Pietism (and not principally negative) in conjunction with the "cultivation of man's life hidden with Christ in God" in mysticism, with the "contemplative life" of monasticism and with the Eastern church's "humility before the absolute miracle of the . . . risen Christ which calls into question the present form of the world from outside."

control—no longer in its way of transcending the given conditions *via negationis* but now in its way of grasping the transcendent in accordance with the *autopistia* of self-confidence. Thus Pietism was no longer primarily seen in conjunction with mysticism but with Cartesianism. And thus it was virtually seen again through the lens of the first rather than of the second *Epistle to the Romans*.

Are we wrong when we assume a change in Barth's understanding of Pietism along these lines? Someone could say that Pietism is mentioned by Barth so infrequently in the latter part of the 1920s that the view of the *Epistle to the Romans* is not cited more often simply by coincidence. We think, though, that references to the view presented in the *Epistle to the Romans* are not missing by chance. In these years Barth actually arrived as a somewhat different view of Pietism. This change became noticeable at the latest in his explicit portrayal of Pietism in his lecture from the winter semester of 1932 and 1933 in which he totally dispensed with his thesis of Pietism's "negative works and ways."[26] We can only surmise *how* he arrived at this new view. We assume that this change in his view of Pietism had to do with the further development of his thought in the course of these years. It also has to do with the fact that he became more of a systematic theologian. As a result of his extensive studies in the history of theology during these years a somewhat different view of the history of Neo-Protestantism was unavoidable for him. Furthermore this change had to do with the fact that in the following years Overbeck's theses that had especially influenced him in the period of the *Epistle to the Romans* and had been a part of his particular understanding of Pietism in the *Epistle to the Romans* increasingly lost their significance for him. But all of these assumptions are perhaps still not sufficient to fully explain this change in his understanding of Pietism. However, it would become explicable if one further assumption were correct. The Pietists who took issue with Barth in the 1920s never grappled with his special understanding of Pietism in the *Epistle to the Romans* or even mentioned it in their writings, as we have seen. In addition, their determination to assert their opposition to him was decisively defined not by the idea of the "negative way and work"; rather, as we have seen, it was that they were mainly interested in affirming that they could experience and see "in themselves" the reality of God and his grace. So we now assume that Barth was motivated to change his understanding of Pietism not least by the reaction of the community people to his *Epistle to the Romans,* which he partially knew, and by the self-understanding that they expressed in the 1920s. If they committed themselves to this self-un-

---

[26] *Die prot. Theologie im 19. Jahrhundert. Ihre Vorgeschichte und ihre Geschichte,* pp. 92ff. (first published in 1946).

derstanding, he too no longer had any reason to repeat the thesis of the *Epistle to the Romans* as original as it was. Thus it is understandable why he now saw Pietism somewhat differently and criticized it from a different angle. Since he discontinued the aspect of his interpretation of Pietism in the *Epistle to the Romans* that made it seem at least somewhat praiseworthy to him, it is also understandable why his aforementioned statements about this theological counterpart created the impression in the further course of the twenties that his criticism of it on the whole had become even sharper.

His Thesis on the Affinity Between Pietism and the Enlightenment

After all of this it is no coincidence that Barth's historical thesis emerged more clearly at the same time in the late 1920s. This thesis (or better, its dogmatic presupposition) was laid out in the second *Epistle to the Romans* but was nowhere explicitly mentioned, although its roots are found further in the past. They can be traced back beyond the first *Epistle to the Romans* to Barth's theological infancy. This theory posits *the affinity of historical Pietism with Rationalism, or better with the Enlightenment* and claims that both together can be seen as forerunners of Schleiermacher's theology. This thesis has already been touched on in the two aforementioned points, and Barth deduced it directly from those two main reservations he held toward Pietism. It was intellectually akin to Cartesianism in its concentration on finding the assurance of Christian truth in self-awareness; and it was close to the Enlightenment in its attempt to conjure away revelation in favor of its "independent" interest in man; and it opens the gates to semi-Pelagianism together with rationalism by turning grace into a *bonum* of man. A statement written by Barth in 1925 can be added to the evidence cited for this theory in his writings. "In Protestant theology we are really not in a classical era whose possibilities could induce us to open our mouths too far. Rather we are actually *between* the times, burdened with the unhappy Pietistic-Rationalist inheritance of the last two centuries. It is not as easy to get rid of it as many would imagine who are not closely involved."[27] With regard to this inheritance that weighs on Reformational Protestantism, Barth in 1928 could at least distinguish between Pietism and Rationalism. "It [this Protestantism] has ceased being churchly *and* it has ceased being Protestant, the former more in the Rationalist form, the latter in its Pietistic form." Of course, he immediately added, "but the boundaries between these two forms are fluid and in Schleiermacher completely eliminated."[28] Barth's verdict on

---

[27] *Ges. Vorträge* 2, p. 100.
[28] Ibid., p. 350.

"Neo-Protestantism" understood in these terms was that in its interest in the human person seen as an autonomous being and in its transformation of grace into a human good, it fell away from the Reformational recognition of the authority of God's Word and permanently free grace. At the same time it is dilettantish in the inadequate way it advocates this interest compared to the Roman Catholic advocacy of the same concern.[29] In appreciating this thesis we have to consider the fact that the concept of "Pietism" (as well as the Enlightenment) is used here as an ideal type in which a diverse historical phenomenon is reduced to a somewhat "dogmatic" concept, which as such must leave room and does leave room for an historically discriminating and nuanced view. We must further notice that the thesis of the affinity between Pietism and rationalism only applies to the claim that they are close to each other at those material points we mentioned. This means that on the one hand, it must not exclude the finding of differences or even opposite positions between both phenomena. On the other hand, this proximity is not invalidated by stating such differences between both phenomena.

If Barth explicitly espoused and emphasized this thesis in the period after the *Epistle to the Romans,* this could have been due to the fact that he now increasingly turned his attention to researching *historical theology.* He did not yet focus on the eighteenth century but on the nineteenth century and here especially on Schleiermacher, but also various revivalist theologians.[30] In his intensive Schleiermacher studies his theology became for Barth the key to interpreting the historical theology of the period preceding him as well as the period subsequent to him; that is the key to interpreting Pietism and the revivalist movement. For Barth it was precisely Schleiermacher who furnished proof for the correctness of his thesis about the proximity of Pietism and the Enlightenment. It was also proof that the basic concerns of both could be harmonized not only by learning from both schools but by trying to combine both.[31] At the same time he considered Schleiermacher's theology to be the unmasking of the inmost concerns of both these movements. "The classical

---

[29]Ibid., pp. 362-63.

[30]On Schleiermacher, compare the lecture on him in 1924 (unpublished); the essay on Schleiermacher's Christmas celebration (1924) possibly comes from this, in *Ges. Vorträge* 2, pp. 106ff. See further *Vorlesung über die Geschichte der prot. Theologie im 19. Jahrhundert,* 1926 (the part on Schleiermacher published in *Ges. Vorträge* 2, pp. 136ff.) and 1929. See also the review of Brunner's book on Schleiermacher in *ZdZ,* 1924, pp. 49ff. On the revivalist movement, compare the lecture "Das Wort in der Theologie von Schleiermacher bis Ritschl," in *Ges. Vorträge* 2, pp. 190ff. See further "Geschichte der prot. Theologie" (lecture of 1929-1930), duplicated in typewritten form in 1943, pp. 244-45.

[31]"Geschichte d. prot. Theologie" (1929-1930), 1943, pp. 180-81.

representation which Christian teaching had found in the great moment of its completion and conquest of the 18th Century meant that in its approach, in the relationship of God and man, a darkness had settled in where all recognizable signs indicate that here man alone remained on the scene, that he alone became theology's subject, but Christ his predicate."[32] Or was Barth perhaps mistaken in this interpretation of Schleiermacher? His study of the theology of the revivalist movement became a test case for this interpretation. The results were negative for him. Not only the "rationalists, but also the revivalist theologians and Biblicists were basically bosom friends with Schleiermacher and his followers."[33] "Even more crassly than he," their theology "moved pious humanity into the center of theology with the force of not just ostensible but real enthusiasm. If it were quite honest as in the case of Rothe, it would make the discovery that pious man resembled modern man."[34] Therefore Barth believed he could state "that revivalist theology does not distance itself from the theological problems of its time but, on the contrary, powerfully participates in its center as it was fixed by Schleiermacher."[35] "On the contrary it has a strong investment in its center as defined by Schleiermacher. It was too close to its alleged opponents to be able to overcome them inwardly."[36] We are of the opinion that Barth's thesis about the affinity between Pietism and the Enlightenment, espoused more frequently and emphatically in the period after the *Epistle to the Romans,* was in part a working hypothesis deduced from dogmatic premises which had to be verified by his studies in the history of theology but was also in part the result of these extensive historical studies.

There might have been another reason for stressing this thesis in this period. The thesis was confirmed in the theological struggle of the 1920s in which the author of the *Epistle to the Romans* got to hear objections both from Pietists and liberals in which both sides raised an objection that basically had the same content. This should be verified by the example of a prominent, liberal critic. I am thinking of the Barth paper by B. Dörries.[37] He was clearly not a Pietist. "Repentance" and "conversion" as defined by the Pietists were foreign to him.[38] Conversely his critical approach to Scripture would have been foreign to them.[39] This is why his closeness to them on the issues that

---

[32]Ibid., p. 207.
[33]*Ges. Vorträge* 2, p. 197.
[34]Ibid.,p. 200.
[35]"Geschichte der prot. Theologie" (1929-1930), p. 241.
[36]Ibid., p. 247.
[37]B. Dörries, *Der ferne und der nähe Gott,* 1927.
[38]Ibid., pp. 18-19.
[39]Ibid., pp. 57ff.

were also central to them in their opposition to Barth is all the more surprising. "We can sum up the difference between Barth and us in these terms.
Barth proclaims a God who is distant. We believe in a God who is *near*."[40]
For, "in him we live and move and have our being."[41] How could someone
ever "fall for the idea of talking about him in negations!"[42] Certainly Barth is
right "in pointing out that a human being experiences the nearness of God
when he experiences the grace of God in judgment, when he finds life in
death."[43] But precisely in this way he *experiences* grace, he *finds* life. Barth
"sees every human experience as something insignificant." But the opposite
is true. "What does not become an experience for us is not available to us."[44]
Barth's "self-laceration" and "brooding introspection" are overcome with such
experience. Rather there is "the certainty of faith," a believing "possession."[45]
Therefore Barth's endeavor to move "everything God does in man" into the
eschatological future is wrong, a future "that must never be felt as present, as
a real existence and possession even for only a moment."[46] Was all of what
Dörries presented here meant to be seen in terms of an "idolatrous flight of
fancy" "which seeks to reach God from the vantage point of man" regardless
of what label the Pietists thought they could use to distance themselves from
liberalism? But no, "Barth is absolutely right when he never tires of emphasizing that all this is a work of God," that "man can always only be the one
who receives."[47] No, in this respect Dorries wanted to be distinct from Barth
as little as the Pietists did, but like them he wanted to be distinct from Barth
even more decisively in affirming that human beings must surely receive
something that is "now really ours," that the gift supports the idea that we
can see what we have.[48] (This was considered here too as the true "paradox"
of which dialectical theology knows nothing in its only apparent dialectics.[49])
We can also observe similar ideas in the work of W. Bruhn (*Vom Gott im Menschen,* 1926). It was also his concern to stress the "immanence of the divine,"[50] "something external to man in man,"[51] not dependent on the person

---

[40]Ibid., p. 54.
[41]Ibid., pp. 9, 37, 88.
[42]Ibid., p. 9.
[43]Ibid., p. 21.
[44]Ibid., p. 142.
[45]Ibid., p. 43.
[46]Ibid., p. 23.
[47]Ibid., pp. 21, 42. Compare p. 143.
[48]Ibid., p. 34.
[49]Ibid., p. 112.
[50]W. Bruhn, *Vom Gott im Menschen,* 1926, p. 24.
[51]Ibid., p. 28.

but occurring in him.[52] Thus grace was understood as "the most personal experience of a living divine reality pouring into the soul."[53] We conclude from all this that the argumentation of explicitly liberal theologians who likewise distanced themselves from Barth in the 1920s was unmistakably close to the essential point of the Pietists' objections, as we laid them out above.[54] Although the author of the *Epistle to the Romans* actually saw them at somewhat different locations, we could also say that the Pietists of that era put themselves in the exact corner where Barth had to see them in conjunction with the liberals. That is why we can understand him when he felt that his opinion about the affinity between both schools of thought was confirmed by the objective parallelism of the objections raised by both sides.

Now it is clear that Barth primarily *rejected* the *objections* that were raised against him by both sides and that he basically felt were the same. It is just as clear that he basically rejected the concern of both schools of thought precisely at the point where they were in harmony with one another, even in the period after the publication of the *Epistle to the Romans*. What he said in a "polemical epilogue" about the book by the liberal W. Bruhn, and thus indirectly about "what has often been said already by somewhat different voices,"[55] can also in fact be understood as a rejection of the Pietists' basic objection: "Existential thought on my terms naturally excludes any talk of placing 'a experiential bracket around God and man.' However, I also know a 'bracket.' But neither is it a bracket 'around God and man.' God is the bracket around man, but not vice versa. Neither is it 'an experiential bracket.' For any effort to 'plumb the depths' of *my* life is of no help. I do not find the bracket *there,* rather what I always find in the inmost depths are only the bad things about my own existence." Thus if Bruhn examines me to find out whether I can "somehow have God," I answer, *"No,"* for if I *believe* that God has *me,* I confess that I do *not* "have" him, that I have had enough of such having. He sticks to the idea "that Cartesianism in theology is utter nonsense, that God cannot be *identified* in 'humanity,' neither by way of reflection nor by way of experience, but only as the One who identifies himself (while we were still sinners) as the One who could be recognized as the mediator of the covenant of grace."[56] These statements are also unmistakably a rejection of the Pietists'

---

[52]Ibid., p. 55.
[53]Ibid., p. 9.
[54]Compare the largely friendly review of Dörries's work by W. Knappe (regardless of a verbal rejection of liberalism) in *Licht und Leben,* 1927, pp. 670ff.
[55]"Polemisches Nachwort," in *ZdZ,* 1927, p. 33.
[56]Ibid., pp. 37ff.

objection to Barth, a rejection which basically insists on the validity of arguments used to critique religious experience that were presented in the second *Epistle to the Romans*. The two critical viewpoints Barth advanced against the Pietists in the period after the *Epistle to the Romans,* which we cited at the beginning of the chapter, confirm the fact that this assumption is not wrong. The form in which both viewpoints are advanced shows that the sharpness of his critique of Pietism more likely increased than decreased after the *Epistle to the Romans* was written. But looking at them from the perspective of their objective content, they also show that they derive from the discoveries made in the *Epistle to the Romans*. It is not hard to recognize in these two critical viewpoints both objections that were raised against Pietism in the second *Epistle to the Romans*. He objected to limiting the freedom of grace (by asserting a "negative" way and work that enable the believer to feel happy that he has passed beyond the experience of submitting to God's judgment). He also objected to including the idea that the divine partner lives in the human being as a result of this experience.[57] In short, in the period after the *Epistle to the Romans* Barth talked about and against Pietism in such a way that we have to ask whether he learned anything positive by looking at this opponent and perhaps by observing the Pietistic discussions about him.

Our negative answer to this question seems to be confirmed by the vehemence of the clash that was engendered by the discussion of Barth's lecture "The Word in Theology from Schleiermacher to Ritschl" on October 19, 1927, in Elberfeld. The "evidence" he provided in it that "the revivalist theologians and the biblicists were as much bedfellows of Schleiermacher as Wegscheider, de Wette and the Hegelians"[58] met with decisive opposition, especially from the Pietists. In response Barth bluntly described the "wailing of the injured" to be "powerless from the very outset."[59] For the time being a rapprochement, let alone an understanding between the different viewpoints, seemed to be out of the question from Barth's side. Given this impression, it must be puzzling that a short time before in neighboring Meiderich a discussion took place on the occasion of a "youth festival" that took a different turn. Here he encountered Christians for whom "Pietists played about the same role as worldly people in customary preaching, that is, they were consigned to the wrath of God as "enemies of grace." The author of the *Epistle to the Romans* reacted to this differently than expected. For he attempted to talk them out of their condemnation of Pietism

---

[57]See pp. 105-6.
[58]K. Barth/E. Thurneysen, *Briefwechsel* 2, 1974, pp. 537-38.
[59]Ibid.

in the interests of pure doctrine.[60] This statement seems to me to be a small indication that he evidently left his critique of Pietism somewhat open, and that he did not simply learn nothing positive at all in his relationship to the community movement and their concern since the days of the *Epistle to the Romans*.

Barth's Shift of Emphasis in the Direction of a Tacit Consideration of Pietistic Concerns

We can see that the aforementioned indication is not misleading if we once again return to the two critical viewpoints Barth advanced against Pietism in the period between 1923 and 1929. We cannot claim that his critique of Pietism lost its sharpness in this period. But the arguments he used to make this critique were now made in such a way that some change in his theological language is noticeable; and this change in language also fit with a change in his theological understanding. Somewhat of a change! Claiming a conflict or contradiction between the second *Epistle to the Romans* and Barth's subsequent theological work would mean that we have not properly understood either the former or the latter. But just as a certain shift of emphasis (apart from their main concern that stayed the same) can be noticed in the Pietistic literature of the late 1920s, a *shift of emphasis* can also be observed in Barth's literature during the same period. Let us make it clear to ourselves that the arguments Barth used to defend his two reservations were no longer fully in harmony with the arguments he used in the *Epistle to the Romans*. In addition, we think the shift of emphasis that can be observed tended to move a little in the direction of considering the concerns advocated by the Pietists in contradistinction to him!

Concerning the first argument: According to Barth's famous adage the "system" of his *Epistle to the Romans* was that "as persistently as possible I kept in mind what Kierkegaard called 'the infinite qualitative difference' between time and eternity in its negative and positive significance. 'God is in heaven and you

---

[60]Ibid., pp. 535-36. With regard to these critics Barth took offense at what was probably what he called the "Pharisaism of the tax-collector," and it resembled what the community people took offense at in Barth; as Thurneysen reported to him, they claimed, "we are so far along that we prayed with the Pharisee, I thank you, God, that I am not like one of these Pietists! A nice reversal of the present situation, right?"(p. 572, letter from April 9, 1928). Moreover, it is interesting and once again illuminates the change in Barth's understanding of Pietism that the charge of a "Pharisaism of the tax-collector," which was targeted at the Pietists in the second *Epistle to the Romans* (p. 84) in its later use was no longer targeted at them but rather at their critics. In the *Church Dogmatics* 1/2, p. 282, he objected to the teaching alleged to be true of the second *Epistle to the Romans:* "God is everything, man is nothing and you are an idiot!" In *Church Dogmatics* 4/1, p. 688, we even read that compared to such a Pharisaism "the first . . . Pietist who comes along could return to his house . . . justified, of course, not because of his 'works,' but because real faith could stand behind them in hidden form."

are on earth.' The relationship of *this* God to *this man,* the relationship of *this*
man to *this* God is for me the subject of the Bible and the sum of philosophy
wrapped in one."[61] In interpreting the second *Epistle to the Romans*—in contradistinction to the majority of interpreters—we must certainly not overlook the
fact that this "difference" also has a "positive significance" encompassing a "relationship" between God and man. But a further step was taken when in the
post-*Epistle to the Romans* period, a period in which Barth was distancing himself from Pietism, he now used the concept of "revelation" or "the Word of God"
in the precise sense of the "Word of *God* directed to *man*" at precisely those
places where he earlier spoke of the "otherness" and the deity of God, including
its positive meaning. Thus he did not speak of something else, but he did speak
differently than he did in the *Epistle to the Romans,* and he advanced a somewhat different, new argument, especially against the Pietists. He did not take
back his previous understanding, but he did go a bit further with it. Equipped
with a more salient conceptuality, he now countered the suspicion that the God
shown in the *Epistle to the Romans* whose unmistakable divinity was still to be
retained, was a general, abstract being and not rather the God who specifically
reveals himself. In so doing, he simultaneously countered the suspicion that the
man described in the *Epistle to the Romans* was a being left to his own devices
and God's free grace would not actually reach him,[62] even though he still insisted that this man was not divine and took back nothing of his fallen nature.
His critique of Pietism was not dropped, and its solution to the problem of the
"believer" was disputed. But the fact that he "took up the problem" of humankind in general and of the "believer" in particular, in the latter case thereby addressing the specifically Pietistic problem as "important and necessary" in and
of itself, could now be said more clearly and emphatically. So although Barth's
critique of Pietism had lost nothing of its sharpness, he actually did take a step
in the direction of a reconciliation with Pietism and a positive appreciation of
its concern.

Concerning the second argument: In a much contested image in the second
Epistle to the Romans he answered the question of *how* the divine being affects
human beings, *how* 'the new world of the Holy Spirit" touches "the old world
of the flesh" by saying, "it touches it as the tangent touches a circle without
touching it and precisely by not touching it; it touches it as its frontier."[63] It

---

[61] *Der Römerbrief,* Vorwort zur 2. Aufl., p .xiv.
[62] J. Fangmeier, *Erziehung in Zeugenschaft,* 1964, p. 96, speaks of "an anthropological widen-
ing" Barth struggled to achieve in these years.
[63] *Der Römerbrief,* 2. Aufl., p. 6.

touches it not as a radius touches the center of a circle *(gratia infusa)*. In his argumentation with Pietism on this second point Barth took back nothing of the insight expressed in this image. However, the questions he asked in dealing with the problem of the "point of contact" between the divine and the human did shift. Barth now asked less *how* this contact happens but *what* happens when "the new world of the Holy Spirit touches the old world of the flesh." In his answer the image of the tangential touching of the circle in his second "letter to the Romans" is replaced with the concept of *"grace"* which was certainly present in the second *Epistle to the Romans* but now emerges more prominently in his post-*Epistle to the Romans* theology, and not only in his argumentation with Pietism. The idea expressed by the image of the tangent was preserved in his definition of the concept of "grace" in so far as it was essentially defined as free grace that remains free. But now he was more explicitly concerned to define "grace" as the decisive content of God's love and affection for man. Barth was preoccupied with reflecting on the concept of "grace" precisely in the period (around 1927) when the Pietists' preoccupation with Barth began. His crucial insight was that "grace" must be dialectically defined by stressing two different but related aspects of it. Otherwise it would not be real and it would not be free grace. "Grace" essentially means two things at the same time: that the person is saved by *grace* alone because he is totally a *sinner* and that the person is and remains totally *bound* to grace when it is given to him because he is saved by *grace* alone. We can only talk correctly about God's grace when both sides are considered at the same time. But this means "the law stands beside the gospel with the same dignity as the Word of the same eternal goodness. The call for repentance stands beside absolution at the same level, sanctification stands beside justification—in the same act of revelation and reconciliation. This act is richer, more exciting, even more contradictory and more in need of eschatological completion that it seems in Lutheran dogmatics. We cannot wish to reduce everything to a common denominator."[64]

Thus Barth demonstrated and probably learned to see more clearly that there is a difference between the problem of justification and sanctification and that both may not be assimilated into each other. In practical terms this meant that

---

[64] *Christliche Dogmatik im Entwurf,* 1927, pp. 327-28. In the same year Barth developed what he had presented programmatically with these statements in his lectures: "Justification and Sanctification" and "The Keeping of the Commandments," which were strangely varied in content but thematically related. Compare also his critique of Kohlbrugge (in his *History of Protestant Theology,* 1929/30). What was new was that he could see a *danger* in the fact that in Kohlbrugge "obedience . . . in faith, the grace of sanctification" is in danger of disappearing in the grace of justification!

one could not be replaced by the other. Moreover, the dual problem could be viewed from a different perspective and in different terms than was customarily the case with the Pietists. It can and must be viewed from the perspective of permanently free grace. From this vantage point he distanced himself from Pietism more clearly than in the *Epistle to the Romans*. But it was somewhat of a novelty that he was now doing it from a position where he was no longer under suspicion of neglecting "sanctification" by focusing on "justification" or by allowing sanctification to merge into justification. Rather he assumed a position where he recognized "justification" *and* "sanctification" as a *dual* problem that had to be taken very *seriously* from both sides. Although he still criticized Pietism, even more than before, he had in fact moved forward a bit in the direction of a positive reception of its concern.

Let us add that we are not just entertaining an assumption here. There is one clear reference for it in Barth's writings of those years. An amazingly positive appreciation of Pietism is found in one place (pp. 406ff.) in his lecture on ethics (published in 1978) from the winter of 1928/29. As in the second *Epistle to the Romans,* he conspicuously saw it again in conjunction with mysticism and monasticism. Of course, he also saw it in opposition to the Reformation but now believed that "the matter of Pietism was not settled by pointing out that it largely signified a betrayal of the Reformation's central theme." It was *also* to be understood as "a reaction" to an eschatologically defined impulse that was originally present in Protestantism but had since waned. One could summarize its concern "by characterizing it as an attempt to achieve a *Christian inwardness* which at its core can be understood as a concern of the conscience." From the perspective of this central theme it also specifically "attempts to achieve a holy church, an ascetic holiness of life, and an inner calm etc." Barth speaks of the danger, the great danger Pietism runs by presenting its concern in this way. But what is exciting is that he now considered this concern (among others) as thoroughly legitimate, even to the extent that he could say, "Pietism can be a possibility, it can well be obedience to the command of the promise. Those who have time only to disapprove of Pietism should consider how *they* intend to do justice to the concern behind Pietism. Could their disapproval not come from the fact that they themselves have not yet noticed this concern although it truly concerns them as well?" Therefore this text shows that we truly do not go wrong by noticing the shift of emphasis in Barth's thought at the end of the 1920s in the direction of bringing his point of view closer to Pietism, by moving toward engagement with the problem of the believing person on the one hand and of sanctification on the other.

The fact that he actually took a step in this direction in his theological writings after the publication of the *Epistle to the Romans* is also confirmed by W. Knappe, an alert representative of the community movement who immediately noticed and welcomed this step that Barth had taken.[65] Certainly Knappe saw how Barth still voiced his opposition to what is important to the Pietists as "experience" and the "assurance of salvation,"[66] and thus to "Cartesianism" in Pietism.[67] But he primarily saw progress in Barth's *Christian Dogmatics* compared with the *Epistle to the Romans*. Knappe was "delighted that the fog of confusion was beginning to lift." In place of the many ambiguities and misunderstandings he noticed how Barth had clarified his theology.[68] It was no actual "correction" but a "clarification"! Knappe saw this clarification primarily on the following points. (1) The thesis that "theology must dare to put God's revelation at the beginning."[69] (2) His somewhat new appreciation for "biblical history," for the fact that God reveals himself in history.[70] (3) His acceptance of the problem of how salvation is mediated—man as "a vessel, a very earthen vessel, of course, but man as a vessel of revelation" comes into view.[71] Knappe believed that Barth was becoming more sympathetic to the Pietists' concern by making such clarifications in his theological understanding, more sympathetic than his historical opinion on this phenomenon would allow us to assume. "On the basis of the clarification in Barth's theology that he made in the dogmatics, we are essentially one with Barth. A dogmatic issue is not at stake in his position on Pietism, but a historical issue . . . which, of course, touches on the practical aspect of modern Pietism. Here our opinions diverge."[72]

New Criteria for Evaluating Pietism

As far as Barth's *historical opinion* of Pietism is concerned, it can in fact be said that the period between 1923 and 1930 gave rise to a somewhat different *view* of this movement. But at that time he did not revise his *judgment* on it. The

---

[65]One could point out the touching confession of another representative of the movement who approached Barth's interpretation of 1 Corinthians 15, having come from the *Epistle to the Romans:* "I approached the task of reading this book with mixed feelings . . . but I was pleasantly surprised." He was told that men such as Schlatter and Michaelis flatly rejected him. And "I don't doubt that men such as Schlatter can see more than I." But he himself no longer really knew what he could object to in Barth (review of Barth's *Die Auferstehung der Toten,* in *Der Ölberg,* 1926, p. 61).

[66]W. Knappe, "Klärung in der Barthschen Theologie," in *Licht und Leben,* 1929, p. 271. Compare also the report of Dr. Fuchs, "Klärung in der Theologie Karl Barths?" in *Rhein. Altfreunde-Dienst,* 1928, pp. 24ff., 30ff.

[67]W. Knappe, "Klärung in der Barthschen Theologie," p. 254.

[68]Ibid.

[69]Ibid.

[70]Ibid., pp. 255-56.

[71]Ibid., p. 270.

[72]Ibid., p. 271.

place where he made his judgment had become a somewhat different one, but the critical intensity of the judgment had also increased somewhat. Of course this statement cannot be the last word on this relationship. A certain shift in emphasis made itself felt in his thought as that time, not concerning the judgment itself but concerning the criteria according to which such a judgment could be made and in the direction of a more favorable understanding of Pietism. While dealing with the history of theology in the nineteenth century he was led to formulate criteria by which the process of examining the history of theology could be guided. Those theological "clarifications" had an unmistakable impact in formulating these criteria. His research on the history of theology in conjunction with the application of these criteria probably also moved forward those theological clarifications.

Barth listed the following criteria. (1) All voices deserve to be *heard* in the church, where the "community of the saints" is active, where the mutual sharing of burdens between sinners gathered there in Christ takes place. The voices of the dead also deserve to be heard because "they still speak and want to be heard as living members of the church," not only our "favorite voices" but "all those of the previous centuries," "we perhaps especially need to hear these very imperfect voices first of all."[73] (2) Such listening in the church can only take place if we do *not* stand *above* but *alongside those* whom we have heard, certainly questioning them but in turn always questioned by them as well. As we encounter these voices, it must remain clear that we do not sit on a "judgment seat" above them. "Although the modern era *can* be right compared to the previous centuries, the question of whether it *is* actually right cannot be answered by us. If this is forgotten, then listening to the voice of the past will become objectively insincere in spite of all our subjective sincerity."[74] (3) As a working hypothesis we at least have to assume as we listen that we *objectively* stand *on the same Christian foundation* as our historical theological partners. If they have been Christian theologians, Christian faith "as the prerequisite for the common conversation between us and them cannot ever be doubted," "always considering the fact that I myself together with my theological work am in the Christian church only on the basis of forgiveness." Even if we have much to take issue with in hearing these voices from the past, we are at any rate not authorized to understand them from a vantage point that is ultimately and decisively other than our own, the place at which we too would like to be understood."[75] (4) In

---

[73]"Geschichte der prot. Theologie," in *Vorlesung 1929-1930*, 1943, pp. 2-3.
[74]Ibid., p. 5.
[75]Ibid., p. 12.

listening to these historical partners we also have to meet them in such a way that we respect their individual *uniqueness*. If the common ground between us and them must not be denied, we can also not deny "the differences between us and them." In that Christian truth is eternal but not timeless truth, then we can a priori expect that they have translated and interpreted "the same text differently than we."[76] This does not rule out criticism, but we must not take offense at its *distinctive features*. This also does not rule out our attempts to see broader perspectives, particular tendencies or similarities, but it puts an end to our "all too popular practice of drawing lines between them and compartmentalizing them." If we were tempted to house all the theologies of a particular era in one structure that is designed for them all, we would be violating their integrity and doing them a great injustice. Such a systematized examination of history would invariably become a "collection of rules that could only be broken."[77]

Imagine a conversation with the Pietists in their historical and contemporary form being carried on in conjunction with a serious application of these criteria! What a positive attitude toward them would be possible then! It seems to me that these bold criteria for a theological examination of the history of theology have broad implications, but Barth did not have the opportunity at that time to examine the history of theology using these criteria. At least in the era we are reporting on, he did not come to terms with the community people alive at that time, nor did he portray the Pietism of the eighteenth century using these four criteria. But at least he established the *criteria* in that era. If he had applied them, certainly a more positive view of the older and more recent Pietism would have emerged than the one that was possible from the perspective of the theology of the *Epistle to the Romans* and especially in the late 1920s. However, I wonder whether the portrayal of the older Pietism he presented in the written lectures of 1932/33 fully met the standard of these criteria. In these lectures he understood Pietism formally "as individualism," taking the view of the second *Epistle to the Romans* less than the view of the first one. However, for him this no longer signified a separation from a living organic whole as it did there, but an attempt to level the objectiveness of the theological object, an attempt to transform an essentially nonparticular theology into one that was particular to the people of that era.[78] Filling it with such content, this characterization clearly took up his critique of Pietism made in the late 1920s and now applied it sys-

---

[76]Ibid., p. 13.
[77]Ibid., pp. 14-15.
[78]"Die Geschichte der prot. Theologie," *Vorlesung, 1932-1933,* 1946, pp. 92ff.

tematically. What was new was that he saw another line in Pietism which did not fit into such a characterization, which at the same time presented it in a different, more favorable light. In view of this fact he thought, "In so far as this second factor was also at work in Pietism, it was, in spite of everything, something like Noah's ark in which the doctrine of justification by faith alone was then rescued from the flood of a pious and reasonable Pelagianism."[79] By considering this aspect as well, Barth certainly demonstrates his effort to do justice to this movement by applying those four criteria. Of course, we must pay attention to the fact that in Barth this other aspect was not a part of the "program" of Pietism but only a disruption of its program that happened to it against its intention. Its "program" was *in itself* only its serious attack on the object of theology.[80] If there was something else in it, then it was only *in spite of* what it wanted, because the attack failed *against* its will, it "remained only an attempt" and turned out to be an "offensive that never got beyond its early stages."[81] Therefore Barth continued to fully reject its program as such. Nothing could be learned from it. We would like to think that if he had fully applied those four criteria, it could be seen in a more positive light on its own terms. Instead, Barth saw only what was in Pietism *in spite of* its Pietism. Why was Barth prevented from advancing further in this direction during that era? It seems to us that it was mainly due to the fact that in portraying the eighteenth and nineteenth centuries, another viewpoint was in play. It was evident that already in the winter of 1932/ 33 he was forging the weapon that was to become so important in the subsequent struggle of the Confessing Church as he viewed it. One of the crucial assertions he made in this struggle was that the error of the "German Christians" could be resisted in principle only by acknowledging that their error was to be understood as a mere eruption of the anthropocentric Neo-Protestantism that had been devastating the church for the past two hundred years.[82] And if Barth also saw a failure of the "attack on the object of faith" in the eighteenth century, we may also view this as an expression of his confident certainty in the midst of the struggle that the new attack in the providence of God would once again fail. Therefore this struggle that was already looming in 1932/33 may have been the reason why he did not reach a more precise and yet also more positive view of the Pietistic program itself by fully applying those four criteria then.

Within the time frame of our report, however, a document from his hand has

---

[79]Ibid., p. 113.
[80]Ibid., p. 64.
[81]Ibid., pp. 103-4.
[82]Compare, for example, the issues of Barth's "Theologische Existenz heute," nr. 2, p. 14; nr. 3, pp. 23-24; nr. 4, pp. 4ff.; all come from 1933.

been found in which this more precise and more positive view was at least hinted at, a document that points beyond the lecture of 1932/33 and whose thesis bore fruit more than ever in Barth's treatment of Pietistic concerns in volumes 4/2 and 4/3 of his *Church Dogmatics* during the 1950s. We are speaking of the only text of the late 1920s to our knowledge in which he examined Pietism in more historical detail. We are thinking of the discussion of the "spiritual awakening" of the early nineteenth century in his lecture from the winter of 1929/30 on the history of theology where he takes up Tholuck's portrayal of that revival.[83] Based on the observations he made there this movement made two significant theological contributions. (1) It helped the church remember that there are "no theological truths in general" but only those that "empower witness from" the lips of those who have been *deeply* touched by these truths. (2) It "brought to the surface a particular insight of the Christian tradition": the knowledge of the depth of human *sin* and faith in God's *mercy* outside of ourselves. Of course, Barth also saw dangers looming in both of these noteworthy points. (1) Modern theological "anthropologism" reached its apex in this movement in so far as "revivalist theology taught man to become preoccupied with himself and revolve around himself." (2) This whole teaching on sin and grace ends up with the common denominator of a human possibility in spite of all the excellent details. But at the same time Barth also saw a *promising* new beginning in *the same* two points. (1) Revivalist theology so profoundly mobilized those people who were touched by Christian truth that we must ask if, contrary to their own explanations, they were to be understood not as messengers of their own hearts' experiences but as witnesses of Christ in spite of all foolishness. (2) They were able to speak of the corruption of humanity but also of the "assurance of salvation" that lies outside of humankind, as well as of the grace on which those who have been pardoned depend, in such a way that "their emotional excitement did not lack a knowledge of what is more than excitement." So on the one hand this theology ultimately has said the *same thing* as the prevailing anthropological theology, but simultaneously it has known "the idea of the free grace that has been lavished on the sinner, even if it has not actually reflected on this truth." Certainly he also declared in this lecture that the revivalist theologians stressed that aspect of grace "contrary to their own statements." A somewhat different nuance but in the end a more consequential nuance than was implied here emerged from the dialectical position Barth took on its concern compared

---

[83]"Vorlesung über die Geschichte der prot. Theologie 1929-1930," 1943, pp. 244-47. Of course, our remarks can be modified in so far as Barth literally adopted this text in his lecture of 1932-1933 (pp. 465ff.).

with the lecture of 1932/33. The promising aspect of their theology was not merely found *beside* the truth but *in* the truth that was central to them. It was not simply an adverse part of their program but was actually a part of their concern itself. We think this shows the first signs of a more positive appreciation of Pietism (in its other historical appearances as well). It was a new beginning that had to have an impact on the theological discussion between him and the Pietists. Now he could not simply say the same thing in the way he had intended, nor could he simply say something different. Instead he could say *the same thing in a different way.*

All in all, Barth's evaluation of Pietism (in its form as a revivalist movement) had remained *critical* at the end of 1929/30, but at the same time it had become critical in a new, *irenic* way. So we may say that he had obviously *learned something new* in the course of the 1920s after the publication of his *Epistle to the Romans.* He responded positively to the difficulty of arriving at a balanced view of Pietism and affirmed the possibility of taking a more open-minded, more friendly attitude toward the historical phenomenon of Pietism, in spite of his continuing critique and even in spite of the new reasons he used to critique it. He was on the path that led a few years later to the following scene (in the discussion after his "Declaration on the Proper Understanding of the Reformational Confessions in the Contemporary German Evangelical Church" at the Free Reformed Synod on January 3-4, 1934, in Barmen.) A participant regretted that Barth had not also distanced himself from Pietism at the same time. He responded to that remark (not without a subsequent critical remark) by declaring, "The front against Pietism is now obsolete."[84] Of course, this remark pointed to a distant future and to a still untrodden path.

If we want to *learn* from Barth's opening to the concern of Pietism that has been heralded here, we would not learn in a fruitful way if one only picked out what he liked: the non-Pietists what was still left of his critique, the Pietists what has been reported here about his irenic attitude. Rather for those who sincerely do *not* wish to be *Pietists, fruitful* learning would mean that they take seriously this partner they encounter in Pietism in the arena of the church. Despite all the criticism they may have and perhaps have to have, they should not give up on this partner, not let him go, not be "finished" with him, but instead always ask how he could be and perhaps must be understood even better and differently than he had been before. Fruitful learning on this side would be

---

[84]"Free Reformed Synod, January 3-4, 1934," ed. K. Immer, 1934, p. 27. The critical remark he made in addition was: what is not good in Pietism has now woken up with the "German Christians."

possible only if they would stop questioning this partner without allowing themselves to be questioned by him. It would only be possible if the other side allows the Pietists to remind them that Christian faith is in fact about becoming "children of the Spirit" however much they may have reason to ask *what* spirit the Pietists actually represent. On the other hand, for those who sincerely wish to be *Pietists,* fruitful learning would mean that they are also prepared to not let the others go and not be "finished" with them and are willing to tolerate their questions as well without immediately disqualifying these questions as unspiritual. For them fruitful learning would only be possible if they do not simply see Barth's incipient opening to their concern as grist for their mills, if they do not simply interpret it as self-affirmation but respond to this (self-critical) opening by moving in the direction of a similar (self-critical) opening. It would be even more of a blessing for them if the conversion experience they stress would not make them unconvertible in this respect, if their knowledge of being children of God would neither deny nor neutralize this pointed question: *Of what spirit* are these individuals who intend to be pious? Like all other Christians they are also invited to repentantly and happily take to heart the wisdom one man expressed whom they feel is one of their own, Nikolaus von Zinzendorf: "The king desires to teach those people who cheerfully know that they are students and have to learn."

Hope for the Conversion of the Converted

Karl Barth and Pietism
by Eberhard Busch

Translated by Daniel W. Bloesch, Christian T. Collins Winn and Ruth Rhenius

1. Considerations on a Christian Willingness for Dialogue

On the death of the Pietist Heinrich Gelzer in Basel in 1963, with whom Karl Barth had maintained a faithful bond of friendship for almost fifty years, Barth called him a "prominent representative of a great tradition in its own way to which I am also deeply indebted from the point of view of some of my ancestors, and then on the basis of my studies as well, in spite of any reservations I may have."[1] This may sound surprising to those who for a long time saw Barth as a "severe critic of Pietism." However, it can be clearly verified that with one exception, he actually left the door open to Pietism for his entire life, though with certain reservations! He was not really a follower of the Pietists and did not become one, nor was he their opponent, but rather more like their critical friend or friendly critic—or, as the community man Ludwig Thimme recognized in the 1920s, a "troublesome friend of the Pietists."[2] Troublesome, one must add, because as a friend he had to ask several important questions of Pietism that were aimed not at refuting and abolishing it but at making a repentant self-correction in it. Addressing his question to it as a friend, Karl Barth's theology is especially suitable for engaging in an open discussion with Pietists. One cannot pose questions to them from this theology without at the same time taking them and their special concern seriously, as well as when they point out serious shortcomings in the church. On the other hand, the Pietists can engage in this discussion without fear of encountering an ignorant rejection, yet only by being willing to make a repentant self-correction if necessary. All this must be done under the assumption that not one side or the other but God may get what is his by right, and that the gospel of Jesus Christ must be victorious!

---

[1] K. Barth *Briefe 1961-1968* (Zurich, 1975), p. 205.
[2] L. Thimme, "Das Problem der Kirche und die reformatorische Lösung," in *Im Kampf um die Kirche* (Gotha, 1930), p. 33.

Of course, I cannot help but point out that Pietism in particular has always had a lot of trouble engaging in such an inner-Christian discussion. I will illustrate this difficulty first of all by citing a case from the eighteenth century that in many ways is comparable to the confrontation between Barth and Pietism. The Hallensian Pietists refused to dialogue with the orthodox theologian Valentin Ernst Löscher. Löscher was also somewhat of a "troublesome friend of the Pietists," convincingly refuting the dogma about "dead orthodoxy" and its merely polemical theology. He even agreed with the Pietists that it is not enough to believe right doctrine but that there is a need for an awakening, for conversion and the new birth—a need not only for justification but also for growth in sanctification. Therefore, he was not satisfied with preaching alone but strongly supported youth and lay ministry, personal edification, and so on. He was so sympathetic to the Pietists that even today their circles enjoy singing Löscher's songs. And yet at the same time he asked the Pietists some serious questions in view of the unimportance they attached to evangelical doctrine compared to pious praxis, in view of their indifference to a salvation that has occurred outside of us in favor of an event in the inner being of man, in view of their limitation of the repentance we need to a fixed time in life, in view of their idea that there is a goodness in our own deeds, causing either arrogance or despair, and so on. After years of trying to reach an agreement with the Hallensian Pietists on these problematic points, Löscher finally ended up having a discussion with them. It soon ended in disaster, however, because Francke blocked any discussion of the points by demanding that Löscher would first have to convert. No matter how much Löscher protested that he was already converted, Francke challenged him. What is important to me here is his argument, for "if someone is truly with Christ, he cannot possibly be against us (Pietists)."[3] This virtually means that he cannot ask us any questions. Here Francke almost equated Jesus' words about one's stance on himself with one's stance on Pietism. Whoever is not for us, is against us and therefore against Christ!

I believe that a specific Pietistic refusal to enter into dialogue became evident here for the first time. To a greater or lesser degree this refusal has since then been a part of the tradition of a movement that thinks along these lines: Questions coming from outside Pietism can be explained only by the fact that the questioner is not at all concerned about a revival of Christianity and that the questioner himself is probably not truly converted. What is actually behind this

---

[3]M. Greschat, *Zwischen Tradition und neuem Anfang. Valentin Loscher und der Ausgang der lutherischen Orthodoxie* (Witten, 1971), p. 300. Compare to K. Barth, *Die Protestantische Theologie im 19. Jahrhundert* (Zurich, 1946), pp. 118ff.

is the claim that God's cause and the cause of Pietism belong so closely together that any serious question addressed to it can ultimately be understood only as casting doubt on God's cause. This then leads to a situation in which basically only one question can be asked about non-Pietistic Christians by the Pietistic side: Can they be co-opted for our own cause, or must they be dropped? What is not even a possibility for them is that these others might have something to say that must be taken seriously as a further inquiry into their own position. We ourselves have the truth; we only have to examine whether others have it as well, not whether what they say could mean that we allow them to ask us to what extent we actually have the truth.[4] Whenever one thinks in terms of these assumptions, it is, of course, almost impossible to carry on a serious discussion: being willing to subject one's own understanding to the discussion and calmly listening to the other side. And if, in my opinion, Pietism has always been at least in danger of refusing to accept such a discussion, this probably has very deep roots; one can even ask whether or not limiting the repentance and conversion we need to a specific time in our lives does not actually have the significance of henceforth making a person impervious and invulnerable to any further questions that would seriously affect him.

On this issue the situation is somewhat different for the one who can be considered here as a dialogue partner with the Pietists. Karl Barth was certainly not someone who was indifferent to what was being taught in the church, who in this sense spoke up for tolerance in the church, claiming that "everything" must be possible there. Armed with his knowledge of the truth, he offered criticism in all directions in a most decisive fashion, and once even dared to make this statement:

> It is in a theological conflict that we are especially in Christ and thus also together in the church, if we are clear about the fact that especially in Christ we are also separated. We are not fighting about the rights of a church, or even about the right to hold a personal opinion, but about the right of the church to fight heresy and thus necessarily to fight one another. . . . Whenever we oppose one another in true dogmatic intolerance, especially then and only then, we will always be able to talk to one another, we will be able to have a fruitful dialogue because then and only then . . . we will have something to say to each other."[5]

However, precisely these statements show that even when we most emphati-

---

[4] A typical example of this is the Pietistic work by H. Jochums targeted at Karl Barth, *Die grosse Enttäuschung. Karl Barth und die Theologien, Philosophien, Antropologien und Ideologien der Gegenwart, sonderlich im deutschen Sprachraum* (Wuppertal: Verlag und Schriftenmission der EGD, 1986). Of course, a similar critique, more discriminating and refined, was made by L. Gassmann, *Karl Barth. Das Verhängnis der Dialektik* (Berneck, 1995).
[5] K. Barth, *Kirchliche Dogmatik* (=KD) I/2, p. 924.

cally stand up for our own understanding in the church of Christ, we will not go our separate ways but talk to one another, though we can do this only when our understanding is not just any private opinion, not a special revelation or a special discovery, but a serious claim to be the knowledge of the gospel of Jesus Christ.

In Barth's thinking there were two additional prerequisites for being able to talk to each other in the church of Christ, and these two are inextricably linked. First, such a dialogue between Christians, even if it has the form of an argument with each other, occurs in the brackets of the assumption that both are in the church of Christ. This gives the discussion its true seriousness but also marks the clear boundaries of the argument. Barth once said that the person we should drop completely could "only be an arch-heretic who is totally lost to the invisible church as well." But he adds, "We do not have the ability to ascertain such lost arch-heresy, we do not have this ability even in the case of Christians who are perhaps under strong suspicion."[6] Barth concludes that this is true of two theologians with whom he especially took issue: "For me, Schleiermacher also belongs (in the community of the saints) and Bultmann does too; there is no question about that."[7] This approach has some immediate specific consequences. As a Christian I can criticize other Christians only if I am also in solidarity with them. Furthermore, when I criticize others I can distance myself from them not in a tone of harsh indignation but only in a tone of sad dismay at a threat that had somehow turned into a temptation for me as well. And finally, believing that Israel's shepherd does not slumber or sleep even in the church, I have to keep myself open to the possibility not only that the "favorite voices" I like to hear testify to the truth of God in the church, but "that we need . . . totally unexpected voices even though these voices may at first be quite unwelcome."[8]

The other prerequisite for talking to each other and having an argument with each other is this: Even when I boldly stand up for my understanding of the truth, I can do so only by paying attention to the boundary that is drawn by the fact that God's truth and my understanding of it are always two completely different things. At the very moment I forget this border, it will shift, and the border between my understanding of God's truth and other Christians' understanding of it will become absolute. At that very moment the other person and I no longer stand before our common judge, rather I become the judge of the other. By contrast we must remember what Karl Barth learned especially from the Reformed

---

[6]K. Barth, *Die Protestantische Theologie,* p. 3.
[7]Dialogue with Rhenish young pastors on November 4, 1963 (tape recording).
[8]K. Barth, *Die Protestantische Theologie,* p. 3.

fathers: As a matter of principle I can only advance my understanding, as firmly
as I may hold it, "if I am open to being taught better by the Scriptures in the future." At any rate, this insight so defined Barth's theology that it was not a system
but a path on which he was always en route, in order to say the same thing again
in a different way. More than ever we must remember Jesus' words about judging, which keep me from mistaking my understanding of God's truth for this
truth itself. Whenever I criticize others, I am in the greatest danger of condemning the speck in my brother's eye while ignoring the plank in my own eye (Mt
7:3-5). This insight had such a formative influence in Barth's theology that it was
constantly accompanied by very specific inquiries into his own work. He in-
quired not only if this or that could have been done better but if as a whole it
was not a flight from God—if in doing so he had not ignored 95 percent of the
Bible. Looking at modern theology, he could say when the confessing movement
rallied against it, "I would not like to make the assumption of an almost general
impenitence, but prefer to ask what we might not have done so well."[9] And, I
must add, any idle observer who uses Barth's self-critique to discredit his theology instead of allowing it to be contagious is a fool, for it should lead him to
make a similar effort not to ignore the plank in his own eye. And whoever understands this kind of thinking as skepticism and no longer as truly humble theology is also a fool, for this theology knows that nothing can be said against our
Lord, but a lot can be said against the way we speak about him and treat him.

I think it is clear to all those involved on either side of the issue of the church
and Pietism that by raising only these preliminary questions for the dialogue between Pietistic and more or less non-Pietistic Christians I did not mention anything of minor importance but virtually the most crucial thing of all (especially
considering the present state of affairs). I am of the opinion that such a dialogue
is meaningful and fruitful only when these two principles are recognized on
both sides, though I see on the part of modern Pietism little willingness to recognize these principles.[10] Hoping and assuming that modern Pietism is not so
close-minded that it could not recognize these two principles, it makes sense
not to stop now but to continue.

2. Stages on Barth's Journey in His Relationship to Pietism
As I have already said, Karl Barth's theology cannot be described as a system
but only as a journey on which he time and again tried to say the same thing in
a different way. This way of thinking is modeled on Israel's wanderings on the

---

[9]Barth, *Briefe 1961-1968,* p. 55.
[10]Compare note 4.

way to the Promised Land; it is modeled on the Holy Place that was kept in the tabernacle, which had to be taken down over and over again and put up in new locations. Time and again something different can be said, and yet always only the same thing can be said. These two things actually rule each other out. But time and again it was Barth's aim to say the same thing in a different way. Therefore, it is also a fact that he had a different relationship to Pietism at various stages along the way. At any rate, it is interesting that he took Pietism so seriously that this subject constantly accompanied him on his journey and occupied his mind. Again, when one appeals to Barth and argues with him, one must pay attention to the context in which he made the respective remarks as well as to the period on his journey when he made them. It is certainly true as well that there are links from his earliest work to his later work and vice versa. This is why the positions of the younger Barth on Pietism are not simply outdated in his later theology but also do not simply rule out the later new emphasis.

Generally speaking, the change in Barth's relationship to Pietism is well known. The portrait of this change looks something like this: In his second interpretation of the epistle to the Romans from 1922 he sharply attacked and fought Pietism. At that time he so overemphasized the distance between God in heaven and humanity on earth that he denied all of God's activity in this world and thus had no appreciation for sanctification, the new birth and the conversion of humankind. The battle lines shifted in the 1930s. To be sure, he did teach about God's action in this world, but he so emphasized the objective aspect of salvation that in the process he forgot the subjective aspect—the taking hold of salvation—or did not stress it enough. Only in the 1950s, especially in *Church Dogmatics* IV/2, did he make close contact with Pietism by talking in detail about sanctification, conversion, spiritual awakening and discipleship. Barth actually explains in the foreword of this volume that he tried to do justice to the concern of the Pietists, even if he was not able to become one of them.

As widespread as this portrait of Karl Barth's journey and the change in his relationship to Pietism is, and although even he himself occasionally spread this portrait,[11] on the whole I do not consider it to be correct. Therefore, I will attempt to portray the journey he made in greater detail by making several concise suggestions and distinguishing six stages on the journey.

First, after growing up in a mildly Pietistic parental home, as he himself

---

[11]In his dialogue with community people in 1959 Barth talks as if he had only recently cut short his dispute with the Pietists. Compare K. Barth, *Gespräche 1959-1962* (Zurich: TVZ, 1995), pp. 15ff. He could actually talk just like this more than twenty years earlier in the early 1930s. Compare K. Immer, *Freie reformierte Synode,* January 3/4 (1934): p. 27: "The front against Pietism is now one of the obsolete fronts."

stated, he first became a decidedly liberal theologian. At that time the key concept for him was "the individualistic religious experience,"[12] as it was put in the
common language of his time. From this perspective his avowed opponent was
any form of dogmatic, orthodox Christianity in which one was supposed to
think that certain doctrines, truths or distant "facts" were true, following an external authority. As he said at that time, the divine truth can make itself strictly
and purely known only in the fact of personal experience, mediated by other
inwardly alive human beings, initially through what he called the "inner life of
Jesus," that is, through the living impression his person personally makes on us.
It was a short summary of his theology when he appealed then to the aphorisms
of Angelus Silesius, which he later called "pious impertinences"[13] but which at
first were "perfectly right" to him.[14] "If Christ were born a thousand times in
Bethlehem / And not in you: you would remain eternally lost." It is remarkable
that he also appealed directly to Pietism at that time—to Tersteegen[15] in an especially intense way—and that he believed he could actually combine the Pietistic concerns with his liberal interests. When he espoused the thesis of the
affinity between Pietism and liberalism (or better, the Enlightenment) in the
1930s, this was also a reminder that he was aware of having sat in the same boat
with the Pietists in his liberal period. He saw the objective common ground between both phenomena in the modern (and then, later for him, unbiblical) conviction that what can be proven and understood to be true in the court of the
individual self and his experience is the only thing that can be recognized as
true, as divinely true.

The second stage is the first interpretation of the epistle to the Romans in
1919 (mostly unnoticed by the Pietists). It is supported by the key concept of
the kingdom of God already "growing" in our midst, binding human beings together in an organic whole. One immediately notices that this key concept is
clearly in opposition to the concept of individual, personal experience from
Barth's initial period. The book is, in fact, a fierce debate with the liberal theology that he himself had previously espoused, but at the same time it is defined
by an equally intense rejection of Pietism. This is the one exception where Barth
spoke against Pietism head on. Pietism essentially means individualism here
(think again of Barth's own, earlier key concept of individual religious experi-

---

[12]Discussed earlier in this volume.

[13]K. Barth, *KD* II/1, p. 316.

[14]Compare K. Barth, "Der christliche Glaube und die Geschichte," *Schweizer Theologische
Zeitschrift* 29 (1912): 57.

[15]Compare K. Barth, "Gerhard Tersteegen," *Gemeinde-Blatt für die Deutsche reformierte Ge-
meinde* 7, nr. 38 (1910): 1-3.

ence!). It is concerned about individual conversion, individual sanctification, individual salvation.[16] But in this way it participates in the dark, unredeemed, evil nature of the world that consists of egotism, self-glorification and a life revolving around the self. Even if Pietism separates itself from other human beings, as long as it revolves around itself, around a satisfaction of self-centered human desires (even if they be of a religious nature), his supposedly new life is only a special case of thinking that is profoundly conformed to the world. Therefore, "How is the Pietist supposed to know what to say or do against mammon, war, sickness . . . when his deepest nature consists of the same apostasy from God as the nature of those powers?"[17]

This is a critical question that Barth addressed to Pietism, and in a certain sense it was always on his mind. The question makes us aware of the remarkable alliance in which Pietism's interest in the private salvation of the soul was so often combined with its willingness to reach an accommodation with the unholy powers ruling this world. This explains their great interest in the "little," private sins and their habit of turning a blind eye to their own involvement in social sins. This combination was not a coincidence for Barth. For example, we can illustrate what he means by examining what modern research has extensively documented.[18] In the Hallensian Pietism of the eighteenth century, sanctification was considered a visible reality manifesting itself in personal successes: abstaining from alcohol, not indulging in excess, not acting out sexually, and so on. The result of this, however, was that individuals then distinguished themselves before others in the social realm as more obedient subjects, more skillful traders, more competent soldiers, and the like. This example shows that the new reality in Pietism, limited to the individual, not only does not cast doubt on the "old," unholy world but as a result merely anoints it so that it can work better. The question Barth addressed to Pietism did not aim merely at a social expansion of their interest in individual salvation. It expressed the suspicion that the new reality of the individual claimed by Pietism was as such only an illusion, in fact only a refinement of the "old life" in that it only had the effect of affirming and reinforcing the conditions of the "old world." When Pietists subsequently found fault with Barth for lacking a doctrine of sanctification, they usually ignored the fact that his theology was not waiting to be supplemented by a doctrine of sanctification on their terms. Instead, his theology was a protest against it—a protest seeking

---

[16]K. Barth, *Der Römerbrief* (Bern: G. A. Baschlin, 1919), p. 205.

[17]Ibid., p. 214.

[18]C. Hinrichs, "Der Hallische Pietismus als politische-soziale Reformbewegung des 18. Jahrhunderts," in *Zur neueren Pietismusforschung,* ed. M. Greschat (Darmstadt, 1977), pp. 243-58.

to reveal that the different quality of life claimed by those who were personally sanctified in relation to the old, godless world was only an apparent change, since it actually guaranteed its continued trouble-free existence.

Of course, Barth made this critique of a supposedly new life in Pietism while advocating a position in which the new life pursued in vain by Pietism is given when one allows himself to be taken into the power of the kingdom of God that is already growing now. Only a short while later he realized that this view was firmly based on the tradition of Swabian Pietism in particular, for example, the Pietism of Friedrich Christoph Oetinger. Precisely in the book in which he most passionately spoke against Pietism, he was objecting to only one tradition and tendency in Pietism, while at the same time being unaware that he was strongly dependent on another tradition in Pietism. The view that caused him to remain dependent on this other tradition, and separate himself from the Reformation together with it, was that the new reality so transforms us human beings "as we grow" that our sinful state is temporally more and more a thing of the past for us. When Barth soon became aware of the problematic nature of this view, he believed he had to learn that this view would not endure if one takes seriously the Reformational insight that even the person who is justified always remains a sinner before God.

This happened in the totally new second interpretation of the epistle to the Romans, which was published shortly after the first one in 1922. It marks the third stage in his relationship with Pietism. His critique of Pietism in it now focuses on a very subtle point.[19] Assuming that Pietism was understood correctly—that a self-righteous "Pharisaism" does not count for anything before God—Barth thinks that Pietism then turns this correct knowledge into a surefire method by which man believes he is able to "earn" God's grace on his own initiative. Barth later calls this the "Pharisaism of the tax-collector,"[20] of which he accuses Pietism here. The critique is targeted at the opinion that man can secure a right to God's forgiveness and goodness not by his works but by his repentance, his humility and his awareness of sin.

As far as the basic theme of the second *Epistle to the Romans* is concerned, it is astonishing to see the lack of understanding H. Jochums reveals in his little book, when he once again laments Barth's talk of otherworldliness and even understands it as the root of today's atheism.[21] For of all of Barth's books, this

---

[19]K. Barth, *Der Römerbrief,* 2nd ed. (Munich: Chr. Kaiser Verlag, 1922), p. 84.

[20]K. Barth, *KD* IV/1, p. 688; here, though, with the dialectical twist that a Pietist could stand justified compared to a Pharisaical tax-collector!

[21]H. Jochums, *Die grosse Enttäuschung*, pp. 18, 73-76.

is the one most deeply influenced by a prophetic protest against the matter-of-factness with which the Germans, as well as the German Pietists, marched into the First World War with the slogan "With God for the people and the fatherland." Barth's protest was targeted at the use of the word *God* to gain a clear conscience for a thoroughly sinful, godless enterprise. He said it was about time to become an atheist against this would-be god[22] precisely for the sake of the real God's honor! Therefore, the whole struggle of this second *Epistle to the Romans* focused on Barth's endeavor to, so to speak, extricate God from the hands of human beings who used him to sanction, implement and approve of actions undertaken without God. God is indeed otherworldly in the face of this abuse. In expressing this view Barth denied, however, only that man can reach God and come to him on his own; he clearly did not deny that, conversely, God can reach man and come to him. This book also clearly speaks of the immanence of God—the fact that God lives in this world, however in such a way that God clearly takes man into his hands—but denies that on the basis of this fact man can in turn take God into his hands.

Barth's critique of the concept of "experience" can also be seen in this context if experience becomes a pretext for man to once again enlist God in the cause of furthering his own purposes. In all of this, Barth's critique is now decisively targeted at liberal theology. He charges it with misusing God in order to accommodate him to the spirit and business of this world. And Pietism? This is the big surprise! On the whole Barth speaks of it in an astonishingly friendly way in, of all places, the second *Epistle to the Romans*. This was not a coincidence. A new, positive approach to Pietism was opened up for him by Franz Overbeck, one of the midwives of his new theology and an astute mocker of the modern, liberal Christianity that was conformed to the world and affirmed the culture. Overbeck saw the Pietists as the phenomenon that had the critical spirit to free itself from the liberal secularization of Christianity.[23] In fact, a positive view of Pietism similar to Overbeck's can be observed in the second *Epistle to the Romans*, including a reasonable appreciation for what conversion and "new man" should mean.

Yet it is perhaps one of the tragic moments of Pietism that it largely overlooked the book's open-mindedness to its cause; that it rather understood the book as a challenge to itself; that it felt is was being attacked where it was not

---

[22]K. Barth, *Das Wort Gottes und die Theologie. Ges. Vortr.,* vol. 1 (Munich: Chr. Kaiser Verlag, 1924), p. 14.

[23]Compare F. Overbeck, *Christentum und Kultur. Gedanken und Anmerkungen zur modernen Theologie,* ed. C.A. Bernoulli (1919; reprint, Darmstadt, 1963), pp. 179, 286; quoted by K. Barth, *Die Theologie und die Kirche, Ges. Vortr.,*vol. 2 (Munich: Chr. Kaiser Verlag, 1928), p. 7.

attacked at all; that in its numerous polemics against the second *Epistle to the Romans*[24] it placed itself right where Barth did not see it: namely on a course that had very much accommodated to the spirit of the time (in spite of its insistence, e.g., on the new birth). It is astonishing to see that the liberal polemics against the second *Epistle to the Romans* defended the phenomenon of "experience" and "God in us" as something sacred in a manner quite similar to the Pietistic polemics.[25] Both equally accused Barth of skepticism for calling this phenomenon into question. Apart from new emphases in his own theological thinking, it is possible that these reactions by Pietists in the 1920s caused him to take another, now somewhat more critical view of Pietism, namely in his lecture on the history of Protestant theology (1932/1933, first published in 1946).[26] With this turn of events the fourth stage in his relationship to Pietism begins. The premise of his new relationship to it is the fact that Barth is now emphasizing the presence of God in this world more strongly and more clearly than in the second *Epistle to the Romans*. Yet he emphasizes it by saying that God becomes so present in this world that he reveals himself to human beings, and in doing so he makes himself a partner in dialogue with human beings. He who devotes himself to them in free yet costly grace makes himself a partner who does not let go of them but whom we in turn cannot get the better of. From there Barth understands Pietism in two ways.

On the one hand, Pietism is the attempt to fight against the Lord as the One who faces us, the attempt to abolish this partner who is opposite us—to so appropriate him that he can be passed off as something that is our own: present, demonstrable, available in the inner being of man. It is the attempt to take all of those elements of Christianity into man which in themselves signify what is external, the partner who is opposite us.[27] Barth sees this attempt in the context of modern man's enterprise of humanizing Christianity, that is, of passing off the reality of God as a reality that is in fact only in man. He gives evidence of this process by providing all kinds of examples:[28] how the actual birth of Christ takes place in our heart, how the Bible is used to affirm man and serve what he wants to hear from it (and this is actually the birthplace of modern biblical criticism), how furthermore the commanding authority of God is replaced by an inner voice (leading to all kinds of extraordinary habits in our lives through which we

---

[24]Discussed earlier in this volume.

[25]Compare, for instance, B. Dörries, *Der ferne und der nähe Gott. Eine Auseinandersetzung mit der Theologie Karl Barths* (Gotha, 1927).

[26]K. Barth, *Die Protestantische Theologie im 19. Jahrhundert* (Zurich, 1946).

[27]Barth, *Die Protestantische Theologie*, p. 95.

[28]Ibid., pp. 94-103.

really want to stand out from others), how furthermore the mystery of the divine truth is so internalized that man discovers himself as a mystery, becoming a sacrament himself, the visible sign of an invisible grace, and so on. We can say that Barth is basically objecting to the same thing in Pietism that he later had on his heart with regard to Bultmann's demythologizing and existentialism.[29] He actually called Bultmann a secret Pietist, in the belief that his project amounts to what has just been described.

Of course, on the other hand, Barth believes something else can be said about Pietism at the same time.

> It is impossible to read its documents without having to say to oneself that its really living Christianity is still found beyond the scope (of what has been described here). But all this means that the attempt I have just described has only been partially successful, that it has remained an attempt.[30]

He also mentions several examples: Pietism has not forgotten the justification of the sinner by God, despite their inclination to understand it only as a transitional stage on the way to gradually making the believer righteous and good. Despite their inclination to reinterpret Jesus' blood and wounds as the subject matter of all kinds of psychological and emotional conditions, they kept alive the memory of Jesus Christ, the crucified One who is the source of all the strength we need, the source of help and change through unmerited grace. Finally, eschatology (the hope of God's ultimate coming that will make everything new) has even been rediscovered, despite the blurring of this hope by rashly anticipating what is hoped for. In short, in those days Barth saw both sides of Pietism: both light and shadow. Even though he said many things worth taking to heart and also expressed critical insights on which he did not change his mind, he could basically not stay with this position. He saw light in Pietism and much that was justified, but he saw it only in those elements that contradicted its actual concern—indeed, in the failure of its true and, as such, only problematic intentions.

At the same moment the portrait had to shift again, as he gave credence to the insight that a very legitimate concern could be found not only in what ran counter to the Pietistic concern but also in its concern as such, which theological thought must respond to positively if it claims to be thinking done truly for the sake of the church. It is really a matter of recognizing what Pietism actually wants and what can be described by the terms that are so important to it, such as *sanctification, spiritual awakening, conversion, new birth* and *discipleship.*

---

[29]K. Barth, "Nachwort," in *Schleiermacher-Auswahl,* ed. H. Bolli, Siebenstern-Taschenbuch 112/114 (1968): 298ff.
[30]Barth, *Die Protestantische Theologie,* p. 103.

The affirmation and positive reception of this concern of Pietism determines the character of the fifth stage of Barth's relationship to it, particularly in his *Church Dogmatics* IV/2 (1955), within the framework of his doctrine of reconciliation that deals with the sanctifying work of Christ. Generally speaking, he first gained access to this reorientation by focusing his theology more and more christocentrically, that is, on the figure of Jesus Christ. With this new focus he actually moved closer to Zinzendorf's theology, whom he now called the greatest and perhaps the only fully authentic christocentric theologian[31] (which he actually was in his era, though he was unanimously rejected by the Hallensian, Swabian and Lower Rhenish Pietists). Of course, Barth emphasized more strongly than Zinzendorf that if I say Jesus Christ, then I am saying true God and true man. Therefore, in Jesus Christ these two things are true: God is for man, but also man is for God. In Christ, not only does God make his way to man, but man is also set free and claimed to come to him and rise up to have fellowship with him. In Christ God not only justifies the sinner but also sanctifies him, awakens him to turn back to God, to follow Jesus—even to do good works and bear the cross. It is this latter theme that Barth expounds in great detail in *Church Dogmatics* IV/2,[32] expressly agreeing with the concern of the Pietists.[33] We can illustrate how far he moved toward their concern by examining the following quotations: "Whoever believes in God thereby also believes in an awakening of man to turn back to Him; He expects such an awakening: no, he expects God to give, to create such an awakening and make it real."

It is not a matter of "improvement, but . . . of a new life. The change is called conversion—we cannot avoid the loaded word: conversion."[34] Sanctified by Christ, the sanctification of Christians is a "real change in their life,"[35] in such a way that they "are really different from the world."[36] Here at the latest Pietism should correct its opinion that Barth (as Fritz Rienecker said)[37] espoused a one-sided objectivism that was a pillow for a sleeping conscience, and that he knew nothing of the subjective acceptance of salvation in repentance, conversion and faith.

However, Barth's warning in the same book must not be forgotten. He said he had not become one of the Pietists.[38] In a certain sense he is highly critical

---

[31]Barth, *KD* IV/1, p. 763.

[32]*KD* IV/2, pp. 578-694.

[33]Ibid., p. vii.

[34]Ibid., p. 633.

[35]Ibid., p. 598.

[36]Ibid., p. 593.

[37]K. Barth, "Biblische Kritik am Pietismus alter und neuer Zeit," in *Badener Konferenz* (Basel: H. Majer, 1952), pp. 15ff.

[38]Compare *KD* IV/2, pp. 578-694.

of the Pietists' concern here as well by at least no longer talking here as if there were a gap in his theology at this point but by claiming that one can talk biblically about conversion, sanctification and spiritual awakening without becoming a Pietist. Thus he lifted the discussion with the Pietists to a new and different level, on which it can no longer be enough for them to say: "You are talking in fully biblical terms only if you talk about conversion," and so on. Rather on this level information must be given on how we can talk about all of this in a biblical, evangelical way. In any case, by deliberately taking up the concern of the Pietists, Barth deliberately talked about it differently in various ways. What follows are two of the perhaps most important points.

1. The new reality (the new man, our sanctification) is definitely not something in us and in our actions but given to us in Christ and his work that he did "in our place, for us."[39] We can say with Paul: "Christ Jesus . . . has become for us wisdom from God—that is, our righteousness, holiness and redemption" (1 Cor 1:30), and we are saints "in Christ Jesus" (1 Cor 1:2; Phil 1:1). We can say with Jesus in John: "For them I sanctify myself, that they too may be truly sanctified" (Jn 17:19). And we can say with the letter to the Hebrews: "We have been made holy through the sacrifice of the body of Jesus Christ once for all" (Heb 10:10)! It is not as if by saying this our participation in it were ruled out! Rather our sanctification consists solely of our participation by faith in our sanctification, which is already real in Christ. Just as reflectors on the road flash at night when light hits them, we are new human beings, in ourselves as well, when we do not look into ourselves but in faith we are focused on Christ. The reality of our sanctification is decisively not in us but outside of us, and the more firmly we focus in faith on Jesus Christ, the more clearly we will participate in it. On the other hand, by actively participating in our sanctification in Christ, we are actually only recognizing what in Christ already applies to all human beings in advance.

2. What God's holiness is, is defined by his will to enter into a covenant: "I will be your God, and you will be my people."[40] Here an understanding of holiness as mere separation from others is transcended. It is not primarily someone or other who is holy; rather it is primarily the people of God, the holy church, who are holy. But there is even more, or perhaps it is the reason for this idea: God's holiness itself contains the freedom to "go beyond" oneself (without doing away with oneself) in order to form a bond with someone who is totally

---

[39]*KD* IV/2, pp. 583ff. Nikolaus von Zinzendorf once stressed the same thing in a memorable debate with John Wesley. Compare H. Lindstrom, *Wesley und die Heiligung* (Frankfurt, 1961), pp. 93ff.

[40]*KD* IV/2, p. 565. Quotation from Jer 7:23; 31:33; Ezek 36:28.

different from oneself, someone who is unholy. In Barth's view this is God's holiness, that although he is "different from (the world), he is devoted to it."[41] This is why our participation in God's holiness revealed in Christ, our participation in the sanctification accomplished for us in him, will not consist of a mere separation from others. Rather, no longer belonging to the world or in thrall to it, but living in it, we will be devoted to it. This indicates to what extent Barth did not become one of the Pietists in his deliberate response to their concern. His affirmation of their concern and his positive response to it tacitly contained a clear critique and correction of their concern.

During his last years at the end of the 1960s Barth again took a further step toward Pietism. He took this step with the expectation that a "theology of the Holy Spirit" would be produced in Christianity. This expectation clearly means that he was willing to call his own christocentric theology into question, as long as it was only a matter of questioning his own attempt at doing theology. Of course, the person of this Christ was not to be replaced by another or by something else. Only this theology he hoped for would testify to Christ in the present, reviving, transforming and renewing power of the Holy Spirit in a way that was quite different from what he saw himself being able to do. He explicitly cherished this hope "in favor of the Pietists," so that their old concern would shine and come to fruition in a whole new way in the church—not as truths of the individual whose life revolves around himself but as truths of the Holy Spirit who touches his heart.[42] Undoubtedly the statement he made at the end of 1967 belongs in this context: "What we need today is a new kind of Pietism," not simply a repetition of the old Pietism but its emergence in a new, inwardly renewed form, in such a way that its concern becomes understandable and prevails as an outpouring of the Holy Spirit, as a new Pentecost.[43]

For the sake of completeness it must be mentioned that as Moses in his old age was looking for the Promised Land, Barth did not, for instance, see this expectation fulfilled in the appearance of the confessing movement "No Other Gospel." As far as he was concerned, it was "the big disappointment" in this expectation he held. He did not see it as a step forward but as a reactionary relapse into the nineteenth century.[44] Why? Because he saw them sharing the same crucial assumption in their thinking that they accused their "enemies" of making. In one way or another, be it in their fear that the validity of the gospel could be

---

[41]Ibid., p. 579.

[42]Barth, "Nachwort," pp. 310ff.

[43]Barth, *Briefe 1961-1968*, p. 488.

[44]Compare "Kirche und Theologie heute," in *Zeichen der Zeit, 20 Jahrgang* (Berlin: DDR, 1966), pp. 285-89; reprint in: K. Barth, *Gespräche, 1964-1968* (Zurich: TVZ, 1997), pp. 212-15.

shaken by human beings or their assumption that its validity depends on our defense against such shockwaves, the same questionable assumption is being made. They both assume that the reality attested in the gospel is put into the hands of Christians and even into the hands of theologians. The old Pietistic belief that the reality of Jesus Christ is not valid for us independent of our appropriation of it is taking its toll here. Where this opinion is prevalent, this reality can actually be threatened or rescued by us; its validity becomes dependent on how we handle it. From Barth's point of view the confessing movement was the epitome of the spirit it wanted to combat.

But notice the almost Pietistic language (and it is more than just a form of speech) in which he registered his reservations about the confessing movement: "We do not have to take care of our dear God, rather he takes care of us. In every respect we must take this into account and live free of anxiety in response to this truth: . . . He ensures that his truth will not go by the board, but continue to be heard." We would much rather "put our hope and trust in the Holy Spirit who has always made sure that the truth remains the truth whatever human beings may say against it."

> There's no stopping the Holy Spirit. . . . I would like to describe what I have against the confessing movement with this (saying by Albrecht Goes): A servant does not make any noise. The confessing movement is a noisy movement . . . (but) nothing is accomplished by making noise, with these mass demonstrations, . . . where brass ensembles start to play their instruments against Bultmann. This is . . . not the delicate, quiet course the Spirit takes. The Holy Spirit does not move at large-scale events that are popular with the masses . . . but goes his quiet way, I would almost say, his unassuming, but confident way. Whoever knows a little something about the new birth, about new life . . . is assured of his cause.

This is why he does not have to keep grimly opposing others or stress that he has the right confession. Rather one sees that he does, and he offers evidence by the Spirit's power that the confession has him.[45] One notices in these statements that Barth is basically not speaking against Pietism but is thinking entirely in terms of its foundational concern, from the point of view of the new birth, new life and the Holy Spirit. This is why he expects Pietism to be able to once again live its faith quite differently and more persuasively than was the case in the confessing movement. But this would certainly be "a new kind of Pietism." From there it can be said that if the confessing movement was a disappointment of that expectation for Barth, this disappointment was not an impediment to his

---

[45]Dialogue with Mennonites on December 13, 1967; printed in Barth, *Gespräche 1964-1968,* pp. 423-26.

expectation of a "theology of the Holy Spirit" and thus also not to his hope that this old Pietistic concern would once again shine brightly in the church.

I hope that it has become clear that at every stage of his journey Barth could not get the question of Pietism out of his mind, and at no stage did he see it as being settled—even if it may have become clear that he was in fact a troublesome friend of Pietism. But it should also be clear that in critiquing Pietism, Barth took it very seriously at the same time and was always open to learning from its concern. His criticism was not petty, and he was not quick to find fault with any "excesses" it may have had. Following this historical overview I have selected several questions, expressed more systematically, that are addressed to Pietism by Barth's theology. It is basically true of all these questions that he did not ask them simply in opposition to Pietism but in a spirit of solidarity. At the same time he wanted to take a position on several essential concerns of Pietism.

3. Barth's Questions Addressed to Pietism

1. On the understanding of the objective and subjective reality of salvation. Barth could say that this is the problem with Pietism: The unshakable reality and validity of God's work for us in Christ exists prior to our faith and independent of it, but this so-called objective aspect of salvation becomes unimportant here in comparison to the "subjective" aspect, that is, personally taking hold of salvation. In short, Pietism distorted Christianity by overemphasizing the subjective aspect. In contrast to this it had been Barth's intention since the 1920s to stress that the objective and subjective reality of God's revelation and salvific act belong together.[46] Since the objective reality must necessarily be seen in conjunction with the subjective reality, he believed he had an open door from there to what occupies the Pietists' attention. Their concern was summarized for him in personally taking hold of salvation. In his view this concern must be seen as dangerous in its isolated emphasis but as legitimate in conjunction with the objective reality of the salvation that has been revealed and that must be stressed first.

What at first glance seemed to simplify the dialogue in fact made it more difficult. The Pietists accused Barth for decades of being the one who reduced Christianity by developing a one-sided "objectivism." Conversely, it was Pietism's intention to stress "the creative unity of subjectivism and objectivism."[47] The dialogue is not easy here because unfortunately one cannot conclude that the whole difference of opinion was based on a misunderstanding; in fact, both

---

[46]Compare for example K. Barth, *Die christliche Dogmatik im Entwurf. I. Die Lehre vom Wort Gottes, Prolegomena zur christlichen Dogmatik 1927* (reprint, Zurich: TVZ, 1982), p. 380.

[47]F. Rienecker, in Barth, "Biblische Kritik am Pietismus," p. 16.

sides evidently meant the same thing. On the one hand, Barth did not deny that Pietism knows "something objective." But he called the way in which this "unity" of the subjective and objective is understood a form of subjectivism. On the other hand, the Pietists did notice something that is correct, even if they saw a form of "objectivism" in the way Barth linked these two aspects.

As far as the latter side is concerned, if we now understand the subjective realization of salvation, in somewhat narrow terms, as the human decision for God and Christ, then Barth's theology was in fact defined by this insight. The question whether we say yes to God is secondary compared to what we can only be amazed at and never cease being amazed at. It is the fact that the great and holy God should truly say yes to the wretched creatures that we are, that he has already said yes, already decided for us. The worst statement in Jochum's work is where he says that the grace of God so emphasized by Barth is a foregone conclusion.[48] In Barth's view, if there is anything that is absolutely not a foregone conclusion and never will be, it is this basic truth that is unshakably true, valid even "when we were still enemies" (Rom 5:10). "When I was not yet born, you were born for me and were chosen to make me your own before I even knew you." This accent that was not invented by him is in fact the accent that permeates his theology. This does not mean that the subjective realization of this reality, and thus particularly our decision for Christ, is for this reason superfluous; rather, in his view this overwhelming miracle makes it all the more possible to also convert us to this reality. But this truth is not expressed as "Accept it, otherwise it is not real for you," but as "Because it is real for you too, accept it!"

This leads to the other point, the charge of subjectivism made against Pietism. Once again, Barth did not argue that Pietism did not know anything objective. Rather he raised the objection that it understands this as an object just lying on the table: as long as it lies there, it does not yet have anything to do with me; only when I grab it does it gain real significance for me. In the opinion of the Pietists I am standing in front of the object, in sovereign freedom of choice, and have the "fate" of the object in my hand. If I do not take it to myself, it is completely useless for me. Along these lines the objective aspect of salvation is basically only a sheer possibility. It becomes real salvation when I "realize" this possibility by my appropriation of it. In doing so, does not man himself ultimately achieve his own salvation? It is precisely this combination of the objective and the subjective that Barth calls a form of subjectivism. Barth once said that in this context the crucial question is

---

[48]Jochums, *Die grosse Enttäuschung*, p. 39.

whether God and man are dialogue partners opposite one another, an encounter that cannot for a moment be thought of as being terminated by anyone other than God, or whether one wants to think of man in such a way that he has the power— whether by natural ability or by appropriation—to terminate this encounter.[49]

Barth considered the former to be correct; and thus it becomes clear how he thinks of the objective aspect of salvation. First of all, it is for him no mere possibility that is only realized when man appropriates it. Whenever the divine reality is thought of in such a way that it is only given reality by some kind of human behavior toward it, we get on a slippery slope, on which the divine reality must be understood in the end as having been created by human beings and thus as illusionary. Then all allegedly new human uprisings and movements are only refinements of the unchanged, "old" man. Since from the outset Barth does not care to get on that slippery slope, the divine reality (the objective aspect of salvation) in his view has the basic form of being beyond the reach of human beings who want to first attain it. It absolutely resists its transformation into such an accessible object with which man then knows how to "do" something or else thinks he cannot do anything. The fact that the objectively real revelation also becomes subjectively real for us can therefore not be a matter of our reaching out but is a matter of God reaching out for us. The subjective reality of revelation is "objective revelation breaking into our realm."[50] Since the objective aspect of salvation enables and gives rise to itself and, on its own initiative, enables and causes us to be grasped by it, and since we only perceive it after that, it ensures that we are not dealing with any illusion. This is the purpose of Barth's doctrine of the Holy Spirit. The criticism also made of Barth's theology apart from this context claimed that he was lacking a doctrine of the Holy Spirit or that it was underdeveloped. But his doctrine of the Spirit must ask this critique if it intends to claim what was ruled out by it: the idea that man on his own has an openness to God or some other opportunity to take hold of God's revelation. In Barth's view the doctrine of the Holy Spirit means that revelation is not an object we can reach for in sovereign freedom of choice. The doctrine of the Holy Spirit means that revelation in turn reaches out beyond itself to us. In this way God's salvation and revelation really come to us and enter into us. It is not that in this process we "take hold of it" but that we are taken hold of. We may say that the new birth, understood as a pure event that is granted to us, precedes our turning to it in faith. So this is Barth's first question

---

[49]K. Barth, *Die Theologie und die Kirche. Ges. Vortr.*, vol. 2 (Munich: Chr. Kaiser Verlag, 1928), p. 192.
[50]*KD* I/2, p. 274.

addressed to the Pietists: Can we not agree on this? The reality of God's decision for us first makes our decision for him possible; our decision does not first make a mere possibility real.

2. On the understanding of grace and sin. The second question underscores the first one, but with a new accent. It is phrased here with reference to the charges the Pietists made against Barth, as Jochums summarized them. They claimed he espouses a doctrine of universal reconciliation; it follows that in his theology everything is excused and sin is no longer called sin. He "no longer knows any sin, any hell, any devil."[51] "Along these same lines we find the fact that Karl Barth does not know what to do with demons."[52] This is spoken rather blithely when one considers that the author keeps from his readers the fact that Barth actually filled several hundred pages in his *Church Dogmatics* with a description of the reality of sin. But we must first say here that somehow Jochums struck a raw nerve in his theology. He certainly did not want to magnify the reality of sin as much as God's eternal compassion for us sinners. He did not for that reason espouse a doctrine of universal reconciliation, as Jochums claimed; even Jochums could not come up with a single quotation. Instead, he knew why Barth did not support such a doctrine (which is, strangely enough, alive in a particular Pietistic tradition): It was because it claimed an automatic mechanism in God's compassion. Nevertheless, he had somewhat of a penchant for putting his finger on particular verses of Scripture: "God was reconciling the world to himself in Christ" (2 Cor 5:19) and "He is the atoning sacrifice for our sins, and not only for ours but also for the sins of the whole world" (1 Jn 2:2). Or this: "For his anger lasts only a moment, but his favor lasts a lifetime" (Ps 30:5). Or take Colossians 1:20 as well: "For God was pleased to have all his fullness dwell in him, and through him to reconcile to himself all things" (*ta panta*, the universe). It is also true that Barth stressed, in terms of these Scripture verses, that the truth attested here is unconditionally valid, that is, not only when we have produced certain positive or negative preparatory works so that the objective aspect of salvation is true only after that.

The evidence for this truth, however, cannot and should not mean for Barth in any way that sin is being downplayed. On the contrary, he says[53] with Psalm 130:4: "But with you there is forgiveness, therefore you are feared." Only when one knows the God of mercy does one truly realize the magnitude of one's sin and truly know against whom one has sinned. Before, one probably understood

---

[51]Jochums, *Die grosse Enttäuschung*, p. 55.
[52]Ibid., p. 47.
[53]Barth, *Gespräche 1959-1962*, pp. 71ff.

by "sin" any deviation from a general code of decency and, in any event, had a hard time understanding one's sin in any other way than by making excuses for it, shifting blame to others, and even being able to say in the worst case (as the Germans said after 1945 of all times), " Once more it was a close shave!"[54] On the other hand, only when one knows that "you have borne all my sins" does one realize in dismay that our sin is too great for us to bear ourselves or to apologize for it. Then one also knows that this same Jesus Christ is also the judge whom I cannot approach without first beating my own breast and not anyone else's: "Lord, have mercy on me, a sinner!"[55] Without being able to anticipate the judge's verdict—according to whose word the first shall be last and the last shall be first—there is only one consolation: this judge "presented himself beforehand to the judgment of God for me."[56] Or to echo 2 Corinthians 5:10: "We must all appear before the judgment seat of Christ." This is very roughly Barth's understanding of sin. It may be problematic for some, but it cannot be said that he did not have any. Likewise, it cannot be said that he did not have any doctrine of the devil, for he said this of him: "Since man thinks he can and should make a stand against the devil on his own initiative, the devil has already triumphed over him. . . . In so doing man has already become a great fighter in his battle."[57] This tells us again that just as sin is so great that I cannot reconcile myself to God, the devil is so powerful that only the mercy of God in Christ is a match for him. But he is a match for the devil by virtue of Christ's resurrection from the dead. In Barth's view it follows from this for the proclamation of the gospel and our Christian witness to others that we must not first demonstrate to them that we are sinners, that they are lost, and so on, thus beating them up so that they are ready for the gospel. Rather, we have to first show them the gospel and then they will become aware that they are sinners, just as Peter did in Luke 5:8 when he exclaimed, "Lord, I am a sinful man!"[58] after the good deed the Lord had done for him. And even more, we must not confront human beings with the alternative: Do you want to be lost or be saved? Here again a neutral freedom of choice is assumed, as if man were not actually lost and his decision to persist in sin were a serious freedom. "Everyone who sins is [not a free man but] a slave to sin" (Jn 8:34). Humanism, which Pietists so often see in others, is a

---

[54]Compare K. Barth, *Die christliche Lehre nach dem Heidelberger Katechismus* (Zollikon: EVZ, 1948), pp. 38ff.

[55]K. Barth, *Das christliche Leben. Die Kirchliche Dogmatik IV/4. Fragmente aus dem Nachlass* (Zurich: TVZ, 1976), pp. 37, 113.

[56]The Heidelberg Catechism, question 52, included by Barth in *KD* IV/1, p. 231.

[57]*KD* IV/1, p. 500.

[58]Compare K. Barth, *Predigten 1921-1935* (Zurich: TVZ, 1998), pp. 330-32.

threat to them because they assume that this "slave to sin" still has the freedom to choose which has decisive significance for his salvation or his damnation.[59] At this point Barth stood together with Luther in stressing the bondage of the will against the teaching of Erasmus, the first teacher of the Enlightenment. He believed that man was free to choose between good and evil. But Barth believed that as long as man claims such freedom of choice, he remains captive in the bondage of his will.[60] Moreover, Barth appealed here to the structure of Jesus' loving care for sinners in the gospel. Where did he abstractly tell sinners, "You could be lost"? Where did he speak of the real threat of being lost other than in the context that he had come to seek and save what was lost?[61] This then is the second question: Can Pietists speak seriously of sin in a different way, giving priority to the divine mercy and its predominance over the power of evil?

3. The significance of a decision of faith. The third question has to do with our personal consent, the personal relationship with Christ we have to enter into, the personal decision we have to make for him. In this respect as well Barth seems to have a disturbing gap in his theology; in the Pietistic interpretation he seems to want only to enlighten human beings about what they do not at all have to know because it is already valid anyway.

Certainly Barth had reasonable questions in view of the reduction of the gospel only to the individual and his personal life. He spoke of the danger that in the process the "self" so easily moves from the periphery to the center, and Jesus moves from the center to the periphery. He spoke of the danger that one so easily forgets the "for us" because of the "for me," and of the danger that God is so easily used to serve one's own cause instead of one's own cause being used to serve God. But his warning about these dangers did not put an end to "his serious agreement with the Pietists" in stressing that the gospel is of great personal concern to each individual, in such a way that "Jesus Christ in person encounters each individual in person on his or her journey, becoming a conscious element of his life story."[62] I would like to cite two significant texts in this context:

> The gospel in its [Christian] expression can be transformed into a lifeless, empty communication that does not really, but only apparently, proclaims the message of salvation. A biblical foundation [and] . . . continuity with the traditions of the church's past . . . do not formally have to be missing from such communication. It

---

[59]Discussed below; see n. 86.

[60]Compare on this subject W. Krötke, *Sünde und Nichtiges bei Karl Barth* (Berlin: Evangelische Verlagsanstalt, 1971), pp. 69ff.

[61]Compare on this subject Barth's dialogue with community people in *Gespräche 1959-1962*, pp. 22-27.

[62]*KD* IV/3, p. 584.

can also appear to have the character of being a message about Christ or preaching on the Kingdom of God or praise of free grace . . . and why should it not also be presented . . . with earnest zeal? It will only be missing one thing in this distorted form. . . . This communication will not be meant as an invitation and call to decide to concretely believe and obey.[63]

So not only is it missing something, but everything is distorted. A second text is also personally addressed to human beings:

Are we really born again, converted, renewed? . . . This question goes further and is really more threatening than all those questions that could make a Christian feel unsettled by a philosophy or world view. In contrast to all such questions it is of personal concern to him. "Brother, how is your heart?", as the elderly Tholuck used to address his students privately.[64]

Therefore, God's decision for us and the greatness of his mercy does not do away with man's response but calls for it. In response to this call, he now for his part renounces his old life and begins to obey God as his Lord. This is why Barth was also for the idea that baptism should regain the purpose it had in the New Testament accounts. In baptism one publicly gives this response. Therefore, there is no longer any infant baptism!

If a Pietist may have followed Barth up to this point, the matter certainly becomes more difficult when one notices that he speaks not in legal but in evangelical terms of this human response to the gospel, of conversion to it. It is not made in fear and anxiety—that "I" must now do something to save myself from destruction—but in gratitude that Jesus Christ saves even me, a sinner, from destruction. Therefore, I do not have to convert; I am allowed to convert. And I do not have to force anyone to convert, but I may bring people joy so that they desire to convert. "It is clearly and exclusively the gospel, the grace of God revealed to him by which conversion . . . is offered to [humankind]." "Let us be clear about the fact that all mere obligation is a completely frightful, demonic thing." "The obligation that man follows in conversion . . . is the obligation of a permission that has been freely given to him." Indeed, the new thing about conversion is "that the one who previously vegetated towards death under a truly hellish obligation, has the permission from now on."[65] This permission takes place in the freedom for which he was liberated by God's grace so that it neither disregards nor coerces his own personal approval nor leaves up to him the arbitrary choice of another "possibility." Consequently, this is Barth's third ques-

[63]Ibid., p. 931.
[64]Ibid., p. 777.
[65]KD IV/2, p. 654.

tion addressed to Pietism. Do we agree that all talk of personal decision, of conversion, must not be under the law of a "you must" but has to speak of a free permission opened up by the gospel?

4. The conversion of believers. The fourth question has to do with the problem of whether the one who is converted is really a new person, or to what extent he is still a sinner who must continually repent and turn back to God. Pietism tends to stress the former and often accused Barth of holding the latter view. Pietism missed the statement in his theology that in the Christian life there is a clear and lasting distinction between the past, when the Christian was a sinner, and the present—when he is saved.[66] This critique, though, does not really affect Barth. Let us once again remember that for Barth as well the believer in Christ who has been converted to him is a new person who has really been changed and is really different from the world. So from Barth's point of view as well we can talk about a past and present, a then and now, when looking at the Christian life. Yet we must consider two more things here.

First, since we only realize the full scale and reality of our sin in the light of the gospel and by believing in it, it is out of the question that one ever gets over the need to repent in the Christian life. Being a Christian is demonstrated by the fact that one is even more willing to repent. Barth pointed out that the fierce critique of the Old Testament prophets was not primarily targeted at the unbelievers or pagans who believed in idols but first and almost exclusively at their own people, the people of God. In a similar fashion Jesus himself pronounced his harsh judgment not on the tax-collectors and sinners but on the Pharisees, not on the weak but on the strong, calling them to repentance.

Second, even the believer has every reason to pray time and again not only half-heartedly but in total earnestness, "Forgive us our sins," "Be merciful to me, a sinner." Barth stresses in agreement with Luther that the person of faith is always at the same time entirely a justified saint and entirely a wicked sinner.

> The entire person is still the old person and again the entire person is already the new person, both in conflict with one another. How neatly arranged everything would be if we could say instead of this: man is still partially the old person, and already partially the new person! But then we would be missing the point! . . . How powerful is sin which played such a dominant role in the past, and how even more powerful is grace which will play such a dominant role in the future. The person who is really in the process of being converted knows himself in these terms.[67]

---

[66]This point emerges as the main criticism of Barth's theology in his dialogue with community people in 1959: *Gespräche 1959-1962*, pp. 14-33.

[67]Ibid., p. 647.

Precisely because this is the way it is in the Christian life, Barth would prefer not to talk about the converted—that is, those who have been through this once and for all—but about those who are in the process of being converted,[68] those who after their initial conversion turn to the Lord again and again in a spirit of repentance. To put it more precisely, they can always only live in repentance and conversion. At no point in their lives could they have experienced this process as already being finished. This then is the fourth question addressed to the Pietists: Does the converted person, in their view, still have to turn back to God anew or does a once-in-a-lifetime conversion make further conversions in a proper spirit of repentance superfluous? Or would the assumption of a once-in-a-lifetime conversion even lead to an attitude that rules out real conversions in the future, no longer allowing a real spirit of repentance?

Something else must be said to underscore this question, not to take delight in the misfortune of the "others" but because Pietism today has assumed an unpleasant form in a number of places, in which it acts as the constant judge of other Christians outside its own ranks: now more or less expelling Karl Barth from the church, then totally expelling Rudolf Bultmann from the church; now accusing Pastor X of "humanism" (because he seeks to feed, clothe and welcome the least of these brothers and sisters of Jesus); constantly pointing fingers at others ("Lord, have mercy on this sinner!") but never really pointing the finger at themselves ("Lord, have mercy on us Pietists!"). This is precisely why we must be reminded of a certain fact for once: they have some reason to put their own house in order! Take, for example, the magazine *Light and Life,* the mouthpiece of these circles. If one examines the issues from the 1920s, one can be taken aback by the way the Pietists largely thought and spoke in terms of accomodating to the "spirit of the world," that is, in accomodating to the spirit of a coming "Third Reich" that was dawning then.[69] Moreover, they did it with a political zeal that surpasses in intensity the Christian "humanism" that is so lamented today. One sees in dismay how Germany's great national culture and traditions were extolled and how the democratic experiment of the Weimar Republic was systematically torpedoed, how the so-called bread basket interests of the workers were ridiculed, how Hitler and Ludendorff were celebrated as "the ones anointed by the people," how above all the Jews were constantly slandered as parasites on the German people. All of this was interspersed between articles on the new birth and new life in equally large capital letters! And when 1933 came, one of the leading Pietists (of whom even today many people have fond

---

[68]Ibid., p. 634.
[69]More detailed examples of this appear earlier in this volume.

memories) wrote this poetry: "Forward, brothers, fall in step! We will stride side by side / with Adolf Hitler, Germany's most faithful son."[70] And in 1936 another head of Pietism defended the essence of Pietism in a book, sharply contradicting Karl Barth and explaining it quite correctly, only making the point that the life of the one who has been converted and born again must prove its worth today by God's love being poured out "into his German heart"—by responding with a strong yes to "blood and race" and planting both feet in the national community of the Third Reich with a burning heart, in true, grateful love for the Führer (Adolf Hitler), a love which here too signifies the "fulfillment of the law, without trying to please man!"[71] Remembering such a burden in Pietism's past history is truly not in itself a matter of condemning it, but it is a matter of pointing out that the Pietists' repeated call for others to repent would begin to be credible only if it were to come from a willingness to first beat their own breast. If this can seldom be seen here or not at all, we must ask why this is so. Is it perhaps because the idea of a once-in-a-lifetime conversion prevents them from henceforth being able to turn back to God in a genuine willingness to repent?

5. His relationship to the existing church. Looking at the existing church, Barth was marked by a dissatisfaction that would bring a warm smile to the face of a real Pietist. Asked about the condition of the church in God's eternity, he sighed in 1956, "Please not eternally this church, which is so terribly boring to people even on earth!"[72] And in 1946 he said, "One could often be disgusted at the whole situation of the church. In the church one is only like a bird in a cage, bumping against the bars time and again. Something greater is at stake than our little bit of preaching, namely the Kingdom of God."[73] But mind you, this is targeted at any form of church community, not only at the "established Protestant church." Nevertheless, Barth did not only entertain a general dissatisfaction with the church but asked very specific questions about the form of the established church and believed that it was finally time to terminate the traditional alliance between the church and the world, in which the church seeks protection from the world (the state). Barth longed for the day when the church would walk on its own two feet in relation to the state and society.[74] Although this critique of the

---

[70]H. Prolingheuer, *Kleine politische Kirchengeschichte. 50 Jahre evangelischer Kirchenkampf von 1919 bis 1969* (Köln: Pahl-Rugenstein, 1984), pp. 55ff. The man in question is Paul Humburg.

[71]F. Mund, *Pietismus-Eine Schicksalsfrage an die Kirche heute,* 2nd ed. (Marburg: Spener-Verlag, 1938), pp. 14ff.

[72]In Barth's dialogue on June 1, 1957, in Rummelsberg with the Bavarian Pastors' Brotherhood, based on the notes of Ch. von Kirschbaum, in the Karl Barth Archives, Basel.

[73]K. Barth, *Dogmatik im Grundriss* (Zurich: EVZ, 1947), p. 172.

[74]K. Barth, "Das Evangelium in der Gegenwart," *ThExh* 25 (Munich, 1935): esp. pp. 33ff.

church coincided with what many Pietists had on their heart against the institution of the church, Barth expressed two reservations about the old Pietistic desire
(which, again, seems so relevant today) to go its own separate way in its relationship with the church. First of all, even though he called Pietism individualistic, he did not ignore the fact that there is also strong fellowship in it. But he
asked if the idea of fellowship there is not entirely built on the individual believer, and he made the comment that in Pietism "my neighbor, my brother in
Christ . . . is in principle no longer supposed to be the other. . . . He is no longer
supposed to disturb me by being different. . . . It is possible that I could find
myself in him." I want to have him the way I am myself.

> The fellowship should not disturb me, but should affirm me. . . . Then and under
> these conditions the individualist can and wants to love, to have brothers and be
> in the church. The very real aversion of the original Pietist to the established Prot-
> estant church and the world church belongs here. This aversion often appears in a
> subtle form, but often in a very sharp form as well . . . especially against their cel-
> ebration of the Lord's Supper where they expect me to be a brother or sister to any
> Tom, Dick or Harry who comes to the table unexamined.[75]

Barth's dissatisfaction with the church does not mean he is dissatisfied with
the disturbing fact that in the real church of Christ I will always be together with
people who are different from me, very different. So this is the first question
Barth addressed to the Pietists: Does not your inclination to go your own separate way in relation to the church mean that you are fleeing from being together
with the one who is really different from you because you prefer to be undis-
turbed "among kindred spirits"?

But we should also consider the other reservation: Precisely in the context in
which Barth speaks of his dissatisfied longing to get beyond the church, he surprisingly continues in this way: "But [even then] you do not abscond, you do
not simply run away. By cherishing the hope of the Kingdom of [God], we do
not allow them to deny us the privilege of serving in the company of God as a
simple soldier. Then we will not be ashamed of the church."[76] This does not
mean that we have to give up now and submit to the church as it is. But it does
mean that even when we have to criticize it like this, this criticism is credible
only when it does not come from the safe distance of an observer like Jonah,
who from afar awaits the destruction of a world that is impossible to bear.
Rather, "serious objections to it . . . can only be raised from a position of solidarity in which we subject ourselves to criticism and then only it [the church],

---

[75]Barth, *Die Protestantische Theologie,* p. 95.
[76]Barth, *Dogmatik im Grundriss,* p. 173.

for the church is subject to criticism by its living Lord." "A legitimate . . . attack on the church [can] only be made on its own foundation, in the name of Jesus Christ, with the intention of re-establishing it better on this foundation which it is perhaps about to deny."[77] So this is the other question: Are you making your critique of the church not merely because this or that need of yours is not being met but really in the name of Christ, and therefore not from a safe distance but in solidarity with the church?

6. Ministry for the "world." There is still a sixth question that has to do with the church's relationship with the world. As has already become clear, the actual intended target of God's salvific will is, for Barth, not the church but the world. "God so loved the world" (Jn 3:16). "God was reconciling the world to himself in Christ" (2 Cor 5:19). And "God our Savior . . . wants all men to be saved" (1 Tim 2:4). Barth emphasized this in such a way that it was almost an embarrassment to him to realize what the church should still be doing according to God's will but is not. His answer is that it has a purpose only when it is not an end in itself but understands itself as being sent out in ministry to testify to Jesus Christ and his reconciliation in the rest of the world.[78] This is why conversions too have a purpose for Barth only when they are not an end in themselves (where one believes one has looked out for number one and may now retreat into one's shell) but are understood in terms of stories in which converts have an actual calling.[79]

This ministry, however, will take different forms, without one form of ministry being depreciated in comparison to another. For instance, in the modern sense of evangelism, the gospel is directly declared to merely nominal Christians by those who are committed Christians.[80] But Barth puts his emphasis on this:

> May it [the church] only proclaim the gospel and not say anything else! Being anxious to achieve successes that are not real, may it not stray from the proclamation of freedom into the propagation of a law, from the promise of life (supposedly for educational reasons) into threatening the horrors of hell, from the declaration of what is eternally undeserved into giving instructions on how to achieve laudable moral rearmament, from a defenseless announcement of the truth into some kind of clever or sensational apologetics![81]

Instead, the church must proclaim the gospel! If it really is the gospel, then it

---

[77]*KD* IV/1, p. 773.
[78]*KD* IV/3, pp. 872ff.
[79]Ibid., pp. 662-78.
[80]Ibid., pp. 999-1002.
[81]Ibid., p. 1002.

will be clear in evangelism that the good news that God has already loved them is far more important and has a higher priority than the unbelief of those who are listening to the message. Therefore, I have to speak to them not in a tone of indignation or condemnation but in the kind spirit of the love of Jesus Christ for them, in the hope that they will come to an understanding of the truth, that they will wake up from their sleep, that those who are blind will open their eyes to see what is true for them.[82] For Barth, the ministry of witnessing definitely continues to take the form of foreign missions as well. Barth praises Pietism for actually rediscovering the missionary task for Christianity, seeing it as an advantage of Pietism over the Reformation. However, he also thinks that from its Pietistic beginnings mission was overshadowed for a long time by having been less a witness to God's love than an act of Christian self-recommendation, in which they believed they were able to bring the poor heathen what would actually be the crowning event of their lives that would meet their true needs,[83] not to mention the fact that in the process mission was in remarkable proximity to the economic conquest of the rest of the world by the European trading nations.

But it is important to notice that what Barth called the social work (*diakonic*) of the church of Jesus Christ was one form of Christian witness, equal in value to the others. In this ministry it not only speaks but acts in practical ways to, first of all, help people suffering from physical and material hardship. In its social ministry it stands by Jesus Christ precisely in these its brothers and sisters, according to Matthew 25:31ff. It stands by the man Jesus Christ, who in the end is only hungry, thirsty, homeless, naked, sick and imprisoned. In its social ministry it makes its witness to him clear as the selfless ministry of kindness "commanded by him, serving those who have fallen into the hands of the robbers, with him, the Good Samaritan, who was a neighbor to this lost person. In its social ministry it goes and does likewise."[84] It is not enough to just give alms, rather the church must raise its voice when engaging in such ministry, and "by proclaiming the gospel it must make the world listen to reason about social injustice and its consequences, calling on them to change those conditions."[85] Thus the social ministry is a signpost pointing to the cosmic character of Christ's reconciliation and his kingdom. This is what Barth could also call the political service Christians render to God, or what we could call the socio-political ministry of the church. Mind you, it is not a matter of the church somehow combining any political slogans or

---

[82]For example, referring to Eph 5:8, ibid, pp. 584-91.
[83]*KD* I/2, p. 368.
[84]*KD* IV/3, p. 1022.
[85]Ibid., p. 1023.

party programs with the Christian faith. It is a matter of serving God not just in organizations within the church but also on the political, social stage, because he is Lord of all realms. It is not a matter of Christianity going along with any prevailing spirit or any prevailing winds of the time. Rather, as a rule it will swim against the stream because it sides not with something that is now in fashion but with what has been crushed by those in power. It sides with forgotten, suppressed truths, with forgotten, oppressed and threatened human beings. And for Barth, taking sides is not a luxury about whose purpose Christians may, in principle, have different opinions. Christianity would deny Christ if it would not proceed to make this courageous witness through its deeds. By taking such action it is determined not to prolong the misery and the threatening conditions by merely treating the symptoms but to overcome them as far as human beings are able. And this is the gist of the sixth question that Barth would address to modern Pietism: Why do you always so quickly denigrate this activity compared to evangelism and mission and so often dismiss it as mere "humanism"?[86] Does this really come from the Spirit of the gospel? Or could it even be a sign that apart from your verbal activity you have from time to time reached an accommodation with the ruling powers of the day? Or why does one sense in your lives so little of the contagious spirit of Jesus' compassion for a humanity afflicted by disease, marked by hardship and threatened with destruction? Why do you as Christians apparently feel so little challenged where sin in the narrow sense of the word is not at stake but where the misery and despair of humanity, the threat to peace and justice in this world, are at stake? Why are you only concerned about the private, little things in your acts of penance—about breaking the habit of smoking cigarettes or drinking beer, for example—but you are so conspicuously little concerned about turning away from social sins in which Pietists after all are also entangled, in which they are implicated, be it by sharing an attitude that says, "If you're not for us, you're against us," an attitude reflected in their relationship to those who think differently, believe differently and act differently, or be it by their involvement in the exploitation of the poor in the relationship of the Northern with the Southern hemisphere? The questions Barth addressed to Pietism in the so-called second stage of his journey remained relevant to him as he interacted with Pietism even in his later years.

---

[86]Jochums, *Die grosse Enttäuschung,* pp. 70, 74, and more cautiously L. Gassmann, *Karl Barth,* p. 80, accuse Barth of having opened the door to the "humanistic spirit of the time." Since in Barth's thought God "disappears" into the beyond, and he supports relativism and skepticism because of his dialectics, atheistic "humanism" can or must spread over the earth. In Jochums's view, the result of this humanism is that God is dissolved into brotherly love and, for instance, pornography or dictatorships run rampant.

We have now finished our discussion of the questions Barth addressed to Pietism! I hope it has become clear that he asked these questions in genuine solidarity with the Pietists and with an open mind to their concern. I hope it has also become clear that in his critique of them he did not practice petty nit-picking and did not make it his aim to eliminate the Pietist movement. If he was not one of them, he was indeed a troublesome friend of theirs. However, a positive answer to the question of whether there will be the "new kind of Pietism" he spoke of and hoped for could perhaps depend on those who count themselves as Pietists being willing to expose themselves to the troublesome aspect of his friendship. I do not mean that they should endorse "his" theological opinions but that they, the "converted" ones, should allow his questions to stimulate their thinking so that they themselves might continue to be in the process of conversion.

A Brief History of German Pietism in the Nineteenth and Twentieth Centuries

by Daniel W. Bloesch

A significant spiritual awakening occurred in the German states between 1815 and 1830. Its enormous influence continued into the twentieth century and formed the basis for Pietism in twentieth-century Germany. At the beginning of the nineteenth century, Germany was occupied by Napoleon's troops. Hearts were being prepared for the seed of the gospel in the wake of French domination. Revival quickly spread to many regions throughout Germany. A number of powerful revivalist preachers emerged, and many pastors were converted. Württemberg and the lower Rhine areas experienced a renewal of the older Pietism and Biblicism begun by Spener and Francke in the late seventeenth and early eighteenth century. In Franconia, Berlin and Pomerania as well as a large section of central and northern Germany the remaining orthodox Lutherans, Pietists and those converted in the revivals formed a confessional movement that revitalized the churches.

Beginning in 1780, Württemberg's Pietists established links to the Herrnhut movement founded by Zinzendorf. In 1818 the Free Evangelical Church of Korntal (near Stuttgart) was founded by G. W. Hoffmann following the model of Herrnhut. This community of faith became the focal point of Württemberg's Pietism and developed several missionary and social service organizations that are still active today.

One of the earliest revivalist preachers was Ludwig Hofacker (1798–1828). In 1826 this sickly young pastor began his ministry in Rielingshausen. He preached his last sermon on Easter Sunday in 1828 and died in the fall of that year. Yet even though Hofacker barely preached more than one hundred sermons, he transformed the Württemberg state church. He did not travel around; instead thousands of people would walk or ride for hours to hear him. He preached without theatrics, simply expecting Christ's presence and his promises to work in the hearts of his people. His sermons consisted of two parts: first, law and damnation, and second, grace and the balsam of God's mercy in Jesus Christ.

His own sufferings made him a compassionate pastor and kept him from being spiritually proud. Thousands were converted through his preaching, and tens of thousands came to faith by reading his books of sermons. The poet and singer Albert Knapp (1798–1864) and Hofacker's younger brother, Wilhelm Hofacker (1805–1848), followed in the great preacher's footsteps, and through their leadership the revival spread throughout Württemberg and even reached the capital city of Stuttgart. In the wake of this renewal many pastors gained the courage to preach the gospel in an uncompromising fashion and succeeded in reintegrating a large number of the separated Pietists into the established Protestant church. During this period both domestic and foreign mission work prospered, Bibles and devotional literature enjoyed wide distribution, and homes and institutions for delinquent youth, orphans, the sick and handicapped shot up like mushrooms throughout the country. In Württemberg alone there were twenty-two of these rescue missions by 1845.

Johann Christoph Blumhardt (1805–1880), the "miracle pastor" of Möttlingen, was filled with this same revivalist spirit. The yearlong spiritual struggle of a both physically and mentally ill woman, Gottliebin Dittus, came to a dramatic conclusion when she was completely healed through Blumhardt's ministry at the end of 1843, strengthening his conviction that Jesus is the Victor. This experience proved to be the turning point in Blumhardt's life, and his church experienced a powerful movement of the Spirit that led to the repentance and faith of thousands. On Good Friday in 1845, visitors from 176 cities and towns came to Möttlingen, and on Pentecost Sunday the youth of the village counted two thousand guests from elsewhere in the region. This great awakening of repentance and faith reached into the far corners of the Black Forest. From 1852 to the end of his life Blumhardt devoted himself to the "spiritual sanatorium" he established in the castle of Bad Boll. Through the numerous healings he witnessed during the revival he anticipated the arrival of God's kingdom, and this conviction grew stronger in the latter years of his life. He exclaimed, "This fact remains eternally true—Jesus is the Victor and the whole world will be His!"

From Württemberg the revival spread to the Lower Rhine, Siegerland and Wittgenstein. Weisgerber and Siebel were the leaders of the movement there. A lively give and take existed between Wuppertal and Siegerland. In the lower Rhineland and in Bremen, Reformed Pietism was dominant, and the influence of Tersteegen was still felt. In the course of the 1830s the followers of Tersteegen and Collenbusch as well as those of an orthodox Reformed and Lutheran persuasion found a home in the numerous flourishing congregations served by revivalist pastors.

In the grand duchy of Baden the revival was carried on by the Catholic priest

Aloys Henhofer (1789–1862). Excommunicated in 1822, he became a Protestant pastor in Baden. At the suggestion of Henhofer the Baden Association for Foreign Missions was founded, and in 1849 the community movement of Baden was organized. Due to his influence as well as the influence of seminary president W. Stern, the revival in Baden remained within the orbit of the established Protestant church.

The uniqueness of the spiritual awakening in Bavaria flows from several factors. First, in the Franconian church of northern Bavaria the Reformational faith remained untouched by rationalism in many of its rural villages and parsonages. Second, the Erlangen pastor and professor Christian Krafft (1784–1845) was the main initiator of the Bavarian awakening. Thus the Franconian-Bavarian revival began in Nürnberg and at the University of Erlangen. The central Franconian village of Neuendettelsau became a focal point of the Lutheran revival through the ministry of Wilhelm Lohe (1808–1872) and the Deaconess Hospital located there. The revival had a profound and lasting impact on the church in Bavaria. It was known for its ecumenical vision, and its leaders recognized that although the subjective experience of conversion was crucial, the church's confession was also an important element in the assurance of salvation and the church's renewal. They realized that only the combination of Lutheran doctrine and revivalist fervor could overcome the Enlightenment and lead to lasting change in the church. Their openness to idealistic and Romantic thought also increased their appreciation for the historical Lutheran confessional documents. Thus the Reformational confession was revived in Bavaria and the awakening gained an orthodox component. The central figure of this development was Adolf von Harless (1806–1879), a professor in Erlangen. A peaceful separation of the Lutheran and Reformed churches took place under his leadership. The unity of the church came to expression in the Lutheran confessional standards to which the pastors had to pledge their allegiance. This combination of revivalist faith and Lutheran confession quickly led to a strong sense of unity in the established Bavarian Protestant church.

Berlin, the capital of Brandenburg-Prussia, became the focal point of the revival in northern Germany. At the beginning of the nineteenth century there were still numerous Pietistic circles in the city that were mainly recruited from the lower classes of society. An early center of the revival emerged with a group of young nobles in the Bohemian-Lutheran Bethlehem Church pastored by Johannes Janicke. In 1800 he founded the first German mission school. The pioneer of the China mission, K. Gruzlaff, was one of its graduates. Soup kitchens for the poor and a Bible society were also important ministries initiated by this circle.

A second focal point of the Berlin revival was associated with Hans Ernst von

Kottwitz (1757–1843) and closely followed the tradition of Herrnhut. Kottwitz came from the Silesian nobility and assumed control of his father's estates at a young age. But then the needs of the impoverished weavers of his homeland touched his heart, and he began to collect funds to alleviate their suffering and even used a considerable portion of his own wealth. Then he turned his attention to Berlin, where the misery was even greater. In 1806 Prussia was defeated by the French at the battle of Jena. Ten days later Napoleon marched into Berlin as the victor. Hunger and unemployment spread throughout the city. So in 1807 Kottwitz opened a spinning mill; a year later he was permitted to occupy a vacant barracks with the approval of the French city commander. With his "volunteer employment agencies" and factories he provided work for more than one thousand unemployed workers. His goal was to help these men and their families "help themselves." Kottwitz recognized that begging could not be stopped by just distributing alms but by providing people with steady jobs. Although he affirmed the principle of self-help and personal responsibility, he did not just do social work. He himself had a conversion experience through the ministry of A.G. Spangenberg and knew that man does not live by bread alone. Therefore he held regular evening services in the barracks. As a gifted pastoral counselor he also addressed the needs of the city's students who honored him "as father Abraham." His influence on the Prussian royal family, on countless nobles who were converted during the revival and on a number of theologians made a lasting impact on the church in northern Germany. Tholuck, Rothe, Neander, Wichern, Zahn, Hengstenberg and Harms were brought to faith through his ministry. Kottwitz shaped a whole generation of revivalist theologians. It is a merit of this "pious baron" that the Berlin revival did not end in separation but participated in the renewal of the established Protestant church. Wichern was also committed to Kottwitz's program when he spearheaded the movement for prison reform in Prussia.

The revival in Berlin and Prussia achieved a dramatic breakthrough when several young nobles converted in the revival joined forces with the sons of the rationalist court preacher Sack. In 1816 they made a pilgrimage to Munich to get to know the Catholic revivalist priests Gossner, Boos and Lindl and to inform themselves about the revival in Bavaria. The young Pietists returned to Berlin deeply impressed by what they had seen and heard. Some of these men, such as Adolf von Thadden (1796–1882) and the brothers H. and G. von Below, transplanted the awakening to the large estates of Pomerania. Bismarck experienced his conversion in Thadden's house. Since the landed gentry also sponsored the churches, they were able to appoint pastors who identified with the revival. From 1820 on the majority of pastors in Berlin were converted in the revival and were gifted pulpit orators who attracted large crowds. For example, Schleiermacher's wife attended the worship services of Gossner in the Bethlehem Church instead of listening to the sermons of her husband! Although the revival did not reach the majority of the population, its connections to the crown prince and later king Frederick William IV were intact. The revivalists did not remain without success in journalism as well. The *Evangelical Church News* founded in 1827 and edited by Professor E. W. Hengstenberg turned into a sharp weapon against liberal currents in theology, church and society, and its influence extended far beyond the borders of Prussia.

In the Prussian revival the conservative element was predominant. Hengstenberg approved Frederick William IV's policy of restoration and the so-called unity of the throne and the altar. Agrarian traditions and values were predominant in a movement shaped by the nobility and farmers.

In Minden and the countryside of Ravensburg the revival took on a distinctly Lutheran and more cosmopolitan flavor. The churchman Johann Heinrich Volkening (1796–1877) in Gütersloh and his colleagues were the leaders of the movement in this region. Through Volkening's influence most of the pulpits of the area were filled with pastors who were converted in the revival. Their influence was profound and long-lasting. The Gütersloh publishing company Bertelsmann placed itself in the service of the revival with its tracts and books that found wide distribution. Volkening's collection of revival songs called "The Little Missionary Harp" went through almost one hundred printings! The revival in Ravensburg later became the driving force behind the Bodelschwingh Institutions and the Bethel Mission. Friedrich von Bodelschwingh (1831–1910) saw that the epileptics' problem was not only their disease but the fact that no one was willing to give these people shelter and a place to work. He founded a community of faith that provided work, room and board and spiritual care to the epileptics, the handicapped and the homeless, restoring the dignity of these forgotten people. The Bethel Mission in Bielefeld continues its vital ministry on an even larger scale to this day.

One of the earliest figures of the revival was Johannes Falk (1768–1826) in Weimar. He was the son a Danzig wig maker. Rich sponsors as well as the Danzig city councilmen made it possible for him to study at the university. As he departed, an old city councilman said to him, "Never forget that you were a poor boy. If poor children should ever knock on your door one day, think of us, the old, gray city councilmen of Danzig. When you see them, do not turn them away." The rationalist theology in Halle left him unsatisfied, so he turned his attention to literature. Sponsored by Wieland, he settled down with his well-to-do wife in Weimar, where he also got to know Herder and Goethe. He eventually became a high official at the court of the grand duke of Saxony-Weimar. There he encountered the most unbelievable contrasts between the rich and the poor in Weimar's society. On the one side, he saw the profligate life of the court (Goethe) and on the other side, the neglected children and the dirt-poor workers and peasants. It seemed to him that the court had a greater interest in breeding horses than in educating the people. Later he wrote, "I was one of a thousand other scoundrels in German literature who thought they could help the world by sitting at their desks." When the French withdrew after the Battle of the Nations in Leipzig, virulent epidemics spread through the region. Falk himself became mortally ill and lost four of his own children. His agonizing grief and profound sense of loss reminded him of the words spoken by that Danzig city councilman, so he decided to spend the rest of his life rescuing orphans. In 1813 he founded the Society of Friends in Need, granting favorable loans to those who wanted to rebuild their homes destroyed in the Napoleonic wars. He placed hundreds of homeless orphans in the homes of godly craftsmen and provided for their needs. In 1819, as he was weeping with his wife at the casket of his nineteen-year-old son, he heard someone knocking at his door. A ragged fourteen-year-old boy asked if he could enter. Falk took him in as if he were his own child. Two years later their last child, a sixteen-year-old daughter, was taken from them, and they were told they had to leave their home.

So Falk bought a piece of property with a dilapidated building on it that was called the Lutherhof. Making the greatest personal sacrifices imaginable, he built a rescue mission with his homeless boys. The work and discipline required to complete the project brought the boys under control and gave them the training and stability they needed. This is what was written on the commemorative plaque attached to the Lutherhof. "After the battles of Jena and Leipzig 'the Friends in Need' built this house with the labor of 200 rescued orphans. It is to be an eternal altar of thanksgiving to the Lord." He found little sympathy for his mission among the leading circles of Weimar. He recognized that adults do not educate young people by beating them but by giving them role models to emulate. Falk became the role model for J. H. Wichern, the founder of the Homeland Mission. He first sang his famous Christmas song, "O du Fröhliche"("O Thou Joyful, O Thou Wonderful"), with his children. The melody comes from an old Marian song from Sicily that a dying Italian boy was humming to himself as Falk held him in his arms. Johannes Falk was called home in 1826. He wrote an inscription on his own grave that reads: "Under these green lime trees/Mr. Johannes Falk can be found/set free from sin by Jesus Christ./ Lord, because he took in children/let him with all believers/also come to you as Your child."

This spiritual awakening regained for Germany a considerable part of the spiritual life it had lost to the rationalism of the Enlightenment. This took place through the establishment of numerous Bible societies and missionary societies. World mission in the nineteenth and twentieth centuries is unthinkable without the sacrificial spirit of the revivalists. The social component of the homeland mission is also a child of the revival. Wichern said, "Love is just as much a part of me as faith." Thus the revival called its institutions "rescue missions." Those converted during the revival did not limit themselves to caring for souls; they ministered to the whole person. As they said, "Being saved gives you the desire to save."

The awakening produced a great number of powerful spiritual personalities who fought for spiritual renewal, using their considerable gifts yet aware of their limitations. The diversity of leaders demonstrates that the revival did not proceed in a uniform fashion. This nineteenth-century revival took a less turbulent course than the eighteenth-century Baroque Pietism of Spener and Francke. The converts consciously sought to remain affiliated with the established Protestant church, although church leaders too often made it difficult for them to carry on their ministries. Yet their integration into the established Protestant church greatly reduced the potential for fanatical groups to emerge.

The Protestant church regained a measure of the respect it had lost during the Enlightenment through this resurgence of spiritual life. The church was renewed as the rationalist pastors died out and young, converted pastors took their place. As a result, the public gained a new appreciation for the church. Thus the revival signified a noticeable rechristianization of Germany. Church attendance increased significantly, and powerful biblical preaching, joyful congregational singing and free prayer became hallmarks of Pietistic worship, replacing the formalistic liturgy of the state church. The astonishing surge in the number of students who studied theology contributed to the revitalization of the clergy. Wherever the revival gained a foothold, the consumption of liquor decreased, and the number of suicides, divorces and illegitimate children declined sharply.

However, in contrast to the Methodist revival in England led by John Wesley, the German revival did not succeed in reaching the whole nation. It created many regional focal points but also left many blank spots on the map. For example, Thüringia, Oldenburg, Mecklenburg and Hessen remained largely untouched. The awakening met with the fierce resistance of rationalist and idealist theologians. The free, autonomous personality resisted a return to the old order and the authoritative claim of the biblical, Reformational message.

The revivalists were heavily involved in social action but less involved in the pursuit of social justice. Thus they were unable to reach the masses of the working class. Moreover, the close connection between the throne and the altar shut doors to the workers as well as to liberal circles. While the revivalists linked up with the cause of political restoration and expected the throne's help in evangelizing the population, members of the working class were running into the arms of Marxism.

Like Baroque Pietism, the evangelical revival made great achievements in the area of practical theology, the study and distribution of the Scriptures, pastoral care and church leadership, but it showed less interest in tackling basic issues in science, culture and systematic theology. Its intellectual paths were too narrow. Problems that could arise for modern people in dealing with the Bible hardly drew their attention. Thus the upper middle class and the intelligentsia were reached by the wars of liberation and the German national movement of the liberals, but in terms of a liberal and Romantic-idealist Christianity espoused by Fichte and Schleiermacher. These segments of society easily sailed from the Enlightenment into the waters of liberalism. Thus the Enlightenment with its problems was overcome or replaced not by a single movement but by a great diversity of movements. However, this disastrous splintering of the German people which marked the whole nineteenth century continued to have a profound effect on Germany throughout the twentieth century.

This book documents and analyzes the dialogue the great Reformed theologian Karl Barth carried on with the Pietists before World War II. His chief partners in this dialogue were found among the ranks of the Community Movement in Germany (die Gemeinschaftsbewegung). This movement is a child of Pietism and the nineteenth-century spiritual awakening in Germany described on the preceding pages. It was also influenced by the evangelical awakenings and holiness movement in America and England. It reached its first peak in the 1880s, but its origins reach back to the middle of the nineteenth century. Strong influences emanated from the Anglo-Saxon countries, where tens of thousands of converts were won in mass evangelistic meetings and mission campaigns led by men such as Charles Finney and Dwight L. Moody. Württemberg's Pietism shaped by Hofacker, Blumhardt, Bengel and Herrnhut as well as the northern German revival shaped by Kollwitz and Wichern also had a considerable impact on modern Pietism. However, in spite of the Anglo-Saxon influences the community movement understands itself as a child of the German Reformation. This reform movement within the Protestant state church was given its name by stressing the importance of community for the life of believers in an era when the masses were becoming increasingly unchurched.

The American glass manufacturer Robert P. Smith traveled to England in 1874 and popularized the doctrine of the baptism of the Holy Spirit. He held large holiness meetings in Oxford and Keswick. At the invitation of the Bonn theology professor Theodor Christlieb, Smith traveled through German-speaking Europe. Carl Heinrich Rappard (the Pilgrims' Mission at St. Chrischona in Basel, Switzerland), Otto Stockmayer (the Hauptwil Castle in Switzerland), Elias Schrenk and others were deeply moved by his teaching. The initiatives of Theodor Christlieb gained special importance. Together with F. Fabri, president of the Rhineland Mission in Barmen, he founded the German branch of the Evangelical Alliance in 1880. In 1882 he introduced his friend Adolf Stocker to Pastor F. von Schlumbach, a German-American student of Moody. Stocker then invited him to hold a mass evangelistic campaign in Berlin. The first YMCA grew out of this large-scale campaign that lasted five months. Subsequently Schlumbach evangelized in Hamburg and Württemberg and paved the way for Elias Schrenk (1831–1913) to become the first full-time evangelist in Germany. The Hamburg urban missionary and friend of Wichern, Baron Jasper von Oertzen, promoted the work of the community movement in northern Germany.

Jonathan Paul but also missionaries from St. Chrischona evangelized eastern Germany. In 1884 Christlieb, von Oertzen, Schrenk and others founded the German Evangelistic Association to promote the church's mission to the German people. This association became the cradle of the Johanneum in Wuppertal, a training school for evangelists. In contradistinction to the holiness movement the founding fathers of the community movement stressed the Reformation doctrine of justification by faith and wanted to make friends with the pastors of the state church. However, in general, these pastors preferred to close their eyes to the disturbing fact that the masses were becoming increasingly secularized.

At the Pentecost Conference in 1888 Christlieb, Schrenk, von Oertzen and others started the Gnadau Association of (Pietistic) Communities (Gnadauer Gemeinschaftsverband) at the Herrnhut colony of Gnadau near Magdeburg. Christlieb summed up Gnadau's position on the established Protestant church in these terms: "We are in the church, work with the church whenever possible, but we are not under the church."

At the initiative of the orphanage director Anna Thekla von Weling, twenty-eight participants from various denominations founded the Blankenburg Alliance Conference in 1886 at Blankenburg in Thüringia. General Georg von Viebahn, Carl Rappard from Chrischona, Elias Schrenk and somewhat later Pastor Ernst Modersohn were among the speakers at this annual conference. Methodist and Baptist churchmen also supported this event, but the actual father of the conference was Dr. F. W. Baedeker, an evangelist to Russia from England. Therefore the influence of the English free churches and the holiness movement was especially palpable there. In 1905 the American evangelist R. A. Torrey preached the baptism of the Holy Spirit in Blankenburg.

Pastor Ernst Modersohn (1870–1948), the director of the Blankenburg Alliance House from 1906, was also the cofounder of the Pastors' Prayer Brotherhood. The Chrischona man Jakob Vetter (1872–1918) evangelized in circus tents and discovered the method of the tent mission to reach the secularized masses. It is true that the revival only reached a small percentage of the working class that the church had lost, but a stream of spiritual blessings flowed into the country through this new wave of revival, especially where individual pastors in the established Protestant church opened their hearts to the cause of evangelizing the German people. Even a brief list of Pietistic organizations illustrates the wealth of pioneering achievements associated with the Gnadau Community Movement: the White Cross, the Youth Federation for Decisive Christianity (EC), the Prayer League of German Women, the German Tent Mission, the Association of Christian Teachers, the German League of Christian Technicians, as well as Christian associations for farmers, civil servants, bakers, factory owners, architects, businessmen, soldiers, policemen, postal and railroad workers. The imaginative and sacrificial social work of the Gnadau Christians is also well known. The majority of deacons and deaconesses were recruited from these Pietistic circles. In addition, the countless Bible camps and retreat centers, mission schools and schools for evangelists in Germany were creations of the Gnadau Community Movement.

The Pietists' relationship to the Pentecostal movement has been strained. In 1909, fifty-six representatives from the community movement and the free churches signed the Berlin Declaration and characterized the spirit of the Pentecostal movement as a spirit "from below." They declared, "We do not expect a new Pentecost; we are waiting for the Lord to return." This controversy led to a split between the Pentecostals and the Pietists. Only in 1996 did the Federation of Pentecostal Churches and the Evangelical Alliance reach an agreement, but the tense relationship between Gnadau and the Pentecostals continues to this day.

The theology of the community movement is not uniform. The Blankenburg Alliance Conference was shaped more strongly by Anglo-Saxon influences, and the Alliance magazine expressed sharp criticism of the established Protestant churches and moderate theologians, especially between 1903 and 1914. Otto Stockmayer and Ernst Stroter advocated Darby's premillennial teaching on the rapture, which led to their separation from the Evangelical Alliance. The "Alliance Conferences to Deepen the Life of Faith" gathered three thousand to five thousand participants in the 1920s and 1930s. Since 1990 the Blankenburg Alliance Conference has been the central conference of the German Evangelical Alliance and once again draws several thousand participants each year, mainly young adults.

In the first half of the twentieth century, the movement gained a new appreciation for its roots in Württemberg and Rhineland Pietism as well as its Lutheran heritage, but it sought to restrain the influence of the holiness movement and distanced itself from Pentecostalism. In the second half of the century the community movement received new impetus from the mass evangelistic campaigns of Billy Graham, Gerhard Bergmann, Wilhelm Busch and the Janz Team. In the 1990s Ulrich Parzany's "Pro-Christ" evangelism events gained tens of thousands of new converts. Gnadau also became one of the most loyal supporters of the Jewish state of Israel and made Jewish-Christian and Jewish-German reconciliation one of its priorities, having overcome the anti-Semitism latent in so many of its public pronouncements in the first half of the century, especially during the Nazi era. But Pietism also faced serious challenges in the latter half of the twentieth century, including Bultmann's theology, the culture of the 1968 generation and the growing pluralism and secularization of the established Protestant church. It has been in the forefront of the battle against the ordination of avowed, practicing homosexuals and the blessing of homosexual "unions" and has stood firm in its opposition to the false doctrines of the *Zeitgeist* while at the same time being at least partially open to moderate biblical criticism.

The approximately five thousand local groups and communities within the Gnadau Association perform their ministry at present in three forms. The first model is called "complementary ministry." The Gnadau community performs its ministry within the framework of the local, Protestant congregation and assumes particular areas of responsibility within the congregation. In the second model, the community preacher performs pastoral duties such as confirmation, baptism and the Lord's Supper apart from the local congregation but with its approval. The third form is called "semi-separation." Several of the Gnadau associations are moving in the direction of this free-church style of ministry. In this increasingly popular model arrangements are made between the state church and the Gnadau association to allow local communities to function as congregations with a special status. These Gnadau congregations are not limited by parochial boundaries. The local Pietistic preacher conducts activities such as confirmation, baptism and the Lord's Supper independent of the local established Protestant churches. These "semi-separate" congregations also support their own missions and organize their own outreach programs. A fourth "free-church" model is now being discussed, where the local Pietistic congregation would be completely independent of the established church. However, this model is discouraged by the Gnadau leadership. The ministry of the Gnadau communities originated in the environment of the established Protestant church, and it has made a conscious choice to remain within it. The president of the Gnadau Association, Christoph Morgner, believes Pietism will continue to affirm its place and its purpose within the Protestant Church of Germany (Die evangelische Kirche in Deutschland, EKD).

At present, the Gnadau Association represents about 300,000 Christians in Germany and is also a member of the Evangelical Alliance, which has 1,300,000 members out of a total population of 82,540,000. Gnadau consists of 83 associations: 38 regional community associations, 11 theological training centers, 7 missionary societies, 16 deaconess homes for single mothers and their children, as well as 12 organizations with specialized ministries. Pietism continues to exercise a considerable influence within the largely liberal Protestant Church of Germany (EKD) and is its primary source of spiritual renewal and vitality as well as evangelistic outreach and support for foreign missions. The Protestant Mission Organization (the EKD's mission board) supported 701 missionaries in 2000, but the Association of Evangelical Missions (AEM) has sent out 2,600 missionaries, and the Association of Pentecostal-Charismatic Missions has sent out 400. Thus the Pietists and Pentecostals combined support 80 percent of all German Protestant missionaries. Similarly, evangelicals participate in the life of the church to a much greater degree than other members of the established Protestant church. In 2003 the Protestant Church (EKD) had 26,300,000 members, but only 4.2 percent attend church regularly. A total of 1,600,000 Protestants attend church on a regular basis in Germany, and over 80 percent of them are either Pietists or other evangelicals in free churches. Clearly Pietism continues to play an essential role in the German church and society.

For further information on Pietism see E. Beyreuter, *Erweckungsbewegung* (2 A. 1977); U. Gabler, *Auferstehungszeit* (1991); W. D. Hauschild, *Lehrbuch der Kirchen-und Dogmengeschichte* 2 (1999), 765ff., *Der Pietismus im neunzehnten und zwangzisten Jahrhundert* = *Geschichte des Pietismus* 3, herausgeber U. Gabler (2000); A. Sierszyn, *2000 Jahre Kirchengeschichte, Die Neuzeit,* 4; F. Hauss, *Väter der Christenheit* (1991), 316ff.; St. Holthaus, *Fundamentalismus in Deutschland* (1993); R. Hempelmann, *Licht und Schatten der Erweckungsbewegung* (1998); H. von Ehmer und U. Strater, herausgeber, *Geschichte des Württembergischen Pietismus* (1998); T. Sorg, *Er das Haupt, Wir seine Glieder, Kirche und Pietismus in Württemberg* (2000); "Pietisten und Kirche, Ein Modell für die Zukunft" in *ideaSpektrum,* nr. 23, 3 June 1998; "Eine Trendwende beim Gottesdienstbesuch?" in *ideaSpektrum,* nr. 37, 11 September 2002; "Immer mehr alte Christen, immer mehr Atheisten," in *ideaSpektrum,* nr. 45, 7 November 2003.

Translator's Note

"Landeskirche" and "Gemeinschaftsbewegung"

The two major Christian churches are the dominant force in the religious life of Germany; 26,300,000 Germans are members of the Protestant Church in Germany (die Evangelische Kirche in Deutschland, or EKD). It was founded in 1948 as an umbrella organization for the twenty-four Lutheran, Reformed and United regional member churches. (The United churches are a merger of the Lutheran and Reformed churches in Prussia that took place in the early nineteenth century.) The EKD is governed by a synod (Synode) that is appointed by a council (Rat) and Conference of Churches (Kirchenkonferenz). The other major church is the Roman Catholic Church with 26,500,000 members.

Although the Basic Law of the Federal Republic (article 1) rejected the idea of an officially established state church, the two main Christian churches enjoy a privileged legal status as public institutions *(Körperschaften des öffentlichen Rechts)*. The word used to describe these two major churches is *Landeskirche*. To convey the idea that the Landeskirchen are still privileged by the state, I have translated Landeskirche throughout the book as the "established Protestant church." The word *Landeskirche* can also refer to the twenty-four regional churches.

Their special legal status entitles them to many privileges other churches do not enjoy. For example, this status entitles them to tax revenue levied by the state. German taxpayers contribute between 8 and 9 percent of their total income tax to the established church, depending on the state in which they pay the church tax *(Kirchensteuer)*. The only way they can avoid paying the tax is to formally leave the church *(Kirchenaustritt)*. This government-generated tax revenue makes it among the richest churches in the world. Other privileges include their responsibility for compulsory religious education in the state schools and providing social services alongside the state (the so-called dual system of welfare). They also provide pastoral care for the armed forces. The Contract to Provide Pastoral Care to the Military *(Militärseelsorgevertrag)* was signed in 1957 and commits the government to provide the framework and financing for such care in the Bundeswehr. The churches also train their pastors at state universities and have a say in appointing the professors in the theological faculties.

Despite this privileged legal status they are not state churches as such because the Basic Law guarantees freedom of religion. There are numerous small free churches, as well as sectarian groups such as the Jehovah's Witnesses and Mormons. New Age groups are also proliferating, and the large number of Muslims in the major cities have made mosques a common sight in the urban landscape.

The privileged status of the two major churches has also not halted their declining influence in German society. Since 1950 the EKD has lost about 17,000,000 members, about one-third of its total membership. Now only 64 percent of the population belong to the two established churches, and in the eastern states only 29 percent are affiliated with them. As recently as 1986 the EKD had 30,000,000 members. In just the last sixteen years it has lost an additional 4,000,000 members, and only 4.2 percent of the remaining members attend church on a regular basis. Most members only attend for key events in life such as baptism, confirmation, marriages, funerals or personal crises. Because of its diminished influence in German society, it has been called a *Volkskirche ohne Volk* (a peoples' church without people) in a recent book by Hans Apel, a former cabinet member in Helmut Schmidt's government.

As I have explained in appendix I, the various Pietistic organizations in Germany have joined together in the Gnadauer Gemeinschaftsverband (the Association of Pietistic Communities). The Pietistic movement in Germany is called *die Gemeinschaftsbewegung,* which I translate as "community movement." Its name reflects the claim of the Pietists that those who have experienced the new birth are called to live together as brothers and sisters in the community of faith; hence the term community movement, stressing the idea of the communion of the saints *(die Gemeinschaft der Heiligen)* that is so prominent in Reformational theology. The Pietists stress that if you are a committed Christian, you will be an active participant in the community of faith, which consists of the regenerate, those who have made a personal commitment to Jesus Christ as Lord and Savior. Therefore I also translate *Gemeinschaftsleute* as community people, those who are part of this community movement of born-again believers. This is also the English terminology used by John Bowden to describe the Pietistic movement in his translation of Eberhard Busch's standard work on Barth's life and thought titled *Karl Barth: His Life from Letters and Autobiographical Texts* published by Fortress Press in 1976. Finally, the translations of the quotations from the *Epistle to the Romans* are my own and the page numbers cited in the footnotes refer to the second German edition.

Bibliography

Literature by Karl Barth

Predigten 1907–1912, handwritten copies in the Karl Barth Archives, Basel

Predigten 1913, 1976

Predigten 1914, 1974

Moderne Theologie und Reichsgottesarbeit, in *ZTK,* 1909, 317ff.

Antwort an D. Achelis und D. Drews, in *ZTK,* 1909, 479ff.

Zu den beiden Gedichten, in *Gemeinde-Blatt,* Genf, 1910, nr. 34

Ob Jesus gelebt hat? ibid., 1910, nr. 36

Gott im Vaterland, ibid., 1910, nr. 38

Gerhard Teerstegen, ibid., 1910, nr. 40

Novalis, ibid., 1910, nr. 43

Pour la dignite de Geneve, in *Basler Nachrichten,* 1911, nr. 119

Wir wollen nicht, dass dieser über uns herrsche, in *Kirchenblatt für die reformierte Schweiz,* 1911, nr. 21

John Mott und die christliche Studentenbewegung (1911), in P. Grüner, *Menschenwege und Gotteswege,* 1942, 437ff.

Jesus Christus und die soziale Bewegung, in *Der freie Aargauer,* December 23 and 30, 1911.

Der christliche Glaube und die Geschichte, in *Schweizer Theol. Zeitschrift,* 1912, H 1 and 2

Auf das Reich Gottes warten (1916), new printing in *Suchet Gott, so werdet ihr leben,* 2nd ed., 1928

Religion und Leben (1917), in *EvTh,*1951/52, 437ff.

Suchet Gott, so werdet ihr leben! 1917

Der Römerbrief, 1919

Vergangenheit und Zukunft (1919), republished in J. Moltmann, Anfänge der dialektischen Theologie 1, 1962, 37ff.

Der Römerbrief, 2nd ed., Christian Kaiser Verlag 1922; ET, *The Epistle to the Romans,* Oxford University Press, 1935

Komm Schöpfer Geist! Christian Kaiser Verlag, 1924; ET, *Come, Holy Spirit,* T & T Clark and Round Table Press, New York, 1935

Das Wort Gottes und die Theologie, Christian Kaiser Verlag, 1924; ET, *The Word of God and the Word of Man,* Harper Torchbooks, New York, 1957

Autobiographische Skizze, 1927, in K. Barth-R. Bultmann, *Briefwechsel 1922–1966*, 1971, 301ff.

Erklärung des Philipperbriefes, Christian Kaiser Verlag, 1927; ET, *The Epistle to the Philippians,* SCM Press and John Knox Press, Richmond, Va., 1962

Die Lehre vom Wort Gottes: Christliche Dogmatik im Entwurf, Christian Kaiser Verlag 1928

Polemisches Nachwort, in *ZdZ,* 1927, 33ff.

Die Theologie und die Kirche, Gesammelte Vorträge 2, 1928

Ethik 1, 1928, 1973; *Ethik* 2, 1928/29, 1978

Brief an Karl Heim (June 12, 1928), in *Furche,* 1928

Geschichte der protestantischen Theologie (lecture 1929/30), published in typewritten form in 1943

Brief an G. F. Nagel, in *Evang. Allianzblatt,* 1930, nr. 1, 9-10

Brief an Karl Heim, in *ZdZ,* 1931, 451ff.

Die protestantische Theologie im 19. Jahrhundert: Ihre Vorgeschichte und ihre Geschichte, Evangelischer Verlag, 1947; ET, *Protestant Theology in the Nineteenth Century,* SCM Press and Judson Press, Valley Forge, Pa., 1972

Erklärung über das rechte Verständnis der reformatorischen Bekenntnisse der DEK der Gegenwart, in *Freie reformierte Synode,* January 3-4, 1934, in *Barmen;* edited by K. Immer

Gespräch mit Karl Barth, in Lebenszeichen aus dem Kreis der evang., Predigerschule in Basel, 1936

Kurze Erklärung des Römerbriefes, 1956, Siebenstern-Taschenbuch 94, 1967; ET, *A Shorter Commentary on Romans,* SCM Press and John Knox Press, Richmond, Va., 1956

Die Menschlichkeit Gottes, *Theologische Studien* nr. 48, 1956; ET, *The Humanity of God,* Collins and John Knox Press, Richmond, Va., 1961

Dank und Reverenz, in *EvTh,* 1963, 337ff.

Autobiographisches Fragment, 1967, typewritten in the Karl Barth Archives, Basel

Nachwort. Zu: *Schleiermacher-Auswahl.* Siebenstern-Taschenbuch 113/114, 1968, 290ff.

Die Kirchliche Dogmatik 1/2, *Die Lehre vom Wort Gottes,* Evangelischer Verlag, 1939; ET, *Church Dogmatics* 1/2, *The Doctrine of the Word of God,* T & T Clark and Scribner, New York, 1956

Die Kirchliche Dogmatik 2/1, *Die Lehre von Gott,* 1940; ET, *Church Dogmatics* 2/1, *The Doctrine of God,* T & T Clark and Scribner, New York, 1957

Die Kirchliche Dogmatik 4/1, *Die Lehre von der Versöhnung,* 1953; ET, *Church Dogmatics* 4/1, *The Doctrine of Reconciliation,* T & T Clark and Scribner, New York, 1956

Die Kirchliche Dogmatik 4/2, *Die Lehre von der Versöhnung,* 1955; ET, *Church Dogmatics* 4/2, *The Doctrine of Reconciliation,* T & T Clark and Scribner, New York, 1958

K. Barth-R. Bultmann, *Briefwechsel 1922–1966,* 1971

K. Barth-E. Thurneysen, *Briefwechsel 1, 1913–1921,* Evangelischer Verlag, 1973

K. Barth-E. Thurneysen, *Briefwechsel 2, 1921–1930,* Evangelischer Verlag, 1974; ET, *Revolutionary Theology in the Making,* ed. James D. Smart, John Knox Press, Richmond, Va., and Epworth Press, 1964 (this contains only extracts from both volumes)

Briefe 1961–1966, 1975

The German edition of this book contains at this point two further bibliographies headed "Literature by Representatives of the Community Movement" and "Further Literature." Most of the works cited are only available in German libraries. Interested readers can consult the original German edition.

Abbreviations of periodicals referred to in the text

CW	*Christliche Welt*
EvTh	*Evangelische Theologie*
KRS	*Kirchenblatt für die reformierte Schweiz*
RGG	*Die Religion in Geschichte und Gegenwart*
ThExh	*Theologische Existenz heute*
ThSt	*Theologische Studien*
ZTK	*Zeitschrift für Theologie und die Kirche*
ZdZ	*Zwischen den Zeiten*

Index